The 1.5 Billion People Question

The 1.5 Billion People Question

Food, Vouchers, or Cash Transfers?

Harold Alderman, Ugo Gentilini, and Ruslan Yemtsov
Editors

WORLD BANK GROUP

Contents

Figures

Preface

Food is not simply a collection of nutrients. It is an integral part of our economy, culture, history, cognitive capacity, and spirituality. For instance, the word "food" appears more than 100 times in the holy books of Buddhism, Christianity, Islam, and Judaism. As this volume shows, in some countries commodities like rice or bread are considered the barometer of the economy, and spikes in food prices have ignited riots and protests. Food is a key priority among people living in poverty, often absorbing most of their financial, mental, and emotional resources. Uncertainty about "where the next meal is coming from" generates profound stress and anxiety, with the net result of focusing on here-and-now thinking. Planning for the future is seldom an option for hundreds of millions of people across the planet.

Understanding the pivotal role of food security is, therefore, central to any poverty response. Food security strategies have traditionally centered on enhancing agricultural production and productivity. This has yielded enormous benefits for farmers and communities across the world. And yet, providing access to food—or the purchasing power to access available commodities—remains a key challenge for social protection, one that both fast-paced urbanization and the current wave of famines underscore even further.

It is against such a backdrop that this book explores how to genuinely integrate the agendas of social protection and food assistance. To be clear: over the past decades, efforts to introduce, expand, and upgrade social protection systems in low- and middle-income countries primarily revolved around cash transfers—and for good reasons. At the same time, about 1.5 billion people worldwide have been covered by in-kind food programs, 1 billion of whom live in countries examined in this volume. In-kind transfers have been a key vehicle to provide income support to poor consumers; but, on average, they have often done so at high cost and as part of broader agricultural support and food price risk management efforts. In other words, in-kind programs can generate technical and political economy quandaries that go well beyond income support to poor consumers. Given those complexities, the "1.5 billion people question" comes to mind: What can we learn from countries' experiences using food, vouchers, or cash transfers to meet people's food needs?

The book provides a long-awaited and very much-needed analysis on such a shift: when viewed through the lenses of history, countries are increasingly moving from in-kind provisions to cash-based transfers, often with vouchers as an intermediate step. Yet this process is far from straightforward, and it is checkered by the bumpy and erratic pathways of evolution. In particular, the book argues that many of the precursors of current cash transfer programs were in-kind measures and that such measures are still relevant in certain circumstances. The volume's analysis—one at the intersection of economics, political economy, politics, sociology, and history—would help debunk some long-standing myths about food assistance, highlight the complex and intertwined objectives pursued by well-intentioned food programs, and identify insightful lessons from reform processes that are, regrettably, seldom available internationally.

Part of the success in answering the 1.5 billion people question would hinge on our prior mindset toward both interventions. To this end, we hope this book will contribute to efforts to move away from the traps of ideology that have sometimes stifled policy debates and instead help to embrace a systemwide, pragmatic, and evidence-based approach to different social protection measures.

Michal Rutkowski
Senior Director
Social Protection and Jobs Global Practice
The World Bank Group

Acknowledgments

The work presented in this volume is part of an initiative supported by the Nutrition Window of the Rapid Social Response (RSR) Multi-Donor Trust Fund at the World Bank, with generous financial contribution from the Russian Federation. Precious time, knowledge, and support were provided by the Economic Research Service at the U.S. Department of Agriculture.

The task was led by Ugo Gentilini under the guidance of Michal Rutkowski, Arup Banerji, and Anush Benzhanyan in their current and past senior management capacities at the World Bank's Social Protection and Jobs Global Practice.

The editors of the volume are extremely grateful to its peer reviewers, namely Margaret Grosh, William Wiseman, John Hoddinott, and Cem Mete, as well as to participants of technical workshops held in November 2015 and March 2016. The book benefited enormously from precious advice by Alessandra Marini, Bénédicte de la Brière, Carlo del Ninno, Changqing Sun, Cindy Paladines, Diego Arias Carballo, Elena Glinskaya, Francesca Lamanna, Gabriela Inchauste, Gustavo Demarco, Hideki Mori, Jehan Arulpragasam, John Blomquist, Kathy Lindert, Kenn Crossley, Leslie Elder, María Concepción Steta-Gándara, Nandini Krishnan, Nora Lustig, Pablo Gottret, Paul Dorosh, Philip O'Keefe, Robert Chase, Robert Palacios, Robert Townsend, Susan Bradley, Thomas Walker, Tim Mahoney, Vivi Alatas, and Xiaoqing Yu. We are thankful for the support provided by Helena Makarenko, Boban Varghese Paul, Zaineb Majoka, Vanessa Co, Ngoc-Dung Thi Tran, Francine Pagsibigan, Nadege Nouviale, Alies van Geldermalsen, Mary Fisk, and Jewel McFadden at various stages of the book production process.

The editors of the volume include a team drawn from both the World Bank and the International Food Policy Research Institute (IFPRI), with the book feeding into the World Bank's Safety Nets Global Solutions Group, as well as from the CGIAR Research Program on Policies, Institutions, and Markets (PIM). The opinions expressed here belong to the authors only and do not necessarily reflect those of the World Bank, IFPRI, PIM, or CGIAR.

About the Editors and Authors

Moustafa Abdalla is a health specialist with expertise in health economics, policy, and financing. He has a medical degree from the Faculty of Medicine Suez Canal University (FOMSCU) and an MPH degree from the London School of Hygiene and Tropical Medicine (LSHTM). Before joining the Middle East and North Africa Region Health, Nutrition, and Population family, he worked as a social protection specialist and a health consultant at the World Bank in the Arab Republic of Egypt and the Republic of Yemen. Earlier, he worked with various organizations, including the Islamic Development Bank, the World Health Organization, the Misr El-Kheir Organisation, and the LSHTM in countries in the Middle East and North Africa and in Sub-Saharan Africa. In his cross-sectoral work, he continues to support the Social Protection team in diverse interventions, including the Egypt disability work under the cash transfer Karama Program, the Egypt Social Registry, and the Food Subsidy Study. He currently works on a number of countries, such as Egypt, Jordan, Libya, Pakistan, and Yemen. He is also a visiting lecturer of postgraduate health economics and health insurance at the University of Cairo.

Harold Alderman holds an MA in nutrition from Cornell University and a PhD in economics from Harvard University and has gravitated to research on the economics of nutrition and food policy. After spending 10 years at the International Food Policy Research Institute (IFPRI), he joined the World Bank in 1991, where he divided his time between the Development Research Group and the Africa Region, advising on social protection policy. He returned to IFPRI in 2012. His recent publications include contributions to *The Lancet* state-of-the-art review on early child development (2011) and *The Lancet* review on nutrition-sensitive investments (2013) as well as editing of the book, *No Small Matter: The Interaction of Poverty, Shocks, and Human Capital Investments in Early Childhood Development* (2011).

Sherine Al-Shawarby is a professor of economics at the Faculty of Economics and Political Science (FEPS) in Cairo University, where she also is vice dean for community affairs and environment development. She is a member of the board of the National Planning Institute and has worked as the economic adviser to the president of the Central Agency for Public Mobilization and Statistics (CAPMAS) on economic and mobilization statistics (April–September 2015), the deputy minister for economic justice, and the executive director of the Economic Justice Unit at the Ministry of Finance (2013–14). She was a senior economist at the World Bank office in Cairo (2001–13) and an adviser to numerous international, regional, and national organizations. She has published numerous research covering a wide range of economic issues in Egypt: exchange rate, trade, inflation, fiscal sustainability, subsidies, poverty, and inequality.

Shrayana Bhattacharya is an economist in the World Bank's Social Protection and Jobs Global Practice, based in New Delhi, India. She recently led a series of state-level assessments of safety nets in India, with a focus on the public distribution system. Before joining the World Bank, she worked with the state government of Delhi on mission convergence and with the International Labour Organization (ILO), the Self-Employed Women's Association (SEWA), and the Centre for Policy Research on a range of issues in the areas of urban bureaucracy and social protection, poverty measurement, and impact evaluation of public programs. She completed her postgraduate education in public administration and economics at Harvard University.

Vanita Leah Falcao is a public policy analyst from India who is currently a Marie Curie Doctoral Scholar at King's College London. Her work centers on antipoverty and food security programs. In the past, as a member of the World Bank's Social Protection and Jobs Global Practice, she conducted state-level assessments of safety nets in India. She has also assisted the Office of the Food Commissioners of the Supreme Court of India in monitoring the implementation of the National Food Security Act, 2013. She is a Fulbright Nehru fellow and holds an MA in public policy from the University of Michigan, Ann Arbor.

Ugo Gentilini is a senior economist with the Social Protection and Jobs Global Practice at the World Bank. His interests encompass the analytics and practice of social protection, including as they relate to food security and nutrition, fragility and resilience, activation and labor markets, political economy of redistribution, universal basic income, urbanization, human development, and the nexus between safety nets and humanitarian assistance. Before joining the World Bank in 2013, he spent more than a decade with the United Nations World Food Programme, working on policy, implementation, and evaluation of cash- and food-based social assistance. He holds a PhD in development economics and has dozens of publications in books, academic journals, working paper series, and the blogosphere.

Hastuti is a researcher at the SMERU Research Institute, based in Jakarta, Indonesia. She holds an undergraduate degree in the socioeconomics of agriculture from Bogor Agricultural University (Institut Pertanian Bogor). Before joining SMERU, she worked as a researcher with the Centre for Policy and Implementation Studies. She has been involved in studies on poverty-related issues and social protection programs in Indonesia. Her publications include "The Use of Social Protection Card (KPS) and the Implementation of the 2013 Temporary Direct Cash Transfer (BLSM) Program," "The Effectiveness of the Raskin Program," and "Child Poverty and Disparities in Indonesia: Challenges for Inclusive Growth."

Citlalli Hernández holds a BS in economics from the Tecnológico de Monterrey (ITESM, Mexico) and an MSc in social development in practice from the University College London, United Kingdom. From 2000 to 2009, she worked in the federal conditional cash transfer program Prospera (formerly called Oportunidades/Progresa) and was the liaison director for the Evaluation Unit for the past three years, coordinating the overall evaluation process of the program in collaboration with the World Bank and the Inter-American Development Bank technical staffs. As a World Bank consultant since 2010, she has participated in research projects related to conditional cash transfer programs. As an external researcher for the Universidad Nacional Autónoma de México, she has been involved in a series of evaluations regarding the Cruzada Nacional Contra el Hambre (National Crusade Against Hunger), the current administration's main strategy for combating hunger in Mexico.

Victor Oliveira is an agricultural economist with the Food Assistance Branch in the Food Economics Division of the United States Department of Agriculture, where he conducts research on food assistance-related topics, focusing primarily on the Special Supplemental Nutrition Program for Women, Infants, and Children (WIC). He has an MS in agricultural economics from Pennsylvania State University.

Mark Prell is a senior economist in the Food Assistance Branch of the Food Economics Division of the Economic Research Service (ERS), which examines the United States Department of Agriculture's domestic food and nutrition assistance programs and issues related to them. His recent research has focused on expanding the research applications of administrative records. His long-term research themes include dietary and nutritional outcomes, food program targeting and delivery, and program dynamics and administration. He served as assistant deputy director at ERS from 1999 to 2003. He taught at the Johns Hopkins University, the University of California—Los Angeles, and the University of Southern California and served on details at the U.S. Bureau of Labor Statistics and the U.S. Office of Management and Budget. He received a PhD in economics from the Massachusetts Institute of Technology.

Raghav Puri is a PhD student at the Maxwell School of Citizenship and Public Affairs, Syracuse University. His research focuses on the design and implementation of social programs (food security, social pensions, and health insurance) in India. Previously, he worked with the World Bank's Social Protection and Jobs Global Practice in New Delhi for five years. He has conducted extensive field research on the Public Distribution System (PDS) in India over the past decade as a volunteer with the Right to Food Campaign. He holds a postgraduate degree in public policy from the Lee Kuan Yew School of Public Policy, National University of Singapore, and an undergraduate degree in economics from St. Stephen's College, University of Delhi.

John Scott is a professor-researcher in the Economics Department at the Centro de Investigación y Docencia Económicas (CIDE) in Mexico City and academic researcher at the Consejo Nacional de Evaluación de la Política de Desarrollo Social (CONEVAL). He has a BA in philosophy from New York University, an MA in philosophy in economics, and doctoral studies at the University of Oxford. His principal research areas include the distributive incidence of social spending, poverty and inequality analysis, and evaluation of social policy, rural development policies, agricultural and energy subsidies, and health and social security.

David Smallwood is chief of the Food Assistance Branch in the Food Economics Division of the United States Department of Agriculture (USDA), where he manages and directs research on USDA's domestic food and nutrition assistance programs including the Supplemental Nutrition Assistance Program (SNAP, formerly the Food Stamp Program), school feeding programs, and the Special Supplemental Nutrition Program for Women, Infants, and Children (WIC). He has more than 30 years of experience in applied economic analysis of food programs and policies, including studies of the effects of food assistance programs on food spending, food prices, meal costs, diet quality, and program participation. He received his PhD from North Carolina State University in Raleigh.

Chinthani Sooriyamudali is a research assistant in the Poverty and Social Welfare Policy Unit of the Institute of Policy Studies of Sri Lanka. She holds a BA in economics from the University of Colombo, Sri Lanka. Her research interests include poverty and development policy, econometrics, and economic modeling.

Sudarno Sumarto is a senior research fellow at the SMERU Research Institute, an independent institute for research and public policy studies, and policy adviser for the National Team for the Acceleration of Poverty Reduction (TNP2K), Office of the Vice President of the Republic of Indonesia. He has a PhD and an MA from Vanderbilt University and a BS from Satya Wacana Christian University (Salatiga), Indonesia, all in economics. He was a visiting fellow at Shorenstein Asia-Pacific Research Center at Stanford University from 2009 to 2010 and for almost 10 years served as the director of SMERU. He was also a lecturer at the Institute of Agriculture (IPB) in Bogor, Indonesia. He has contributed to more than 60 coauthored articles, chapters, reports, and working papers. He has worked closely with the Indonesian government, giving advice on poverty issues and poverty alleviation programs.

Laura Tiehen is an economist with the Food Assistance Branch in the Food Economics Division of the USDA, researching the use of federal food assistance programs, including as they relate to poverty, food security, and health-related behaviors. She received her PhD in economics from the University of Wisconsin-Madison. She is a member of the American Economics Association and the Association for Public Policy Analysis and Management.

Ganga Tilakaratna is a research fellow and head of the Poverty and Social Welfare Policy Unit of the Institute of Policy Studies of Sri Lanka. Her key research interests include poverty, social protection, financial inclusion, and labor, where she has carried out various research projects. She has worked as a consultant to international organizations such as the World Bank, the Asian Development Bank, and the ILO. She holds a PhD in development policy and management from the University of Manchester, an MA in economics from the University of Cambridge, and a BA in economics from the University of Manchester.

Peter Timmer is an authority on agricultural development, food security, and the world rice economy who has published scores of papers and books on these topics. He has served as a professor at Stanford University, Cornell University, three faculties at Harvard University, and the University of California, San Diego, where he was also the dean of the Graduate School of International Relations and Pacific Studies. He is the Cabot Professor of Development Studies, emeritus, at Harvard University, a core adviser on the World Bank's *World Development Report 2008: Agriculture for Development,* and a nonresident fellow at the Center for Global Development. He was awarded the Leontief Prize in 2012 for advances in economic thought and delivered the 18th annual United Nations University World Institute for Development Economics Research (UNU-WIDER) lecture at the United Nations in New York in 2014. His research and advisory work focuses on three main themes: lessons for low- and middle-income countries from the historical experience of structural transformation in Europe and Asia; the impact of modern food supply chains on smallholder farmers and poor consumers; and approaches to stabilizing rice prices in Asia with minimum spillover to the world market and to producers and consumers in Africa and Latin America.

Ruslan Yemtsov is a lead economist in the Social Protection and Jobs Global Practice of the World Bank. He is coordinating the work of the Global Solutions Group in the area of social safety nets. Prior to his current position, he was lead poverty economist in the Middle East and North Africa Region and in the Europe and Central Asia Region. His experience includes leading and coauthoring publications on social safety nets and targeting, including major flagship reports on the state of social safety nets in the world; leading South–South learning forums and global training programs on poverty, data analysis, social protection, and labor; conducting country poverty assessments; managing fuel subsidy reform dialogue; and leading regional flagship reports on poverty, subsidy reforms, and spatial disparities in development. He has written and coauthored more than 25 research papers, articles, book chapters, and monographs.

Abbreviations

AAY	Antyodaya Anna Yojna
ABAWD	able-bodied adult without dependents
AFDC	Aid to Families with Dependent Children, United States
AIDIS	All India Debt and Investment Surveys
APL	above the poverty line
APMC	Agricultural Produce Marketing Committee, India
ARRA	American Recovery and Reinvestment Act of 2009, United States
BANSEFI	Banco del Ahorro Nacional y Servicios Financeiros (National Bank of Financial Services), Mexico
BB	baladi bread
BDT	Basis Data Terpadu (Unified Database), Indonesia
BKKBN	Badan Koordinasi Berencana Nasional (National Family Planning Coordination Board), Indonesia
BLSM	temporary direct cash assistance, Indonesia
BPKP	Badan Pengawasan Keuangan dan Pembangunan (Finance and Development Supervisory Agency), Indonesia
BPL	below the poverty line
BPS	Statistics Indonesia
BSM	poor students assistance, Indonesia
BULOG	Badan Urusan Logistik (State Logistics Board), Indonesia
CAPMAS	Central Agency for Public Mobilization and Statistics, Arab Republic of Egypt
CCT	conditional cash transfer
CIP	central issue price
CNCH	Cruzada Nacional Contra el Hambre (National Crusade Against Hunger), Mexico

CONASUPO	Compañía Nacional de Subsistencias Populares (National Company of Popular Subsistence), Mexico
COPLAMAR	Coordinación General del Plan Nacional de Zonas Deprimidas y Grupos Marginados (General Coordination of the National Plan of Depressed Zones and Marginal Groups), Mexico
CORE PDS	centralized online real-time electronic PDS, India
CT	cash transfer
CV	coefficient of variation
DBT	direct benefit transfer
DCGS	Department of Commissioner General of Samurdhi, Sri Lanka
Diconsa	Sistema Social de Abasto de Distribuidoras Conasupo (Social Supply Distribution System of Conasupo), Mexico
DIF	Sistema Nacional para el Desarrollo Integral de la Familia (National System for Integral Family Development), Mexico
DS	district secretariat, Sri Lanka
D-SNAP	Disaster Supplemental Nutrition Assistance Program, United States
E&T	employment and training
EBT	electronic benefit transfer
EHCSS	Egyptian Holding Company for Silos and Storage
EITC	earned income tax credit, United States
FAM	Fondo de Aportaciones Múltiples (Multiple Contributions Fund), Mexico
FCI	Food Corporation of India
FDPIR	Food Distribution Program on Indian Reservations, United States
Fidelist	Fideicomiso para la Liquidación del Subsidio a la Tortilla (Trust to Eliminate the Tortilla Subsidy), Mexico
FOSA	food-oriented social assistance
FPS	fair price shop
FSS	food subsidy system, Egypt
GAIN	Global Alliance for Improved Nutrition
GASC	General Authority for Supply Commodities, Egypt
GDP	gross domestic product
GPS	global positioning system
HCFI	Holding Company for Food Industries, Egypt
HIECS	Household Income, Expenditure, and Consumption Survey, Egypt
ICT	information and communication technology
IMF	International Monetary Fund
IPPG	index of pro-poor growth
J-PAL	Abdul Latief Jameel Poverty Action Lab

JPS	Jaring Pengaman Sosial (social safety net programs), Indonesia
KPK	Komisi Pemberantasan Korupsi (Corruption Eradication Commission), Indonesia
KPS	social protection card, Indonesia
Menko PMK	Coordinating Ministry for Human Development and Culture, Indonesia
MGNREGA	Mahatma Gandhi National Rural Employment Guarantee Act, India
MOPMAR	Ministry of Planning, Monitoring, and Administrative Reform, Egypt
MOS	Ministry of Supply, Egypt
MOSIT	Ministry of Supply and Internal Trade, Egypt
MOSS	Ministry of Social Solidarity, Egypt
MPS_{SB}	marginal propensity to spend (on food) out of SNAP benefits
MSP	minimum support price
NAP	Nutrition Assistance Program, Puerto Rico
NCAER	National Council for Applied Economic Research, India
NCP	Coordinación Nacional Prospera (National Coordination of Prospera), Mexico
NFSA	National Food Security Act, India
NSSO	National Sample Survey Organization, India
OPK	Operasi Pasar Khusus (Special Market Operations), Indonesia
PAL	Programa de Apoyo Alimentario (Food Support Program), Mexico
PAR	Programa de Abasto Rural (Rural Food Supply Program), Mexico
PASL	Programa de Abasto Social de Leche (Social Milk Supply Program), Mexico
PDS	public distribution system, India
P.L.	Public Law
PMJDY	Pradhan Mantri Jan Dhan Yojana (National Mission for Financial Inclusion), India
POS	point-of-sale
PPLS	Social Protection Program Census, Indonesia
PRI	panchayati raj institution
Procampo	Programa de Apoyos Directos al Campo (Direct Support for Farmers Program), Mexico
Pronasol	Programa Nacional de Solidaridad (National Solidarity Program), Mexico
PRWORA	Personal Responsibility and Work Opportunities Reconciliation Act of 1996, United States
PUCL	People's Union for Civil Liberties, Rajasthan, India

RC	ration card
RPDS	revamped PDS
RT	group of neighborhood households, Indonesia
RW	group of RTs, Indonesia
SASL	Samurdhi Authority of Sri Lanka
Sedesol	Ministry of Social Development, Mexico
SNAP	Supplemental Nutrition Assistance Program, United States
SNAP-Ed	SNAP nutrition education
SNAP E&T	SNAP employment and training
SSI	Supplemental Security Income, United States
SSN	social safety net
Susenas	Statistics Indonesia National Socioeconomic Survey
TANF	Temporary Assistance for Needy Families, United States
TKPK	Tim Koordinasi Penanggulangan Kemiskinan (National Team for Poverty Reduction), Indonesia
TNP2K	Tim Nasional Percepatan Penanggulangan Kemiskinan (National Team for the Acceleration of Poverty Reduction), Indonesia
TPDS	targeted public distribution system, India
UCT	unconditional cash transfer
USDA	U.S. Department of Agriculture
VAT	value added tax
WIC	Special Supplemental Nutrition Program for Women, Infants, and Children, United States

CHAPTER 1

The Evolution of Food as Social Assistance

AN OVERVIEW

Harold Alderman, Ugo Gentilini, and Ruslan Yemtsov

INTRODUCTION

India's state of Chhattisgarh faced a daunting challenge in the mid-2000s. About half of its public food distribution was leaked, meaning that it never reached the intended beneficiaries. Such a situation was not unique to that state and fed into a broader skepticism toward in-kind assistance: many observers predicted that the days of food transfer programs were numbered. By 2012, however, Chhattisgarh had nearly eliminated leakages, doubled the coverage of the scheme, and reduced exclusion errors to low single digits.[1] The country as a whole continued to consider public food distribution as a pillar of its rights-based social protection system.

Such challenges and improvements are not unique to India, and any discussion of food transfers invariably leads to the question, "Why not provide people with cash instead?" When policy makers consider a new social assistance program, it is likely to be a cash transfer. To be clear, there are solid arguments to support such an inclination. Above all, cash can, under the right circumstances, provide choice, empower recipients, and generate local economic multipliers. Modern policy making benefits not only from sweeping technological advances in cash delivery but also from evidence sparked by a revolution in empirical inquiry. In particular, the recent extension of experimental techniques to social protection evaluations shows that cash transfers are, *on average*, more cost-effective at delivering resources to households than are in-kind alternatives (Gentilini 2016a; Margolies and Hoddinott 2015). Yet those arguments alone have not always offered a convincing basis for fully replacing food and voucher schemes with cash.

This book addresses the thorny and fascinating question of how food and voucher programs, despite theory and evidence generally favoring cash, remain relevant, have evolved, and, in most circumstances, have improved over time. In doing so, we take an evolutionary and pragmatic view; we are interested in understanding *why* food-based programs exist and *how* countries can benefit from transformations such as that of Chhattisgarh, not in determining whether those programs *should* exist.

In *The Panda's Thumb*, Stephen Gould (2010) observes that pandas have an extension of their wrist that serves a function similar to that of an extra and opposable digit. Gould points out that the physical modification is hardly a planner's best solution to the problem of stripping bamboo leaves; the evolutionary process has jury-rigged a solution, but this does not necessarily mean that it is an ineffective one. Quite the opposite in Gould's example. The analogy is apt for several in-kind instruments that have evolved from government efforts to stabilize prices or to address real or perceived market failures.

By studying the antecedents of current policies and the lessons that emerge from their implementation, we show that decision making is rooted in a wide array of factors. Investigating the political economy and path dependency of programs as well as the interplay of different objectives and conflicting incentives reveals an intricate world. A fuller appreciation of those complexities may help to explain why governments often opt for what is feasible rather than what is desirable and why they may embark on gradual improvements rather than radical overhauls—although substantial reforms do happen. The broader point is that failure to account for those forces may hinder the process of reform, even if proposals are technically sound.

Why focus on food? Some of the issues explored in this book may find broader relevance and applicability than in the food realm alone, such as in energy subsidy reforms (see, for example, Verme and Araar 2017). Yet the motivation for the topic is grounded in the simple fact that food, which claims about 61 percent of the poor's expenditures,[2] is a pressing, daily concern for persons at the bottom of the income ladder. An effective food-based social assistance program can make a tangible difference; it can help to release household resources and unleash individuals' biological capabilities, talents, and mental bandwidth to compete on a more level playing field and pursue upward mobility. If individuals' minds are on food, however, and most of their limited money goes for it, there is little room for anything else.

While global knowledge on food-based social assistance is significant in scale and compelling in purpose, there are gaps in evidence and interpretation. This book highlights trends from a 30-year interlude, representing one of the first cross-country reviews since the late 1980s (Pinstrup-Andersen 1988). It does so by presenting case studies of six countries with long histories of food-based transfers, namely, the Arab Republic of Egypt, India, Indonesia, Mexico, Sri Lanka, and the United States. These experiences were chosen because of the diversity in their contexts, program origins, pathways of reform, and design parameters; however, they all offer lessons of global relevance. Although each of the countries has a range of other food-based programs, we focus on a core, salient one—in most cases, the largest-scale intervention—and study its evolution and implementation.

Although the case studies include middle- and high-income countries, the lessons are relevant to lower-income settings for four reasons. First, most of the countries examined were relatively low income at the time they introduced the food interventions; hence, their situation resembled the current conditions of countries at lower levels of development.

Second, while lower-income countries are increasingly investing in social protection systems—a relatively new development in many countries in Sub-Saharan Africa (World Bank 2015)—some have revived food price subsidies that were popular after independence, such as Ghana and Tanzania in the 1970s and 1980s (Devereux 2001).[3] For example, although the government of Ethiopia has significantly injected cash into its social protection system, the 2008 global food crisis led to the introduction of an urban wheat subsidy program costing about US$271 million per year (Kiringai and others 2016).

Third, this book might be useful for countries with large-scale international humanitarian assistance. While up to 94 percent of humanitarian aid is still provided in kind, the humanitarian landscape is transitioning decisively to cash assistance (Gentilini 2016b). Also, about 73 percent of donor-financed, multilateral food aid is now procured in low- and middle-income countries (WFP 2016), creating a local constituency for those measures to be institutionalized in government budgets. These then may lay the basis for future domestic food programs in a range of low-income settings.

Finally, this book is not a toolkit with checklists and handy prescriptions; these can be useful in fields where automation and procedure are defining requisites. The notion of ready-made menus drives counter to the concept of complex systems that permeate the change process. As this initial section suggests, the reform of food-based programs is indeed a systemic matter. In this vein, the growing literature of complex systems underscores the key role of iteration, adaptation, and feedback loops (Andrews, Pritchett, and Woolcock 2016; Green 2016; Ramalingam 2013).

Hence, instead of prescriptions, this book offers data, traces reform path-ways, and identifies lessons that, we hope, may energize and inspire policy makers engaged in social protection reforms.

The remainder of the chapter is structured as follows. After setting out basic concepts and providing a brief overview of global programs as well as empirical evidence, we track countries' underlying evolution or directions of change, identify the channels through which such direction occurred, and lay out the results emerging from those trends. In discussing those issues, we enrich and extend the case study findings with historical examples from coun-tries not covered in this book that nevertheless offer insights into the issue at hand. A final section reflects on future issues related to preparing for and acting on reforms.

UNBUNDLING FOOD-BASED SOCIAL ASSISTANCE

Basic Concepts and Stocktaking

Governments have several options to pursue food-related objectives, includ-ing two broad classes of measures. First, public authorities may opt to enhance the supply of food. These measures could take both direct and indirect forms. Direct measures would include interventions to support farmers (inputs, credit, and insurance) and agricultural infrastructure. Indirect measures would include those managing prices, including price subsidies for producers or intermediaries involved in milling, transport, and storage. They would also include macro levers like the calibration of exchange rates and open-market sale of food from either imports or storage.

Second, public authorities may opt to influence demand. Demand-side interventions, which we call "food-oriented social assistance" (FOSA), are the focus of the book. These interventions also include direct and indirect mea-sures. Direct ones encompass noncontributory transfers as part of wider social protection systems (World Bank 2015). In particular, transfers can take the form of commodities provided to beneficiaries as part of unconditional public distribution programs or conditional interventions such as school meal programs. A particular in-kind modality is known as rationing, whereby governments limit the quantity of food commodities purchasable on markets. Such quotas reemerge in times of crisis, including during world wars and during the post-1990 war period of sanctions in Iraq and in the planned economies of the former Soviet Union and the Democratic People's Republic of Korea (World Bank 2005).

Direct FOSA programs can include vouchers, also known as "near-cash" or stamps, which provide access to food for a given value or quantity in pre-defined private or public outlets. These interventions lie midway on the continuum of transfer modalities where cash and in-kind constitute the extremes. Furthermore, FOSA encompasses parts of the cash transfer family, including cash programs where targeting, transfer size, and performance metrics are devised based on food security objectives and data. For example, under the Ethiopia Productive Safety Net Program, the cash transfer is calibrated to provide enough money to purchase 15 kilograms of cereals and 4 kilograms of pulses per participant per month. In contrast, most cash transfer programs—for example, social pensions or many conditional cash transfers (CCTs)—are not generally calibrated in terms of a basket of goods. Finally, indirect FOSA measures include price subsidies for consumers, which provide commodities at a lower price than their market value. With the exception of cash, all direct FOSA programs are nudges away from pure consumer sovereignty—that is, all of these programs attempt to influence consumer behavior and shape incentives. The full suite of options is laid out in a taxonomy presented in table 1.1.

The performance of social assistance programs has been studied in numerous contexts and reveals a significant impact on well-being. For example, it is estimated that social assistance has lifted between 136 million and 165 million people out of extreme poverty (Fiszbein, Kanbur, and Yemtsov 2014). Similarly, there is ample evidence documenting the effectiveness of these

TABLE 1.1 Taxonomy of Interventions Pursuing Food-Related Objectives

TYPE OF INTERVENTION	SUPPLY SIDE	DEMAND SIDE (FOOD-ORIENTED SOCIAL ASSISTANCE)[a]
Direct	• Support to farmers (inputs, fertilizers, credit, insurance) • Infrastructure (irrigation)	• Food commodities: 　– Unconditional food transfers (public food distribution) 　– Conditional food transfers (nutritional supplements, school meals) 　– Food-for-work activities 　– Generalized rationing • Food vouchers or stamps: 　– In most cases, unconditional 　– Value-based or quantity-based • Cash transfers (*when strictly intended and designed to access food*)
Indirect	• Price subsidies to producers • Price subsidies to intermediaries (millers, transport, storage) • Open-market sales of commodities (Egypt, Arab Rep., in World War I) • Exchange rates, tax, and trade policy	• Price subsidies to consumers

a. Most interventions covered in this book are demand side.

programs on dimensions such as food security and nutrition, human capital accumulation, climate resilience, social cohesion, and physical assets, as well as their success in sparking economic spillovers (Alderman 2016; FAO 2015; IEG 2011; World Bank 2015).

While some FOSA interventions like school feeding have received significant recent empirical and operational scrutiny (Alderman and Bundy 2011; Beegle, Galasso, and Goldberg 2015; Drake and others 2016), measures like public food distribution programs and food subsidies have elicited much less attention in recent years. To fill this gap, we examine those programs and how they evolved into other interventions, particularly vouchers and, in some cases, cash transfers.

While countries are increasing their provision of cash transfers (World Bank 2015), food and vouchers assistance is still a predominant modality in low- and middle-income countries. Based on administrative data from programs in 108 countries, food and vouchers programs cover 20.4 percent of the population in those settings (figure 1.1). This is 13 percentage points higher than unconditional cash transfers (UCTs). Disaggregated analysis reveals that in low-income countries, the mean coverage of the population by food and voucher programs is 8 percent, double that of UCT programs; coverage rises to 22 percent in middle-income countries.[4] In the 13 high-income countries for which data are available, the highest coverage is achieved by UCTs (16 percent), followed by food and vouchers (6.5 percent).

FIGURE 1.1

Coverage of Social Assistance Programs in 108 Low- and Middle-Income Countries, Latest Available Data

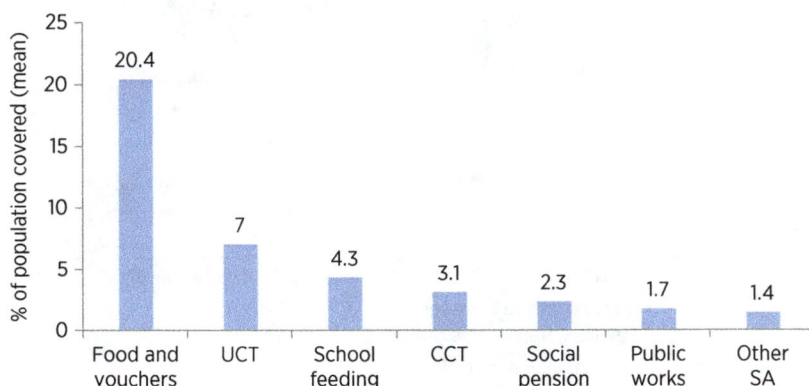

Source: World Bank (ASPIRE database).
Note: The ASPIRE database presents combined data for food and vouchers (both are generally unconditional transfers); UCTs = unconditional cash transfers; CCTs = conditional cash transfers; SA = social assistance. The analysis includes China and India, which are not included in ASPIRE and were added for the analysis.

Programs in the six case studies examined in this volume reach about 1 billion beneficiaries. Global coverage, including relatively large programs in countries like Bangladesh and the belt of countries stretching from Morocco to the Islamic Republic of Iran, clearly adds appreciably to this estimate. The 1 billion figure, for instance, does not include beneficiaries enrolled in programs like school feeding and labor-intensive "food-for-work" activities, which reach 368 million and 22 million beneficiaries, respectively (WFP 2013a, 2013b). Moreover, approximately 57 million people in European and other high-income countries are supported by informal mechanisms such as food banks, soup kitchens, and food pantries operated by civil society, communities, and faith-based organizations (Gentilini 2013).[5] Taken together, the studied interventions, as well as other international programs, reach almost 1.5 billion people, a remarkable number that motivated the title of this volume.

Snapshot of Case Studies
The six case studies presented in chapters 2–7 discuss the evolution, design, and performance of some key programs. These include the targeted public distribution system (TPDS) in India; the ration cards (RCs) and *baladi* bread programs in Egypt; the *Samurdhi* food stamp program in Sri Lanka; the *Programa de Apoyo Alimentario* (PAL, Food Support Program) in Mexico; the Supplemental Nutrition Assistance Program (SNAP) in the United States; and Raskin (now Rastra) in Indonesia. Combined, these programs involve more than US$90 billion annually. The programs are core components of wider safety net programs in these countries and provide a critical source of food for participating households (for example, more than 40 percent of food expenditures for poor households receiving assistance in India). The main features of the schemes are laid out in annex 1A.

The TPDS in India is the largest-scale social assistance program worldwide. In chapter 2 of this volume, Bhattacharya, Falcao, and Puri show that the scheme reaches about 800 million individuals who receive a set of subsidized food commodities accessible in designated food shops. While India's assistance offers the highest absolute coverage, Egypt's schemes—which Abdalla and Al-Shawarby study in chapter 3—offer the highest rate of national coverage, reaching almost 90 percent of the population.

As in Egypt, in Sri Lanka the antecedents of the in-kind program, examined by Tilakaratna and Sooriyamudali in chapter 4, reached 90 percent of the population before being transformed into a food voucher program. This was subsequently converted into a cash-based program reaching about 16 percent of the population. In chapter 5, Scott and Hernández describe the evolution of food-based programs in Mexico, which occurred in parallel with—and in complement to—the better-known conditional cash transfer (CCT), *Prospera* (originally named *Progresa*). PAL currently reaches about 2.5 million people with a combination of cash and voucher transfers.

As Oliveira, Tiehen, Prell, and Smallwood document in chapter 6, SNAP in the United States currently reaches 14 percent of the American population or 45.8 million people. About half (49 percent) of U.S. children are estimated to be in a SNAP-participating household at some point during their childhood. SNAP is a value-based voucher similar to a debit card that can be used in more than 261,000 outlets. The program is part of wider—mostly in-kind—social assistance programs, such as school meals and the Special Supplemental Nutrition Program for Women, Infants, and Children (WIC). Finally, in chapter 7, Timmer, Hastuti, and Sumarto describe the Raskin program in Indonesia. The scheme was established in 1998 and covers more than a quarter of the population, accounting for more than 40 percent of Indonesia's social assistance budget. In contrast to SNAP, which gives beneficiaries a choice, Raskin provides a fixed quantity of rice (15 kilograms) per household at subsidized prices, which is delivered by the government at the community level. Yet, recent developments in Indonesia signal the beginning of a significant transition toward a voucher modality.

A Rapid Tour of Global Evidence
Even in antiquity, public provision of commodities was considered an obligation of the state, including well-known food distribution programs in Egypt and Rome. Yet cash assistance has a similarly ancient history. For example, Garnsey (1988, 26) documents that in the 100s BC, "Famine relief came to Edessans in the form of money." Fast-forward to the 17th century, when England's seminal Old Poor Law expanded "the quantity of cash in the hands of those whose vulnerability was exposed to high prices in dearth years" (Smith 2011, 88). Over the centuries, the relative merits of cash versus food continued to be debated. While others have recently discussed the quandary in more detail (Gentilini 2016a) we provide a succinct overview of key issues in order to frame the ensuing discussions on the evolution and design of food-based programs. Additional considerations around theory and evidence are offered when discussing nutritional issues later in this chapter.

In-kind assistance reduces household choice, but from a normative public policy standpoint, such paternalism may be the intended goal (Currie and Gahvari 2008). For example, a food or voucher program may be more aligned with the specific objective of altering consumption patterns to favor certain types of nutritious foods than a generic transfer in cash.

The use of in-kind transfers may also reflect broader societal preferences toward redistribution, with average taxpayers deeming in-kind as more "reassuring" than cash, despite evidence that recipients spend cash wisely (Evans and Popova 2017). According to Reinhardt (2013, 6), "The preference among voters for bestowing on the poor benefits in-kind rather than cash transfers ... may rest in good part on that characteristic of the typical taxpayer's utility function." That is, FOSA may reflect the interests of nonrecipients as much as those of recipients.

The case for in-kind transfers can also occasionally be made in terms of implementation conditions. For example, in the context of weakly integrated markets or high food prices, such as in the immediate aftermath of a covariate shock or during a lean agricultural season, the capacity of in-kind transfers to keep purchasing power constant can make them preferred—and technically appropriate.

Gender roles and intrahousehold decision-making processes also tend to be among the factors that shape preferences, including the degree of control that women exert over household resources. Moreover, people's experiences can shape their preferences. In India, for example, poor people prefer to receive cash when the public food distribution system works poorly; however, they prefer to receive food when distribution is timely (Khera 2011, 2014). This preference has also been noted in Ethiopia (Sabates-Wheeler and Devereux 2010). Moreover, the majority of participants in a trial in Ecuador who received either cash, vouchers, or in-kind transfers of equal value expressed a preference for the program into which they had been randomly assigned, with such preference being highest among the cash recipients (Hidrobo and others 2014).[6]

What does the empirical evidence reveal about the *comparative* effectiveness and efficiency of noncontributory cash assistance and in-kind food transfers? Results from 14 comparative, randomized and quasi-experimental trials in 11 low- and middle-income countries—all of which were designed to attain food security goals—showed mixed impacts; that is, the *effectiveness* of cash and food transfers was similar on average (Gentilini 2016a). Indeed, differences are often not statistically significant and tend to depend on objectives such as ensuring calorie availability and dietary diversity, and the indicators used to measure them (for example, food expenditures, food consumption scores, and dietary diversity index). The comparative performance of transfers also appears to be a function of the organic and fluid interactions among various factors (for example, profile and "initial conditions" of beneficiaries and capacity of local markets), instead of the inherent merits of a modality.

Instead, assessments of relative *efficiency* lean more favorably toward cash transfers. For example, four randomized trials found that the cost was two to four times higher for food transfers than for cash (Margolies and Hoddinott 2015). Moreover, increasing the value of the transfer did little to change the cost per transaction—thus costs per dollar of transfer declined markedly with value, but this was not the case with food (Alderman 2016). However, in some contexts, economies of scale from the procurement of large amounts of food can offset the higher logistical costs of in-kind provision.[7]

Most large-scale, food-based programs are part of a wider set of objectives, including supporting agriculture and managing price fluctuations and supply risks, in addition to playing a social assistance function. As such, food transfers likely involve more political economy than cash transfers (or vouchers) because of the intertwined, multiple-actor nature of those objectives. And yet, as our case studies show, change is possible and does occur over time—sometimes dramatically, but most often at the margin. In the following sections, we explore these programs and patterns of change in more detail.

While the case studies differ in their reform pathways, they are presented in a consistent structure. In particular, they provide a narrative on the context and factors behind the historical evolution of the core FOSA program, its main design features, and current performance. The chapters also provide insights on institutional coordination with other social protection programs, and their connections to supply chain issues (logistics and agriculture) as well as nutritional matters. In addition, each chapter identifies lessons learned from current experiences and past evolution.

BROAD DIRECTIONS OF CHANGE

From Generalized Subsidies to Targeted Transfers, with Transitions from Food Transfers to Vouchers or Cash Transfers

The trajectories of reform among the six case studies can be charted along two basic axes: (a) whether programs feature a generalized provision[8] or are more targeted and (b) the type of intervention—here, for simplicity, including food subsidies, food transfers, vouchers, and cash transfers. While we focus on the six country examples, we interpret them within global experiences and international literature. Plotting countries' reforms against those metrics reveals some stylized pathways, which are traced in figure 1.2 and include the following:

- Moving from a generalized to a targeted scheme, with a switch from food subsidies to, respectively, food, vouchers, and eventually cash transfers (Sri Lanka)

FIGURE 1.2
Stylized Evolution of the Pathways of the Case Studies

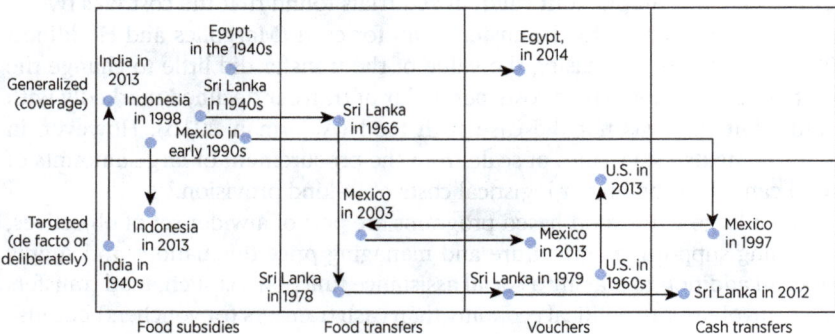

Note: Evolution refers to the examined programs, not necessarily to countries as a whole.

- Moving from generalized to targeted provisions, within the same subsidy modality for a defined bundle of food (Indonesia)

- Maintaining generalized scope, with a switch from a subsidy for commodities to a subsidy similar to vouchers (Egypt)

- Improving scalability and targeting performance (coverage and accuracy), with innovations within a voucher modality (the United States)

- Moving from generalized to targeted provisions, with cash complemented by food and subsequently vouchers (Mexico)

- Moving from a de facto targeted approach (urban biased) to more generalized provision, with emerging innovations within food subsidy provision (India).

In its first two decades (1942–1960s), India's public distribution system (PDS) was de facto spatially targeted. The government initially retained the structure of wartime ration shops to ensure that a regular supply of basic food commodities was widely available in cities, while the country was a net importer of grain. In other words, the PDS was originally conceived to function as a secure market channel and was largely urban. From the early 1970s and following the introduction of the Food Corporation of India (FCI) in 1965, the program evolved into a more general provision, expanding its coverage to rural populations. During the 1990s, structural reforms, skyrocketing costs, and limited performance (including high leakage) led to a shift toward targeting and the introduction of different quotas and prices depending on income—first in 1992 with the revamped PDS (RPDS), followed in 1997 by the targeted PDS (TPDS).

Since the 2000s, the scheme has been part of a broader movement toward generalized and rights-based approaches. India broadened public distribution coverage with the National Food Security Act of 2013. Although debates are unfolding on whether such commitments can be fulfilled, a legacy of droughts and local shortages and the renewed role of rights-based approaches may influence the direction of future reforms and will remain the starting point for many social protection considerations in the country.

At the same time, states such as Chhattisgarh have been innovating with the technical delivery of food subsidies without, for the moment, fully shifting to vouchers or cash transfers. Those experiments have led to remarkable improvements in delivery and accountability, in no small measure due to the application of technology that allowed for beneficiary choice, program monitoring, and competition among participating shopkeepers. We return to these improvements later in the chapter.

Like India, Egypt's RC program has swung between targeting and more general provision. Egypt, however, has maintained a relatively steady course of near-universality through the baladi bread subsidy and expansion of RC coverage. Programs in the Maghreb countries like Algeria, Morocco, and

Tunisia have evolved along the lines of Egypt's system (World Bank 1999, 2011);[9] throughout the Middle East and North Africa more generally, providing food at low (and stable) prices to everyone is regarded as a responsibility of the state and a key ingredient for social contracts. That retention, however, does not mean that systems in the region have been static. In Egypt, changes toward targeting have tended to follow a "U shaped" curve, with coverage starting from extremely high levels (more than 90 percent in 1981), then declining remarkably (although never below serving at least half of the population), and then expanding again. As shown in annex 1A, the subsidy system reaches about 90 percent of Egyptians.

As previous attempts to limit costs opened new opportunities for diversion of flour from subsidized bakeries to the open market, in 2014 the government devised new means to monitor offtake at bakeries, including the experimental use of smartcards. The move both assisted in reducing leakage and allowed a new individual, record-based incentive system, which can be viewed as a major step toward a voucher-type program. More fundamentally, for baladi bread, Egypt moved from subsidizing inputs to bakeries (flour) to subsidizing outputs, that is, up to five loaves per beneficiary per day. At the same time, the RC system was changed from a fixed-quantity-based approach for three commodities to a value-based approach that allows beneficiaries to choose among more than 100 food items. Recent reforms have deliberately connected the baladi and RC systems, including a system whereby unused baladi bread quotas are converted into "points" usable under RC.

The Sri Lanka experience illustrates a more dramatic shift along the dimensions of both targeting and transfers. In that country, a universal system that provided low-price—or free—food on quota for nearly four decades was transformed into a means-tested voucher program over a six-year period. The voucher was only a way station toward a program of cash transfers. Such a conceptually clear evolution was, on closer inspection, fraught with reverses and setbacks.

From 1942 to the early 1970s, the basic structure of the Sri Lankan food subsidy scheme remained largely intact. Then the 1973 global food crisis sparked a major reform, which led to less generous benefits and the introduction of means-tested targeting. The latter was meant to inhibit the better-off individuals from accessing part of the subsidy and, by 1976, to exclude them from the scheme altogether. Other means-tested criteria were subsequently established to target the poorest, while by 1979 the food subsidy scheme was replaced with a voucher program. The voucher program remained in place for 33 years—way longer than in countries like Zambia that tried, briefly and unsuccessfully, to shift from price subsidies to stamps (Grosh 1994; Suryanarayana 1995).

The performance of Sri Lanka's voucher scheme was severely hindered by inflation (the benefit's real value shrank 50 percent in 1982) and hampered by several targeting and recertification challenges. Starting in 1989, two consecutive programs, Janasaviya and Samurdhi, substituted part of the voucher scheme with cash, providing a mix of transfers linked to work and training requirements. By 2012, vouchers were replaced with cash transfers, although several implementation challenges remained.

In the mid-1990s, Mexico brought to a halt its long-standing generalized food subsidy programs. These programs have antecedents in policies initiated in 1938. From the 1960s through the 1990s, they were largely implemented by the government agency CONASUPO. In 1997, the government launched the Progresa CCT program replacing 15 food subsidies (Levy 2006). Such a major step (a) built on a series of smaller reforms that dismantled government retail outlets over time, (b) explored alternative means of subsidizing tortillas (a main food staple), and (c) involved several different transfer modalities.

In particular, within an overall shift toward cash, vestiges of food-based transfers remained after Progresa and its successors scaled up. Indeed, an unconditional food transfer component was retained to serve places that Progresa could not reach. Gradually, that component was phased out and replaced by a voucher scheme operating in tandem with cash. Yet links with previous arrangements were preserved. The voucher distributed by the program (PAL–Sin Hambre, meaning PAL–Without Hunger) could be used at Diconsa stores involving a network of more than 27,000 government-run subsidized retail outlets. That measure revealed a deliberate preference for maintaining some level of in-kind instruments to complement the pure cash-based model.

In the United States, although modifications have been made to SNAP since its inception, it retains its basic function as a targeted voucher program. SNAP originated in an agricultural measure that provided surplus products to low-income families in the Great Depression and evolved into a high-performing countercyclical safety net following its establishment in 1964 (with a pilot in 1961 and roots in a 1939 program). The scheme became an entitlement program and dramatically expanded its coverage of the poor through considerable outreach efforts, while maintaining high cost-efficiency and standards of targeting accuracy.

Finally, Indonesia's approach to food-based social assistance is intrinsically linked to its strategy of maintaining a high level of domestic food prices. Rather than addressing price volatility through targeted social safety nets, a seemingly less administratively taxing approach was to address the "root" cause of food unaffordability through upstream interventions in the rice market and supply chain. In this regard, BULOG, a food logistics agency, was created in 1966 with a mandate similar to India's FCI, including a responsibility to achieve food (rice) self-sufficiency and use stocks to smooth fluctuations in production and consumption. In 1998, however, a massive devaluation occurred at the same time as an El Niño event that negatively affected agriculture; with the skyrocketing cost to stabilize prices, the country was forced to adopt an explicit targeted program to provide subsidized rice to poor households (even though this proclaimed objective remains challenging to achieve).

The program, Raskin (now called Rastra), has persisted as the core domestic safety net even as the country has launched several cash transfer schemes. As mentioned, Rastra is moving in the the direction of a voucher scheme, with ongoing experimentation in 44 cities.

From Agricultural Objectives to Social Protection

Imperatives of food self-sufficiency have been a key factor motivating an in-kind approach to food security. Over time, many countries have transformed food price stabilization policies into social protection programs aimed directly at poverty reduction. Such an evolution was possible only with changing politics, governance reforms, and modifications to the social contract, and it was enabled by technological changes.

For example, during the 1970s and 1980s, some countries in Latin America used overvalued exchange rates to reduce the price of food, a practice that lowered the cost of living for the poor and kept urban wages low enough to encourage private enterprise. The same was true in many African countries after independence, with detrimental impacts on agricultural development (de Janvry and Subramanian 1993; Krueger, Schiff, and Valdés 1988). Other measures, such as mandatory procurement at prices below those that would clear an open market as well as export bans, were also used to achieve many of the goals covered elsewhere by ration shops and food distribution via state-supported retail networks. Although such policies are still employed—especially to stabilize prices in the wake of significant spikes (Barrett 2013)—they are more likely to be used as temporary emergency measures rather than as core instruments designed to influence price levels (Pinstrup-Andersen 2015).

The presence of direct targeted cash support or a willingness to use fiscal resources to place a wedge between consumer and producer prices for food has helped to lessen the inherent tension between the interests of the two groups. For example, fiscal subsidies to consumers allowed Egypt to relax procurement quotas (Von Braun and de Haen 1983) and enabled Morocco to support wheat producers without imposing major increases on consumer prices (Azzam 1991; World Bank 2003). A similar wedge permitted the Islamic Republic of Iran to pursue a self-sufficiency strategy with price incentives for producers as well as controlled prices for bread (Amid 2007). Additionally, before implementation of the North American Free Trade Agreement, Mexico simultaneously offered prices to producers that were above world market prices and provided subsidized tortillas to urban consumers.

The interaction of consumer and producer policies in India is particularly complex and has evolved appreciably over time. A key moment in its evolution stems from the petition filed in the Supreme Court by the People's Union for Civil Liberties in Rajasthan in 2001. The petition demanded that the government use the country's considerable food stocks to address hunger, citing a clause in the country's constitution that ensures the right to life and personal dignity. The court responded with an "interim order" (since renewed) that converted benefits from existing nutrition programs into entitlements.[10] The trend to lower prices for commodities distributed in the TPDS represents a shift of objectives from assuring the functioning of food markets to transferring income to the poor (Khera 2011).

While the interplay of objectives still plays an important role, food-based programs are becoming better aligned with social protection systems. SNAP contains features that connect it to other national FOSA programs. For example, the electronic benefit transfers card of the WIC program has a strong functional overlap with SNAP cards. In addition, more than 50 percent of WIC beneficiaries also participated in SNAP in 2009.

In Indonesia, an evaluation of Rastra led to the eventual adoption of a "social protection card," which allows access not only to the food subsidy but also to other cash-based and education-related programs. Rastra's data and targeting classification criteria are, since 2012, aligned with the Unified Database for Social Protection (earlier criteria followed a 10-point scale based on National Family Planning Coordination Board data). In 2013, Rastra became part of the Acceleration and Broadening of Social Protection Program, a program to alleviate the impact of rising fuel prices, with the government providing households with brochures that contained further information about Rastra.

In addition to integrating baladi and RC programmatically, Egypt recently introduced *Takaful*, a new CCT scheme. The program automatically ensures eligibility for the food subsidy program. Thus, it currently administers a subsidy scheme in parallel with a targeted transfer. As mentioned, Indonesia also has a policy of cash transfers that coincides with its program of in-kind distribution. In Mexico, the PAL program was gradually integrated with Prospera: after an initial period of separate organizational arrangements, the program was eventually incorporated into Prospera's institutional framework. Yet, Mexico maintained a food distribution program for many years after institutionalizing CCTs and continues to distribute subsidized milk, and it has not completely phased out its retail arm, Diconsa (which remains a key institution). On balance, in Mexico, the benefits reaching the poor increased fivefold in the past two decades. The food-based PAL is a stepping stone to CCTs once the preconditions of available services are met and the budget is authorized (1.3 million beneficiary households of PAL have moved to the mainstream CCT, a sizable influx).

A similar approach has been taken in Bangladesh, which has successfully administered cash transfers for education for decades and eliminated food rationing in 1993 (Ravallion and Wodon 2000; Ryan and Meng 2004). However, in the spring of 2016, the country reintroduced a rural grain-rationing scheme, which is intended to avoid upheavals such as those of the 2008–09 global food crisis through an aggressive domestic food stock policy (Dorosh, forthcoming).[11]

These examples show a degree of commonality within a set of programs that are all easily categorized as elements of a safety net strategy, often with clear administrative overlap. In other cases, free or subsidized food distribution occurs outside of social protection programs. For example, in Sri Lanka, the

Ministry of Health provides Thriposha, a formulated infant nutritional supplement, on the basis of nutritional need and has done so as food rations have
evolved into food stamps and subsequently into direct income support. India
provides in-kind commodity transfers—as well as prepared meals—as part of
its Integrated Child Development Services, which is administered by the
Ministry of Women and Child Development, with eligibility not affected by
whether or not the household is below the poverty line. Eligibility is not dependent on the level of subsidy the household receives in the TPDS.

The insights emerging from case studies also shed light on an intriguing,
yet understudied, aspect of social assistance provision—that is, its role in facilitating a process of structural transformation from an agrarian to a more
industrial economy (Timmer 2007). While the issue requires further examination, suggestive evidence indicates that food subsidies have been used to
accelerate the transformation process.

The initial urban bias of formal social assistance could be interpreted
in this vein (Lipton 1977). For example, for most of Indonesia's history, the
main social safety net has been a public guarantee that rice would be available in urban markets at affordable (and stable) prices. In Mexico, the Social
Milk Supply Program—the country's oldest targeted food program—began as
an urban program, while in India the PDS began operations in urban centers
with a population of more than 100,000. Perhaps more explicitly, in Egypt
in the 1950s–60s, food subsidies were intended to finance industrialization
and the provision of inexpensive food to urban consumers. In Sri Lanka, the
role of agriculture and the coverage of food subsidies seem particularly
attuned: over the past half-century, the share of agriculture in gross domestic
product (GDP) declined 75 percent and the coverage of food subsidies
declined 80 percent (figure 1.3).

The considerations dovetail transformation strategies whereby agriculture is
protected in the early stages of the process, with farmers later becoming a
potent voting bloc in newly formed democratic societies. In Indonesia, many
poor households remain—in both rural and urban areas—but they may not be
numerous enough to outvote key coalitions. These may include urban middle-class households that want guaranteed supplies of rice in their local markets
and farmers who want higher rice prices to compensate for the loss of economic
competitiveness in the production of labor-intensive crops, especially rice.

Such perspective might also provide a useful lens to understand how, for
instance, vouchers are connected to the growing and diversified retail sector
(and its political clout)—which in itself is the result of wider transformations
in supply chains. The rise of supermarket chains across low- and middle-
income countries epitomizes those underlying structural forces (Reardon and
Timmer 2014). As a result, food vouchers do not necessarily need to be
redeemed in small food shops, like relatively small-scale vendors in the
West Bank and Gaza and the precrisis Syrian Arab Republic (Omamo,
Gentilini, and Sandström 2010); instead, a wider gamut of outlet options

FIGURE 1.3

Food Subsidy Coverage and Agriculture as a Share of GDP in Sri Lanka, 1960–2014

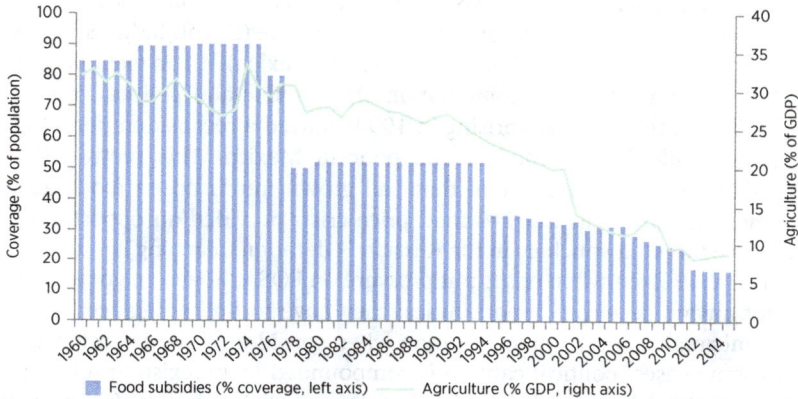

Source: Chapter 4 in this volume (Tilakaratna and Sooriyamudali 2018) and World Development Indicators online database.
Note: GDP = gross domestic product.

have emerged, with Ecuador illustrating how a voucher program could be used in commercial supermarket chains (Hidrobo and others 2014). SNAP is a premier example of how a voucher program can operate in an increasingly sophisticated retail sector, with implications for procurement standards. Under the program, 49 percent of the total transactions occur in superstores and 33 percent in supermarkets. Groceries or similar stores account for only 12 percent of total outlets used.

CHANNELS FOR CHANGE

Crises as Critical Junctures

In the preface to his 1962 book, Milton Friedman suggested, "Keep options open until circumstances make change necessary. ... That, I believe, is our basic function: to develop alternatives to existing policies, to keep them alive and available until the politically impossible becomes politically inevitable." Almost every crisis is a reminder for policy makers of the volatility of markets and ensuing risks for producers and consumers. Often, but not always, a crisis opens the political space and creates opportunities for reform. These opportunities are what Acemoglu and Robinson (2012) call "critical junctures" in the course of policy making. Macroeconomic crises can serve as catalysts for this makeover, but it is very difficult to stabilize prices or find the resources needed to ring-fence food-based transfers when the macroeconomy is out of control. For example, when the costs of imports rise due to either oscillations in grain markets or movements in exchange rates, countries may be forced either to increase subsidies with the attendant budgetary impact or to redesign consumer support policies.

Most of the flagship food-based programs examined in this book were introduced or significantly reformed during wartime (Egypt, India, Sri Lanka) or after severe economic shocks (Indonesia, Mexico).[12] For example, Levy (2006) maintains that the combination of economic and political pressures that followed the Chiapas uprising in 1994 spurred a reconsideration of how support should be provided to the poor in Mexico. This motivated the rethinking of a complex system that had grown into a dozen food subsidy schemes. Similarly, the 2007–8 food price crisis provided an opportunity to introduce targeted vouchers in the Russian Federation, reaching about 19 million people.[13] Even when crises put pressure on FOSA, however, governments do not always seize the opportunities; they have to find a balance between economic realism and political caution when considering sudden reforms.

In some cases, political caution is compounded by preexisting sentiments regarding the role of food provision in forging social contracts. In Egypt, for example, the legitimacy of the ruling regime often became conditioned on its commitment and ability to provide food and basic goods at affordable prices. Similarly, in Sri Lanka, interfering with the subsidy program was not politically feasible without risking political capital. Moreover, the shift in power in 1970 could be attributed largely to the government's change in the food subsidy structure (that is, halving the quantities provided, although providing them for free instead of at subsidized prices), which was partially superseded by the incoming administration.

Technology Can Help to Seize Reform Momentum
Change, however, does not need crises to occur. Technology is a case in point. The use of electronic platforms to transfer cash to bank accounts, smartcards, and mobile phones has transformed the ability of governments to introduce and manage cash transfer programs. The same technology that delivers cash can also be used for vouchers, eliminating most of the expense of redeeming them. Available technology can even make in-kind systems more efficient. For example, Egypt uses card readers that record the number of bread loaves a family purchases. This technology not only reduces the opportunity for diversion of flour, but also incentivizes savings (that is, a family that purchases less bread is entitled to more purchases at other outlets providing ration card commodities).

Although technology can cut transaction costs, the willingness and capacity to adopt such measures are central. Mexico introduced the electronic tracking of purchases of free tortillas a quarter of a century before Egypt sought to use such tracking. Moreover, the recent reduction in the leakage of rations in Bihar, India, was made possible, in part, by the distribution of coupons that could be used at any time during the existence of the program (Drèze, Khera, and Pudussery 2015). In particular, table 1.2 shows the key

TABLE 1.2 Technology and Problem Solving in India's Targeted Public Distribution System (TPDS)

PROBLEM	TECHNOLOGY-BASED SOLUTION	COMMENT
Manual entry of data and missing documents	End-to-end computerization of transactions involving the procurement, storage, and transportation of food grains	As a result, in Bihar the leakage of food grains declined from 92.9% in 2004–05 to 29.1% in fiscal year 2011–12.
Abuse by TPDS shopkeepers	Beneficiary choice and performance-based allocation of grain to participating shops	In Chhattisgarh, the centralized online real-time electronic PDS (CORE PDS) allows beneficiaries to use smartcards and choose shops, an innovation that enhances portability of benefits and fosters competition. In turn, the model allows states to allocate grains to shops on a performance basis—that is, based on online-recorded transactions.
Food not arriving at ration shop	Doorstep delivery and global positioning system (GPS)–based monitoring	This monitoring includes simple solutions like replacing private delivery trucks with yellow-painted government trucks, which addressed a key source of leakage. In Bihar, for example, a Bangalore-based information and communication technology (ICT) company designed a software that allows district and state officials to track the movement of grain, as well as to obtain detailed information from each truck, like the weight of grain it is carrying.
Double dipping	Digitization of the ration card database	Digitization has increased transparency by making available an easily accessible database and allowed the government to apply other technologies, such as bar codes and biometric smartcards, to remove bogus or "ghost" beneficiaries. The digitization process has been carried out for more than 320 million cards, of which more than 25 percent have been seeded with Aadhaar.
Lack of feedback loops	Grievance software and call numbers	In Chhattisgarh, complaints are directed to a toll-free call center where they are recorded on a web portal. The web portal redirects complaints to the respective district food offices, which send them to the associated food inspectors. Food inspectors are expected to investigate and respond within 15 days.

Source: Based on chapter 2 in this volume (Bhattacharya, Falcao, and Puri 2018).

role of technology in addressing five sources of leakage. Furthermore, many countries are moving to a common registry of current and prospective beneficiaries that allows coordination and integration across programs (Leite and others, forthcoming). Along these lines, India is making progress in providing a unique, biometric *Aadhaar* identification number to every citizen. That use of technology may revolutionize the business of record keeping and verification in all social safety nets, including the TPDS.[14] Clearly, the use of technology has also helped to move away from approaches that direct beneficiaries to specific shops and toward a system that allows beneficiaries to *choose* where to spend their entitlement. This has helped to eradicate patronage and abuse by shopkeepers, while fostering competition among them. In other words, beneficiaries became customers.

In addition to the Chhattisgarh case mentioned in table 1.2, the recent experience of Egypt is noteworthy. In chapter 3, Abdalla and Al-Shawarby show that the number of reported violations by bakeries in regard to underweight loaves and loaf specifications decreased from 37,000 and 46,000 pre-reform incidents, respectively, to 12,000 and 14,000 incidents in 2015. Similarly, a key ingredient for the merger of the baladi and RC schemes was the presence of an automated smart system to monitor both financial transactions of the bakeries and accrued saving points of the beneficiaries. A private sector partnership consolidated the system and rolled out the model nationwide within about a year, starting with a pilot in Port Said in 2013.

Technology also assists in improving the efficiency of targeting. Computer-assisted data collection, for example, makes proxy means testing easier to implement. Targeting, however, still requires incentives for administrators, because bureaucratic management and quality assurance of data take resources (Duclos 1995). But in some cases, targeting breaks down because the community and the administrators may favor universal distribution (of smaller allotments for everyone), as in some areas of Indonesia. In such a case, decentralization potentially improves information, but it also allows local implementation to deviate from the central government's preferred approach.

Political Economy

One well-known model of collective action posits that comparatively small groups, with large benefits for a given individual, can organize more effectively to promote their interests than can the general population, with larger total benefits but relatively small expected benefits for a given individual (Olson 2009). Even in primarily agrarian economies, a few surplus-producing estates can dominate trade, and, thus, the estate stratum has an incentive to advocate for pro-producer policies. But if poverty is widespread, food absorbs a large share of household budgets and consumers are unlikely to be indifferent to high producer prices, as is often the case in higher-income countries. Hence, many countries (including India and Indonesia) have sought to reconcile those interests by simultaneously supporting producers and subsidizing consumers.

But the alignment of incentives and the ability of different groups to assert their interests is fluid, with crises that can reorder social priorities and reweight concerns. Longer-term trends in the economy can also reorient priorities for food policy. For example, the overall balance of consumer and producer interests often shifts over time. A declining share of agriculture in the economy, usually accompanied by increasing national income, is a hallmark of agricultural transformation. The concentration of agricultural production does not reduce the ability of the rural economy to organize politically, but the associated reduction in the number of poor households and the share of the budget they devote to food could make a targeted transfer program more feasible to administer and a broader food policy less compelling. Indonesia fits this pattern most closely.

Changing market circumstances also helped Bangladesh to revisit its food policy, where fitful attempts to reform the ration system eventually reached fruition in 1992, aided by a 20 percent decline in rice prices in the wider market (Chowdhury and Haggblade 2000). Similarly, Pakistan was able to abolish flour rationing in 1987 with no consumer resistance, in part because the share of flour that even low-income consumers obtained from ration shops had been declining for a decade (Alderman 1988). In the United States, SNAP vouchers are supported by a coalition of rural and urban interests, in part because the common goal is to increase the size of the food budget (Beghin and Elobeid 2015; Wright 2014). By placing the reauthorization of SNAP vouchers within a comprehensive farm bill that is scheduled to be renewed every five years, sponsors can rely on a share of urban representatives to work with farm lobbyists to enact the legislation.

However, rent seeking by a small set of participants can also slow or dilute reform. As is commonly observed throughout the world, two-tier price systems can invite corruption (Mehta and Jha 2014). Government officials at the head of the distribution channel and shopkeepers at its tail may have an incentive to divert subsidized commodities to the higher-priced open market and, thus, have an interest in blocking reforms that remove that opportunity. The reforms in Chhattisgarh included doorstep delivery to ration shops, a procedure that reduced the potential for upstream diversion of supplies and made it difficult for shopkeepers to blame the warehouse for partial delivery of rations (Drèze and Khera 2010).

Even bakers' interest in having access to subsidized flour, which they can divert, appears to have been an obstacle to bread policy reforms in Egypt, at least until recently. Moreover, even if the retailers do not divert grain, their livelihoods may depend, in part, on their participation in the subsidy system. Thus, the distribution of dealerships became a means of political patronage in Bangladesh, one that was lobbied effectively through a dealers' association (Chowdhury and Haggblade 2000). Although such an arrangement was not able to thwart the abolition of ration shops in 1992, an earlier attempt at reform in the former East Pakistan in 1956 was reversed largely due to the efforts of disenfranchised departmental employees who were rehired when rationing was restored (Haggblade 2000). Bangladesh's derationing in 1992 and Pakistan's similar step in 1987 prompted ration shopkeepers to protest; however, they received little broad consumer support (Alderman 1988).

Relatedly, in India various attempts to replace grain distribution with flour, which can be fortified with micronutrients, have been challenged by small mill (*chakki*) owners (Fiedler and others 2012). The millers could lose business if flour were processed at a more convenient central location.

How do consumers and producers make their voices heard? While coalitions of support for food policy do not always interact in the public arena, the public expresses its interest in food policy at the ballot box and in the streets. Regarding the former, both India and Sri Lanka have used promises of increases in transfer programs as part of the election process, reflecting a common, indeed global, pattern of clientelism in democratic states (Fukuyama 2014). Edirisinghe (1988) presents a specific illustration of the interplay of elections and stymied program reforms. In an attempt to improve targeting, the Sri Lankan government set up administrative guidelines for publicizing names in order both to discourage false reporting and to allow local committees to screen applicants. However, after the president declared that no family receiving stamps would lose access to them, it was no longer possible to pare off ineligible beneficiaries, and the number of recipients increased 6 percent.

Democratic processes can, however, also make substantial reforms possible. For example, Jamaica introduced targeted food stamps following opening of the economy in the 1980s endorsed by the ballot (Grosh 1992). Voters may also reward politicians who are seen as promoting equity through efficiently targeted transfer programs. For example, mayors in Brazil who were more successful at transparent implementation of the country's cash transfer had a greater probability of reelection (de Janvry, Finan, and Sadoulet 2012). Such a result is consistent with the various laboratory studies indicating an innate preference for fairness. In partial contrast to this perspective, Gelbach and Pritchett (2000) argue that if middle-class voters do not share in a portion of a transfer program, they will not support it. This view is in keeping with an analysis of Colombia's food coupon, which was launched in 1975 and discontinued by 1982 (Uribe Mosquera 1993). That program was relatively small yet complex; with no clear political constituency, it withered from lack of interest.

A different form of voice can be heard in the streets, although the role of riots in blocking reforms is not clear. Bread riots have ignited mass protests from the Greek and Roman empires to the tumultuous days of the Arab Spring (Barrett 2013; Garnsey 1988; Tannahill 1988). However, few governments fall as a result of food riots, in part because these riots are often spontaneous rather than a product of an organized opposition (Bienen and Gersovitz 1986). Perhaps, but this provides little consolation to a minister whose job was sacrificed to mollify public opinion. Moreover, one reason why governments survive food riots is that they often rescind reforms or offer new subsidies in the wake of protests. This was part of the response to the riots that broke out in Alexandria and Cairo in 1978 after the government announced that it would reduce—not abolish—subsidies (Alderman 1986). Moreover, the government kept those disturbances in mind when considering reforms over subsequent decades.

Although food prices may be a focal point for consumers, some food riots may reflect a general discontent and challenge a government's legitimacy or overall economic management. Seddon (1986) maintains that this was the case for the 1984 food riots in Morocco and Tunisia, both of which led to the withdrawal of previously announced price increases. This is also likely a valid observation in regard to food riots during the Arab Spring of 2010 and 2011. For example, deadly riots in Algeria were sparked by 20 percent increases in the prices of cooking oil and sugar (*Wall Street Journal* 2011), although such price movements were unlikely to have had a substantial impact on real income. Nevertheless, regardless of the mix of factors that feed into food riots, most governments remain acutely sensitive to the potential for consumer unrest to become unmanageable.

Somewhat less visible, or at least less dramatic, than public protest is the long-term involvement of civil society outside the ballot box. Civil society played a major role in ensuring that the Indian TPDS was viewed as an entitlement when it brought suit in court. Here we refer to entitlement in its narrow legal sense (as opposed to the concept introduced by Indian economist A. K. Sen, which embodies opportunities as well as rights). Claiming public assistance as a right does not work without a legal system that enforces the law and a budget that is adequate to make good on individual claims; SNAP fits these criteria effectively. India's situation, however, stands out because civil society uses the courts not merely to monitor the implementation of laws—indeed, implementation of court orders appears spotty—but also to set the agenda.

Civil society plays an additional role in reforming the implementation of a program by increasing transparency. For example, the state of Chhattisgarh has reduced ghost or fake recipients and reduced mistargeting by publicly posting information on cardholders, a policy that both increases program awareness and provides a measure of public shaming of ineligible beneficiaries (Drèze and Khera 2010). In addition, a grievance hotline was established in the state to increase the voice of previously disenfranchised households. Moreover, the government of Chhattisgarh, as well as the government of Tamil Nadu, sends text messages to households informing them when grains have been delivered to ration shops (Khera 2011). Finally, reforms in Chhattisgarh have placed ration shops under community councils (*gram panchayats*) and self-help groups.

Community monitoring of performance may be enhanced by the inclusion of a broad spectrum of the population. Drèze and Sen (2013) maintain that states where families with incomes somewhat above the poverty line can draw rations often have less leakage than states where only marginalized households have a stake in the system. Similarly, they speculate that, although the gap between the ration price and the open-market price might be a motivation to divert supplies, that same price premium is also an incentive for communities to scrutinize delivery more closely.

STEPS FORWARD, STEPS NOT TAKEN

Average Performance Has Improved, but Challenges Remain

Today, food-based social assistance programs are a long way from the stereotype of food assistance that fueled past perceptions of wastage and inefficiency. Since the mid-2000s, most programs made significant progress along key performance metrics. For example, SNAP consistently exceeds global standards of program performance: 85 percent of eligible beneficiaries participate in a typical month, 4.7 million people were lifted out of poverty in 2014, and the program has an economic multiplier factor of 1.79—that is, national GDP increases US$1.79 billion for every US$1 billion worth of SNAP, with a resulting creation of 17,900 full-time jobs.

SNAP program features are designed to offset potential work disincentives. These include, for example, an earned income deduction and dependent care deduction; a simplified eligibility process, with relaxed asset limits to allow for vehicle ownership; restrictions on the participation of nonworking adults without dependents; and work registration (and training) requirements. Program participation is highly dynamic, making SNAP one of the most countercyclical social assistance programs worldwide (figure 1.4). For example, between 2008 and 2012 the median spell of continuous participation was one year. About two-thirds of beneficiaries exited within two years; among those who exited, almost half reentered within one year. Also, provisions are included for disaster response (D-SNAP), with the delivery of an additional month of benefits to disaster-affected participants.

In India, some noticeable improvements occurred between 2004–05 and 2011–12. For instance, there was a steady decline in the leakage of TPDS food grain, from 55 to 38 percent; coverage of the program doubled from 22.4 to 44.5 percent of Indian households; and coverage among the bottom 40 percent increased from 33 to 58.3 percent. Nominal monthly benefits transferred to the poor also increased from Rs 46 to Rs 184.

Improvements in TPDS functioning have been attributed to a range of innovations initiated by state governments, especially low-income ones. In Chhattisgarh, for example, measures were put in place to capture in real time the transactions between beneficiaries and food shops. Field surveys suggest that leakages decreased from 51.8 to 1.5 percent. Similarly, Indonesia has significantly reduced exclusion errors. Between 2002 and 2014, the share of households in the bottom decile that received Rastra soared from 60 to

FIGURE 1.4

SNAP Participation, Poverty, and Unemployment in the United States, 1980–2014

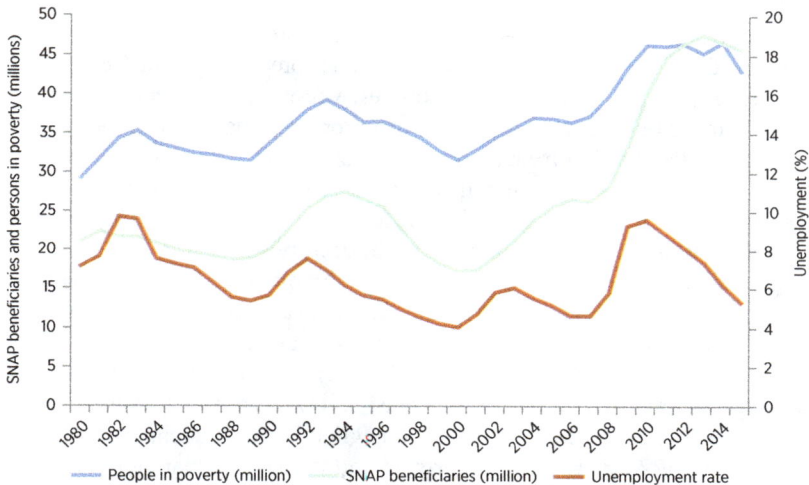

Source: Oliveira and others 2016.

72 percent. Also, steps were taken for a more user-friendly distribution, such as stipulating that rice packs could be provided with a capacity aligned with the household's entitlement quantity (15 kilograms).

In Egypt, the reform of the food subsidy system has been associated, in the case of baladi bread, with a reduction in the amount of nonmilled wheat from 15 to 7–8 percent a year. At the same time, coverage grew from 56 million to 82.2 million people, with the provision of bread moving from a "first come, first served" basis to smartcard preregistration. Waiting time for beneficiaries decreased from "several hours" to less than 15 minutes. Moreover, coverage of RC grew from 66 million to 71 million people. There are early indications that the RC program's choice-based approach brought a 30 percent increase in dietary diversification.[15]

There is also emerging evidence of economic benefits from the broad Egyptian reform: for example, the government launched a new franchising chain of 14,000 shops (called My Cooperative), where young entrepreneurs get concessional loans to equip their shops with commodities in line with government specifications; simultaneously, Egypt's three state-owned grocery chains doubled their sales between 2013 and 2015, from LE 0.7 billion to LE 1.5 billion, respectively. The fact that the food subsidy scheme is now open to the private sector has enhanced the negotiating power of the government in procurement, leading to wholesale prices that are generally in line with those obtained by large retailers. This translated into significant discounts for grocers licensed to receive RC commodities (up to 15 percent for some products), hence making their business profitable. Like Egypt, other countries in the region are attempting to use modern technology for program implementation (especially for identification and payment) and for making more explicit the links between food-based assistance and the rest of the social protection system. These efforts may generate mutual learning opportunities. Morocco, in particular, is attempting to gear the reform of its system toward promoting better nutrition.

In Sri Lanka, the shift from a cash plus voucher in the Samurdhi program to a pure cash regime was accompanied by a simplification of beneficiary categories (reduced to four groups) and a transfer of the cash grant directly into beneficiaries' Samurdhi bank account. The shift occurred because of long delays in the provision of voucher-related goods, their poor quality, abuse by shopkeepers (who were charging higher prices), and limited availability of commodities.

While the emerging evidence from the case studies is encouraging, significant challenges remain. For instance, while coverage has been enhanced and exclusion errors have improved, inclusion errors are still significant. In Chhattisgarh itself, exclusion errors are negligible, while inclusion errors are at a sobering 22.1 percent. Similarly, in Indonesia, the planned number of Rastra-participating households is 15.5 million. Although the overall program is progressive, in 2014, actual beneficiaries were double that level, or some 33.4 million households.

Moreover, household survey data show that Rastra recipients only receive about one-third of their entitlement. This stems from several factors, like "missing rice" on the order of 39–48 percent of total allocation; extra costs incurred by beneficiaries (for transporting rice from the distribution point to the local center); inadequate information and awareness about the program; and inadequate sharing of practices within receiving communities. Finally, Rastra rice is often inferior quality, the purchase of that rice by beneficiaries occurs with manual cash payments.

Although qualitative indications for the new system in Egypt are positive, recent reforms have yet to be evaluated rigorously. There is evidence, for example, that while the move toward a value-based entitlement provided more choice, inflation decreased its real value by about 18 percent compared with that of the quantity-based system. Beneficiaries also experienced shortages of commodities: for example, between July and December 2015 shortages of cooking oil accounted for about one-third of total supply among affiliated groceries. The near-universal nature of the scheme is also evident in its targeting performance, with 77.4 percent of the richest decile participating in the program. Although the reforms seem to have reduced the leakage of wheat flour, the supply chain of procurement, warehousing, and milling of wheat is still facing some issues.

Similarly, Mexico's PAL has historically lacked some key performance indicators, making performance monitoring challenging. Its recent absorption into the

Prospera framework was intended to raise the evaluation standards for that component, placing them on a par with those applied to the CCT arm. In Sri Lanka, the targeting performance of the Samurdhi program has deteriorated over the years. In 1995–96, nearly two-thirds of households in the bottom two deciles were beneficiaries; in 2012–13, this share had declined to around 36 percent of households in the poorest decile. The lack of clearly defined criteria for selecting beneficiaries and limited systematic entry and exit mechanisms may help to explain the persistence of targeting errors in the Samurdhi program.

Evidence Can Facilitate Change

The discussion of performance is closely connected to the role of evidence in decision making. Attributing a policy change to any specific study or new information is challenging. The principals involved in a policy decision are rarely fully conscious of the role that facts and analysis play in shifting objectives or changing instruments. These individuals may be even less likely to articulate the decision-making process. For example, when the state secretary for agriculture, Sartaz Aziz, announced the end of flour rationing in Pakistan in 1987, he cited evidence of grain leakage. However, it is not possible to ascertain whether the data directly motivated the policy change or merely assisted in the justification to the public (Alderman 1988). In other words, evidence can be an instrument to further policy choices made on other criteria rather than a tool to determine them.

In Pakistan, the path from evidence to an interested policy maker was direct; the evidence was not transmitted through either academic publications or the wider media.[16] Although academic studies and the media do produce evidence that informs policy, there is often a gradual diffusion of general knowledge over time, knowledge that is generally not attributable to a single study or report. Indeed, the relevant information often crosses borders. For example, Kenya does not have a ration shop for maize partially because of evidence accumulated from the PDS in India. The Kenyan government had considered an urban ration in 2008 as prices spiked, and it set up a food policy advisory group to consider the proposal before ruling out the option.[17] Similarly, Behrman (2010) attests that the specific body of research used to evaluate Progresa has as much or more value to the global community of practice as to Mexico itself. That opinion does not imply that the reforms in Mexico were not based on evidence—indeed, the 1997 watershed reflected a careful evaluation of a pilot program and other reforms. Subsequent modifications of the CCT have also used studies from earlier phases.

Additionally, the evidence accumulated in trials of smartcards, cash, and in-kind programs from Mexico is used in discussions of safety net programs around the world. However, Mexico did not conduct a pilot before introducing a form of voucher redeemable at government retail outlets (Diconsa), signaling policy makers' interest in continuing to provide food transfers alongside cash-based programs.

Reforms in Tunisia in the late 1980s and early 1990s illustrate the additional role of information. Although the government employed detailed studies of consumer budgets in its programs, including using a combination of (a) subsidies on commodities preferentially consumed by low-income households and (b) price increases on higher-quality varieties of commodities purchased by wealthier families, it also used a strategy of broad dissemination of information (Tuck and Lindert 1996). In particular, it promoted the distribution of data on the budgetary implications of subsidies as well as the rationale for reforms that would be implemented in advance of the actual reforms. Unlike the experience six years earlier, the government was able to reduce the subsidy without public unrest. However, similar attempts to change the subsidy regime after the Arab Spring have not resulted in a recasting of the scheme, even though it has largely lost its original rationale.

Promising, but Largely Untapped, Linkages to the Nutrition Agenda
Interventions or programs that address the immediate determinants of fetal and child nutrition and development—adequate food and nutrient intake, feeding, caregiving and parenting practices, and low burden of infectious diseases—may be necessary steps toward reducing malnutrition, but they are likely only part of a larger strategy. For example, simulations of the impact of scaling up 10 effective nutrition-specific interventions to cover 90 percent of children in the world's most malnourished countries would diminish stunting only 20 percent globally (Bhutta and others 2013). Thus, investments in "nutrition-sensitive" sectors will be critical components of any global strategy to eliminate undernutrition (Ruel and Alderman 2013).

Those interventions or programs will address the underlying determinants of fetal and child nutrition—food security; adequate caregiving resources at the maternal, household, and community levels; access to health services; and a safe and hygienic environment. Social protection can be a nutrition-sensitive investment by virtue of the fact that it targets families at risk of malnutrition. Moreover, social protection programs are often at a scale far more comprehensive than nutrition-specific programs. Few countries have been able to scale up all of the recommended nutrition-specific interventions at levels similar to the coverage of social protection programs.

In some contexts, in-kind transfer programs may have a limited impact on the amount or diversity of food consumed. A key reason is that they often provide a small fraction of consumption needs even for the poor: as shown in annex 1A, transfer programs in Egypt, Indonesia, and the United States range between 2 and 10 percent of household food consumption or expenditures. As such, most transfer programs are "inframarginal"—that is, they provide an amount of food (or specific commodity) smaller than the household would consume in the absence of the program. These inframarginal transfers do not influence consumption through a price response, although they do increase the amount of income at the household's disposal.

While the size of transfers might be limited, households often consume more food from transfer programs than from other sources of income. Indeed, what is noteworthy about the global experience with food-oriented transfers—whether a voucher, food, or even a cash transfer—is that such transfers often nudge consumers to devote more of the additional income to food purchases than they would from other sources of income. This tendency has been noted in Colombia, Ecuador, Mexico, and Nicaragua (Attanasio, Battistin, and Mesnard 2012), as well as in studies of SNAP. Beatty and Tuttle (2015) find that the expansion of SNAP in 2009 led to increases on food expenditure greater than predicted by an assumption of fungible income sources. This increase may be the result of social marketing or labeling (Kooreman 2000). Alternatively, or additionally, the shift of budgets toward food purchases may be linked to female control of income and bargaining power (Angelucci and Attanasio 2013; Schady and Rosero 2008).

Although this "nudging" holds for all transfer modalities—that is, for both cash and in-kind transfers—in some cases, in-kind transfers generate an additional effect relative to cash. This "cash out puzzle" has been widely observed in the literature on SNAP: according to Barrett (2002, 54), "Virtually every study finds [that] food stamps increase household nutrient availability at 2–10 times the rate of a like value of cash income." Chapter 6 discusses this surprising evidence in more detail.

Another major puzzle is why the unmistakable impact of transfer programs on food consumption does not readily translate into improvements in anthropometric measures of nutrition. Meta-analyses of trials of conditional and unconditional transfers have found that these programs have relatively little consistent impact on child stunting or underweight (Manley, Gitter, and Slavchevska 2013; Ruel and Alderman 2013). Many explanations have been offered for that limited impact. Some of these reflect research design. For example, the children studied often are outside the age of greatest growth velocity and vulnerability to malnutrition. Moreover, many interventions, or at least the evaluations of them, cover too short a period of time to capture the cumulative nature of the program. In addition, systematic reviews are based predominately on studies of Latin American programs.

More substantially, however, there is some question as to the quality of the supply side of health services available to beneficiaries. Demand-side interventions have not generally been matched with programmatic considerations, making these transfers nutrition sensitive (Alderman 2016). As discussed, one approach to improving the nutritional sensitivity of transfer programs is to include an in-kind component within the broader social protection system. For example, children participating in Progresa in Mexico who benefited in terms of increased stature also benefited from a package of interventions including increased access to health services, improvements in maternal nutrition knowledge, and a calorie- and micronutrient-dense food supplement (Behrman and Hoddinott 2005).

Nutrition education is another potential means to enhance the nutritional impact of increased food consumption. SNAP Ed, a program within SNAP, aims to encourage participants to make healthier food choices through public education and messaging. It remains, however, a small component of SNAP (less than 0.5 percent of the total budget) and is far exceeded by the advertising of major food producers and retailers, which often nudges consumers into less-healthy food choices. Other forms of enhancing the nutritional effects of SNAP include price subsidies for "healthy" products and more frequent payments to beneficiaries to sustain more frequent purchases of perishable (and more nutritious) foods. Such programs remain for the moment as pilot programs and, in the case of payment frequency, at the proposal stage. In Mexico, the "nutrition colors" campaign at Diconsa stores helps consumers to understand the nutritional content of food items: green is associated with items whose consumption is encouraged daily, yellow signals moderate consumption, and red discourages consumption.

An additional means of making food transfers—even inframarginal transfers—nutrition sensitive is to fortify the commodities to improve their micronutrient status. For example, Cunha (2014) observes that most of the 10 commodities in the in-kind distribution program in Mexico (known as the Rural Supply Program) substituted for similar goods that would otherwise have been purchased. But because the milk powder was fortified with iron and zinc, the program increased the consumption of micronutrients. A similar result is likely for any program that provides a fortified commodity if the alternative foods obtained from the market are not similarly enriched; in-kind distributions can be sensitive to nutrition when they are vehicles for food fortification.

Various states in India have used the PDS as a vehicle for fortified commodities. Gujarat reduced inadequate intake of iron by 94 percent when it substituted iron-fortified flour for wheat grain in the PDS at an incremental cost of only US$0.48 per ton (Fiedler and others 2012). The measure was introduced gradually between 2006 and 2010, with testing of acceptability as well as a government media campaign. At the same time, the government of India added micronutrient fortification to school meals as well as to items in a children's nutrition program, the Integrated Child Development Services. However, the fortification program was discontinued in 2012. Indeed, with the exception of a long-running fortification program in the state of West Bengal, other state fortification initiatives in India have had short lives. Such was also the case in Egypt, which briefly fortified bread flour with iron and folate between 2008 and 2013.

WHAT'S NEXT FOR THE AGENDA?

This chapter has served as a compass for navigating and contextualizing the six country case studies. We have shown that the core in-kind programs examined in this volume are not static and that underlying forces are, at different paces, moving schemes from generalized to targeted provisions, from subsidies to cash-oriented modalities, and from agriculture to social assistance objectives. Those trends are long-standing and somewhat related to each country's structural transformation process.

Crises have often offered a window for accelerating those changes, with technology playing a key role in facilitating and enabling those accelerations. Political economy, of course, has also been a key vehicle that has, at times, stifled and even reversed the direction of change—but not always. The overall social assistance results are improving on average, ranging from SNAP's impressive performance to Raskin's more modest progress.

Against this backdrop, the basic agenda around the process of reform could revolve around furthering the direction of change, channels, and performance of programs. The transition out of agriculture-related objectives is not yet complete and, unless governments opt for cash transfers, may never be entirely complete by definition. In-kind programs would need to be somewhat procured, but the way in which that happens increasingly points to a voucher-oriented approach of "outsourcing" procurement functions to retailers, with proper government oversight, guidelines, and standards. The direction of change seems to move toward providing choice to beneficiaries, including where to buy (as in India) and what and where to buy (as in the United States). Clearly, countries with more advanced and integrated food systems can provide more ample opportunity for enabling such choice in a competitive and transparent way. The experience of trailblazers like some low-income Indian states calls for governments to be on the lookout for positive outliers. There is plenty of local-level innovation that, if properly nurtured, could serve as a scalable model.

Programs would need to continue their process of integration with social protection.[18] Until recently, one could clearly discern "smart" cash transfer programming from traditional in-kind support, but today that is much harder to do. Both food and voucher programs can often be accessed by beneficiaries through electronic cards that resemble standard consumer swipe cards; they are increasingly underpinned by biometric information to verify beneficiaries' identity; they are supported by online devices allowing beneficiaries to choose retailers; and satellite tracking systems have been leveraged to monitor procurement, storage, and delivery of food programs. This suggests that in-kind transfers can be connected to coexist with cash transfers, and few social protection systems are based entirely on food or cash alone.

More and better evidence is needed on key metrics, particularly regarding comparative cost structures. While there are results, the available data and overall empirical base of in-kind programs are—with the exception of SNAP—a far cry from the quality of evidence available for cash transfers.

Our analysis does not include an extensive review of Sub-Saharan African experiences, which could be a natural follow-up to this book's discussion. Yet the volume has important implications for Africa. The region has been a comparative latecomer to social protection, initially relying largely on state interventions in markets and regulation to achieve food policy objectives. FOSA programs are not uncommon in the region (for example, in the Sahel), but they are more likely conditioned by donor support and emergency response than by long-running national strategies. However, many countries in the continent have recently invested in national social protection systems (World Bank 2015). The timing of this trend has allowed African countries to build on global experiences from outside the continent as well as on innovations in South Africa's social protection system. This trend is reflected in the emergence of cash transfers across Sub-Saharan Africa (Davis and others 2016).

At the same time, a growing share of global food assistance is being procured locally from farmers in host countries. While positive for local economies and cross-sectoral links the practice of local procurement might also create new pressures for maintaining and integrating FOSA throughout the food system (WFP 2017). Moreover, some countries are introducing food subsidy programs ex novo. For this reason, the evolution of social assistance in Africa is likely to be unique, yet not totally immune from the mixed objectives that have characterized FOSA programs across the spectrum of country income. The pathways and models of FOSA in the continent might be an important social protection theme in the years to come.

Relatedly, the social protection system agenda includes multiple stakeholders. In-kind programs would bring to the table even more actors. Identifying cases of where and how stakeholders' incentives and objectives for reform align would be important for assessing the feasibility and direction of reform pathways.

Finally, in-kind assistance has not benefited to the same extent as cash transfers from knowledge-sharing and learning platforms. This is an area where countries could greatly benefit in exchanging experiences from reform processes, program design, and implementation. If FOSA programs continue in their trajectory of alignment with social protection systems, it is important to open up space for sharing knowledge and information.[19]

ANNEX 1A. SUMMARY FEATURES OF THE PROGRAMS EXAMINED IN SIX COUNTRIES

FEATURE	EGYPT, ARAB REP.	INDIA	INDONESIA	MEXICO	SRI LANKA	UNITED STATES
Name of the program(s)	Ration cards (RCs) and baladi bread (BB)	Targeted public distribution system (TPDS)	Raskin (now Rastra)	*Programa de Apoyo Alimentario* (PAL, Food Support Program)	Samurdhi food stamp program[a]	Supplemental Nutrition Assistance Program (SNAP), formerly "Food Stamp"
Current modality	Food subsidy	Food subsidy	Food subsidy	Voucher, cash	Cash	Voucher
Previous modalities	Food subsidy	Food subsidy	Food subsidy	Food subsidy, in-kind food	Food subsidy, in-kind food, vouchers	Voucher
Managing institution	Ministry of Supply and Internal Trade (MOSIT)	Food Corporation of India and States	Ministry of Human Development and Culture	Ministry of Social Development (Sedesol)	Department of Commissioner General of Samurdhi	U.S. Department of Agriculture
Established	1941	1943	1998	2003	1995 (with antecedents in 1942)	1964 (with pilot in 1961 and origins in a 1939 program)
Coverage as % of population	90% (BB: 82.2 million; RC: 71 million)	67% (about 800 million people)	24% (62 million people)	2.50% (2.8 million people)	16.8% (3.4 million people)	14% (45.8 million people)

table continues next page

FEATURE	EGYPT, ARAB REP.	INDIA	INDONESIA	MEXICO	SRI LANKA	UNITED STATES
Eligibility condition	BB: no targeting criteria; RC: mostly income-based	Two types of households are eligible, Priority households and Antyodaya Anna Yojana households. They receive 5 kgs per family member and 35 kgs per month, respectively. Both categories receive wheat at INR2/kg and rice at INR3/kg. Some households not eligible for NFSA benefits are provided rations by the state government. Quantity and price vary by states.	"Poor and vulnerable" from unified database (bottom 40%)	Same targeting method as Prospera CCT (but in areas with limited service supply)	Income criteria, varying by family size (Rs 100–Rs 1,000 per month)	Gross income <130% of poverty; gross income minus deductions (net income) <100% of poverty; assets <US$2,250 (US$3,250 if elderly or disabled)
Targeting performance (coverage)	RC: 91.9% of poorest decile	58.3% of households at bottom 40% of the population	72% of households in poorest decile	37.5% of households at bottom 40% of the population	36.5% of households in poorest decile	85% of the eligible participate
Benefit amount	6.8% of household food consumption (10.5% for poorest decile)	43.4% of household food expenditures[b]	2% of household expenditures	27.8% of household income	n.a.	More than 10% of food-at-home spending in the United States
Cost as % of GDP	1.3% (US$2.2 billion); 59.8% of social assistance budget	0.4% (US$7 billion); 53% of social assistance budget	0.2% (US$1.5 billion); 43.1% of social assistance budget	0.03%; 7% of Prospera budget	0.17% (US$102.9 million)	0.47% of GDP (US$79.9 billion); 13% of budget for major federal social assistance programs

Note: GDP = gross domestic product; kg = kilogram; n.a. = not applicable; NFSA = National Food Security Act.

a. Figures refer to 2012–13 (before the program became cash only).

b. Calculations of average beneficiary TPDS purchases in six states based on data from NCAER (2015, 30–31).

NOTES

1. An "exclusion error" occurs when a potentially eligible person or household does not participate in a program.
2. Data refer to 16 low- and middle-income countries presented in Banerjee and Duflo (2011), with estimates based on average spending on food by rural households living on less than US$2 per day.
3. See also Cornia and Stewart (1995) for a discussion on the phaseout of general food subsidies in Jamaica in 1984 as well as their reinstatement in 1986–88 and eventual abolishment in 1989.
4. Given that estimates are population-weighted, excluding China and India would reduce the coverage of food and vouchers to 8.6 percent, still almost as high as that of an unconditional cash modality.
5. For example, see Feeding America, http://www.feedingamerica.org/. Although a more comprehensive stock taking might be required, in Europe, FOSA remains outside formal welfare regimes (Silvasti 2015). In some cases, these are supported by public funding, such as the European Union's Food Aid for Deprived Persons Program.
6. This may be related to an endowment effect; see Kahneman, Knetsch, and Thaler (1991).
7. For numerical examples, see the cases of Ecuador and the Republic of Yemen presented in Gentilini (2016b).
8. We intentionally avoid referring to "universality" and instead refer to "generalized" provision. The concept is often used erroneously and refers to a specific form of provision (that is, reaching 100 percent of the population) (Devereux 2016). The examined programs, instead, are far-reaching (even more than 90 percent of the populace), but not designed nor intended to reach everyone.
9. Since the 1970s, those countries took a more deliberate stance toward subsidization of agriculture; since 1996, they targeted specific groups of poor farmers and guaranteed low consumer prices for some basic commodities (bread, oil, sugar, at times milk, and canned fish) available on a generalized basis with an element of self-targeting (Alderman and Lindert 1998).
10. See the Right to Food Campaign, http://www.righttofoodcampaign.in/.
11. See also "Village Rationing from July to Cover 5.0 Million Poor," *Financial Express* (Dhaka), April 4, 2016 (http://www.thefinancialexpress-bd.com/2016/04/04/24649 /Village-rationing-from-July-to-cover-5.0m-poor).
12. For example, in response to trade disruptions during World War II, many countries, including Egypt and Great Britain as well as Great Britain's South Asian colonies of Ceylon and India, rationed basic goods that, it was argued, untampered markets could not be trusted to provide for the entire population. Great Britain dismantled its food rationing completely by 1954; however, even three decades after the end of World War II, ration systems in the three countries partitioned from British India, as well as ration systems in Egypt and Sri Lanka, still bore a strong resemblance to the structures designed as emergency measures.
13. With the food price crisis in 2008, several regions have introduced targeted food vouchers for consumers and subsidies to retailers. At the time of finalizing this book, legislation was drafted with the inclusion of parameters similar to the SNAP program. There are however, significant opportunities to deepen learning and ensure coordination with the rest of Russia's social protection system (World Bank 2016).
14. According to Drèze (2016), growing pains with the introduction of the Aadhaar have set back reforms of the PDS. He laments the "juggernaut" that has not heeded evidence on the roll out.
15. This may be attributed to consumer choices or the shortage of some basic commodities where customers have no choice but to go for the available ones.

16. For other anecdotes on pathways between research, policy, and accountability in the 1970s and 1980s, see Alderman (1995) and Marshall (1990).
17. Meetings attended by Harold Alderman, one of the authors of this chapter. Initially, the prime minster had a favorable impression of the PDS stemming from a visit to Gujarat earlier that year. This was countered, however, by reports of extensive leakage throughout the country. The final "nail in the coffin" was a report by the Indian Ministry of Planning, rather than an academic quibble, that documented extensive flaws in the program's implementation.
18. It is interesting to note that in India, a "reincarnation" of the cash vs. in-kind debate is now occurring around whether and how to introduce a universal basic income—that is, an unconditional cash transfer program for every citizen—replacing the TPDS and other social assistance interventions (Gentilini and Yemtsov 2017; Government of India 2017).
19. For example, the U.S. Department of Agriculture's Economic Research Service maintains a web database of more than 1,000 peer-reviewed reports and operational guidelines on food assistance programs.

REFERENCES

Abdalla, Moustafa, and Sherine Al-Shawarby. 2018. "The Tamween Food Subsidy System in the Arab Republic of Egypt: Evolution and Recent Implementation Reforms." In *The 1.5 Billion Question: Food, Vouchers, or Cash Transfers?*, edited by Harold Alderman, Ugo Gentilini, and Ruslan Yemtsov, ch. 3. Washington, DC: World Bank.

Acemoglu, Daron, and James Robinson. 2012. *Why Nations Fail: The Origins of Power, Prosperity, and Poverty*. New York: Crown Business.

Alderman, Harold. 1986. "Food Subsidies and State Policy in Egypt." In *Food, States, and Peasants: Analysis of the Agrarian Question in the Middle East*, edited by Alan Richards. Boulder, CO: Westview Press.

———. 1988. "The Twilight of the Flour Ration in Pakistan." *Food Policy* 13 (3): 245–56.

———. 1995. "Information as an Input into Food and Nutrition Policy Formation." In *Child Growth and Nutrition in Developing Countries: Priorities for Action*, edited by Per Pinstrup-Andersen, David Pelletier, and Harold Alderman. Ithaca, NY: Cornell University Press.

———. 2016. *Leveraging Social Protection Programs for Improved Nutrition*. Washington, DC: World Bank.

Alderman, Harold, and Donald Bundy. 2011. "School Feeding Programs and Development: Are We Framing the Question Correctly?" *World Bank Research Observer* 27 (2): 204–21.

Alderman, Harold, and Kathy Lindert. 1998. "The Potential and Limitations of Self-Targeted Food Subsidies." *World Bank Research Observer* 13 (2): 213–29.

Amid, Javad. 2007. "The Dilemma of Cheap Food and Self-Sufficiency: The Case of Wheat in Iran." *Food Policy* 32 (4): 537–52.

Andrews, Matt, Lant Pritchett, and Michael Woolcock. 2016. "The Big Stuck in State Capability for Policy Implementation." CID Working Paper 318, Harvard University, Cambridge, MA.

Angelucci, Manuela, and Orazio Attanasio. 2013. "The Demand for Food of Poor Urban Mexican Households: Understanding Policy Impacts Using Structural Models." *American Economic Journal: Economic Policy* 5 (1): 146–205.

Attanasio, Orazio, Erich Battistin, and Alice Mesnard. 2012. "Food and Cash Transfers: Evidence from Colombia." *Economic Journal* 122 (559): 92–124.

Azzam, Azzeddine. 1991. "Food Subsidies and Market Interdependence: The Case of the Moroccan Soft Wheat Subsidy." *Agricultural Economics* 5 (4): 325–39.

Banerjee, Abhijit, and Esther Duflo. 2011. *Poor Economics: A Radical Rethinking of the Way to Fight Global Poverty*. New York: PublicAffairs.

Barrett, Christopher. 2002. "Food Security and Food Assistance Programs." In *Handbook of Agricultural Economics*, edited by Bruce Gardner and Gordon Rausser. Amsterdam: Elsevier.
———, ed. 2013. *Food Security and Sociopolitical Stability*. New York: Oxford University Press.
Beatty, Timothy K. M., and Charlotte J. Tuttle. 2015. "Expenditure Response to Increases in In-Kind Transfers: Evidence from the Supplemental Nutrition Assistance Program." *American Journal of Agricultural Economics* 97 (2): 390–404.
Beegle, Kathleen, Emanuela Galasso, and Jessica Goldberg. 2015. "Direct and Indirect Effects of Malawi's Public Works Program on Food Security." Policy Research Working Paper 7505, World Bank, Washington, DC.
Beghin, John C., and Amani Elobeid. 2015. "The Impact of the U.S. Sugar Program Redux." *Applied Economic Perspectives and Policy* 37 (1): 1–33.
Behrman, Jere. 2010. "The International Food Policy Research Institute (IFPRI) and the Mexican Progresa Anti-Poverty and Human Resource Investment Conditional Cash." *World Development* 38 (10): 1473–85.
Behrman, Jere, and John Hoddinott. 2005. "Programme Evaluation with Unobserved Heterogeneity and Selective Implementation: The Mexican Progresa Impact on Child Nutrition." *Oxford Bulletin of Economics and Statistics* 67 (4): 547–69.
Bhattacharya, Shrayana, Vanita Leah Falcao, and Raghav Puri. 2018. "Public Distribution System in India: Policy Evolution and Program Delivery Trends." In *The 1.5 Billion Question: Food, Vouchers, or Cash Transfers?*, edited by Harold Alderman, Ugo Gentilini, and Ruslan Yemtsov, ch. 2. Washington, DC: World Bank.
Bhutta, Zulfiqar A., Jai K. Das, Arjumand Rizvi, Michelle F. Gaffey, Neff Walker, Susan Horton, Patrick Webb, Anna Lartey, and Robert Black. 2013. "Evidence-Based Interventions for Improvement of Maternal and Child Nutrition: What Can Be Done and at What Cost?" *The Lancet* 382 (9890): 452–77.
Bienen, Henry, and Mark Gersovitz. 1986. "Consumer Subsidy Cuts, Violence, and Political Stability." *Comparative Politics* 19 (1): 25–44.
Chowdhury, Tawfiq-e-Elahi, and Steven Haggblade. 2000. "Dynamics and Politics of Policy Change." In *Out of the Shadow of Famine: Evolving Food Markets and Food Policy in Bangladesh*, edited by Raisuddin Ahmed, Steven Haggblade, and Tawfiq-e-Elahi Chowdhury. Baltimore, MD: Johns Hopkins University Press for the Food Policy Research Institute.
Cornia, Giovanni Andrea, and Frances Stewart. 1995. "Food Subsidies: Two Errors of Targeting." In *Adjustment and Poverty: Policy and Choices*, edited by Frances Stewart. New York: Routledge.
Cunha, Jesse. 2014. "Testing Paternalism: Cash versus In-Kind Transfers." *American Economic Journal: Applied Economics* 6 (2): 195–230.
Currie, Janet, and Firouz Gahvari. 2008. "Transfers in Cash and In-Kind: Theory Meets the Data." *Journal of Economic Literature* 46 (2): 333–83.
Davis, Benjamin, Sudhanshu Handa, Nicola Hypher, Natalia Winder Rossi, Paul Winters, and Jennifer Yablonski, eds. 2016. *From Evidence to Action: The Story of Cash Transfers and Impact Evaluation in Sub Saharan Africa*. Oxford, U.K.: Oxford University Press.
de Janvry, Alain, Frederico Finan, and Elizabeth Sadoulet. 2012. "Local Electoral Incentives and Decentralized Program Performance." *Review of Economics and Statistics* 94 (3): 672–85.
de Janvry, Alain, and Shankar Subramanian. 1993. "The Politics and Economics of Food and Nutrition Policies and Programs: An Interpretation." In *The Political Economy of Food and Nutrition Policies*, edited by Per Pinstrup-Andersen, 3–21. Baltimore, MD: Johns Hopkins University Press.
Devereux, Stephen. 2001. "Transfers and Safety Nets." In *Food Security in Sub-Saharan Africa*, edited by Stephen Devereux and Simon Maxwell. London: ITDG Publishing.
———. 2016. "Is Targeting Ethical?" *Global Social Policy* 16 (2): 166–81.

Dorosh, Paul. Forthcoming. *Promoting National and Household Food Security in Bangladesh: The Evolving Roles of Public Stocks, Cereal Distribution, and Private Trade.* Washington, DC: International Food Policy Research Institute.

Drake, Lesley, Alice Woolnough, Carmen Burbano, and Donald Bundy. 2016. *Global School Feeding Sourcebook: Lessons from 14 Countries.* London: Imperial College Press.

Drèze, Jean. 2016. "Dark Clouds over the PDS." *Hindu,* September 10.

Drèze, Jean, and Reetika Khera. 2010. "Chhattisgarh Shows the Way." *The Hindu,* November 13.

Drèze, Jean, Reetika Khera, and Jessica Pudussery. 2015. "Food Security." *Economic and Political Weekly* 50 (34): 45.

Drèze, Jean, and Amartya Sen. 2013. *An Uncertain Glory: India and Its Contradictions.* Princeton, NJ: Princeton University Press.

Duclos, Jean-Yves. 1995. "Modelling the Take-Up of State Support." *Journal of Public Economics* 58 (3): 391–415.

Edirisinghe, Neville. 1988. "Recent Targeting Attempts in Sri Lanka's Food Stamp Scheme." *Food Policy* 13 (4): 401–02.

Evans, David, and Anna Popova. 2017. "Cash Transfers and Temptation Goods." *Economic Development and Cultural Change* 65 (2): 189–221.

FAO (Food and Agriculture Organization of the United Nations). 2015. *The State of Food and Agriculture: Social Protection and Agriculture—Breaking the Cycle of Rural Poverty.* Rome: FAO.

Fiedler, John L., Sunil Babu, Marc-Francois Smitz, Keith Lividini, and Odilia Bermudez. 2012. "Indian Social Safety-Net Programs as Platforms for Introducing Wheat Flour Fortification: A Case Study of Gujarat, India." *Food and Nutrition Bulletin* 33 (1): 11–30.

Fiszbein, Ariel, Ravi Kanbur, and Ruslan Yemtsov. 2014. "Social Protection and Poverty Reduction: Global Patterns and Some Targets." *World Development* 61 (September): 167–77.

Friedman, Milton. 1962. *Capitalism and Freedom.* Chicago: University of Chicago Press.

Fukuyama, Francis. 2014. *Political Order and Political Decay: From the Industrial Revolution to the Globalization of Democracy.* New York: Farrar, Straus, and Giroux.

Garnsey, Peter. 1988. *Famine and Food Supply in the Graeco-Roman World: Responses to Risk and Crisis.* New York: Cambridge University Press.

Gelbach, Jonah, and Lant Pritchett. 2000. "Indicator Targeting in a Political Economy: Leakier Can Be Better." *Policy Reform* 4 (2): 113–45.

Gentilini, Ugo. 2013. "Banking on Food: The State of Food Banks in High-Income Countries." Working Paper 415, Institute of Development Studies, Brighton, U.K.

———. 2016a. "Revisiting the 'Cash versus Food' Debate: New Evidence for an Old Puzzle?" *World Bank Research Observer* 31 (1): 135–67.

———. 2016b. *The Other Side of the Coin: The Comparative Evidence of Cash and In-Kind Transfers in Humanitarian Situations.* Washington, DC: World Bank.

Gentilini, Ugo, and Ruslan Yemtsov. 2017. "Being Open Minded about Universal Basic Income." *Let's Talk Development* (blog), January 6. http://blogs.worldbank.org /developmenttalk/being-open-minded-about-universal-basic-income.

Gould, Stephen J. 2010. *The Panda's Thumb: More Reflections in Natural History.* New York: W. W. Norton and Company.

Government of India. 2017. "Universal Basic Income: A Conversation with and within the Mahatma." In *Economic Survey 2006–17,* ch. 9. New Delhi: Government of India.

Green, Duncan. 2016. *How Change Happens.* Oxford, U.K.: Oxford University Press.

Grosh, Margaret. 1992. "The Jamaican Food Stamps Programme: A Case Study in Targeting." *Food Policy* 17 (1): 23–40.

———. 1994. *Administering Targeted Social Programs in Latin America: From Platitudes to Practice.* Washington, DC: World Bank.

Haggblade, Steven. 2000. "History of Public Food Interventions in Bangladesh." In *Out of the Shadow of Famine: Evolving Food Markets and Food Policy in Bangladesh,* edited by

Raisuddin Ahmed, Steven Haggblade, and Tawfiq-e-Elahi Chowdhury, 121–36. Baltimore, MD: Johns Hopkins University Press for the Food Policy Research Institute.

Hidrobo, Melissa, John Hoddinott, Amber Peterman, Amy Margolies, and Vanessa Moeira. 2014. "Cash, Food, or Vouchers? Evidence from a Randomized Experiment in Northern Ecuador." *Journal of Development Economics* 107 (March): 144–56.

IEG (Independent Evaluation Group). 2011. *Social Safety Nets: An Evaluation of World Bank Support, 2000–2010.* Washington, DC: World Bank. https://ieg.worldbankgroup.org /Data/reports/ssn_full_evaluation.pdf.

Kahneman, Daniel, Jack Knetsch, and Richard Thaler. 1991. "Anomalies: The Endowment Effect, Loss Aversion, and Status Quo Bias." *Journal of Economic Perspectives* 5 (1): 193–206.

Khera, Reetika. 2011. "Revival of the Public Distribution System: Evidence and Explanations." *Economic and Political Weekly* 46 (44–45): 36–50.

———. 2014. "Cash vs. In-kind Transfers: Indian Data Meets Theory." *Food Policy* 46 (C): 116–28.

Kiringai, Jane Wangui, Michael Tobias Geiger, Mesfin Girma Bezawagaw, and Leif Jensen. 2016. "Ethiopia Public Expenditure Review." World Bank, Addis Ababa.

Kooreman, Peter. 2000. "The Labeling Effect of a Child Benefit System." *American Economic Review* 90 (3): 571–83.

Krueger, Anne, Maurice Schiff, and Alberto Valdés. 1988. "Agricultural Incentives in Developing Countries: Measuring the Effect of Sectoral and Economy-Wide Policies." *World Bank Economic Review* 2 (3): 255–71.

Leite, Phillippe, Tina George, Changqing Sun, Theresa Jones, and Kathy Lindert. Forthcoming. "Social Registries for Social Assistance and Beyond: A Guidance Note and Assessment Tool." World Bank, Washington, DC.

Levy, Santiago. 2006. *Progress against Poverty: Sustaining Mexico's Progresa-Oportunidades Program.* Washington, DC: Brookings Institution.

Lipton, Michael. 1977. *Why Poor People Stay Poor: Urban Bias in World Development.* Canberra: Australian National University Press.

Manley, James, Seth Gitter, and Vanya Slavchevska. 2013. "How Effective Are Cash Transfers at Improving Nutritional Status?" *World Development* 48 (August): 133–55.

Margolies, Amy, and John Hoddinott. 2015. "Costing Alternative Transfer Modalities." *Journal of Development Effectiveness* 7 (1): 1–16.

Marshall, Eliot. 1990. "USDA Admits 'Mistake' in Doctoring Study." *Science* 247 (4942): 522.

Mehta, Aashish, and Shikha Jha. 2014. "Pilferage from Opaque Food Subsidy Programs: Theory and Evidence." *Food Policy* 45 (April): 69–79.

NCAER (National Council of Applied Economic Research). 2015. "Evaluation Study of Targeted Public Distribution System in Selected States." NCAER, New Delhi, September. http://www.ncaer.org/free-download.php?pID=262.

Oliveira, Victor, Mark Prell, Laura Tiehen, and David Smallwood. 2016. "The Supplemental Nutrition Assistance Program (SNAP) in the United States: Implementation." Presentation at the World Bank, Washington, DC, March 13.

Oliveira, Victor, Laura Tiehen, Mark Prell, and David Smallwood. 2018. "The Evolution and Implementation of the Supplemental Nutrition Assistance Program in the United States." In *The 1.5 Billion Question: Food, Vouchers, or Cash Transfers?*, edited by Harold Alderman, Ugo Gentilini, and Ruslan Yemtsov, ch. 6. Washington, DC: World Bank.

Olson, Mancur. 2009. *The Logic of Collective Action.* Cambridge, MA: Harvard University Press.

Omamo, Steven Were, Ugo Gentilini, and Susanna Sandström, eds. 2010. *Revolution: From Food Aid to Food Assistance; Innovations in Overcoming Hunger.* Rome: World Food Programme.

Pinstrup-Andersen, Per, ed. 1988. *Consumer-Oriented Food Subsidies: Costs, Benefits, and Policy Options for Developing Countries.* Baltimore, MD: Johns Hopkins University Press.

————. 2015. *Food Price Policy in an Era of Market Instability: A Political Economy Analysis.* New York: Oxford University Press.

Ramalingam, Ben. 2013. *Aid on the Edge of Chaos: Rethinking International Cooperation in a Complex World.* New York: Oxford University Press.

Ravallion, Martin, and Quentin Wodon. 2000. "Does Child Labour Displace Schooling? Evidence on Behavioural Responses to an Enrollment Subsidy." *Economic Journal* 110 (462): 158–75.

Reardon, Thomas, and Peter Timmer. 2014. "Five Inter-Linked Transformations in the Asian Agrifood Economy: Food Security Implications." *Global Food Security* 3 (2): 108–17.

Reinhardt, Uwe. 2013. "Why Economists Are Lousy Lovers: On the Political Economy of Benefits In-Kind." Economics lecture. Princeton University, Princeton, NJ.

Ruel, Marie, and Harold Alderman. 2013. "Nutrition-Sensitive Interventions and Programs: How Can They Help Accelerate Progress in Improving Maternal and Child Nutrition?" *The Lancet* 382 (9891): 536–51.

Ryan, James G., and Xin Meng. 2004. "The Contribution of IFPRI Research and the Impact of the Food for Education Program in Bangladesh on Schooling Outcomes and Earnings." Impact Assessment Discussion Paper 22, International Food Policy Research Institute, Washington, DC.

Sabates-Wheeler, Rachel, and Stephen Devereux. 2010. "Cash Transfers and High Food Prices: Explaining Outcomes in Ethiopia's Safety Net Programme." *Food Policy* 25 (3): 274–85.

Schady, Norbert, and José Rosero. 2008. "Are Cash Transfers Made to Women Spent Like Other Sources of Income?" *Economics Letters* 101 (3): 246–48.

Scott, John, and Citlalli Hernández. 2018. "From Generalized Food Subsidies to Targeted Transfers: The Case of Mexico." In *The 1.5 Billion Question: Food, Vouchers, or Cash Transfers?,* edited by Harold Alderman, Ugo Gentilini, and Ruslan Yemtsov, ch. 5. Washington, DC: World Bank.

Seddon, David. 1986. "Politics and the Price of Bread in Tunisia." In *Food, States, and Peasants: Analyses of the Agrarian Question in the Middle East,* edited by Alan Richards. Boulder, CO: Westview Press.

Silvasti, Tiina. 2015. "Food Aid—Normalising the Abnormal in Finland." *Social Policy and Society* 14 (3): 471–82.

Smith, Richard. 2011. "Social Security as a Developmental Institution? The Relative Efficacy of Poor Relief Provisions under the English Old Poor Law." In *History, Historians, and Development Policy: A Necessary Dialogue,* edited by C. A. Bayly, Vijayendra Rao, Simon Szreter, and Michael Woolcock. Manchester and New York: Manchester University Press.

Suryanarayana, M. H. 1995. "Some Experiments with Food Stamps." *Economic and Political Weekly* 30 (52): A151–59.

Tannahill, Reay. 1988. *Food in History.* New York: Crown Publishers.

Tilakaratna, Ganga, and Chinthani Sooriyamudali. 2018. "Food-Based Social Assistance Programs in Sri Lanka: Evolution of and Transition to Cash Transfers." In *The 1.5 Billion Question: The Evolution and Implementation of Food as Social Assistance,* edited by Harold Alderman, Ugo Gentilini, and Ruslan Yemtsov, ch. 4. Washington, DC: World Bank.

Timmer, C. Peter. 2007. *A World without Agriculture: The Structural Transformation in Historical Perspective.* Henry Wendt Lecture Series. Washington, DC: AEI Press.

Timmer, C. Peter, Hastuti, and Sudarno Sumarto. 2018. "Evolution and Implementation of the Rastra Program in Indonesia." In *The 1.5 Billion Question: Food, Vouchers, or Cash Transfers?,* edited by Harold Alderman, Ugo Gentilini, and Ruslan Yemtsov, ch. 7. Washington, DC: World Bank.

Tuck, Laura, and Kathy Lindert. 1996. "From Universal Food Subsidies to a Self-Targeted Program: A Case Study in Tunisian Reform." Discussion Paper 351, World Bank, Washington, DC.

Uribe Mosquera, Tomas. 1993. "The Political Economy of Colombia's PAN." In *The Political Economy of Food and Nutrition Policies*, edited by Per Pinstrup-Andersen, 50–60. Baltimore, MD: Johns Hopkins University Press.

Verme, Paolo, and Abdelkrim Araar. 2017. *The Quest for Subsidies Reforms in the Middle East and North Africa Region*. Washington, DC: World Bank.

Von Braun, Joachim, and Hartwig de Haen. 1983. "The Effects of Food Price and Subsidy Policies on Egyptian Agriculture." Research Report 42, International Food Policy Research Institute, Washington, DC.

Wall Street Journal. 2011. "Algeria Seeks to End Food Riots." January 10.

WFP (World Food Programme). 2013a. *Building Resilience through Asset Creation*. Rome: WFP.

———. 2013b. *The State of School Feeding Worldwide*. Rome: WFP.

———. 2016. *Annual Performance Report for 2015*. Rome: WFP.

———. 2017. *World Food Assistance 2017: Taking Stock and Looking Ahead*. Rome: WFP.

World Bank. 1999. "Consumer Food Subsidy Programs in the MENA Region." Report 19561-MNA, World Bank, Washington, DC.

———. 2003. "Royaume du Maroc: Croissance agricole et réduction de la pauvreté rurale— orientations de politique economique." World Bank, Washington, DC.

———. 2005. "Considering the Future of the Iraqi Public Distribution System." Economic and Social Development Working Paper, World Bank, Washington, DC.

———. 2011. "Royaume du Maroc: L'economie politique de la reforme du systeme de subventions energetiques et alimentaires." World Bank, Washington, DC.

———. 2015. *The State of Social Safety Nets 2015*. Washington, DC: World Bank.

———. 2016. "The Food Stamp Program in Russia." World Bank, Washington, DC.

Wright, Brian. 2014. "Global Biofuels: Key to the Puzzle of Grain Market Behavior." *Journal of Economic Perspectives* 28 (1): 73–97.

CHAPTER 2

The Public Distribution System in India

POLICY EVOLUTION AND PROGRAM DELIVERY TRENDS

Shrayana Bhattacharya, Vanita Leah Falcao, and Raghav Puri

INTRODUCTION

The targeted public distribution system (TPDS) is the largest safety net program in India, in terms of both government expenditures and number of beneficiary households.[1] The program targets nearly 800 million people (WFP 2014), providing subsidized grain through a network of more than 500,000 fair price shops (FPSs) across the country. The distribution of subsidized cereals through the TPDS was and remains the centerpiece of India's social protection system. Although India has expanded and diversified its social protection programs in the past decade, government spending continues to emphasize the TPDS. The program absorbs US$7 billion, which is almost 1 percent of India's gross domestic product (GDP) (World Bank 2011). As figure 2.1 indicates, subsidies remain key, with food and fuel subsidies accounting for two-thirds of expenditure on social protection programs.[2] In 2014–15, Rs 1,226.76 billion (US$18.9 billion) was spent on food subsidies, an increase from Rs 424.89 billion (US$6.5 billion) in 2009–10 (Ministry of Finance, various years, specifically for 2014–15).

FIGURE 2.1

Social Protection Expenditures in India, 2004–15

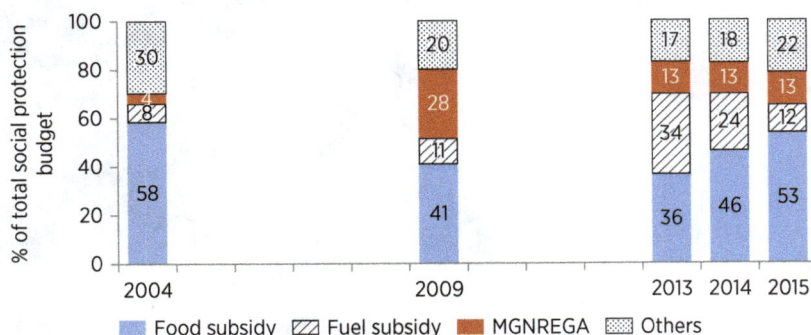

Source: Ministry of Finance, various years.
Note: MGNREGA = Mahatma Gandhi National Rural Employment Guarantee Act.

A ruling by the Supreme Court recognizes the TPDS as a fundamental pillar of food security in the country and defines mandatory basic provisions for it. As discussed in chapter 1, the TPDS has witnessed several shifts in its overall goals and design. Owing to the nature of India's federal government structure, states too have implemented reforms and innovations in the TPDS.

In particular, the TPDS has evolved as a major instrument of government economic policy for ensuring the availability of affordable food grain to the public, especially the poor. The previously universal public distribution system (PDS) was converted into a targeted PDS in 1997, as part of a larger effort to achieve fiscal consolidation. Following this shift, beneficiaries were identified and categorized as being below the poverty line (BPL) or above the poverty line (APL). People in each category were entitled to a set of food grains at differing quantities and prices. In 2000, an additional classification of *Antyodaya Anna Yojna* (AAY, poorest of the poor) was included to provide the abject poor with dedicated food grain allotments at highly subsidized prices.

In 2013, the scope and mandate of the TPDS expanded significantly through passage of the National Food Security Act (NFSA). The NFSA combines entitlements from three core programs: the TPDS, which targets food-insecure households; the Mid-Day Meal Scheme, a school-based feeding program targeting children ages 6–14 years; and Integrated Child Development Services, a supplementary feeding program targeting children between 6 months and 6 years and pregnant and lactating women. The NFSA entitles 50 percent of the urban population and 75 percent of the rural population to receive food benefits under the TPDS, which is the largest of these programs (WFP 2014).

Following a period of high leakage and low uptake in the late 1990s (World Bank 2011), numerous studies have suggested that TPDS administration has improved since 2005 (Khera 2011b; NCAER 2015). National household survey data collected through the National Sample Survey Organization (NSSO) shows a steady decline in the leakage of TPDS food grains, from 55 percent in fiscal year 2004–05 to 38 percent in fiscal year 2011–12. However, this decline in diversion has varied spatially. States such as Jharkhand and Rajasthan continue to report high leakage and poor coverage, while states such as Bihar, Chhattisgarh, and Odisha have achieved tremendous improvements in program outcomes. Improvements in TPDS functioning have been attributed to a range of innovations initiated by state governments to address key bottlenecks that stifled coverage and efficiency. Those measures are yet to be documented comprehensively. Further, within the ambit of TPDS reforms, much less is known about the nutrition-sensitive interventions and their impacts.

Any discussion of India's TPDS has to acknowledge the role played by broader trends within Indian social policy, macroeconomic regimes, technological advances, and political devolution. In particular, four themes are significant in reviewing PDS performance and history.

First, social policy in India has increasingly leveraged citizen engagement and rights-based approaches to codify and simplify the delivery of entitlements. For instance, the right to work is embodied in the Mahatma Gandhi National Rural Employment Guarantee Act (MGNREGA), and the right to food is reflected in the NFSA 2013.

During most of the 1990s, protective programs such as the TPDS and public works predominantly targeted citizens with official BPL status (World Bank 2011). Government officials assumed significant power and discretion in allocating benefits and conferring eligibility, resulting in regressive allocation of BPL cards and eligibility status (Jalan and Murgai 2009). The increasing use of rights as a tool to curb administrative discretion, by reducing power and information asymmetries between citizens and government, is a key theme underpinning the myriad governance reforms in the PDS regime.

Second, the role of state governments in innovation and program administration has gained greater prominence because of the increasing devolution of resources and responsibilities to states for delivery, micro planning, and monitoring. That trend was particularly salient in the management and planning of MGNREGA, which created a parallel block- and village-level administrative cadre to plan and manage public works in partnership with elected *panchayati raj* institutions, nongovernmental organizations, and other civil society actors (Ministry of Rural Development 2012). Beyond public works, state governments have granted greater authority to community-based organizations such as self-help groups and cooperatives in the management of FPSs (Puri 2012).

The role of state governments has been bolstered further by the implementation of recommendations made by the Fourteenth Finance Commission in 2014, whereby funds for eight centrally sponsored schemes have been transferred directly to state governments. Further, the share of state governments in the national tax base has been increased to 42 percent, the highest in the history of Indian fiscal federalism (Ministry of Finance 2015). Before 2014, the Planning Commission allocated central funds to states. The national government replaced the Planning Commission with the National Institute for Transforming India (commonly known as the NITI *Aayog*). The NITI Aayog was created to be an advisory body with limited financial powers to strengthen the role of state governments in determining funding priorities and designing context-specific programs and policies in partnership with the central government. It is important to keep in mind these changes while examining the role of state-level innovation and leadership and the heterogeneity in TPDS performance.

Third, the program has walked a tightrope between its aims to ensure food price stability for farmers and consumers and its aims to ensure food security and nutrition for the poor. Critics have highlighted the distortionary impacts of the TPDS procurement process on agricultural prices and cropping patterns. However, reforms intended to delink the procurement and distribution of the TPDS from prices and planting decisions have been difficult to enact and implement (Kumar 2015). Understanding the role played by the TPDS in the food markets is key to understanding the political economy of TPDS reforms, particularly in the area of procurement and distribution.

Finally, several recent technological advances have improved delivery through the TPDS. Expanded automation through hardware and software, along with expanded rural infrastructure, has brought electricity and connectivity to a majority of India's villages. The Unique Identification Authority of India has biometrically enrolled more than 1 billion Indians and has a policy mandate and authority to give each Indian resident a unique *Aadhaar* identification number (PIB 2016). The use of Aadhaar for the distribution of TPDS rations remains contentious, with critics claiming it is leading to exclusion because of technological failures. Despite this, the role of information and communication technology (ICT) in digitizing beneficiary databases, computerizing supply chain management, setting up transparency portals, and putting in place grievance redress mechanisms has been a key influence in several states where the TPDS has improved its performance. Such practices can provide valuable lessons for other states and countries.

This chapter discusses the PDS experience in India, shedding light on the implementation and recent reforms of the TPDS. After introducing the public distribution system, using information on service delivery from across states, it traces the history of the program, outlines the key role played by citizens and the judiciary in social protection reform since 2005, and outlines major reforms and innovations in the delivery of food subsidies through the TPDS. The discussion focuses on state government ownership and innovations to improve delivery and nutrition outcomes and on a few reformer states that have achieved significant improvements in implementation outcomes. A final section concludes with a discussion of the future of the TPDS.

THE TARGETED PUBLIC DISTRIBUTION SYSTEM IN INDIA: AN INTRODUCTION

India's TPDS is an in-kind food subsidy program that is financed and managed by the government of India. Unlike programs such as the Supplementary Nutritional Assistance Program (SNAP) in the United States, which use vouchers to ensure food security, the TPDS provides subsidized food grain through a large network of government-licensed fair price shops. The government intervenes in the food market in two ways to influence the availability and accessibility of food grain. First, it encourages production by purchasing food grain from farmers at a minimum support price (MSP), a predetermined price floor. Second, it provides highly subsidized food grain to low-income and vulnerable households. This system of procurement and distribution is managed by the Ministry of Food and Civil Supplies through the Food Corporation of India (FCI). Figure 2.2 shows the major stakeholders and processes involved in implementing the TPDS.

Important Stakeholders

The TPDS is a centrally sponsored program that is financed by the government of India and jointly implemented by the central and state governments. The central government is responsible for financing the program, providing food grain (procuring, storing, and transporting), and determining the minimum number of beneficiaries and benefits (amount and price of grain to be distributed). States are responsible for selecting distributors (fair price shops), identifying beneficiaries, and ensuring that food grain is transported to all FPSs and distributed to all beneficiaries.

Decision making and implementation take place at the central, state, and district levels. At the central level, the Ministry of Food and Civil Supplies is responsible for procurement and distribution of food grain, which are managed by the FCI and the Department of Public Distribution, respectively. At the state level, procurement and transportation are managed by the State Food Corporation, while the functioning of the TPDS is managed by each state's Department of Food and Civil Supplies through district food offices.[3] District food offices are headed by a district food officer, a state-level bureaucrat who is responsible for implementing the TPDS in each district. The district food officer is assisted by a team of assistant food officers and food inspectors who monitor procurement and distribution of grain at the procurement centers and FPSs, respectively. A detailed discussion of these two main processes— procurement and distribution—follows.

Procurement

Procurement is an essential part of India's food security policy. Not only does it ensure the availability of food grain for the TPDS, it also provides Indian farmers with an MSP at which the government purchases their food grain.

FIGURE 2.2

The Public Distribution System in India: Stakeholders and Responsibilities

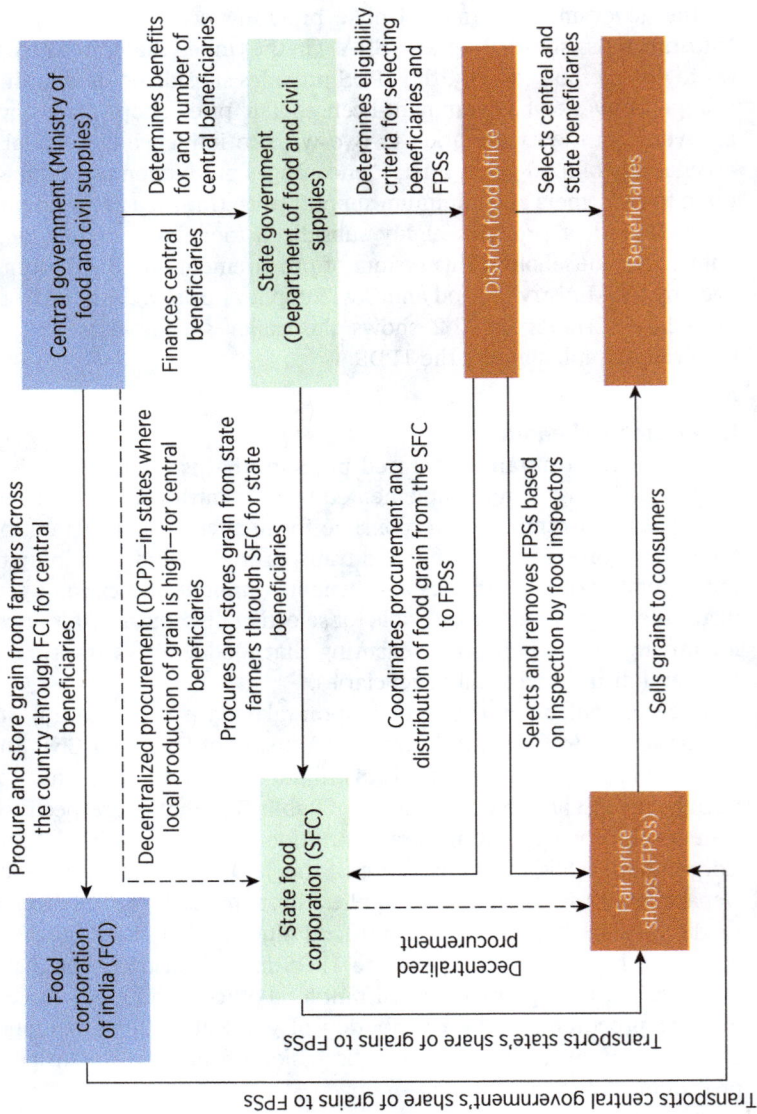

The FCI has procurement centers across the country that purchase paddy (unmilled rice) and wheat from farmers. In 2014–15, the MSP for wheat and rice was Rs 14.5 and Rs 13.6 per kilogram, respectively.[4] Once the food grain is procured, it is transported to FCI storage facilities across the country. It is then allocated according to the number of TPDS beneficiaries in each state.

Although the central government is responsible for procurement, some state governments have started playing a more prominent role in procurement. To improve the efficiency of the procurement process, particularly in states with high production of food grain, India launched the decentralized procurement program in 1997–98 to encourage states to develop their own procurement and storage facilities. More recently, state food corporations (state-level equivalents of the FCI) have proliferated in many states because of state-level expansions of TPDS benefits and coverage. Many state governments have expanded their distribution system by adding "state beneficiaries"—households that are poor or vulnerable but not counted as eligible by the central government. Some state governments have also lowered the price of grain or increased the quantity allocated per household. To make up for the shortfall (that is, to account for the extra food grain needed to meet the expansion of the TPDS), states are procuring food grain for their state-level initiatives. For example, the Chhattisgarh State Civil Supplies Corporation not only plays a major role in procuring food grain directly from farmers, but also is a leader in the use of ICT, such as end-to-end computerization of the TPDS supply chain (Bhattacharya and others 2016).

Distribution

Distribution of food grain is managed by state governments, which are responsible for identifying beneficiaries and selecting fair price shops. Once the beneficiaries are identified, the district food office provides them with a ration card that serves as identification for accessing the TPDS. The card includes information regarding the household's eligibility for the TPDS and a list of eligible members and documents all purchases made from the TPDS. District food offices also select the FPSs. Some states use private shops to distribute food grain; others use government-run TPDS shops (usually through local government bodies such as panchayats), self-help groups, and cooperatives. The district food office is also responsible for monitoring FPSs and has the authority to remove poorly performing ones.

The quantity and price of food grain available to households depend on the type of ration card assigned to them. Once a household receives its ration card, its members can visit their FPS (all households are assigned to a particular FPS) to buy their food grain every month. Before 2013, most households had one of three types of ration cards: above poverty line, below poverty line, and Antyodaya Anna Yojna. In 2013–14, the central issue price (CIP) for households with BPL ration cards was Rs 5.65 and Rs 4.15 per kilogram for rice and wheat, respectively.[5] The corresponding price for households with AAY ration cards was Rs 3.00 and Rs 2.00 per kilogram for rice and wheat, respectively. In most states, households with APL ration cards do not get food grain. Depending on the type of ration card, households may purchase their food grain from their assigned FPS. With implementation of the NFSA in 2013, entitlements for BPL were changed from household to individual entitlements—that is, 5 kilograms of food grain per member of an eligible household.

Trends in Program Delivery
The scale and coverage of the public distribution system expanded significantly in the past decade. Before the all-India implementation of the NFSA in 2015, the TPDS allocated ration cards to 65.2 million BPL families (including 25 million AAY families) as well as to 115 million APL families. Those numbers are being revised following the NFSA's rollout, and the TPDS is expected to reach 190 million households.[6] However, the number of households holding a ration card is not necessarily the number using TPDS services. To explain use, this chapter employs nationally representative data from the NSSO. However, those data are available only up to 2011, before the NFSA rollout, which restricts the discussion of delivery trends after the 2012 period. Based on NSSO analysis, the public distribution coverage rate—that is, the share of households reporting that they purchased food grain from FPSs—increased from 22.4 percent in 2004–05 to 44.5 percent in 2011–12, the highest coverage since the inception of the targeted program in 1997 (figure 2.3). Coverage includes APL and BPL families, which suggests that nearly 111 million households bought subsidized grain from FPSs in 2012. On average, nearly 6 of every 10 poor households purchased grain from the TPDS in 2011–12. TPDS coverage among the bottom 40 percent of the income distribution rose from 33 percent in 2004–05 to 58.3 percent in 2011–12. TPDS also expanded during this period, as indicated by an increase in the number of households holding ration cards (Desai 2015).

At the national level, the benefit incidence of food subsidies and TPDS food grain has changed little since 2004—the poorest 40 percent receives nearly half of food subsidies and food grain. The average amount of grain purchased by all households remained fairly constant at the state and national levels. At the all-India level, the nominal monthly subsidy transferred to households through the distribution of cereals rose sharply from Rs 28 in 2004–05 to Rs 139 in 2011–12 (detailed in figure 2A.1 in annex 2A). In nominal terms, subsidies transferred to poor households expanded from Rs 46 in 2004–05 to Rs 184 in 2011–12. That trend holds for both low-income and higher-income states. Each state reports increases in the size of the subsidy being allocated per household. Rahman (2014) uses deflated prices at the 2004–05 level for comparison. His findings also point to an increase in the size of transfer to households. In real terms, the subsidy amount per household increased from

FIGURE 2.3

Share of Households Purchasing Grain from the Public Distribution System in India, by State, Fiscal Years 2004–05 to 2011–12

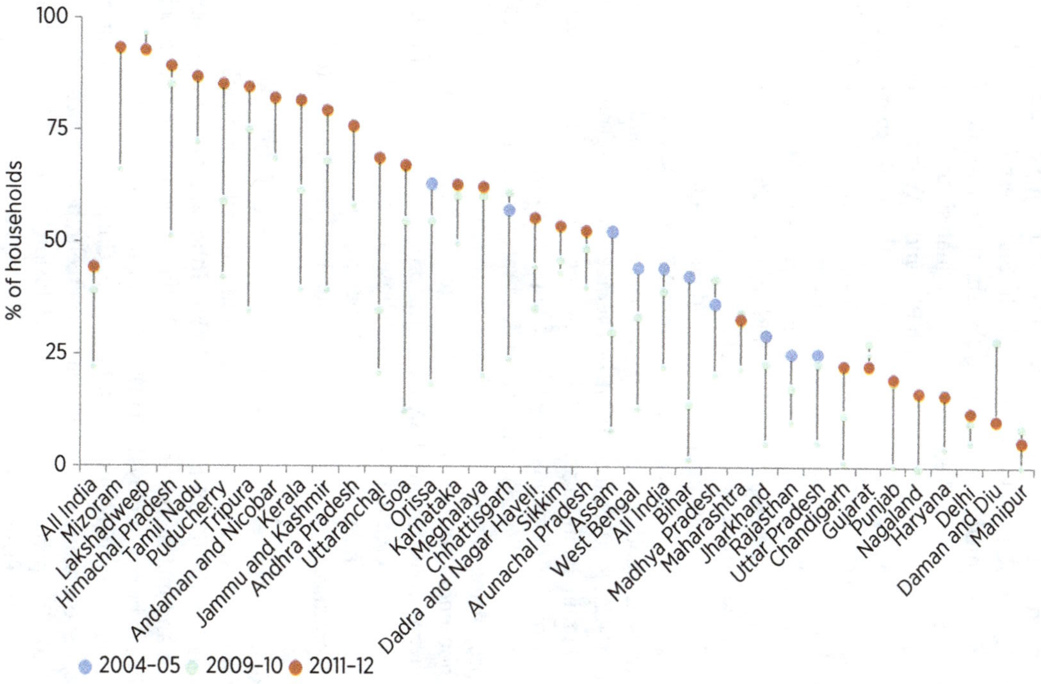

● 2004–05   ● 2009–10   ● 2011-12

Source: National Sample Survey Organization data.

Rs 31.10 per household in 2004–05 to Rs 85.21 in 2011–12. Chhattisgarh reported the highest increase in subsidy transferred per household in this period.

Beyond NSSO data, recent sample surveys conducted in 2014 by the National Council for Applied Economic Research (NCAER) highlight the important role played by the TPDS in providing food for the poor. The survey focused on BPL and AAY ration cardholders in six states: Assam, Bihar, Chhattisgarh, Karnataka, Uttar Pradesh, and West Bengal. The NFSA was being implemented in Bihar, Chhattisgarh, and Karnataka. The survey results corroborate trends picked up in the NSS analysis and reveal high use of the TPDS (more than 90 percent for both BPL and AAY cardholders in six states). Expenditure on food was a major component of total expenditure for families with four to six household members. On average, BPL and AAY families spend 64 and 60 percent, respectively, of their total monthly expenditure per capita on food. In rural areas, the proportion ranges from 53 percent in Assam to 69 percent in West Bengal, and in urban areas it ranges from 40 percent in Assam to 74 percent in Chhattisgarh.

Poor people consume mainly rice and wheat and often cannot afford other sources of basic nutrition. The requirement for those two foods varies across the states, depending on the agro-climatic zone and food habits. The NCAER survey (NCAER 2015) found that, on average, one person needs 8–13 kilograms of food grain, including rice and wheat, per month and that a substantial proportion of the demand for grain of people below the poverty line is met through public distribution at subsidized rates. In non-NFSA states, the average proportion of total household consumption of rice and wheat that a rural BPL household buys from the TPDS ranges from 37 percent in West Bengal to 56 percent in Assam; in NFSA states, the proportion varies from 38 percent in Bihar to 68 percent in Karnataka. Those households either purchase the remaining cereals required from the open market or satisfy the demand from home produce. The latter option is usually available only to households in rural areas.

Identification errors continue to plague the TPDS. The NCAER survey captures exclusion errors, defined as the proportion of people who should be included in the TPDS as BPL or AAY cardholders but who are excluded in reality, and inclusion errors, defined as the proportion of people who are not eligible to be covered by the TPDS but who are included by mistake or through inefficiency. As highlighted in table 2.1, in Chhattisgarh, the best-performing state, the exclusion error is low, at 2.0 percent, but the inclusion error is quite high, at 22.1 percent. In Bihar, the exclusion error is 30.5 percent, whereas the inclusion error is 18.4 percent. The highest inclusion error among the three NFSA states is in Karnataka. In the three non-NFSA states—Assam, Uttar Pradesh, and West Bengal—the exclusion error is 70.8, 63.1, and 29.8 percent, respectively (scenario 2 in table 2.1), whereas the inclusion error is 28.5, 22.2, and 46.7 percent, respectively.

TABLE 2.1 Identification Errors in the Targeted Public Distribution System in India, by State and Scenario

Percentages

STATE	SCENARIO 1 ERRORS ACCORDING TO STATE-SPECIFIC CRITERIA FOR NFSA		SCENARIO 2 ERRORS ACCORDING TO PLANNING COMMISSION ESTIMATED POVERTY LINE	
	INCLUSION	EXCLUSION	INCLUSION	EXCLUSION
Non-NFSA states				
Assam	16.3	27.0	*28.5*	*70.8*
Uttar Pradesh	22.0	36.5	*22.2*	*63.1*
West Bengal	20.5	27.0	*46.7*	*29.8*
NFSA states				
Bihar	*18.4*	*30.5*	27.8	52.3
Chhattisgarh	*22.1*	*2.0*	19.5	55.0
Karnataka	*31.2*	*16.0*	27.1	53.0

Source: NCAER 2015.
Note: State-specific identification criteria are used to calculate identification errors under scenario 1 for Bihar, Chhattisgarh, and Karnataka, and similar eligibility criteria are used for Assam, Uttar Pradesh, and West Bengal. For non-NFSA states, the error estimated under scenario 1 is hypothetical, because those states have yet to switch to the NFSA and are currently using the Planning Commission estimates and criteria for BPL. Figures in italics highlight errors according to criteria of the relevant state government. NFSA states no longer use Planning Commission estimated poverty lines to identify households. NFSA = National Food Security Act.

The leakage of TPDS food grain has declined steadily in a majority of states. Diversion is defined as the amount of TPDS food grain purchased by beneficiaries as a percentage of the total food grain allocated to FPSs for distribution.[7] "Leakage" refers to the amount of TPDS food grain released by the FCI that fails to reach the intended beneficiaries. At the all-India level, leakage declined from 58.6 percent of official TPDS grain offtake in 2004–05 to 43.1 percent in 2011–12 (table 2A.7). However, that decline in diversion is limited to a few low-income states; leakage in states such as Jharkhand, Madhya Pradesh, Rajasthan, and Uttar Pradesh has remained high, with large shares of TPDS grain never reaching the intended recipients. Higher-income states such as Gujarat and Punjab have experienced a rise in leakage. Leakage rates are lower for rice than for wheat and are higher for APL beneficiaries (Drèze and Khera 2015; Ministry of Finance 2015; Saini and Gulati 2015).

TPDS delivery of food grain varies widely by geographic location. The share of urban households using the TPDS to purchase grain is consistently lower than that of rural households. Other than the southern states, the majority of the increase in participation is observed in rural areas of low-income states. However, intrastate variation in participation rates is large within low-income states as well. For instance, regions affected by left-wing extremism in Chhattisgarh and Jharkhand have TPDS participation rates as high as 65 percent.

Despite major expansion in coverage, inclusion of the poorest and most vulnerable groups continues to lag in low-income states relative to higher-income states. As figure 2.4 indicates, of all low-income states, Chhattisgarh and Odisha have relatively lower rates of leakage and better TPDS access for the poorest individuals. Assam, Bihar, Jharkhand, Madhya Pradesh, and West Bengal are catching up with other well-performing states. However, Rajasthan and Uttar Pradesh continue to perform poorly. Coverage is high and leakage is low in southern states, but highly urbanized states in the north are the worst performers in implementing the TPDS. Delhi, Haryana, and Punjab report very high rates of leakage and low rates of participation of the poor. Those differences signal the need to have a spatially nuanced dialogue on the subsidy reform process.

Criticism of the TPDS often revolves around leakage and the uneven quality of implementation, and these are given as reasons for moving toward cash transfers. While considering this, it is important to gauge the contributions that the TPDS and other in-kind food transfers made to poverty reduction between 2004–05 and 2014–15. In a review of the impact of in-kind transfers, Himanshu and Sen (2013) decompose the role of in-kind transfers in reducing headcount poverty rates between 1993 and 2012. To implement these decompositions, they constructed and modified state and national poverty lines and revalued the market price of rice, wheat, and sugar purchased from the TPDS. They then isolated the contribution of subsidies to the number of households lifted out of poverty, comparing out-of-pocket consumption expenditure with

FIGURE 2.4

Spatial Diversity of Trajectories in Coverage of the Targeted Public Distribution System across States in India, 2011–12

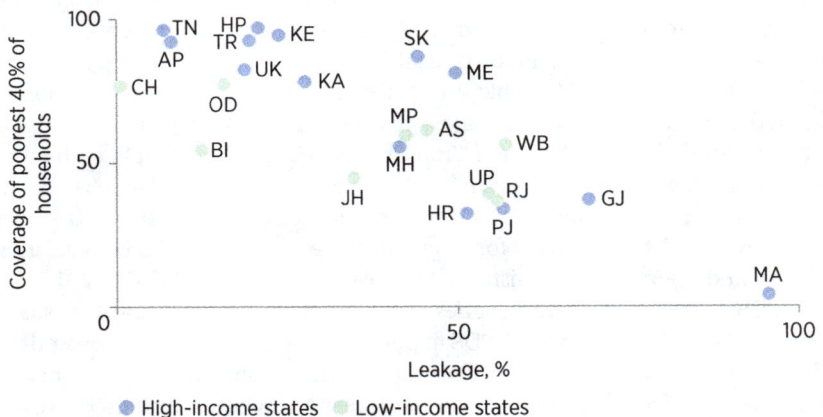

Source: National Sample Survey Organization 2011–12 data.
Note: Central Food Corporation of India offtake data provide conservative estimates of leakage.

and without food transfers. The results highlight the significance of the TPDS during the drought year of 2009–10, when the TPDS transfers served as a safety net that kept 38 million households out of poverty.

Despite the recent phase of program expansion and decline in leakage, critics highlight how in-kind delivery of grain has a distortionary impact on agricultural production decisions and prices. Despite improvements, TPDS leakage rates remain high in the poorest states (Gulati and Saini 2015), and the current mode of delivering subsidies is inefficient and costly because of government involvement in the procurement and distribution of grain. Critics highlight several potentially positive aspects of moving to a system of cash delivery of subsidies, which would dilute the role of the TPDS in food market arbitration. First, they suggest that the incentive to divert grain would not exist under a system of cash transfers, as FPSs would have to sell grain at market price to all customers. Because "a shopkeeper gets the market price even when he is making a subsidized sale, the incentive to defraud is extinguished" (Kotwal, Murugkar, and Ramaswami 2011, 78). Second, under cash transfers, consumers would be free to buy the grain of their choice. Third, moving away from a system of in-kind transfers would eliminate the need for government to engage in procurement, storage, and distribution.

At the heart of this debate is the role of the TPDS in food markets. The current agrarian setup encourages procurement of grains from a few states with large surpluses. As a result, farmers in surplus states are better off economically. Kotwal, Murugkar, and Ramaswami (2011) suggest that the distribution of subsidized wheat and rice in poorer areas exerts downward pressure on the prices of local coarse grain, which hurts local and small-scale farmers of those grains. Such a system triggers inequality between farmers in surplus states and those in arid and semiarid areas. Critics argue that a system of cash transfers would do the opposite, as consumers in poorer areas would choose to spend their cash on local grain. This would boost demand and hence the market prices for local grain (Kotwal, Murugkar, and Ramaswami 2011).

Such debates are not new in the context of the TPDS, which has undergone several changes with respect to coverage, procurement, distribution, and pricing, since its inception. The following section discusses the political economy of these changes and outlines how it evolved to provide both social protection and food market stabilization.

POLITICAL ECONOMY OF PROGRAM EVOLUTION: BALANCING THE DUAL ROLES OF THE TPDS

The First 50 Years of Food Rationing in India

Before economic liberalization, the PDS was designed to ensure food sufficiency and price stability, in keeping with India's policy of nonalignment and geopolitical ambitions. Between 1939 and 1945, nearly Rs 3,500 million (US$53.8 million) was spent on World War II in India (Sohal 2013, 255).

The expansion in public expenditure resulted in rising inflation that significantly affected Indian consumers. Between 1939 and 1945, food inflation rose steeply (table 2.2). The average rate of inflation of wholesale prices during wartime was 33 and 22 percent for rice and wheat, respectively. The highest increase was in 1943, when the wholesale price of rice nearly doubled, increasing 208 percent, and the wholesale price of wheat rose 57 percent. During that time, the sterling securities with the Reserve Bank of India increased from Rs 740 million (US$11.4 million) to Rs 17,240 million (US$265.2 million).

To support its war efforts, the government of India began to intervene in agricultural and food markets. Between 1940 and 1942, it held several price control conferences. At the sixth conference, held in September 1942, a recommendation was made for the centralized purchase of food grain to address the country's food emergency (Knight 1954). Following this, the basic principles of a public distribution system were laid out (Planning Commission 2005). Following establishment of the Department of Food in 1942, the PDS was extended to six other cities. In December of that year, at the First Food Conference, the need for an estimation of food grain requirements and resources was raised, as well as the need for a plan to guide their best possible use. Thereafter, the Food Department defined an All-India Basic Plan to allot existing surpluses from provinces and states most efficiently. The basic plan dealt with "issues such as procurement, contracts for purchasing agents, public distribution, inspection, and storage" (Tripathi 2014, 59).

TABLE 2.2 **Wholesale Price of Rice and Wheat and Inflation Rate in India, 1939–45**

	WHOLESALE PRICE INDEX (1938 = 100)		INFLATION (%)	
YEAR	RICE	WHEAT	RICE	WHEAT
1939	115	132	15	32
1940	123	137	7	4
1941	159	167	29	22
1942	191	216	20	29
1943	589	339	208	57
1944	349	378	−41	12
1945	330	372	−5	−2
Average	265	263	33	22

Source: Mishra 1985, 42, using information from the *Agricultural Census Report 1951*, vol. I, pt. I-B, app., p. 316.

To account for inflation and the deteriorating food situation, in 1943 the Food Grains Policy Committee recommended the "introduction of rationing in urban centers with a population of more than 100,000" (Planning Commission 2005, 1). The quantity stipulated for this purpose was a minimum of 1 pound of cereals per capita per day, "even if imports would be needed" (Mooij 1998, 3). Throughout this period, administrative efforts were focused on urban areas, despite the widespread food crisis unfolding in rural parts of the country. Many point to the apathy of colonial administration as the trigger for the Bengal famine of 1943, in which an estimated 1.5 million to 3 million Indians died (Sen 1981). As the food crisis intensified, the government resorted to requisitioning the harvest, which bred resentment against the British among the agricultural elites, especially in Punjab. Taking advantage of this unrest and the inflation caused by food shortages, members of antiwar campaigns and the Muslim League became more active, leading to the rise of communal tensions and demand for an autonomous Muslim nation. Those tensions particularly affected the fertile, well-irrigated, and agriculturally prosperous province of Punjab. When India gained independence, significant tracts of the agricultural Punjab region were lost.[8] After the end of World War II in 1945, India continued with the rationing system, extending the PDS to 771 cities and towns by 1946. Although largely limited to urban areas, some rural areas facing chronic shortages were also covered (Nawani 1994).

Following independence in 1947, the newly established government struggled to contain inflation in the absence of a consistent food policy. At the time of independence, the country was partitioned to create the new country of Pakistan. The partition resulted in India having 82 percent of its total population before partition, but only 75 percent of its cereal production (Nawani 1994). Two provinces—Punjab and Sindh—that supplied about 1 million tons of food grain to other provinces went to Pakistan. The domestic economic strife was "accentuated by the already prevailing high global prices of food grain at the end of the War, which were around four times higher than the prewar prices" (Nawani 1995, 66).

Despite the advice of the Food Grains Policy Committee in December 1947, all existing food controls were lifted under the influence of Mahatma Gandhi (Mooij 1998, 4). As quoted in Chopra (1988, 67), Gandhi believed that controls "give rise to fraud, suppression of truth, intensification of the black market, and to artificial scarcity. Above all [they] unman the people and deprive them of initiative; [they undo] the teachings of self-help they have been learning for generations." Such drastic reforms, combined with bad weather, led to crop losses and a steep rise in food prices. The situation necessitated the reintroduction of controls on the price, procurement, and distribution of food grain in September 1948 (Mooij 1998, 4). In 1950, the Constitution of India was adopted, declaring India a socialist republic. India modeled its economic growth along the lines of the Soviet Union's planned economy, using five-year plans to set targets and shape the economy.

In keeping with the plan approach to achieving economic development, the Food Grains Procurement Committee of 1950 recommended rationing in all large towns (population over 50,000), informal rationing in smaller towns, and provision of a limited, regulated supply of grain in rural areas. Furthermore, the committee recommended that only the government should trade in food grain (Majumder 2009). In accordance with these recommendations, under the First Five-Year Plan (1951–56), the PDS was extended beyond urban areas to rural areas suffering from chronic food shortages. The PDS had the following objectives (Swaminathan 2008):

- Maintaining price stability

- Raising the welfare of the poor (by providing access to basic food at reasonable prices to the vulnerable population)

- Rationing during situations of scarcity

- Keeping a check on private trade.

During the First Five-Year Plan, food grain prices remained stable, and production grew steadily, increasing from 51.99 million metric tons in 1951 to 66.85 million metric tons in 1956. Owing to the rising rate of agricultural production and the declining rate of imports, which fell from 4.7 million tons in 1951 to 0.8 million tons in 1954 (Chopra 1988, 84–106; Mooij 1998, 4), another phase of decontrol was initiated from 1952 to 1954. During this time, movement of food grain was unrestricted, procurement was nearly stopped, rationing was reduced considerably (Mooij 1998), and regulations governing private trade were removed (FAO 1994). Indian political leaders and advisers believed that India was heading toward self-sufficiency (Chopra 1988).

Production of food grain continued to rise until 1955 (figure 2.5), when bad weather and low food grain prices began to have an adverse effect on production (Mooij 1998, 4). Production recovered to some extent in 1956–57, only to plunge again in 1957–58.

Following the 1957–58 drop in food grain production, the government expanded the PDS. The number of ration shops nearly tripled, increasing from 18,000 in 1957 to 51,000 in 1961 (Nawani 1994). Other essential commodities were added to the PDS, such as kerosene, cooking coal, and sugar. This expansion was possible because large amounts of wheat were being imported from the United States, mostly under Public Law (P.L.) 480 or the Food for Peace Program of 1954 (Mooij 1999). Following the move toward nonalignment and India's criticism of the U.S. intervention in Vietnam (Malhotra 2010), India recognized the need to ensure food sufficiency to support its sovereign geopolitical plans.

FIGURE 2.5

Food Grain Production in India, 1950–1991

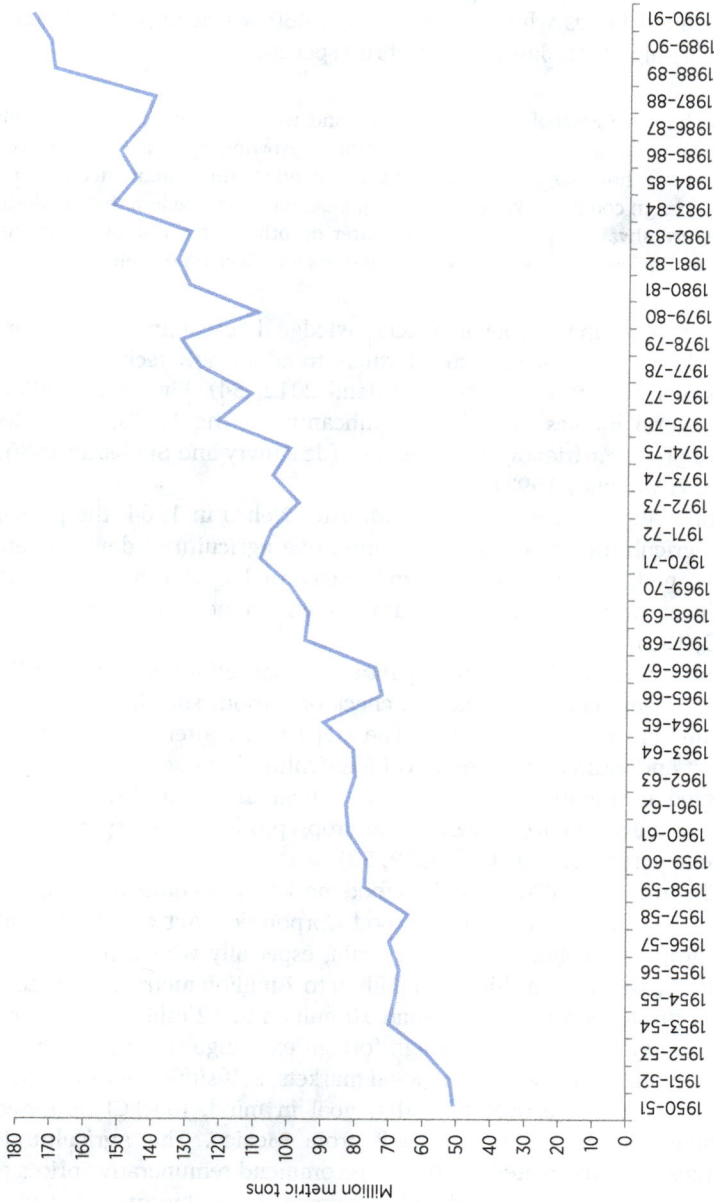

Source: Ministry of Agriculture 2015.

The mid-1960s to 1970s witnessed major changes in the PDS and, more generally, India's agricultural policy. Scholars suggest that these changes resulted from India having to compromise its sovereignty at the hands of the United States while negotiating P.L. 480 wheat imports. Bhatia (1991, 345–46) highlights Jawaharlal Nehru's speech:

> We have sought help from abroad ... and we shall continue to do so under pressure of necessity, but the conviction is growing upon me more forcefully than ever how dangerous it is for us to depend for this primary necessity of life on foreign countries. We can never function, with the freedom that we desire, if we are always dependent in this matter on others. It is only when we attain self-sufficiency in food that we can progress and develop ourselves.

Further, policy makers began to acknowledge that sustained food security was possible only by "incentivizing farmers to adopt new technology and make investments in modern inputs" (Chand 2012, 54). Finally, the influence of agricultural lobbies intensified significantly by the 1960s, which led to a "more producer-friendly price regime" (de Janvry and Subbarao 1986; Mooij 1998, 7; Varshney 1993).

Following the death of Prime Minister Nehru in 1964, the principles of low agricultural prices and labor-intensive agricultural development were abandoned, and India began to undertake rapid agricultural reforms through producer price incentives and investment in new technology (Varshney 1993, 183).

Policy interventions were expanded beyond efforts to facilitate the functioning of markets and to keep a check on various stakeholders, particularly private traders (Chand 2012). The steps taken after the mid-1960s were "direct and indirect interventions in agricultural markets and prices, initially targeted at procuring and distributing wheat and paddy. This [effort] gradually expanded to cover several other crops/products and aspects of domestic trade in agriculture" (Chand 2012, 53).

The role of the TPDS in India's food markets was codified through creation of the FCI in 1965 (under the Food Corporation Act of 1964) against the backdrop of a major shortage of grain, especially wheat. Imports of wheat under P.L. 480 were as high as 6 million to 7 million metric tons, when India's wheat production hovered around 10 million to 12 million metric tons, and the country did not have enough foreign exchange reserves to buy an adequate quantity of wheat from global markets. Self-sufficiency in grain was the most pressing objective; with that goal in mind, the FCI imported high-yielding varieties of wheat seeds from Mexico. The Agricultural Prices Commission was created in 1965 to recommend remunerative prices to farmers, and the FCI was mandated to pursue three objectives: (a) to provide effective price supports to farmers, (b) to procure and supply grain to the PDS for distributing subsidized staples to economically vulnerable sections of society, and (c) to keep a strategic reserve to stabilize markets for basic food grain (Kumar 2015).

The Agricultural Prices Commission (renamed the Commission on Agricultural Costs and Prices in 1985) was set up to define minimum support prices. A year later, in 1966, high-yielding varieties of seeds imported from Mexico were distributed among farmers, and wholesale markets for agricultural produce were administered by the Agricultural Produce Marketing Committee (APMC) Acts (figure 2.6).

The government introduced legislation to ensure that farmers received a fair price for their harvest by "eradicating malpractices from markets, protecting

FIGURE 2.6

Procurement, Offtake, and Stocks of Rice and Wheat in India, 1975–2010

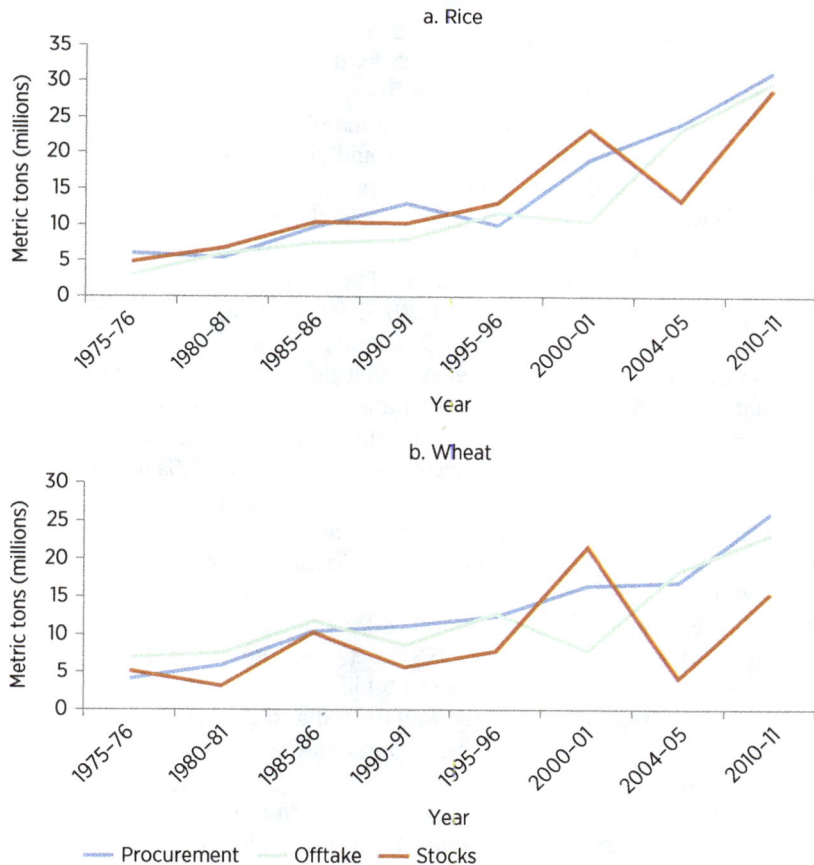

Source: Ministry of Agriculture 2015.

them from exploitation by middlemen, and creating a competitive pricing environment" (Chand 2012, 54). The APMC Acts sought to ensure that certain agricultural commodities could be bought and sold only in designated areas, where appropriate infrastructure is available, prices are determined by open auction in the presence of an official, and commissions and service charges are fixed. This legislation, along with the simultaneous increase in the supply of institutional credit to producers, (a) eradicated several malpractices and imperfections in agricultural markets, (b) created orderly and largely transparent marketing conditions, and (c) gave farmers a fairer deal for their harvests (Acharya 2004; Chand 2012). This combination of technology and market regulatory policy during the 1970s ushered in an era of agricultural growth, often referred to as the Green Revolution. During that time, production of wheat increased from 12 million to more than 26 million metric tons, while imports decreased from 6.5 million to 0.5 million metric tons (Kumar 2015, 10). The Green Revolution also led to the formation of a class of wealthy capitalist farmers who, over time, gained political influence and penetrated political parties and agricultural policy institutions, such as the Commission on Agricultural Costs and Prices (Mitra 1977; Varshney 1993).

Until the mid-1960s, the PDS was used mainly in urban areas as an emergency measure during times of inflation and shortages. Following the food crisis of the mid-1960s, the government of India decided that a subsidized rationing system was needed for all, and in the early 1970s the PDS was expanded and made universal. In October 1972, the government discontinued all private wholesale trade in wheat. The following year, the same policy was implemented for paddy (Kumar 2015). As a result, the procurement of cereals dropped substantially. Dr. N. C. Saxena, commissioner to the Supreme Court in the Right to Food case, believes that the reason for low procurement was that 1973–75 were bad years for Indian agriculture because of drought and poor harvest.[9] In addition, the government was unable to "set up arrangements to buy from the farmer so there was a lot of chaos," Saxena said. The situation was made worse by the international price crisis of 1973–74. India returned to being dependent on imports of wheat, importing 2.4 million metric tons of wheat in 1973, 4.5 million metric tons in 1974, and 7.2 million metric tons in 1975 (Kumar 2015). However, India was no longer receiving P.L. 480 wheat, and the price of wheat in the international market had more than doubled, from US$80.32 to US$166.39 per metric ton. India's foreign exchange reserves ranged from US$1.26 billion to US$2.26 billion between 1972 and 1976 (Kumar 2015), too low for India to depend on imports, and in 1975 the decision was made once again to allow private traders to participate in the wholesale market.

The PDS acquired an important political role in the 1980s because politicians were increasingly using populist subsidy policy to appeal to voters and farmer lobbies (Mooij 1998). The breakdown of the dominant party system (Kothari 1964, 1988; Vanaik 1990) and the development of a more "assertive and demanding" electorate (Manor 1988; Mooij 1998, 11) are part of the explanations for the shift in policy.

From 1965 to the late 1980s and early 1990s, the approach to food security policy in general, and the PDS in particular, expanded greatly (figure 2.7). The quantity of food grain that the FCI managed in a year nearly doubled (table 2.3). The number of ration shops tripled, and the PDS was extended, largely to rural India, with 75 percent of FPSs located in rural areas. Furthermore, of the total rice and wheat sold under the PDS, 70 percent of rice and 55 percent of wheat were sold in rural areas. The amount of food subsidy increased from nearly negligible to more than Rs 25 billion (US$371 million).[10] From the 1970s until 1992, the PDS was uniformly implemented as a national universal program.

Targeting within the PDS

In the early 1990s, the PDS was increasingly criticized for the following (Umali-Deininger, Sur, and Deininger 2005, 5):

* Failure to reach the poor effectively

* Urban bias

* Substantial leakages

FIGURE 2.7

Changes in the Amount of Food Grain Subsidy and the Public Distribution System in India, 1970–95

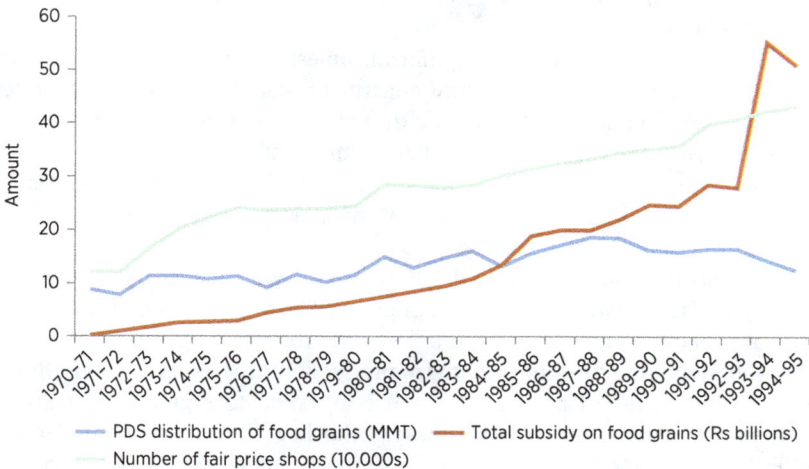

Source: Mooij 1998.
Note: MMTs = million metric tons.

TABLE 2.3 **Changes in the Public Distribution System in India, 1965 to
Late 1980s**

ITEM	1965	END-1980S
FCI-managed food grain (million metric tons per year)	10	>18
Number of ration shops	116,000	>350,000
Amount of subsidy	—	Rs 25,000–Rs 28,000 million

Source: Mooij 1998.
Note: FCI = Food Corporation of India; — = not available.

- Supply of poor-quality grain as a result of deficient inventory management and relaxed specification for procurement
- Lack of transparent and accountable delivery systems
- Lack of availability of stock, negligible coverage, and low offtake in states with a high concentration of poor.

Following a series of structural reforms in 1991, the government introduced the revamped PDS (RPDS) in 1992, which focused on giving higher subsidies primarily to drought-prone, tribal, hilly, and remote areas. Despite that effort, leakages at the national level during 1997–98 were estimated to be 31 percent for rice and 36 percent for wheat. Targeting was introduced in the PDS, and the RPDS was replaced in mid-1997 by the TPDS. The TPDS was unique in that targeting was based on household poverty rather than location (World Bank 2011).

The shift to the TPDS was a significant milestone in India's food security and social protection strategy. Until enactment of the NFSA in 2013, states were required to issue food grain at a difference of not more than Rs 0.5 per kilogram above the CIP for BPL families (Ministry of Consumer Affairs 2016). More recently, however, states have been given flexibility to fix the retail issue price for TPDS food grain, except for AAY recipients. Figure 2.8 shows trajectories of the MSP and the CIP.

To recap the journey, the mid-1960s were watershed years, with India moving toward a consistent food grain policy. The realization that food grain self-sufficiency is crucial for India's progress, the growing influence of the farm lobby, and the need to incentivize production ushered in a pro-producer price regime. The FCI and APMC were established to regulate agricultural markets, procurement, and distribution. Further, the government defined MSPs for wheat and paddy and made institutional credit available to farmers. These initiatives, combined with the introduction of high-yielding varieties

FIGURE 2.8

Minimum Support Prices and Central Issue Prices of Food Grain in India, 1976–2016

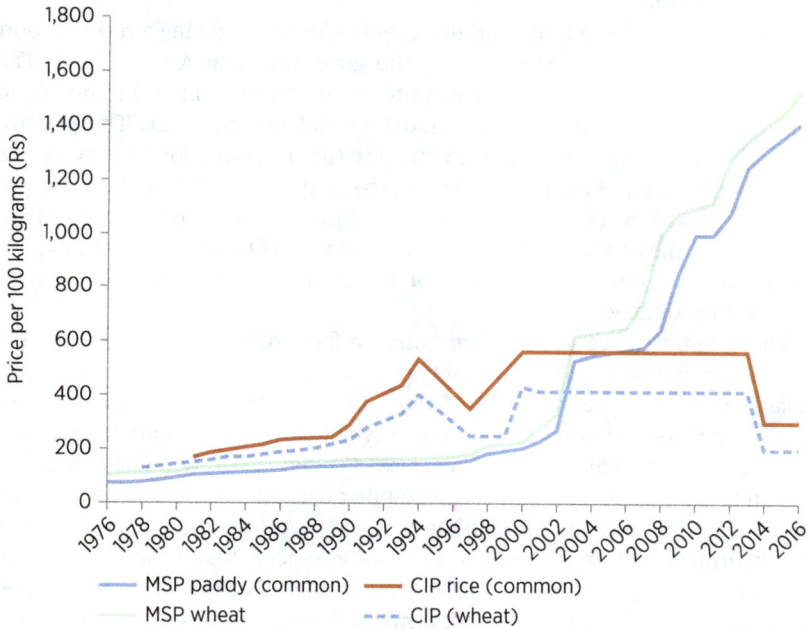

Sources: Ministry of Agriculture data for minimum support prices (MSPs) (Indiastat.com); Department of Agriculture and Cooperation data for central issue prices (CIPs).

of seeds, led to the Green Revolution of the 1960s and created a class of prosperous and politically influential farmers. India began to produce enough food grain to meet its own needs as well as to export.

During this period, the government universalized the PDS and the nature of the PDS changed from being an emergency provision in urban areas to a welfare scheme supporting producers and consumers. The program was expanded considerably in rural areas. However, inefficiencies and high rates of leakage continued to plague the PDS. In the 1980s, the PDS gained populist support because of the decline of the Indian National Congress Party and ushering in of competitive democratic politics. After India adopted a program of structural adjustment in 1997, the TPDS was introduced to target BPL households. In the late 1990s, unfavorable weather conditions resulted in chronic hunger in several parts of the country, despite surplus food grain stocks. To address those conditions, in 2001 the People's Union for Civil Liberties filed a writ petition in the Supreme Court seeking legal enforcement of the right to food. Following a widespread grassroots and civil society campaign, the right to food was recognized with passage of the NFSA in 2013.

Ongoing Debates on FCI Reforms

The role of the TPDS in food markets is set to change following a recent report by a high-level committee set up by the government in August 2014. The committee was asked to suggest ways to restructure or unbundle the FCI to improve its operational efficiency and financial management. The government also asked the committee to suggest (a) measures for improving the FCI's management of food grain overall; (b) measures for reorienting the role and functions of the FCI in MSP operations, in storage and distribution of food grain, and in the country's food security systems; and (c) cost-effective models for storing and moving grain and for integrating the supply chain of food grain in the country.

The committee report on procurement reform recommends delinking the TPDS's role in food markets as a safety net for the poor. It suggests that, despite India's move from the shortages of the 1960s into surpluses of cereals since 2010—"the food management system, of which the FCI is an integral part, has not been able to deliver on its objectives" (Kumar 2015, iv). The benefits of procurement have yet to reach a large number of farmers beyond those in a few states. The NSSO (round 70) data for 2012–13 reveal that only 13.5 percent of paddy farmers reporting sales during July–December 2012 (and only 10 percent of farmers reporting sales during January–June 2013) sold it to a procurement agency. In the case of wheat farmers during January–June 2013, only 16.2 percent sold to any procurement agency. Only 6 percent of all wheat and paddy farmers in the country appear to have gained directly from selling their produce to any procurement agency (Kumar 2015, iv). In addition, the country held surplus grain stocks far above the norms, even though inflation of cereal stocks was hovering between 8 and 12 percent. This situation persisted even after India exported more than 42 million metric tons of cereals in 2012–14, levels not previously seen in India's history (Kumar 2015).

The committee report recommends that the FCI hand over all procurement operations of wheat, paddy, and rice to state governments that have adequate infrastructure and expertise for procurement. Those states are Andhra Pradesh, Chhattisgarh, Haryana, Madhya Pradesh, Odisha, and Punjab. In addition, the FCI should "accept only the surplus (after deducting the needs of the states under NFSA) from the state governments (not from millers) to move them to deficit states" (Kumar 2015, v). The FCI should then assist farmers in the states of Assam, Bihar, Eastern Uttar Pradesh, and West Bengal, which are dominated by small holdings and often resort to distress sales at prices far below the MSP. Furthermore, these states form the belt where the second green revolution is expected and where the FCI needs to be proactive, by mobilizing state and other agencies to provide the benefits of MSP and procurement to more farmers, especially small and marginal ones.

The committee report on procurement reforms, particularly MSP, suggests giving pulses and oilseeds priority and better price support. The MSPs for wheat and rice skew the cultivation choices of farmers in favor of these two crops, while the shortage of pulses and oilseeds (edible oils), which often sell below the MSP, remains unaddressed in the absence of price support. "Further, trade policy works independently of MSP policy; many times, imports of pulses come at prices much below the MSP, which hampers diversification. One suggestion is to dovetail MSP policy with trade policy so that the landed costs of those products are not below their MSP" (Kumar 2015, vi). Ongoing debates in parliament on adopting these recommendations for FCI reform highlight the tensions between the role of the TPDS as a tool to provide social protection and as a tool to stabilize and intervene in food markets.

ENHANCED CITIZEN ENGAGEMENT: USING RIGHTS AND JUDICIAL INTERVENTION

Since early 2000, India's TPDS has been the focus of concerted civil society–led judicial attention. Such judicial activism has triggered and sustained public pressure on central and state government agencies to curb leakage and improve service delivery.[11] In 2006, the government formed a Central Vigilance Committee under the chairmanship of Justice D. P. Wadhwa, a former judge of the Supreme Court of India, to review the public distribution system and identify remedies to operational bottlenecks. In response, the committee made a series of state-specific recommendations, which various state governments have incorporated as they redesigned the business processes of their supply and delivery of food grain.

Codification of Orders for Changing Business Practices

The central government issued Public Distribution System (Control) Order 2001 (amended in 2004) for the effective functioning of the distribution of subsidies and delivery of benefits to India's poorest. The orders codified the following business processes for all state governments in management of the TPDS: identification of beneficiaries and distribution of ration cards, management and distribution of food grain, and end-to-end computerization of PDS records.

Reformulation of Beneficiary Identification and Ration Card Distribution Processes

In 2004, the central government directed all state governments to formulate suitable guidelines for identifying families living below the poverty line, including AAY families, using estimates adopted by the central government. The committee suggested involving *gram sabhas* (village committees) and panchayati raj institutions to validate the list of beneficiaries belonging to BPL and AAY categories. The list would be drawn up by the designated authority in villages and wards. In jurisdictions with no gram sabhas, the orders suggested engaging local area representative bodies.

In response to the government orders, all state governments revised and issued new state-level TPDS (control) orders clarifying the criteria for eligibility for subsidized food grain. State governments were also instructed to issue distinctive ration cards to APL, BPL, and AAY families and to review and check the ration cards periodically to curb inclusion errors. Those orders were a major step, because business rules specifying those processes were missing or outdated in many low-income states. The drive also triggered state-level attempts to identify eligible people who were excluded and to cancel counterfeit cards. For example, Madhya Pradesh Control Order 2009 repealed the Madhya Pradesh Foodstuff (Distribution and Control) Order 1960. The statutory framework governing and regulating various aspects of the public distribution system is contained in the following documents:

- The Essential Commodities Act 1955

- Public Distribution System (Control) Order 2001, as amended in 2004

- Circulars issued by the Department of Food and Public Distribution in the Ministry of Consumer Affairs

- Public Distribution System (Control) Orders issued by various state governments

- Circulars, orders, and notifications issued by various State Civil Supplies Corporations.

Improved Food Grain Management and Distribution
Following PDS Control Order 2001, the central government codified the procedures for distributing food grain by the FCI to the state governments or their nominated agencies (Ministry of Consumer Affairs 2001):

> Fair price shop owners would take delivery of stocks from authorized nominees of the state governments to ensure that essential commodities are available at the FPS within the first week of the month for which the allotment is made. The district authority entrusted with the responsibility of implementing the TPDS must ensure that the stocks allocated to the FPSs are physically delivered to them by the authorized nominee within the stipulated time.

End-to-End Computerization of TPDS Records
Computerizing TPDS records to track transactions in the PDS supply chain would help to stop the large-scale diversion of grain. In 2008, the central government supported a series of pilots in the states of Chhattisgarh, Haryana, Odisha, and Tamil Nadu to test the benefits of automating the supply, distribution, and delivery of rations. In 2012, that computerization drive became a

central scheme whereby the central and state governments shared costs for (a) automating FPS-level data and transactions, warehouse (*godown*) and storage information, data on the transport of grain, and data on beneficiary transactions and (b) creating ICT-based methods for redressing grievances, such as online websites and toll-free numbers.

Passage of the NFSA

The National Food Security Act was intended to alleviate hunger by establishing access to food as a legal right and providing highly subsidized food grain to roughly 70 percent of the Indian population.[12] By law, the central government determines the size of the population to be covered in each state, and the state governments identify eligible households based on published census data. The state governments establish their own criteria for identifying eligible beneficiaries at the local level, but states are required to cover 75 percent of all rural inhabitants and 50 percent of all urban inhabitants. The central government agreed to provide financial assistance to the state governments to support intrastate transportation and handling of food grain and to cover the margins to be paid to the FPSs. It also allowed the states to expand coverage and to introduce fortification of food grain if they chose to do so, but at their own expense.

The NFSA also reduced the monthly entitlement for individual beneficiaries from 7 to 5 kilograms, with one important exception: the "poorest of the poor" households in the AAY program are guaranteed 35 kilograms of grain per household per month. Under the NFSA, beneficiaries are entitled to purchase specified monthly quantities of food grain—wheat, rice, and coarse grains (consisting mostly of millet)—at prices ranging from Rs 1 to Rs 3 per kilogram, with wheat averaging Rs 2 per kilogram (table 2.4). These prices

TABLE 2.4 **TPDS Entitlements under India's National Food Security Act**

BENEFIT	PRE-NFSA (2004–13)	POST-NFSA (2014)
Rate, Rs per kilogram (US$ per kilogram)		
Rice	5.65 (0.08)	3 (0.04)
Wheat	4.15 (0.06)	2 (0.02)
Millet	3.00 (0.04)	1 (0.01)
Quantity (kilograms)		
BPL	25	5 per member
AAY	35	35

Source: Ministry of Consumer Affairs, Department of Food and Public Distribution (http://dfpd.nic.in /public-distribution.htm).
Note: TPDS = targeted public distribution system; NFSA = National Food Security Act; AAY = Antyodaya Anna Yojana (poorest of the poor); BPL = below poverty line.

are highly subsidized and a fraction of their open-market prices, which range from Rs 14 to Rs 18 per kilogram.

The campaign for passage of the NFSA began in 2001 when the People's Union for Civil Liberties (PUCL, Rajasthan) filed a writ petition in the Supreme Court seeking legal enforcement of the right to food (RTFC Secretariat 2008). The petition was filed to challenge the government's decision to maintain large food stocks despite the intensification of chronic hunger in drought-affected areas. While speaking about the large buffer stocks being maintained by the FCI, Jean Drèze said, "When millions of people are undernourished if not starving, hoarding food on this scale—at enormous cost—is nothing short of implicit mass murder" (Drèze 2003, 434).

The petition *PUCL* v. *Union of India and others* (Writ Petition [Civil] no. 196 of 2001) was filed with the belief that "legal action is one of the means that can be used, in a democratic political system, to hold the state accountable to its responsibilities" (RTFC Secretariat 2008). "The petition argues that the right to food is a basic right enshrined in the Constitution of India because it is a logical extension of Article 21, the fundamental right to life. The case initially named the government of India, the FCI, and six state governments but was expanded to include all state governments, holding them answerable 'to the larger issues of chronic hunger and under-nutrition.'" (Falcao and others 2015). Through grassroots and civil society mobilization, the Right to Food Campaign advocated widening the understanding of food security to include "implementation of food-related schemes, urban destitution, the right to work, starvation deaths, maternity entitlements, and even broader issues of transparency and accountability" (RTFC Secretariat 2008).

Implementation of the provisions of the act was slow for the initial two years. In the first three years after its passage, only 28 of 36 states and union territories had implemented the TPDS in accordance with the NFSA. The perennial criticism of welfare programs in India is that they are well intentioned, but that the benefits are limited because of faulty implementation and corruption. The TPDS has a complex organizational structure, which is discussed in the following section.

Beyond the role of rights and the judiciary, several state governments have engaged village-level institutions and community-based organizations in monitoring and direct service delivery. For example, an important reform to make the TPDS more effective involved improving the management of fair price shops. Two important steps in this regard have been (a) shifting ownership of FPSs from private dealers to community-based organizations, such as self-help groups and cooperatives, and to local government bodies, such as panchayatis and municipal bodies, and (b) increasing the commissions paid to FPS managers. Reform of the TPDS has been linked to measures that improved the viability of fair price shops. Further, state governments have also engaged voice organizations and self-help networks in monitoring the TPDS to reduce discretion and diversion in the delivery of benefits.

The central government encouraged such partnerships (DFPD 2016), taking a cue from reformer states such as Andhra Pradesh, Chhattisgarh, and Tamil Nadu. Those states engaged village-level leadership, local health workers (*mitanins* in Chhattisgarh), and self-help groups in monitoring the functioning of the PDS (Misra 2011).

Finally, by relaxing eligibility criteria, state governments have expanded the program's client base and increased the potential of citizen pressure to influence program administration. The politics of program expansion have helped to reduce leakage and increase coverage for the poor, with the TPDS revival being seen as strongly linked with having more citizens become clients (Drèze 2003). As figure 2.9 illustrates, states have been able to cover a larger share of their poor population by covering a larger share of the total population. Activists and academics argue that guaranteeing benefits to a larger segment of the polity activates "pressure from below" (Khera 2011a), whereby a political coalition of the poor and well-off can

FIGURE 2.9

Change in Coverage for All Income Groups versus Bottom 40 Percent in Low- and High-Income States in India, 2004–12

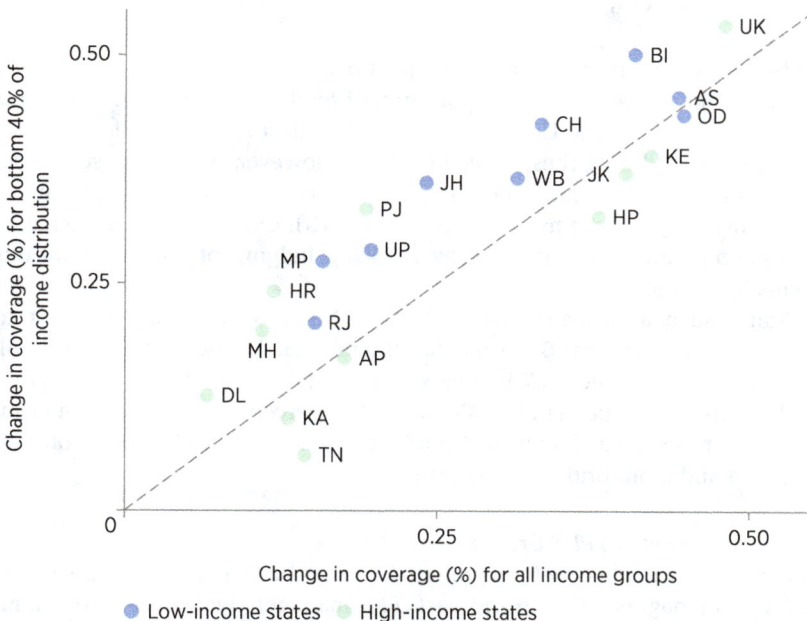

Source: National Sample Survey Organization data.
Note: BI = Bihar; CH = Chhattisgarh; DL = Delhi; JH = Jharkhand; OD = Odisha.

pressure program administrators to ensure that entitlements are delivered (Drèze 2003).

INNOVATIONS IN TPDS DELIVERY: THE ROLE OF STATE GOVERNMENTS, TECHNOLOGY, AND NUTRITION

This section outlines the major nutrition-sensitive reforms undertaken by state governments, particularly in the past decade, that have yielded improvements in program delivery outcomes. The review explores the broad tenets of the overall TPDS experience, drawing on the experience of reformer states such as Bihar, Chhattisgarh, and Odisha to highlight the four ingredients for successful TPDS reforms. As shown in figure 2.9, those states have reported drops in leakage and increases in coverage of the bottom 40 percent of income distribution, providing a useful window into the TPDS reform process.

Information and Communication Technology

Government reforms have deployed ICT tools to make the distribution of food grain transparent through modernization of the TPDS delivery chain. Such ICT-based reforms are aimed at improving implementation in many low-income states, such as Bihar, Chhattisgarh, and Odisha, and are seen to be major contributors to reducing the leakage of PDS food grain (Chatterjee 2014; Khera 2011a; Puri 2012).

End-to-End Computerization of the Supply Chain

Procurement, storage, and transportation of food grain are important points of leakage in the TPDS. Until a few years ago, most states recorded transactions manually during these three processes. However, over the past decade, eight states have computerized all or some of the processes with the aim of improving supply chain management (PIB 2015). Computerization increases transparency and accountability by reducing fudging of entries at various points in the supply chain.

States such as Chhattisgarh and Tamil Nadu were among the first to embrace TPDS reforms; Bihar adopted them later. According to World Bank estimates (annex table 2A.7 in annex 2A), in Bihar the leakage of food grain declined from 92.9 percent in 2004–05 to 29.1 percent in 2011–12. Himanshu (2015) attributes that decline to "simple technological fixes," such as computerization and monitoring of food grain movement.

Online Allocation of TPDS Grain to FPSs

The use of ICT to allocate food grain to FPSs has been a boon for bureaucrats and FPS managers alike. In the past, FPS managers would have to submit detailed accounts of all stock and sales in the previous month to get the next month's allocation of food grain. That process was not only cumbersome, because of the hand-written accounts, but also unreliable, because documents often went missing. Many states have addressed the issue by moving to the online allocation of food grain to FPSs, requiring FPS managers and district food officers to enter stock and sales figures online to get future allocations. According to official records, 16 states and union territories have implemented online allocation of food grain (PIB 2015).

In Bihar, for example, FPS managers are issued an online *challan* (document) that can be printed from the State Food Corporation's website, which they use to pay for their allotment of food grain for the upcoming month. Once this payment is made, the FPS manager can download the store issue order from the same website and use it to get food grain from the warehouse. These documents include all of the details of the allocation to avoid any confusion during the process of payment for and transportation of food grain from the warehouse to the FPS. States like Chhattisgarh have gone one step further, as described in box 2.1.

Doorstep Delivery of Food Grain to the FPS: Use of GPS Monitoring to Reduce Leakage
Diversion of food grain to the open market during its transportation from the warehouse to the FPS has been a major concern in TPDS implementation. In some parts of the country, FPS managers divert TPDS grain by informing beneficiaries that it never arrived. Chhattisgarh addressed this problem by replacing private delivery trucks with yellow-painted government trucks (Puri 2012). By taking responsibility for delivering the food grain, government officials made it their task to ensure that it reached the FPS.

More recently, many states have started using global positioning system (GPS) technology to track the movement of grain from warehouses to FPSs. In Bihar, for example, a Bangalore-based ICT company has designed software

---

BOX 2.1 **Chhattisgarh and CORE PDS**

Chhattisgarh became a front-runner in end-to-end TPDS supply chain modernization when the state government launched the centralized online real-time electronic PDS (CORE PDS) in 2012. The CORE PDS uses smartcards and point-of-sale devices to track transactions between FPSs and beneficiaries in real time. This system allows the state food department to allocate food grain on the basis of the actual distribution of food grain by each FPS. In the previous system, the food department had to rely on information provided by the FPS dealers. Not only does the CORE PDS improve the monitoring of food grain distribution to beneficiaries, but it also allows beneficiaries to choose the FPS from which to buy their food grain—an innovation in benefit portability that encourages competition among FPSs and helps beneficiaries who are migrants. Indeed, FPS dealers can no longer rely on guaranteed purchases from ration card holders who are "attached" to their FPS. Fair price shops must attract ration card holders by providing efficient services and good-quality food grain.

that allows district and state officials not only to track the movement of trucks but also to collect detailed information from each truck, including the weight of grain it is carrying.

Digitization of the Ration Card Database
Most states have made considerable progress in the digitization of their ration card database. Digitization has been helpful in two respects. First, it increases transparency by making available an easily accessible database, and second, it allows the government to apply other technologies, such as bar codes and biometric smartcards, to remove bogus or "ghost" beneficiaries. According to PIB (2015), digitization of ration cards has been completed in 29 states and union territories, with the digitization of more than 320 million ration cards, of which more than 25 percent have been seeded with Aadhaar (connected with the unique database).

Grievance Redress: The Advent of Toll-Free Numbers
and Grievance Redress Software
Although most TPDS beneficiaries still rely on local politicians, bureaucrats, and intermediaries to address their TPDS-related grievances, various state governments have sought to provide grievance redress mechanisms that are easier to access. The most common method has been to introduce toll-free numbers that beneficiaries can call to lodge and follow up on complaints. According to official records, by December 2015 more than 26 states and union territories had implemented online grievance redress systems (PIB 2015).

In Chhattisgarh, for instance, all complaints are directed to a call center where they are recorded on a web portal. The web portal redirects complaints to the respective district food offices, which send them to the associated food inspectors. Food inspectors are expected to investigate and respond within 15 days (Bhattacharya and others 2016).

State Government–Driven Program Innovation with Support from the Central Government
The experience of the past decade shows that innovations and interventions by state governments, with the central government acting as a facilitator, can solve seemingly intractable problems such as TPDS leakage of grain through the use of ICT and enhanced citizen engagement (World Bank 2011). The turnaround of an ailing TPDS has been attributed to the various state-level TPDS reforms that were initially implemented in Himachal Pradesh, Kerala, and Tamil Nadu and eventually taken up by states such as Andhra Pradesh, Bihar, Chhattisgarh, and Odisha. Such initiatives aimed to expand coverage, lower issue prices, and reduce leakage. Although the central government has made modernization of TPDS supply chains a prerequisite for receiving funds to implement the NFSA of 2013, many state governments had initiated TPDS reforms long before the NFSA came into effect.

Beyond the use of ICT, state governments have tailored solutions to their own contexts. For example, the state government of Bihar distributed coupons to all TPDS beneficiaries with the aim of reducing leakages. With coupons in circulation, FPS dealers were paid for the total number of coupons collected; under the old system, dealers could divert food grain by making false entries for households that did not collect their share of TPDS grain (WFP 2014). In Odisha, the state government launched a Zero Hunger Program through the TPDS. The state also piloted biometrically authenticated physical uptake of food grain in Rayagada District, long before the advent of Aadhaar (WFP 2014).

The central government can play an important role in incentivizing and enabling state innovation and initiatives. TPDS reforms provide a case study illustrating the role of central government and state partnerships in improving program implementation. Using results and lessons learned from state reform measures in Chhattisgarh, Kerala, Odisha, and Tamil Nadu, the government of India initiated two important measures to improve the functioning of the TPDS. The first one is the decentralized procurement program that the government introduced in 1997–98 to enhance the efficiency of procurement by reducing the total subsidy (Ministry of Consumer Affairs 2013). Under decentralized procurement, states are encouraged to take responsibility for procurement, storage, and distribution of food grain by building the necessary infrastructure. The FCI purchases any surplus food grain procured by these states. As of 2012, 10 states were implementing decentralized procurement.

The second measure, developed by the government in 2006–07, was a Nine-Point Action Plan aimed at reducing leakages in the PDS. Formulated after consultations with state food ministers, the plan was formalized in 2012 (Gulati and Saini 2015). Table 2.5 summarizes the nine points and their current status of implementation. To provide infrastructure and financial support to states and union territories for implementing the last point of the nine-point plan, the government launched a scheme for end-to-end computerization of the TPDS under the 12th Five-Year Plan (2012–17) (Ministry of Consumer Affairs 2014). The scheme had two components. Component 1 included digitization of beneficiary, FPS, and warehouse databases; computerization of the supply chain; and the setting up of a grievance redress system and online portal. Component 2 involved FPS automation. With Rs 8.8 billion allocated for this project, states such as Chhattisgarh, Kerala, Odisha, and Tamil Nadu benefited from central financial assistance in initiating and piloting ICT-based TPDS reform.

Before 2012, 13 state governments had broadened eligibility and expanded the amount of subsidy. Two states have achieved near-universal coverage of the PDS: Tamil Nadu since 1992 and Chhattisgarh since 2007. More recently, Himachal Pradesh (2007), Andhra Pradesh (2008), Kerala (2008), Rajasthan (2010), and Assam (2010), in addition to Chhattisgarh (2007), have expanded their TPDS coverage by providing "state BPL" ration cards using state finances. Those states have relaxed the eligibility criteria for obtaining a BPL ration card by moving away from income-based criteria that are difficult to

TABLE 2.5 **Nine-Point Action Plan to Reduce Leakage from the Public Delivery System in India, 2006–07**

ELEMENT OF THE PLAN	NUMBER OF STATES AND UNION TERRITORIES THAT HAD STARTED IMPLEMENTATION AS OF JUNE 2014
1. State campaign to review BPL and AAY lists to eliminate ghost ration cards	33
2. Strict action taken against the guilty to ensure leakage-free distribution of food grain	33
3. For the sake of transparency, involvement of elected panchayati raj institution members in the distribution of food grain; fair price shop licenses given to self-help groups, gram panchayats, cooperatives, and so forth	29
4. Display of names of beneficiaries (BPL and AAY lists) by FPSs	32
5. Display of FPS and district allocations of TPDS commodities on websites for public scrutiny	22
6. Doorstep delivery of PDS commodities to FPS	20
7. Timely availability of food grain at FPSs and distribution of food grain by FPSs through vigilance measures	32
8. Training of vigilance committee members	27
9. Computerization of TPDS operations, use of ICT	35

Source: Ministry of Consumer Affairs, Department of Food and Public Distribution (http://dfpd.nic.in/statement-reg-implementation-tpds.htm).
Note: Total number of states and union territories = 35. AAY = Antyodaya Anna Yojana (poorest of the poor); BPL = below the poverty line; FPS = fair price shop; ICT = information and communication technology; TPDS = targeted public distribution system.

enforce on the ground. For example, in Chhattisgarh, the state government excludes all households that pay income taxes or government employees and households with more than 10 acres of irrigated land in rural areas and 1,000 square feet of land in urban areas (DFPD 2016). In Bihar, the state government did not use the central government figure of 6.5 million eligible BPL households and conducted its own BPL survey, which placed the number of households eligible for TPDS food grain at 14 million (Wadhwa 2012).

Balancing of Demand- and Supply-Side Measures
State-level experimentation and innovation in delivery systems remain isolated, with limited scale-up in low-income states. A few leading examples of such reforms have been the states of Bihar, Chhattisgarh, and Odisha, some of the poorest states in the country. In these states, reforms have centered on expanding eligibility criteria to obtain TPDS grain and on using ICT-enabled developments to improve accountability and transparency in the delivery

chain. Low-income states struggle to scale up and use an array of reform instruments in concert. For example, nearly all low-income states have used ICT in modernizing their TPDS supply chain. However, reforms related to simplifying eligibility criteria and FPS management and monitoring have not been stressed equally in all states. Several states have reported limited gains in TPDS delivery because they implemented only a subset of a larger reform package.

The case of Chhattisgarh highlights the need to take a systemic view of TPDS reform. Rather than view the procurement and distribution aspects of program administration in self-contained units, the state government learned from the experiences of advanced states and employed a host of demand- and supply-side reforms, which interacted with each other, yielded gains in coverage, and reduced leakage. Four reform tools were viewed as part of a larger effort to create an integrated food distribution system.

First, by making the TPDS nearly universal, the government of Chhattisgarh simplified eligibility criteria and benefit levels. The state relied on village-level institutions, elected representatives, and local health workers to raise awareness of the changes. Those initiatives expanded the TPDS client base and activated demand-side pressures on program administrators.

Second, the state implemented reforms—using incentive schemes, ICT, and accountability tools—to ensure that the supply chain of grain was efficient and responsive to client demand. Chhattisgarh transferred ownership of FPSs from private dealers to community-based organizations and increased the commissions given to FPS managers. The state invested in computerization of the TPDS supply chain, online allocation of food grain, doorstep delivery of food grain from warehouses to FPSs, GPS monitoring of transportation of food grain, digitization of the ration card database, and grievance redress mechanisms such as toll-free helpline numbers.

Third, the state leveraged a package of reforms (doorstep delivery of food grain and GPS tracking of TPDS trucks) to improve delivery and was very successful in its attempt. Fourth, Chhattisgarh made entitlements portable by combining the use of smart ration cards with real-time monitoring. The reform program CORE PDS was piloted initially in Chhattisgarh's capital city, Raipur, and later extended to four districts. The key element of the reform was to capture in real time the transactions between beneficiaries and FPS operators selling subsidized grain. By August 2014, CORE PDS was extended to 151 shops covering 150,000 ration card holders in Raipur. Some estimates based on field surveys suggest that leakages decreased from 51.8 to 1.5 percent (Joshi, Sinha, and Biraj Patnaik 2015).

In other words, Chhattisgarh policy makers revolutionized the way food was distributed by fostering competition among food distribution points, digitizing assistance though mobile technology, and implementing a series of reforms meant to track food movements along the supply chain.

Making citizen engagement with programs a credible tool for reform requires complementary investments in the capacity of states to respond and deal with larger numbers of clients and their grievances. TPDS reforms that sought to strengthen the supply side have improved program outcomes through simpler program rules, staff training, cross-state learning, ICT-enabled transparency measures, business process reengineering, expanded authority of community groups in FPS management and monitoring, increased numbers of TPDS clients, and involvement of community groups.

Nutrition-Sensitive Interventions

Caloric and income transfers from the TPDS distribution of grain have historically been inframarginal, with small impacts on nutrition (Kaushal and Muchomba 2013; Khera 2011a; Kochar 2005; Tarozzi 2005). Following a period of improvement and reform in TPDS functioning, Himanshu and Sen (2013) and Kaul (2014) revisited the nutritional implications of the food subsidy and found positive impacts during price shocks. Kaul's estimates show that an increase in the monthly rice subsidy by Rs 10 increases the consumption of calories by 126 kilocalories per day. Although the elasticity of cereal consumption with respect to the subsidy value is small, the finding remains positive and significant, stressing that the subsidy has an impact on nutrition. In addition, Kaul's work finds that the subsidy augments the purchase of other nutrients and foods, diversifying the caloric intake of households and that its impacts are much stronger in states where diversion is lower. A study using a border-discontinuity design to investigate the impact of rice subsidies on household nutrition in Chhattisgarh (Krishnamurthy, Pathania, and Tandon 2014) in the period 2004–05 finds significant impacts as well: enhanced availability of subsidized rice in Chhattisgarh resulted in "households increasing their consumption of pulses, animal-based protein, and produce relative to households in districts bordering the state." Further, households eligible for the rice subsidy experienced increases in consumption.

The state governments of Gujarat, Rajasthan, and West Bengal have piloted the distribution of fortified wheat through the TPDS, using the TPDS as an arm of nutrition policy. The pilot project in Bengal, which was conducted through the State Micronutrient Initiative Project, implemented the pilot project in the Sadar subdivision of Darjeeling District to test the effectiveness of fortified wheat flour in improving the iron and vitamin A status of the population. The pilot demonstrated that fortification of high-extraction wheat flour (*atta*) with iron, folic acid, and vitamin A is an effective strategy to address iron deficiency in the population.

Fortification policy was first introduced in Rajasthan in addition to a series of reforms in TPDS policy (Fiedler and Lividini 2015), in particular, to reduce leakages in the APL and urban quota of grains. The first phase, in 2009, aimed at substituting wheat flour for wheat grain among only the APL group of beneficiaries in seven cities of Rajasthan, without any fortification.

Furthermore, to reduce diversion of grains, the government moved the sale of APL grain to privately owned dairy retail outlets, which are common in urban areas of Rajasthan. During this phase, the government invited tenders from the wheat flour millers. Those who were selected were given six-month contracts and allowed to purchase wheat grain from the FCI at Rs 6.1 per kilogram. The contracted millers were required to grind the wheat grain into flour, fortify it with a premix provided by the government, package it in 10-kilogram bags, and supply it to identified outlets in the seven cities at a price of Rs 8.7 per kilogram.

As (Fiedler and Lividini 2015, 99) finds, "In essence, the roller flour mills were fulfilling a job order and taking advantage of their unused capacity. The Rs 3.6 per kilogram differential was intended to cover the millers' cost of the handling, transportation, milling, fortification, packaging, and delivery. The dairy outlets then were to sell one 10-kilogram package per month to APL families for Rs 9.6 per kilogram, giving outlets a margin of Rs 0.4 per kilogram. The price of wheat grain to APL families at the time was Rs 6.8 per kilogram. The level of milling required during this phase was relatively limited and undertaken by a small number of roller mills and *chakki* (wheat processing) plants. The state mandated that the mills could conduct the milling for TPDS only during certain days of the week, so that state officials could monitor it more closely. The participating millers regarded that as an onerous requirement because it disrupted their usual production schedules."

In 2011, the state government of Rajasthan embarked on a second phase of TPDS reform activities in Rajasthan to test the feasibility of scaling-up fortification of wheat flour. The state government introduced the sale of wheat flour fortified with iron, folic acid, and vitamin B-12 in 11 urban areas of the state, with such reforms being restricted to APL beneficiaries of the TPDS. The sale of fortified flour was accompanied by an increase in the price at which millers were allowed to sell the flour to retailers, from Rs 8.7 per kilogram to Rs 9.7 per kilogram. The price at which wheat grain was sold to APL beneficiaries in other urban areas and in rural areas of the state continued to be Rs 6.8 per kilogram.

In August 2010, the Global Alliance for Improved Nutrition (GAIN) signed a grant agreement with the national Roller Flour Millers Federation of India. The partnership aimed to provide technical and financial support to augment state capacity (a) to implement large-scale food fortification activities; (b) to conduct internal and external quality assurance and quality control activities; and (c) to conduct social marketing, communication, and policy advocacy activities using a variety of complementary approaches (Fiedler and Lividini 2015). The agreement also worked through commercial channels and through social safety network programs such as the TPDS, Integrated Child Development Services, and the Mid-Day Meal programs. Shortly after, GAIN started working with the Rajasthan Roller Flour Millers Association.

From late 2011 to mid-2013, approximately 840,000 metric tons of wheat flour was produced annually and sold to APL beneficiaries in the 11 urban centers of Rajasthan (Bhagwat and others 2014). The fortified wheat flour was packaged and sold under the brand name Raj Atta. Over that same period, open-market sales of fortified atta began and grew slowly but steadily, reaching about 84,000 metric tons per year. Total annual sales of fortified atta surpassed 920,000 metric tons in 2013, roughly 20 percent of the atta market.

LOOKING FORWARD: CHALLENGES AND GAPS

A spatially diverse and mixed record on program delivery has stimulated debates among various constituencies, academics, activists, and policy makers on the value of the TPDS within the overall mix of social protection programs (Himanshu and Sen 2013; Kapur 2011; Kapur, Mukhopadhyay, and Subramanian 2008; Kotwal, Murugkar, and Ramaswami 2013; Shah 2008; Svedberg 2012). There are two strands of thought on the future of the program in India. One strand welcomes the move to justiciable rights and the expansion of entitlements. That strand is concerned with issues related to program implementation, urging a focus on administrative constraints that hurt program impacts, particularly in the poorest states. Addressing those constraints entails systematically building awareness, employing tools of e-governance, establishing community-based monitoring, and strengthening local administrative capacity (Khera 2011a; Puri 2012).

The second strand of thought argues for changing the current program mix predicated on replacing the in-kind delivery of grain with the direct delivery of cash benefits to eligible individuals. Advocates of that stream of thinking suggest that cash distribution is simpler and cheaper to implement. They say that cash transfers are less distortionary and achieve poverty reduction objectives for the same budget (Jha and Ramaswami 2010; Kapur, Mukhopadhyay, and Subramanian 2008; Kotwal, Murugkar, and Ramaswami 2011). Recent policy directives and an emphasis on campaigns to open bank accounts—most recently in August 2014, with *Pradhan Mantri Jan Dhan Yojana* (PMJDY, the National Mission for Financial Inclusion)—and to issue national identity cards (Aadhaar), combined with mobile technology, have become known as the JAM trinity (Jan Dhan, Aadhaar, and mobile) and are seen as the backbone of such a social protection system (box 2.2). Supporters of rights-based entitlements worry that the ecosystem for delivering cash effectively to poor households is missing and warn against the adverse intrahousehold and nutritional impacts of replacing food transfers with cash (Ghosh 2011; Sinha 2015; Swaminathan and others 2013) (box 2.3).

TPDS coverage in urban areas lags coverage in rural areas. For example, half of India's rural households use the TPDS compared with only

BOX 2.2 Jan Dhan Yojana and the Direct Benefit Transfer Initiative

In August 2014, Prime Minister Narendra Modi launched PMJDY with the ambitious objective of ensuring that all households in the country have access to banking services through a bank account and affiliated financial services. The government is also pursuing the direct benefit transfer (DBT) initiative, which was started in 2013. The DBT vision focuses exclusively on making fund flows more efficient and timely by using Aadhaar-enabled payments to remove duplicate beneficiaries and unclog the pipeline connecting central financial assistance to citizens. The model is predicated on using online portals to credit electronic payments directly from central coffers to Aadhaar-enabled bank accounts. By doing so, payments bypass intermediaries and minimize leakage. Automation of welfare delivery is thought to reduce expected inefficiencies in the current payment flows and to save the Indian government about Rs 100,000 crore (about Rs 900 per capita) in total annual payments. This savings is almost one-third of the government's spending of Rs 2.9 million on welfare schemes for the poor (Ehrbeck and others 2010, 10). The government considers PMJDY and DBT as integral to creating an environment that supports automated, speedier, and transparent delivery of social protection measures.

Initial results have been mixed. By January 31, 2015, more than 125 million accounts had been opened under PMJDY. A recent assessment found that 86 percent of beneficiaries reported the new bank account as their first (Microsave 2014). However, 64 percent of those new bank accounts were dormant as of December 2014. The DBT phase 1 rollout currently covers 1,665,771 beneficiaries, with a bank coverage rate of 77.5 percent.

The success of the DBT initiative and the PMJDY depends to a large extent on the network of financial intermediaries and banking agents, called bank *mitrs*, who are meant to serve as transaction points for individuals to access basic banking services. However, setting adequate compensation for bank agents is challenging because experts believe that the current structure of commissions is not economically viable. Ensuring a successful rollout of PMJDY requires a reasonable cost of service delivery.

30 percent of urban households. Despite being the dominant urban safety net in terms of spending, the TPDS has a smaller share of urban clients. According to NSSO estimates, only 9 percent of all TPDS users lived in urban areas in 2004–05. This share had increased to 11 percent by 2011–12. Food markets and prices function differently in urban areas than in rural areas. Leakage is highest in urbanized states and cities, possibly because of the lack of demand for subsidized grain in urban areas. Thus, urban areas and mobile populations could be better served by redesigning the use of cash transfers. Current pilots in the states of Chandigarh, Delhi, and Puducherry, all states or union territories with more than 90 percent urban populations, can pave the way for adapting the TPDS to urban environments.

A one-size-fits-all policy and program designed by the central government can no longer overlook the different spatial and growth trajectories of

BOX 2.3 **Considerations for Cash Delivery of Food Subsidies in India**

International experience from 10 low- and middle-income countries and the United States highlights that the type of social assistance needed—food or cash—depends on which instrument is more effective in local contexts. Although cash transfers are more cost-effective and less distortionary, outcomes depend on the following considerations:

- *Financial access and literacy.* The near-term feasibility of cash transfers depends on the depth of financial access. Less than a third of India's population has a bank account (World Bank 2011). Experiments with implementing direct cash transfers in rural areas continue to highlight the constraints faced by citizens in opening and using bank accounts. The ongoing campaign to issue national identity cards and open bank accounts (most recently, under the PMJDY) has significant potential to change the status quo. Several low-income states have reported weak Aadhaar penetration and continue to struggle to assign the poor a financial address.

- *Attitudes toward cash versus food transfers.* Although evidence on the following claims is scarce because of the limited experiments with the delivery of cash subsidies in India, researchers raise concerns about the potential harm to women (Swaminathan and others 2013). A recent study in the slums of Delhi found that 99 percent of women surveyed said that they prefer food transfers to cash because they fear that male family members will misuse the funds (Ghosh 2011). Empirical studies in Bangladesh and the United States show that moving from food stamps or ration cards to cash transfers reduces food consumption in poor households (Ahmed 2005; Breunig and others 2001; Del Ninno and Dorosh 2003), as households use cash to purchase other goods.

- *Integrated and competitive food markets.* A basic level of market functioning is a prerequisite for the effective provision of cash transfers. In some cases, prices may be particularly volatile, with a certain degree of unpredictability in future trajectories. Price volatility could turn a cash transfer program that was efficient in the design stage into a cost-inefficient one during implementation because of the difficulties in indexing transfers to inflation rates. Keeping purchasing power constant in the wake of sharp and protracted price increases may escalate costs as a result of the extensive use of contingency funds, as in Zambia (Harvey and Savage 2006). In India, despite the availability of grain, many poor states contain food-insecure regions and are unable to ensure price protection for consumers in the open market (WFP 2014).

- *Political economy.* Historically, international political economy arguments favor food transfers rather than cash (World Bank 2011). In addition, a majority of states are in the middle of a TPDS revival (Drèze and Khera 2011). Improvements in TPDS coverage and grain delivery weaken the political argument in favor of cash transfers at the all-India level. Surveys highlight citizen preferences for food transfers vis-à-vis cash. In a survey of rural areas across 18 states in India, 80 percent of respondents said that they prefer food transfers (Drèze and Khera 2011). A study conducted by the World Bank in 2014 in urban Chhattisgarh found similar results, with 94 percent of respondents saying they prefer food transfers (Bhattacharya and others 2016).

box continues next page

BOX 2.3 **Considerations for Cash Delivery of Food Subsidies in India**
(continued)

A recent study assessing the impact of a basic income transfer in Madhya Pradesh high-lights the significant investments needed in financial literacy and intermediation for survey respondents to be able to access banks (SEWA 2014). Interacting with financial institutions continues to be a cumbersome process for the poor, who are often discrim-inated against within bank branches and provided limited information and support to access formal financial networks (Mowl and Boudot 2014). Low levels of financial inclu-sion have been reported in nationally representative household-level surveys for decades, most prominently by the National Sample Survey Organization's decennial All India Debt and Investment Survey (AIDIS). Data from the 2002 AIDIS revealed that, despite India's vast network of bank branches and credit cooperatives, less than 27 percent of farm households used formal credit (Rangarajan Committee on Financial Inclusion 2009). More recent nationally representative data from the 2012 Global Finan-cial Inclusion (Global Findex) database reveals that only 35 percent of all adults in India have an account at a formal financial institution (Demirgüç-Kunt and Klapper 2012).

Source: Adapted from Gentilini 2014.

Indian states. This chapter's review shows an increasing divergence between well-performing states and low-income states in terms of program coverage and targeting of entitlements. Distinctions are seen among advanced states as well. Northern regions such as Delhi, Haryana, and Punjab report very high rates of leakage and poor coverage, and southern states report good perfor-mance. Location is integral to the identification of optimal risk insurance instruments. Dealing with such diversity requires an enabling policy and a finance regime whereby state governments are given greater authority and flexibility in shaping their social protection systems.

Given the major improvements in TPDS reported in rural areas and several low-income states in India, the experiences in other countries, and difficulties that rural households have in accessing financial institutions, a phased and spatially sensitive approach to subsidy reform would best suit current condi-tions. The NFSA of 2013 allows state governments to meet nutrition entitle-ments through delivery of cash using the JAM trinity or direct benefit transfer platforms instead of through the direct provision of food. In urban areas, where banking networks are stronger, food market programs can be used to experiment with cash delivery. Officials of each state government could use the results of pilot programs to make more informed decisions on how best to deliver food subsidies in their own jurisdictions. Several urbanized union territories are piloting cash delivery of food subsidies. Results from these experiments can guide future state-level differentiation in the design and delivery of the TPDS.

LESSONS LEARNED

India offers some cautionary tales for the global community, in regard to both the costs of food-based social assistance as well as the loss of flexibility that in-kind systems incur when situated between agricultural and consumer objectives. India also illustrates how civil society and an independent judiciary can strengthen the voice of food security advocates and the potential for decentralization within an entitlement program.

What was once an emergency wartime measure has become a legal entitlement. Many factors influenced this evolution of the PDS—in concept as well as in organization and implementation. Initially, the PDS was limited to urban areas and focused on meeting the needs of the armed forces fighting in World War II. At that point, the colonial administration did not view the food rationing program as a viable option to address the severe shortages facing the rural population.

The politics of food distribution are strongly linked to the politics of sovereignty in India. After its independence, India struggled to provide for its people's food needs, and food shortages were addressed entirely through food aid, especially from the United States under P.L. 480. The dependency on food aid resulted in a trade-off between ensuring the welfare of its people and taking a stand on global events that was independent of the position of India's main donor country, the United States. Despite some years of excess food grain production in the early 1950s, India's food shortages did not cease until the 1970s. That situation was a result of India's faulty policy, its experimentation with reduced control of markets, and what some scholars believe was a deliberate choice to encourage industrialization at the cost of agriculture.

The design and delivery of the PDS have evolved, with state governments and civil society playing a key role in the reform process. Throughout the past two decades, the central government and some states, such as Himachal Pradesh, Kerala, and Tamil Nadu, have been adopting measures to make procurement, transportation, storage, and distribution of food grain entitlements efficient, free of corruption, and transparent. More recently, Andhra Pradesh, Bihar, Chhattisgarh, and Odisha have taken similar initiatives. These measures include decentralizing the procurement and storage process, using ICT tools to modernize the TPDS delivery chain, and engaging citizens and civil society through self-help instruction. They aim to bring about accountability at the village level, relaxing eligibility criteria to encourage citizens to demand program implementation. These measures have been largely successful; however, some challenges continue to plague implementation of the TPDS. Efforts to include the poorest and most vulnerable individuals, expand the coverage of the TPDS in urban areas, and reduce corruption are still needed to enable the smooth implementation of the TPDS.

ANNEX 2A. STATISTICAL INFORMATION

TABLE 2A.1 **Possession of Ration Cards in India, by Type and State, 2004–05 and 2011–12**

% of households

STATE	BPL 2004-05	BPL 2011-12	APL 2004-05	APL 2011-12	AAY 2004-05	AAY 2011-12	NO CARD 2004-05	NO CARD 2011-12
Jammu and Kashmir	18.6	20.5	76.8	70.4	0.5	2.1	4.1	7.0
Himachal Pradesh	10.6	18.1	76.2	64.9	6.1	10.9	7.0	6.0
Punjab	9.3	22.6	78.6	60.5	0.1	1.0	12.0	15.9
Chandigarh	1.3	10.8	61.0	36.9	0	5.1	37.7	47.2
Uttaranchal	19.6	26.4	71.0	63.8	1.7	2.1	7.8	7.6
Haryana	15.1	17.0	72.7	68.4	2.5	2.4	9.8	12.2
Delhi	4.5	3.3	65.0	50.4	0	3.3	30.5	43.0
Rajasthan	12.7	18.8	81.5	73.1	1.8	2.3	3.9	5.7
Uttar Pradesh	12.2	15.3	67.8	58.1	2.4	9.3	17.6	17.2
Bihar	14.1	43.1	60.9	36.0	2.1	4.7	22.9	16.2
Sikkim	38.7	50.1	35.4	34.4	0.9	1.2	25.0	14.3
Arunachal Pradesh	14.0	26.6	62.4	50.9	0.7	4.4	22.9	18.2
Nagaland	5.0	23.5	5.7	18.7	0.2	0.0	89.0	57.8
Manipur	19.5	26.7	14.7	22.8	0.1	4.1	65.7	46.4
Mizoram	24.9	29.5	71.7	60.0	1.0	8.8	2.4	1.7
Tripura	35.7	29.2	60.7	60.9	1.3	6.7	2.4	3.1
Meghalaya	20.7	45.4	48.3	26.1	2.5	2.8	28.5	25.6
Assam	10.2	39.2	64.2	36.3	0.6	5.1	25.0	19.4

table continues next page

TABLE 2A.1 **Possession of Ration Cards in India, by Type and State, 2004–05 and 2011–12** (continued)

% of households

STATE	BPL		APL		AAY		NO CARD	
	2004–05	2011–12	2004–05	2011–12	2004–05	2011–12	2004–05	2011–12
West Bengal	23.1	29.3	65.6	62.4	2.4	2.8	8.9	5.4
Jharkhand	20.9	25.3	50.8	24.5	2.3	5.8	26.0	44.4
Odisha	39.5	44.4	26.0	21.0	1.8	5.3	32.7	29.3
Chhattisgarh	32.7	49.9	35.7	23.1	4.3	5.0	27.3	21.9
Madhya Pradesh	26.8	31.4	42.0	44.4	2.9	5.7	28.3	18.5
Gujarat	27.6	22.5	60.4	60.8	0.7	1.8	11.3	14.9
Daman and Diu	11.0	5.4	80.1	66.0	0.0	0.2	8.9	28.4
Dadra and Nagar Haveli	30.1	29.3	40.1	35.9	9.4	6.4	20.4	28.4
Maharashtra	22.4	18.4	58.6	58.8	2.6	4.8	16.5	18.1
Andhra Pradesh	50.3	75.8	17.7	8.1	2.5	3.0	29.6	13.1
Karnataka	35.3	52.0	30.5	21.4	6.8	5.2	27.4	21.4
Goa	15.4	7.2	67.3	85.2	6.9	2.3	10.4	5.4
Lakshadweep	6.3	11.0	85.7	80.9	1.1	6.3	6.8	1.8
Kerala	26.8	28.0	60.6	63.2	1.6	1.2	11.0	7.5
Tamil Nadu	17.2	30.7	70.5	57.9	1.2	3.7	11.1	7.7
Pondicherry	36.7	29.6	51.1	57.3	0.3	0.4	11.8	12.7
Andaman and Nicobar Islands	8.3	7.6	79.8	83.6	0.7	0.1	11.2	8.7
All-India	22.4	31.1	56.8	48.3	2.3	4.7	18.5	15.9

Source: National Sample Survey Organization, rounds 61 and 68.
Note: BPL = below the poverty line; APL = above the poverty line; AAY = Antyodaya Anna Yojana (poorest of the poor).

TABLE 2A.2 **Possession of Ration Cards in India, by Socioeconomic Status of Households, 2011–12**

% of households

INDICATOR	RURAL				URBAN			
	AAY	BPL	APL	NO CARD	AAY	BPL	APL	NO CARD
Consumption quintile								
Poorest	11.9	48.5	26.2	13.4	5.4	34.9	39.7	20.0
Q2	6.5	40.1	40.7	12.8	2.4	25.2	51.0	21.3
Q3	3.9	36.6	48.7	10.8	2.1	23.2	53.8	20.8
Q4	2.8	29.1	56.8	11.3	1.4	15.1	61.3	22.2
Richest	2.1	21.0	63.6	13.3	0.5	7.2	61.0	31.3
Social group								
Scheduled tribe	8.1	51.1	27.1	13.7	4.8	22.0	44.0	29.2
Scheduled caste	9.7	44.9	33.7	11.7	2.9	22.9	48.5	25.7
Other backward caste	5.0	35.0	47.2	12.7	1.9	22.1	53.8	22.2
Other	3.2	25.5	60.1	11.2	1.1	9.5	62.1	27.4
All India	5.9	36.7	45.2	12.3	1.8	17.1	56.0	25.1

Source: National Sample Survey Organization, rounds 61 and 68.
Note: BPL = below the poverty line; APL = above the poverty line; AAY = Antyodaya Anna Yojana (poorest of the poor).

88 THE 1.5 BILLION PEOPLE QUESTION

TABLE 2A.3 **Household-Level Offtake of TPDS Grain in India, by Quintile and State, 2004–05 and 2011–12**

% of households

STATE	2004–05						2011–12					
	Q1	Q2	Q3	Q4	Q5	POOR/RICH RATIO	Q1	Q2	Q3	Q4	Q5	POOR/RICH RATIO
Andaman and Nicobar	68.2	73.6	76.9	74.1	50.8	1.1	84.8	91.6	88.0	86.8	60.3	1.2
Andhra Pradesh	76.5	74.1	64.8	53.1	23.9	2.0	94.5	89.6	86.4	71.7	38.1	1.7
Arunachal Pradesh	37.6	41.4	47.8	34.1	40.3	1.1	54.6	50.7	52.9	52.4	53.6	1.0
Assam	19.8	11.4	5.9	2.7	2.2	6.3	65.8	56.7	54.8	51.6	34.4	1.4
Bihar	3.4	2.4	1.4	1.0	1.1	2.8	59.8	54.8	41.5	37.3	20.1	2.0
Chandigarh	3.9	0.6	0.0	1.9	0.0	2.3	35.2	32.6	28.9	5.0	11.8	4.1
Chhattisgarh	45.7	22.4	22.8	19.6	10.5	2.3	79.9	73.3	63.0	49.2	21.9	2.2
Dadra and Nagar Haveli	54.7	62.5	43.2	37.5	25.7	1.9	86.4	54.8	78.2	45.9	12.2	2.5
Daman and Diu	31.8	19.6	0.0	3.4	0.0	15.2	21.9	17.4	5.6	4.3	3.5	5.0
Delhi	14.8	4.4	3.0	4.2	1.8	3.2	23.2	21.2	8.3	7.7	1.2	5.0
Goa	33.0	21.5	4.2	0.4	3.4	14.7	90.2	71.7	69.9	55.4	49.7	1.5
Gujarat	46.2	37.2	27.4	13.8	2.7	5.1	45.6	28.4	27.4	8.5	3.5	6.1
Haryana	8.3	7.8	3.2	1.5	0.7	7.2	42.5	21.9	9.9	4.7	1.7	10.0

table continues next page

TABLE 2A.3 **Household-Level Offtake of TPDS Grain in India, by Quintile and State, 2004–05 and 2011–12** (continued)

% of households

STATE	2004-05						2011-12					
	Q1	Q2	Q3	Q4	Q5	POOR/RICH RATIO	Q1	Q2	Q3	Q4	Q5	POOR/RICH RATIO
Himachal Pradesh	69.0	59.9	51.0	48.1	29.9	1.7	98.3	95.5	94.4	88.9	70.4	1.2
Jammu and Kashmir	57.2	46.7	39.8	32.9	21.0	1.9	86.9	91.3	85.8	80.1	53.7	1.3
Jharkhand	11.4	5.8	5.3	2.2	2.5	3.7	53.5	35.8	28.3	21.8	8.3	3.0
Karnataka	74.7	60.9	54.9	44.0	15.6	2.3	83.3	72.9	73.5	58.9	26.8	1.8
Kerala	66.0	44.4	42.1	26.5	19.3	2.4	96.1	92.5	83.7	75.4	61.4	1.4
Lakshadweep	98.1	100.0	99.1	97.6	88.1	1.1	100.0	100.0	100.0	92.5	71.8	1.2
Madhya Pradesh	35.4	28.7	22.1	12.8	4.8	3.6	63.8	42.1	37.0	28.1	11.8	2.7
Maharashtra	40.5	31.1	21.3	13.2	4.5	4.0	65.6	45.3	29.5	18.4	6.4	4.5
Manipur	0.7	0.0	0.4	0.0	0.4	1.8	2.8	5.3	9.1	8.7	3.1	0.7
Meghalaya	33.3	31.5	19.0	13.5	4.9	3.5	82.7	79.2	71.6	47.9	31.5	2.0
Mizoram	75.6	75.5	74.0	64.2	42.8	1.4	98.8	99.5	98.0	91.8	79.2	1.2
Nagaland	0.2	0.0	0.0	0.7	0.0	0.4	20.3	24.9	18.6	14.5	5.3	2.3
Odisha	41.4	25.7	15.2	7.6	3.2	6.2	82.3	72.1	67.6	58.4	36.1	1.6
Pondicherry	73.7	49.9	41.9	24.2	21.0	2.7	98.1	82.5	94.6	78.1	74.2	1.2
Punjab	0.3	0.9	0.8	0.2	0.2	3.3	41.2	26.4	18.8	9.5	3.3	5.3

table continues next page

TABLE 2A.3 **Household-Level Offtake of TPDS Grain in India, by Quintile and State, 2004–05 and 2011–12** (continued)

% of households

STATE	2004–05						2011–12					
	Q1	Q2	Q3	Q4	Q5	POOR/RICH RATIO	Q1	Q2	Q3	Q4	Q5	POOR/RICH RATIO
Rajasthan	20.8	11.1	10.4	5.2	3.5	3.7	47.0	26.2	24.4	22.5	7.0	2.5
Sikkim	82.1	56.8	42.1	27.3	9.1	3.8	90.1	83.5	55.5	33.1	7.0	4.3
Tamil Nadu	91.3	88.9	82.8	65.6	34.7	1.8	97.9	94.4	92.4	86.9	63.7	1.3
Tripura	74.1	50.2	22.8	17.9	8.9	4.6	96.9	87.9	87.8	84.7	66.5	1.2
Uttar Pradesh	11.7	7.2	3.9	3.8	1.7	3.5	45.0	28.8	24.2	18.7	10.4	2.5
Uttaranchal	34.0	23.8	23.6	18.8	4.9	2.4	83.2	81.4	82.9	60.4	36.9	1.7
West Bengal	23.0	16.0	13.3	9.3	4.6	2.8	60.6	51.6	48.0	39.3	23.3	1.8
All India	31.6	27.0	23.2	19.5	10.8	2.5	60.0	49.7	46.4	39.9	26.6	2.0

Source: National Sample Survey Organization, rounds 61 and 68.
Note: TPDS = targeted public distribution system.

TABLE 2A.4 **Household-Level Offtake of TPDS Grain in India, by Rural–Urban Location, 2004–05, 2009–10, and 2011–12**

% of households

STATE	ALL HOUSEHOLDS			RURAL HOUSEHOLDS			URBAN HOUSEHOLDS		
	2004-05	2009-10	2011-12	2004-05	2009-10	2011-12	2004-05	2009-10	2011-12
Andaman and Nicobar	68.9	82.2	82.3	67.6	87.3	86.9	71.5	73.6	74.6
Andhra Pradesh	58.5	76.8	76.1	66.4	87.3	89.3	35.5	50.2	49.0
Arunachal Pradesh	40.2	48.8	52.8	39.6	46.7	52.2	45.3	57.2	55.6
Assam	8.4	30.3	52.7	8.9	31.9	55.2	3.4	16.5	31.4
Bihar	1.9	14.1	42.7	1.8	14.7	44.9	2.3	9.3	22.5
Chandigarh	1.3	11.7	22.7	6.8	0.0	9.4	0.7	13.8	23.7
Chhattisgarh	24.2	61.4	57.5	25.7	66.2	61.9	15.6	39.2	41.6
Dadra and Nagar Haveli	44.8	35.6	55.7	45.7	45.8	72.7	37.8	4.9	32.0
Daman and Diu	11.3	28.5	10.6	14.7	42.0	2.0	4.9	11.8	24.2
Delhi	5.7	10.2	12.3	5.9	40.0	19.5	5.6	8.6	11.7
Goa	12.6	54.8	67.4	14.0	59.6	74.1	10.2	42.6	61.1
Gujarat	25.5	27.9	22.7	34.1	38.2	32.5	8.9	11.1	8.4
Haryana	4.3	16.8	16.2	3.5	19.8	18.4	6.6	9.9	11.0
Himachal Pradesh	51.6	85.5	89.5	54.9	88.4	93.9	20.2	55.4	53.2
Jammu and Kashmir	39.5	68.3	79.6	35.7	68.5	80.8	51.0	67.7	75.4
Jharkhand	5.5	23.1	29.6	5.8	26.4	34.9	3.4	9.9	9.4
Karnataka	50.0	60.6	63.1	60.3	76.2	76.1	26.8	31.3	40.4
Kerala	39.7	61.7	81.8	41.6	64.2	85.0	33.6	54.4	72.9

table continues next page

TABLE 2A.4 **Household-Level Offtake of TPDS Grain in India, by Rural-Urban Location, 2004–05, 2009–10, and 2011–12** *(continued)*

% of households

STATE	ALL HOUSEHOLDS			RURAL HOUSEHOLDS			URBAN HOUSEHOLDS		
	2004-05	2009-10	2011-12	2004-05	2009-10	2011-12	2004-05	2009-10	2011-12
Lakshadweep	96.7	93.0	93.0	98.5	97.4	93.9	94.8	88.7	92.2
Madhya Pradesh	20.8	42.1	36.6	23.5	47.3	40.0	11.8	26.2	26.5
Maharashtra	22.1	34.6	33.1	30.8	49.4	48.1	9.2	13.8	15.2
Manipur	0.3	8.9	5.8	0.4	8.2	6.5	0.2	10.7	3.9
Meghalaya	20.5	60.6	62.6	23.0	66.6	69.6	3.8	31.5	36.5
Mizoram	66.4	93.6	93.5	71.7	95.6	97.7	58.4	91.2	88.6
Nagaland	0.2	0.0	16.7	0.2	0.0	20.7	0.2	0.0	9.2
Odisha	18.6	55.0	63.3	20.6	59.1	68.2	6.5	30.1	35.8
Pondicherry	42.4	59.3	85.5	71.3	81.1	83.1	26.5	47.7	86.8
Punjab	0.5	18.9	19.8	0.3	22.3	25.2	0.8	12.6	10.4
Rajasthan	10.2	17.7	25.4	12.5	18.1	27.7	2.1	16.3	18.1
Sikkim	43.5	46.2	53.9	48.1	53.4	63.4	7.2	1.0	8.8
Tamil Nadu	72.7	87.4	87.1	83.7	95.1	94.7	55.1	77.8	77.6
Tripura	34.8	75.3	84.8	38.3	77.5	88.1	13.5	63.7	66.8
Uttar Pradesh	5.7	23.2	25.4	6.3	23.7	27.0	3.1	21.2	19.7
Uttaranchal	21.0	35.0	69.0	26.6	40.4	73.7	2.9	19.0	55.0
West Bengal	13.2	33.7	44.6	15.0	38.8	51.2	7.6	18.0	26.5
All India	22.4	39.3	44.5	24.8	43.3	50	15.4	28.2	30.7

Source: National Sample Survey Organization, rounds 61, 66, and 68.
Note: TPDS = targeted public distribution system.

TABLE 2A.5 **Share of TPDS Grain Captured in India, by Consumption Quintile, Group, and Rural-Urban Location, 2004–05, 2009–10, and 2010–11**

GROUP	2004–05				2009–10			2010–11		
	AVERAGE 30-DAY OFFTAKE BY HOUSEHOLDS ACCESSING TPDS (KILOGRAMS)	AVERAGE ANNUAL OFFTAKE BY HOUSEHOLDS ACCESSING TPDS (KILOGRAMS)	SHARE OF TOTAL BENEFICIARIES (%)	SHARE OF TOTAL OFFTAKE CAPTURED (%)	AVERAGE OFFTAKE BY PERSONS ACCESSING TPDS (KILOGRAMS)	SHARE OF TOTAL BENEFICIARIES (%)	SHARE OF TOTAL OFFTAKE CAPTURED (%)	AVERAGE OFFTAKE BY PERSONS ACCESSING TPDS (KILOGRAMS)	SHARE OF TOTAL BENEFICIARIES (%)	SHARE OF TOTAL OFFTAKE CAPTURED (%)
Consumption quintile										
Poorest	24.8	301.5	28.2	30.7	25.7	27.4	31.5	27.7	26.9	32.7
Q2	23.1	281.3	24.1	24.5	23.7	22.6	23.9	23.9	22.3	23.3
Q3	22.3	271.7	20.7	20.3	21.3	20.4	19.5	21.7	20.9	19.8
Q4	21.1	256.2	17.4	16.1	20.2	18.3	16.5	19.6	17.9	15.4
Richest	19.9	242.1	9.6	8.4	17.0	11.3	8.6	16.7	11.9	8.8
Group										
Other backward caste	21.7	263.8	44.3	42.2	21.5	44.5	42.8	22.2	45.2	43.8
Scheduled caste	23.3	283.8	24.8	25.4	23.3	24.4	25.5	24.5	23.6	25.3
Scheduled tribe	24.1	293.0	12.7	13.5	24.7	12.0	13.2	25.8	12.0	13.6
Other	23.7	287.9	18.2	18.9	21.7	19.1	18.6	20.6	19.2	17.3

table continues next page

TABLE 2A.5 Share of TPDS Grain Captured in India, by Consumption Quintile, Group, and Rural-Urban Location, 2004–05, 2009–10, 2010–11 (*continued*)

GROUP	2004–05			2009–10			2010–11		
	AVERAGE 30-DAY OFFTAKE BY HOUSEHOLDS ACCESSING TPDS (KILOGRAMS)	AVERAGE ANNUAL OFFTAKE BY HOUSEHOLDS ACCESSING TPDS (KILOGRAMS)	SHARE OF TOTAL BENEFICIARIES (%)	SHARE OF TOTAL OFFTAKE CAPTURED (%)	AVERAGE OFFTAKE BY PERSONS ACCESSING TPDS (KILOGRAMS)	SHARE OF TOTAL BENEFICIARIES (%)	SHARE OF TOTAL OFFTAKE CAPTURED (%)	AVERAGE OFFTAKE BY PERSONS ACCESSING TPDS (KILOGRAMS)	SHARE OF TOTAL BENEFICIARIES (%)	SHARE OF TOTAL OFFTAKE CAPTURED (%)
Location									
Rural	22.8	277.5	82.7	82.9	22.8	80.6	82.2	23.5	80.3	82.5
Urban	22.5	273.7	17.3	17.1	20.4	19.4	17.8	20.3	19.7	17.5
Total	22.8	276.9	100.0	100.0	22.4	100.0	100.0	22.9	100.0	100.0

Source: National Sample Survey Organization, rounds 61, 66, and 68.
Note: TPDS= targeted public distribution system.

TABLE 2A.6 Planning Commission Estimates of Leakage of BPL Grain in the TPDS in India, 2005

STATE	DIVERSION (% BPL GRAIN)	APL SHARE OF BPL GRAIN (%)	TOTAL LEAKAGE OF BPL GRAIN (%)
Andhra Pradesh	20.6	37.0	57.6
Assam	41.7	12.0	53.7
Bihar	81.5	9.6	91.1
Gujarat	42.1	5.0	47.1
Haryana	55.7	11.0	66.7
Himachal Pradesh	31.4	14.5	45.9
Karnataka	43.4	27.5	70.9
Kerala	21.7	17.3	39.0
Madhya Pradesh	62.4	3.6	66.0
Maharashtra	26.5	8.0	34.5
Odisha	23.4	13.0	36.4
Punjab	76.5	13.0	89.5
Rajasthan	32.0	3.0	35.0
Tamil Nadu	15.7	49.9	65.6
Uttar Pradesh	61.3	6.2	67.5
West Bengal	19.2	7.8	27.0
All India	36.4	21.5	57.9

Source: Planning Commission 2005.
Note: TPDS = targeted public distribution system; BPL = below poverty line; APL = above poverty line.

TABLE 2A.7 **Estimated Leakage from Household TPDS Offtake as a Percentage of Official Offtake in India, by State, 2004–05 and 2011–12**

STATE	WORLD BANK		GULATI AND SAINI		HIMANSHU AND SEN		DRÈZE AND KHERA	
	2004-05	2011-12A	2004-05	2011-12	2004-05	2011-12	2004-05	2011-12
Andhra Pradesh	31.1	16.6	23.2	11.1	25.4	7.8	23.2	22.0
Arunachal Pradesh	61.0	46.3	–	17.6	46.5	25.2	0.0	0.0
Assam	89.4	51.8	88.7	60.9	88.1	45.2	88.7	50.7
Bihar	92.9	29.1	91.0	68.7	91.2	12.2	91.0	24.4
Chandigarh	–129.5	68.7	–	75.7	–	–	–	–
Chhattisgarh	51.8	16.9	51.8		49.5	0.3	51.7	9.3
Dadra and Nagar Haveli	–	42.4	–	53.7	–	–	–	–
Daman and Diu	–	91.2	–	95.8	–	–	–	–
Delhi	91.2	85.6	–	82.6	89.5	80.6	–	–
Goa	–62.5	43.5	–	48.7	–	–	–	–
Gujarat	56.7	72.9	51.7	72.2	50.4	69.0	51.7	67.6
Haryana	84.2	52.9	82.7	70.3	83.5	51.1	82.7	49.0
Himachal Pradesh	27.3	26.2	27.0	22.5	24.7	20.6	27.0	27.1
Jammu and Kashmir	48.9	15.3	23.0	2.3	17.4	–12.0	23.0	–3.7
Jharkhand	86.8	51.5	85.2	74.9	84.2	34.5	85.2	44.4
Karnataka	36.1	34.7	28.7	46.4	27.7	27.4	28.7	34.7
Kerala	29.4	29.5	25.6	43.2	27.4	23.6	25.6	37.1
Lakshadweep	–	–5.9	–	–	–	–	–	–

table continues next page

TABLE 2A.7 **Estimated Leakage from Household TPDS Offtake as a Percentage of Official Offtake in India, by State, 2004–05 and 2011–12** (continued)

STATE	WORLD BANK			GULATI AND SAINI		HIMANSHU AND SEN		DRÈZE AND KHERA	
	2004–05	2011–12A		2004–05	2011–12	2004–05	2011–12	2004–05	2011–12
Madhya Pradesh	50.3	50.6		50.1	49.3	46.4	42.1	50.1	51.5
Maharashtra	52.8	47.0		49.3	54.9	47.7	41.3	49.3	48.2
Manipur	98.4	96.2		–	97.8	97.9	95.4	–	–
Meghalaya	71.0	56.4		–	67.0	64.7	49.5	–	–
Mizoram	59.4	8.0		–	15.2	44.7	–5.3	–	–
Nagaland	100.0	93.4		–	94.7	–	–	–	–
Odisha	75.8	30.7		76.3	36.8	74.8	15.5	76.3	25.0
Pondicherry	–438.2	14.2		–	23.1	–	–	–	–
Punjab	94.8	60.3		93.2	60.7	94.2	56.5	93.2	58.8
Rajasthan	59.3	62.2		93.9	66.3	55.3	55.6	93.9	60.9
Sikkim	48.9	55.1		–	–	43.5	44.0	–	–
Tamil Nadu	12.6	14.8		7.3	12.2	–2.4	6.7	7.3	11.9
Tripura	47.8	24.8		–	19.2	45.4	19.3	–	–
Uttar Pradesh	84.9	60.4		58.0	47.9	83.7	54.3	58.0	57.6
Uttaranchal	38.1	24.8		59.4	30.0	32.5	18.6	59.4	34.9
West Bengal	85.9	61.7		80.6	69.4	85.0	56.8	80.6	65.3
All India	58.6	43.1		54.0	46.7	54.0	34.6	54.0	41.7

Source: National Sample Survey Organization, rounds 61 and 68; Gulati and Saini 2015; Himanshu and Sen 2013; Drèze and Khera 2015.
Note: TPDS = targeted public distribution system; – = not available.
a. Calculated using the official Food Corporation of India data for central allocations plus additional allocations made during the year. Using only central allocations gives results similar to Himanshu and Sen's estimates for 2011–12.

TABLE 2A.8 **Estimated Leakage of Rice and Wheat in India, 2004–05 and 2011–12**

% leaked

| STATE | WORLD BANK ESTIMATES | | | | | | ECONOMIC SURVEY ESTIMATES | | |
| | 2004–05 | | 2011–12A | | | | 2011–12 | |
	RICE	WHEAT	RICE	WHEAT			RICE	WHEAT
Andhra Pradesh	30.3	88.2	16.7	6.6			2.0	–21.0
Arunachal Pradesh	56.6	94.2	41.8	89.9			33.0	91.0
Assam	84.6	99.9	40.9	96.8			27.0	96.0
Bihar	87.8	94.3	32.0	24.7			16.0	10.0
Chandigarh	8.5	–	72.9	68.0			73.0	71.0
Chhattisgarh	45.9	82.2	12.2	43.3			–26.0	40.0
Dadra and Nagar Haveli	–	–	39.2	71.2			42.0	83.0
Daman and Diu	–	–	88.6	96.1			96.0	98.0
Delhi	91.5	91.1	90.1	84.2			86.0	82.0
Goa	–43.0	–	43.0	46.5			45.0	55.0
Gujarat	55.9	57.0	66.5	75.2			49.0	67.0
Haryana	–	84.3	–	54.1			–	47.0
Himachal Pradesh	10.0	44.8	23.1	28.2			21.0	27.0
Jammu and Kashmir	27.0	86.7	10.9	25.9			3.0	15.0
Jharkhand	83.9	89.3	51.9	18.1			43.0	53.0
Karnataka	34.3	44.8	35.3	31.5			26.0	21.0
Kerala	5.6	79.2	24.5	50.6			20.0	45.0
Lakshadweep	–	–	–5.1	–			–7.0	–

table continues next page

TABLE 2A.8 **Estimated Leakage of Rice and Wheat in India, 2004–05 and 2011–12** (*continued*)

% leaked

STATE	WORLD BANK ESTIMATES 2004–05		WORLD BANK ESTIMATES 2011–12A		ECONOMIC SURVEY ESTIMATES 2011–12	
	RICE	WHEAT	RICE	WHEAT	RICE	WHEAT
Madhya Pradesh	17.3	56.6	35.3	53.6	22.0	51.0
Maharashtra	48.0	55.6	41.6	50.8	38.0	48.0
Manipur	97.7	100.0	95.7	99.5	96.0	100.0
Meghalaya	68.4	99.7	49.8	98.9	42.0	99.0
Mizoram	54.0	99.1	-1.6	90.0	167.0	90.0
Nagaland	100.0	100.0	91.3	99.6	91.0	100.0
Odisha	73.2	98.7	22.5	74.5	9.0	76.0
Punjab	61.5	95.0	–	60.5	–	62.0
Rajasthan	48.2	59.3	–	62.6	–	58.0
Sikkim	41.3	99.4	51.3	99.4	47.0	97.0
Tamil Nadu	13.0	-3.2	19.8	-104.2	11.0	–
Tripura	41.5	96.8	21.1	82.3	12.0	77.0
Uttar Pradesh	85.5	84.6	52.8	66.6	42.0	69.0
Uttaranchal	46.8	22.0	9.4	36.3	11.0	37.0
West Bengal	70.1	92.8	41.8	74.2	35.0	73.0
All India	45.6	75.2	32.4	57.7	15.0	54.0

Source: National Sample Survey Organization, rounds 61 and 68.
Note: — = not available.
a. Calculated using the official data for central allocations plus additional allocations made during the year. Using only central allocations gives results similar to the estimates of Himanshu and Sen (2013).

FIGURE 2A.1

Monthly Subsidy Transfer (Wheat and Rice) in Select States of India, 2004–05 and 2011–12

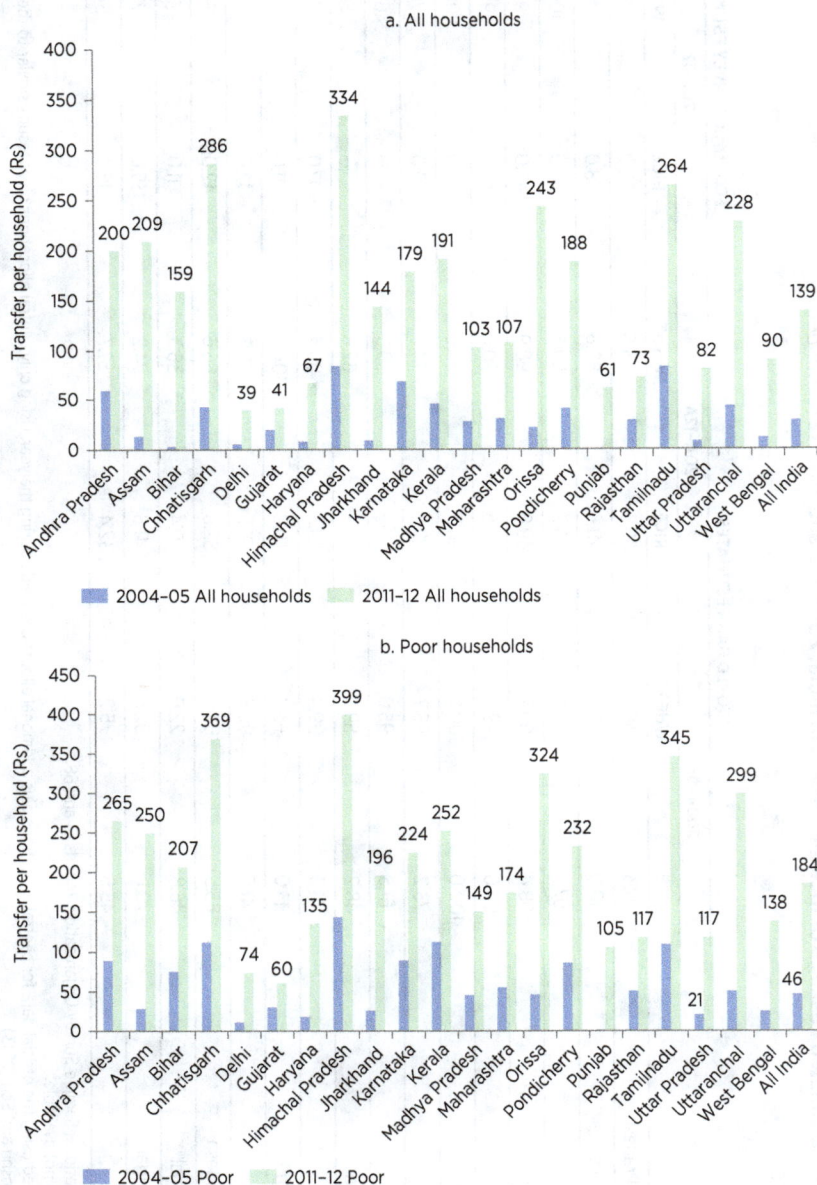

a. All households

b. Poor households

Source: National Sample Survey Organization data, rounds 61 and 68.

NOTES

1. The food grain rationing system in India has been redesigned several times. Before 1997 and the introduction of targeting, it was simply called the public distribution system. This chapter refers to the program as TPDS, except when speaking specifically of the pre-1997 program.
2. The food subsidy is the sum of the consumer subsidy and the cost of maintaining the buffer stock. For further details, see Sharma (2012).
3. Districts are administrative subunits at the state level and are similar to counties in the United Kingdom and the United States.
4. See http://eands.dacnet.nic.in/PDF/MSP17.06.2015.pdf.
5. The CIP is the price at which TPDS food grain is issued or "sold" to state governments.
6. Calculated from administrative data provided by India's Department of Food and Distribution on the intended number of individuals to be covered by the NFSA, divided by state average household size. See http://dfpd.nic.in/writereaddata/images/EstdStatewiseNFSA.pdf.
7. Official offtake data for TPDS (BPL, APL, AAY) are from the Department of Food and Public Distribution (http://dfpd.nic.in/?q=node/829). TPDS offtake is calculated from NSSO rounds.
8. For more on the relationship between the agricultural elites and the colonial administration, see Talbot (1984, 1988); Yong (2005, 284–300).
9. Dr. Saxena is a retired bureaucrat who was the secretary of the Planning Commission in 1999–2000 and secretary of the Ministry of Rural Development in 1997–99. The Right to Food case was *People's Union for Civil Liberties* v. *Union of India and others,* Supreme Court of India, Civil Original Jurisdiction, Writ Petition [Civil] No. 196 of 2001. His opinions, reproduced here, were stated in an interview conducted by the authors on December 14, 2015.
10. US$1 = Rs 67.5.
11. The order was passed in 2001 and enacted and implemented in 2006. See http://www .prsindia.org/uploads/media/Food%20Security/Justice%20Wadhwa%20 Committee%20Report%20on%20PDS.pdf.
12. Other entitlements defined by the NFSA include a conditional cash transfer and supplementary feeding for pregnant and lactating women and a school feeding program. For further information on the Right to Food Campaign and the NFSA, see http://www .righttofoodcampaign.in/food-act.

REFERENCES

Acharya, S. S. 2004. "State of the Indian Farmer: A Millennium Study." In *Agricultural Marketing.* Vol. 17. New Delhi: Academic Foundation for the Department of Agriculture and Cooperation.

Ahmed, Shaikh S. 2005. "Delivery Mechanisms of Cash Transfer Programs to the Poor in Bangladesh." Social Protection Discussion Paper 0520, World Bank, Washington, DC.

Bhagwat, Sadhana, Gulati Deepti, Sachdeva Ruchika, and Sankar Rajan. 2014. "Food Fortification as a Complementary Strategy for the Elimination of Micronutrient Deficiencies: Case Studies of Large-Scale Food Fortification in Two Indian States." *Asia Pacific Journal of Clinical Nutrition* 23 (Suppl 1): S4–S11.

Bhatia, B. M. 1991. *Famines in India 1860–1990.* Delhi: Konark Publishers.

Bhattacharya, Shrayana, Anastasiya Denisova, Raghav Puri, and Changquin Sun. 2016. "Assessment of Centralized Online Real Time Public Distribution System in Chhattisgarh." Draft report, World Bank, Washington, DC.

Breunig, Robert, Indraneel Dasgupta, Craig Gundersen, and Prasanta Pattanaik. 2001. "Explaining the Food Stamp Cash-Out Puzzle." Food Assistance and Nutrition Research Report 12, U.S. Department of Agriculture, Washington, DC.

Chand, Ramesh. 2012. "Development Policies and Agricultural Markets." *Economic and Political Weekly* 47 (52): 53.

Chatterjee, Mihika. 2014. "An Improved PDS in a 'Reviving State.'" *Economic and Political Weekly* 49 (45): 49–59.

Chopra, R. N. 1988. *Food Policy in India. A Survey.* New Delhi: Intellectual Publishing House.

de Janvry, Alain, and Kalanidhi Subbarao. 1986. *Agricultural Price Policy and Income Distribution in India (No. 43).* New York: Oxford University Press.

Del Ninno, Carlo, and Paul A. Dorosh. 2003. "Impacts of In-Kind Transfers on Household Food Consumption: Evidence from Targeted Food Programmes in Bangladesh." *Journal of Development Studies* 40 (1): 48–78.

Demirgüç-Kunt, Aslı, and Leora F. Klapper. 2012. "Measuring Financial Inclusion: The Global Findex Database." Policy Research Working Paper 6025, World Bank, Washington, DC.

Desai, Sonalde. 2015. "Public Distribution System: More People Rely on the PDS Than Ever Before." Research Brief 1, India Human Development Survey, University of Maryland. http://ihds.umd.edu/IHDS_files/ResearchBrief01.pdf.

DFPD (Department of Food and Public Distribution, Government of India). 2016. *Food Grain Bulletin* (January). http://dfpd.nic.in/writereaddata/images/january_2016.pdf.

Drèze, Jean. 2003. "Food Security and the Right to Food." In *Towards a Food Secure India: Issues and Policies,* edited by S. M. Dev, K. P. Kannan, and Nira Ramachandran, 433–43. New Delhi: Institute for Human Development; Hyderabad: Centre for Economic and Social Studies.

Drèze, Jean, and Reetika Khera. 2011. "PDS Leakages: The Plot Thickens." *The Hindu,* 12 August.

———. 2015. "Understanding Leakages in the Public Distribution System." *Economic and Political Weekly* 50 (7): 39–42.

Ehrbeck, Tilman, Rajiv Lochan, Sinha Supriyo, Naveen Tahliyani, and Adil Zainulbhai. 2010. "Inclusive Growth and Financial Security: The Benefits of e-Payments to Indian Society." McKinsey and Company, New York.

Falcao, Vanita Leah, Jasmeet Khanuja, Sonal Matharu, Shikha Nehra, and Dipa Sinha. 2015. "Report on the Study of the Indira Gandhi Matritva Sahyog Yojana." Centre for Equity Studies, New Delhi.

FAO (Food and Agriculture Organization of the United Nations). 1994. *Indian Experience on Household Food and Nutrition Security.* Paris: FAO. http://www.fao.org/docrep/x0172e /x0172e06.htm#P1406_137724.

Fiedler, John, and Keith Lividini. 2015. "An Analysis of Rajasthan's Iron Program Portfolio Options, 2014-2043." HarvestPlus. Unpublished.

Gentilini, Ugo. 2014. "Is Cash King? The Revival of the Cash versus Food Transfers Debate." *Development Impact,* July 30. http://blogs.worldbank.org/impactevaluations/cash-king -revival-cash-versus-food-transfers-debate-guest-post-ugo-gentilini.

Ghosh, Jayati. 2011. "Cash Transfers as the Silver Bullet for Poverty Reduction: A Sceptical Note." *Economic and Political Weekly* 46 (21): 67–71.

Gulati, Ashok, and Shweta Saini. 2015. "Leakages from Public Distribution System (PDS) and the Way Forward." Working Paper 294, Indian Council for Research on International Economic Relations, New Delhi. http://icrier.org/pdf/Working_Paper_294.pdf.

Harvey, Paul, and Kevin Savage. 2006. "No Small Change: Oxfam GB Malawi and Zambia Emergency Cash Transfer Projects; A Synthesis of Key Learning." Overseas Development Institute, London.

Himanshu. 2015. "PDS: A Story of Changing States." *Live Mint,* August 7. http://www .livemint.com/Opinion/TTLqU0Cg2iF4hYtJSHtMRI/PDS-a-story-of-changing-states .html.

Himanshu and Abhijit Sen. 2013. "In-Kind Food Transfers—II: Impact on Nutrition and Implications for Food Security and Its Costs." *Economic and Political Weekly* 48 (47): 60–73.

Jalan, Jyotsna, and Rinku Murgai. 2009. "Intergenerational Mobility in Education in India." Working Paper, Indian Statistical Institute, Delhi.

Jha, Shikha, and Bharat Ramaswami. 2010. "How Can Food Subsidies Work Better? Answers from India and the Philippines." Economics Working Paper 221, Asian Development Bank, Manila.

Joshi, A., Dipa Sinha, and Biraj Patnaik. 2015. "PDS 'to Go'? 'Portability' of Rights through Real-Time Monitoring: The Centralised Online Real-Time Electronic PDS in Chhattisgarh, India." Evidence Report 133, Institute of Development Studies, Sussex.

Kapur, Devesh. 2011. "The Shift to Cash Transfers: Running Better but on the Wrong Road?" *Economic and Political Weekly* 46 (21): 80–85.

Kapur, Devesh, Partha Mukhopadhyay, and Arvind Subramanian. 2008. "The Case for Direct Cash Transfers to the Poor." *Economic and Political Weekly* 43 (15): 37–43.

Kaul, Tara. 2014. "Household Responses to Food Subsidies: Evidence from India." University of Maryland, College Park, MD.

Kaushal, Neeraj, and Felix Muchomba. 2013. "How Consumer Price Subsidies Affect Nutrition." NBER Working Paper 19404, National Bureau of Economic Research, Cambridge, MA.

Khera, Reetika. 2011a. "Revival of the Public Distribution System: Evidence and Explanations." *Economic and Political Weekly* 46 (44–45): 36–50.

———. 2011b. "Trends in Diversion of Grains from the Public Distribution System." *Economic and Political Weekly* 46 (21): 106–14.

Knight, Henry. 1954. *Food Administration in India, 1939–47.* Stanford, CA: Stanford University Press.

Kochar, Anjini. 2005. "Can Targeted Food Programs Improve Nutrition? An Empirical Analysis of India's Public Distribution System." *Economic Development and Cultural Change* 54 (1): 203–35.

Kothari, Rajni. 1964. "The Congress 'System' in India." *Asian Survey* 4 (12): 1161–73.

———. 1988. *State against Democracy: In Search of Humane Governance.* Delhi: Ajanta Publications.

Kotwal, Ashok, Milind Murugkar, and Bharat Ramaswami. 2011. "PDS Forever?" *Economic and Political Weekly* 46 (21): 72–76.

———. 2013. "Some Reflections on National Food Security Act." *Yojana* 57: 25–29.

Krishnamurthy, Prasad, Vikram Pathania, and Sharad Tandon. 2014. "Public Distribution System Reforms and Consumption in Chhattisgarh: A Comparative Empirical Analysis." *Economic and Political Weekly* 49 (8): 74–81. http://www.isid.ac.in/~epu/acegd2014/papers/VikramSinghPathania.pdf.

Kumar, Shanta. 2015. "Report of the High-Level Committee on Reorienting the Role and Restructuring of Food Corporation of India." Government of India, New Delhi.

Malhotra, Inder. 2010. "Swallowing the Humiliation." *Indian Express,* July 12. http://archive.indianexpress.com/news/swallowing-the-humiliation/645168/.

Majumder, Bhaskar. 2009. *Political Economy of Public Distribution System in India.* New Delhi: Concept Publishing.

Manor, James. 1988. "Parties and the Party System." In *India's Democracy. An Analysis of Changing State-Society Relations,* edited by Atul Kohli, 61–98. Princeton, NJ: Princeton University Press.

Microsave. 2014. "Assessment of Bank Mitras under Pradhan Mantri Jan Dhan Yojana." Report submitted to Department of Financial Services, Ministry of Finance, New Delhi. http://www.microsave.net/files/pdf/Assessment_of_Bank_Mitrs_under_PMJDY.pdf.

Ministry of Agriculture. 2015. *Agricultural Statistics at a Glance 2014.* New Delhi: Oxford University Press.

Ministry of Consumer Affairs. 2001. "PDS Control Order 2001." Department of Food and Public Distribution, New Delhi. http://dfpd.nic.in/pds-control-order-1.htm.

———. 2013. "Centre to Encourage Decentralised Procurement." Press release, Ministry of Consumer Affairs, New Delhi, March 5. http://pib.nic.in/newsite/PrintRelease.aspx ?relid=93033.

———. 2014. "Computerisation of TPDS Operations." Status paper, Department of Food and Public Distribution, New Delhi, January 30. http://www.pdsportal.nic.in/Files /Final-Status_Paper.pdf.

———. 2016. "Annual Report 2015–16." Department of Food and Public Distribution, New Delhi.

Ministry of Finance. 2015. "The Fourteenth Finance Commission (FFC)—Implications for Fiscal Federalism in India." In *Economic Survey 2014–15*, ch. 10. New Delhi: Ministry of Finance. http://indiabudget.nic.in/es2014-15/echapter-vol1.pdf.

———. Various years. *Union Budget of India*. New Delhi: Ministry of Finance. http:// indiabudget.nic.in/budg.et2014-2015/ebmain.asp.

Ministry of Rural Development. 2012. "Sameeksha: An Anthology of Research Studies on the Mahatma Gandhi National Rural Employment Guarantee Act, 2005 (2006–2012)." Ministry of Rural Development, New Delhi.

Mishra, Bhagabat. 1985. *Economics of Public Distribution System in Food-Grains*. New Delhi: Ashish Publishing House.

Misra, J. P. 2011. "Evaluation of the Community Health Volunteer (Mitanin) Programme." Draft report, European Union State Partnership Programme, Raipur. http://health.cg .gov.in/ehealth/MitaninFinalReport11thMarch2011.pdf.

Mitra, Ashok. 1977. *Terms of Trade and Class Relations*. London: Frank Cass.

Mooij, Jos. 1998. "Food Policy and Politics: The Political Economy of the Public Distribution System in India." *Journal of Peasant Studies* 25 (2): 77–101.

———. 1999. *Food Policy and the Indian State*. Vancouver: Oxford University Press.

Mowl, Amy, and Camille Boudot. 2014. "Barriers to Basic Banking: Results from an Audit Study in South India." NSE-IFMR Financial Inclusion Research Initiative, Chennai.

Nawani, N. P. 1994. "Public Distribution System in India: Evolution, Efficacy, and Need for Reforms." In *Indian Experience on Household Food and Nutrition Security*. Rome: Food and Agriculture Organization of the United Nations. http://www.fao.org/docrep/x0172e /x0172e06.htm#P1406_137724.

———. 1995. *Towards Food for All: Ideas for a New PDS*. New Delhi: Ministry of Information and Broadcasting.

NCAER (National Council of Applied Economic Research). 2015. "Evaluation Study of Targeted Public Distribution System in Selected States." NCAER, New Delhi, September. http://www.ncaer.org/free-download.php?pID=262.

PIB (Press Information Bureau). 2015. "Year End Review—2015." Ministry of Consumer Affairs, Food and Public Distribution, New Delhi. http://pib.nic.in/newsite/PrintRelease .aspx?relid=133703.

———. 2016. "UIDAI Generates a Billion Aadhaars: A Historic Moment for India." Ministry of Communication and Information Technology, New Delhi, April.

Planning Commission. 2005. "Performance Evaluation of Targeted Public Distribution System (TPDS)." Program Evaluation Organisation, New Delhi.

Puri, Raghav. 2012. "Reforming the Public Distribution System: Lessons from Chhattisgarh." *Economic and Political Weekly* 47 (5): 21–23.

Rahman, Andaleeb. 2014. "Revival of Rural Public Distribution System: Expansion and Outreach." *Economic and Political Weekly* 49 (20): 62–68.

Rangarajan Committee on Financial Inclusion. 2009. "Report of the Committee on Financial Inclusion." Government of India, New Delhi. https://www.sidbi.in/files/Rangarajan -Commitee-report-on-Financial-Inclusion.pdf.

RTFC (Right to Food Campaign) Secretariat. 2008. *Supreme Court Orders on the Right to Food: A Tool for Action—A Primer.* 2nd ed. New Delhi: Right to Food Campaign. http:// www.righttofoodindia.org/data/scordersprimeratoolforaction.pdf.

Saini, Shweta, and Ashok Gulati. 2015. "The National Food Security Act (NFSA) 2013—Challenges, Buffer Stocking, and the Way Forward." Working Paper 297, Indian Council for Research on International Economic Relations, New Delhi. http://icrier.org/pdf/Working_Paper_297.pdf.

Sen, Amartya. 1981. *Poverty and Famines: An Essay on Entitlement and Deprivation.* Oxford, U.K.: Clarendon Press.

SEWA (All India Association of Self-Employed Women's Association). 2014. "A Little More, How Much It Is: Piloting Basic Income Transfers in Madhya Pradesh, India." SEWA, New Delhi.

Shah, Mihir. 2008. "Direct Cash Transfers: No Magic Bullet." *Economic and Political Weekly* 43 (34): 77–79.

Sharma, Vijay Paul. 2012. "Food Subsidy in India: Trends, Causes, and Policy Reform Options." *Indian Journal of Agricultural Economics* 68 (2): 195–221.

Sinha, Dipa. 2015. "Cash for Food—A Misplaced Idea." *Economic and Political Weekly* 50 (16): 17–20.

Sohal, Sukhdev. 2013. "Food Crisis, Inflation, and Political Control in Punjab (1940–47)." *Journal of Punjab Studies* 20 (1–2): 243–72.

Sonna, Thangzason, Himanshu Joshi, Alice Sebastin, and Upasana Sharma. 2014. "Analytics of Food Inflation in India." Working Paper 6174, Reserve Bank of India, Delhi.

Svedberg, Peter. 2012. "Reforming or Replacing the Public Distribution System with Cash Transfers?" *Economic and Political Weekly* 47 (7): 53–62.

Swaminathan, Madhura. 2008. "Programmes to Protect the Hungry: Lessons from India." DESA Working Paper 70, United Nations Department of Economic and Social Analysis, New York.

Swaminathan, Madhura, Bezwada Wilson, Shantha Sinha, Veena Shatrugna, Aruna Roy, Gautam Mody, Jean Drèze, Bina Agarwal, Utsa Patnaik, and Amiya Kumar Bagchi. 2013. "Cash Transfers and UID (Letter)." *Economic and Political Weekly* 48(1).

Talbot, Ian A. 1984. "The Second World War and Local Indian Politics: 1939–1947." *International History Review* 6 (4): 592–610. http://www.jstor.org/stable/40105423.

———. 1988. *Punjab and the Raj, 1849–1947.* Riverdale, MD: Riverdale Company.

Tarozzi, Alessandro. 2005. "The Indian Public Distribution System as Provider of Food Security: Evidence from Child Nutrition in Andhra Pradesh." *European Economic Review* 49 (5): 1305–30.

Tripathi, A. K. 2014. *Agricultural Prices and Production in Post-Reform India.* New York: Routledge.

Umali-Deininger, Dina, Mona Sur, and Klaus W. Deininger. 2005. "Foodgrains Subsidies in India: Are They Reaching the Poor?" American Agricultural Economics Association Annual Meeting, Providence, RI, July 24–27.

Vanaik, Achin. 1990. *The Painful Transition: Bourgeois Democracy in India.* New York: Verso Books.

Varshney, Ashutosh. 1993. "Self-Limited Empowerment: Democracy, Economic Development, and Rural India." *Journal of Development Studies* 29 (4): 177–215.

Wadhwa, D. P. 2012. "Report of the Justice Wadhwa Committee on Public Distribution System." Central Vigilance Commission, New Delhi.

WFP (World Food Programme). 2014. *Targeted Public Distribution System: Best Practice Solutions.* Rome: WFP. http://documents.wfp.org/stellent/groups/public/documents/newsroom/wfp267097.pdf.

World Bank. 2011. "Social Protection for a Changing India: Executive Summary." World Bank, Washington, DC. https://openknowledge.worldbank.org/handle/10986/2746.

Yong, Tan Tai. 2005. *The Garrison State: Military, Government, and Society in Colonial Punjab, 1849–1947.* New Delhi: Sage.

CHAPTER 3

The Tamween Food Subsidy System in Egypt

EVOLUTION AND RECENT IMPLEMENTATION REFORMS

Moustafa Abdalla and Sherine Al-Shawarby

INTRODUCTION

Food subsidies in the Arab Republic of Egypt are as old as the nation's pyramids. Over the many upheavals and spells of stability, Egypt's policy makers have persistently prioritized food subsidies in an effort to achieve social equity and political stability. In the past century, Egypt's food subsidy system (FSS) has evolved from emergency food relief to a core social safety net program,[1] and its importance is reflected in the significant amount of public resources allocated to food subsidies.

The contemporary system (*tamween*) includes two components: *baladi* bread (BB) and ration cards (RCs). Spending on these two programs ranged from a peak of 13 percent of gross domestic product (GDP) in the mid-1960s to a low of 0.9 percent of GDP in the late 1990s, averaging 1.7 percent of GDP in the past five years. Subsidies have become embedded as a citizen's right, and legitimacy of the ruling regime has been conditioned on its commitment and ability to provide food and basic goods at affordable subsidized prices.

This chapter reviews the historical development of Egypt's FSS and high-lights major reforms and innovations that are being implemented today. The chapter builds on a large literature and offers additional information and data, mostly previously unpublished, from official sources—namely, the Ministry of Supply and Internal Trade (MOSIT)[2] and the General Authority for Supply Commodities (GASC). In addition, it uses media reports and a beneficiary survey to fill in some knowledge gaps on the perspectives of beneficiaries.[3]

A large literature on the traditional pitfalls of the FSS has pointed out the well-known challenges regarding leakages, the regressive nature of benefits, and various cost inefficiencies. Attempts to reform the system have always been politically sensitive in Egypt. Indeed, discussions on targeting, for example, contrast with the notion that Egypt's social contract is largely considered an entitlement for the majority of middle-class Egyptians, especially during crises and economic downturns.

However, food subsidies came under renewed scrutiny in the aftermath of the 2011 revolution, especially starting in mid-2014. A significant reform was rolled out, consolidating the two components of Egypt's FSS. The most important measures were replacing subsidized commodity quotas with a monthly cash allotment, allowing RC beneficiaries to choose among a larger number of items, shifting from input- to output-based subsidies, capping the number of loaves per person, and establishing a point-based incentive system that allows beneficiaries to use savings from BB consumption to buy commodities under the RC system.

This last step on a long path of reforms, including several failed attempts, fits into a broader global trajectory of food-based social assistance systems. As discussed in chapter 1 of this volume, Egypt's FSS evolved from the provision of specific goods in-kind (subsidized at different stages of their production and distribution) in dedicated shops to an open voucher-style subsidy. At the same time, modern technology changed the accountability and oversight of subsidy provision, realizing significant efficiency gains. The system has achieved much greater "personalization" and traceability of all subsidized food commodities, yet it remains essentially universal, refraining, at least for the moment, from using the technology for more decisive targeting.

The remainder of the chapter is organized as follows. After placing food subsidies within the context of Egypt's broader social safety net system, it documents the historical evolution of food subsidies, highlighting major reforms and modifications, discusses the innovations of the new system, and sets out the main challenges. A final section draws emerging lessons and conclusions. Annex 3A lays out core milestones of the individual components since their inception. Annex 3B presents the results of a beneficiary survey conducted in 2016.

TAMWEEN FOOD SUBSIDY SYSTEM AND EGYPT'S SOCIAL SAFETY NET

Overview

According to the 2014–15 Household Income, Expenditure, and Consumption Expenditure Survey (HIECS), at least one of every four Egyptians is poor, and one of every two is either poor or near poor (CAPMAS, various years). Furthermore, a large proportion of the middle class is trapped in lower-middle-class status, living very close to the poverty line. Almost 85 percent of Egyptians were living on less than US$5 a day during the first decade of the 21st century (World Bank PovcalNet data). There was also an increase in poverty and a decrease in income of the bottom 40 percent of the population, indicating that GDP growth did not translate into household income growth. The increase in poverty indicates that Egypt needs a more efficient and effective safety net system.

Public spending on subsidies, grants, and social benefits reached LE 200 billion in fiscal year 2015/16 (equivalent to US$27 billion), accounting for 9.7 percent of GDP and 30 percent of average annual public spending for fiscal years 2011/12 to 2015/16. This government spending includes four categories: (a) subsidies for commodities (which include food subsidies, among others), (b) subsidies and grants for social services, (c) subsidies and grants for development areas (or lagging regions), and (d) subsidies and grants for economic activities. Commodity subsidies make up the largest group, accounting for 75 percent of social spending and 7.4 percent of GDP, on average, during the same period (figure 3.1).

FIGURE 3.1

Structure of Subsidies, Grants, and Social Benefits as a Percentage of GDP in the Arab Republic of Egypt's Budget, Fiscal Years 2012/13 to 2016/17

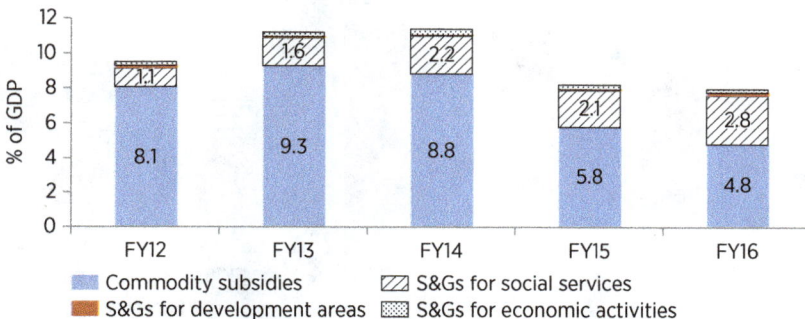

Source: Ministry of Finance financial statement of the fiscal year 2015/16 budget.
Note: S&G = subsidies and grants.

Commodity subsidies comprise six items: (a) subsidies for *tamween* com-modities (food); (b) farmers' subsidies; (c) fuel subsidies; (d) electricity subsidies; (e) subsidies for medicine and children's milk; and (f) transfers to public water companies. Food subsidies have been the cornerstone of Egypt's social safety net, especially when Egypt became significantly vulnerable to global food price shocks and currency exchange rate fluctuations. This vul-nerability was translated into the amounts allocated to food subsidies in the fiscal budget, with food subsidies averaging about 24 percent of total com-modity subsidies and 1.7 percent of GDP in the past five years. The FSS program is the second-largest program in Egypt's social safety net system in terms of public spending (figure 3.2). Fuel subsidies have remained the largest (2.2 percent of GDP), in spite of a significant drop (from 6.3 percent of GDP in fiscal year 2014/15) caused by the decline in fuel oil prices.

Egypt's social protection programs are not only highly fragmented, but also unbalanced. Social assistance cash transfers from the Ministry of Social Solidarity (MOSS), the only program that targets just the poor, were still small, accounting for less than 5 percent of the subsidies, grants, and social benefits segment of the budget and constituting only 0.26 percent of GDP, on average, during the past five years (table 3.1). The expenditure on MOSS was small, despite the considerable increase in the size of benefits and coverage of the program, especially after two new programs, *Takaful* (Solidarity) condi-tional cash transfers and *Karama* (Integrity) unconditional cash transfers were launched in January 2015.[4]

An estimated 9 percent of Egyptians would have fallen into poverty in the absence of food subsidies in fiscal year 2008/09 (Al-Shawarby and

FIGURE 3.2

Structure of Commodity Subsidies in the Arab Republic of Egypt, Fiscal Years 2012–16

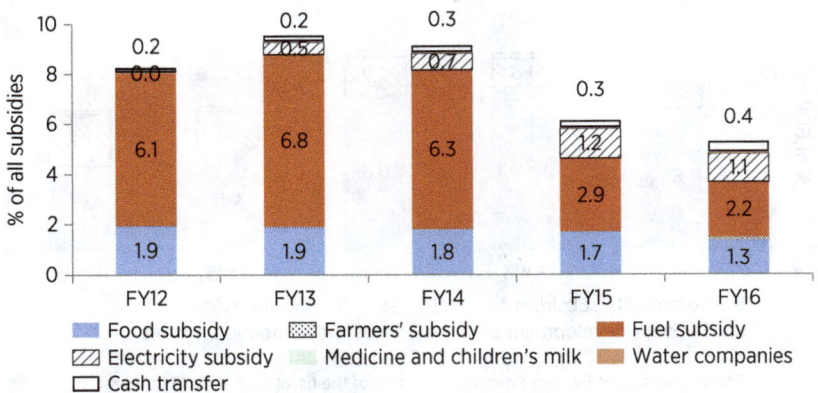

Source: Ministry of Finance financial statement for the 2015/16 budget.

TABLE 3.1 Budget and Number of Beneficiaries of Social Safety Net Programs in the Arab Republic of Egypt, Fiscal Year 2015/16

PROGRAM	BUDGET (LE, BILLIONS)	NUMBER OF BENEFICIARIES
Food subsidies	37.7	71 million (ration cards); 82.2 million (baladi bread)
Cash transfers	11.2	9 million individuals; 2 million families
Free health insurance for the poor	3.7	9 million individuals; 2 million families
Grants for the needy	6.7	0.5 million–1.0 million individuals
Support for wheat farmers	3.7	3.1 million individuals

Sources: Budget data are based on Ministry of Finance financial statements of the fiscal year 2015/16 budget; unpublished data on beneficiaries for 2106 are from the Ministry of Social Solidarity for cash transfer programs, the Ministry of Supply and Internal Trade for food subsidy programs, the Ministry of Health for health insurance for the poor, and the Ministry of Agriculture and Land Reclamation for the farm program.

El-Laithy 2010). In fiscal year 2010/11, although food subsidies accounted for only 4 percent of total household expenditures on food consumption,[5] they represented 22.5 percent of the total calorie consumption of the whole population (32.5 percent for the poor; 20.8 percent for the non-poor) (WFP 2013) and still had a very large impact on poverty. Figure 3.3 shows the effect of food subsidies on the Egyptian poverty rate in fiscal year 2010/11.

Egypt's 2011 and 2013 revolutions came with a new social contract and pressing demands for more inclusive growth and social justice. The policies have emphasized inclusive growth with several important developments: the 2014 constitution, which focused on the social agenda; the strategic Egypt Vision 2030, which stressed social justice; the coordination of social policies through the ministerial Social Justice Committee; and the 2014 subsidy reform measures.[6]

For all social safety net programs, the government adopted a phased approach of improving targeting, efficiency, and delivery before expanding either coverage or benefits. The intention was to shift gradually from universal subsidies to subsidies targeted toward the poor and vulnerable and to improve the quality of social services provided.

In July 2014, the government embarked on a major social and economic reform program and introduced a series of reforms with the objective of fiscal consolidation and protection of the poor. The introduction of comprehensive price increases for fossil fuels and electricity saved LE 51 billion, of which LE 27 billion (US$3.6 billion)[7] was allocated for reforms in health, education, and social safety nets. Concurrently, MOSIT implemented FSS structural reforms.

FIGURE 3.3

Impact of Food Subsidies on Poverty in the Arab Republic of Egypt, Fiscal Year 2010/11

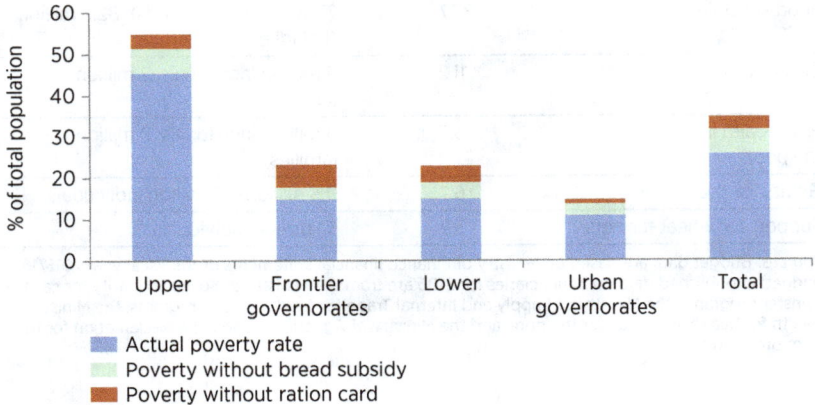

Legend:
- Actual poverty rate
- Poverty without bread subsidy
- Poverty without ration card

Source: WFP 2013, based on Household Income, Expenditure, and Consumption Expenditure Survey fiscal year 2010/11 data.

Parallel to those reforms, MOSS established a tool for targeting the poor (a proxy means test), with the goal of having the two new cash transfer programs—Takaful and Karama—reach 2.1 million households by June 2017. Also, the Social Fund for Development implemented a labor-intensive public works program (supported by the World Bank and the European Union) in the poorest governorates to target the low-skilled unemployed poor. Moving toward modern delivery systems, the Ministry of Planning, Monitoring, and Administrative Reform (MOPMAR) launched an initiative to build a national database for the poor and to integrate social safety net programs and coordinate targeting and delivery mechanisms.

The post-2013 political economy was an enabling factor and a critical element for the successful introduction of these reforms. The 2011 and 2013 revolutions, along with their negative economic consequences, psychologically prepared Egyptians for tough government decisions to fix structural distortions and boost inclusive growth.

Challenges with Baladi Bread and Ration Cards until 2014

Before discussing the evolution of the FSS in Egypt and the current outlook, this section summarizes the main challenges affecting the two core schemes: baladi bread and ration cards.

For BB, a key challenge was related to "leakage," meaning the share of benefits not reaching the intended beneficiaries. Leakage occurred in two ways: first, during procurement of domestic wheat, the weak monitoring capacity and underdeveloped supply chain created an incentive for wheat leakage through what are called revolving barns, or *shawna dawwarah*. Once domestic wheat was bought by the government committee and warehoused, it was discharged and procured by another committee and stored in another shawna, and so on. As a result, government accounted and paid for the same domestic wheat more than once. The exact size of leakage caused by revolving barns is not known, but some estimates put it at 15–20 percent of domestic wheat. Between 2009 and 2015, Egypt procured a total of 58 million tons of wheat, of which 6.5 million tons (11.2 percent) was not milled.[8]

A second area prone to leakage was input-based financing, whereby the government's provision of subsidized wheat flour to bakeries opened the door for a black market for flour. For instance, a metric ton of BB flour was sold on the market at LE 1,750–LE 2,000, whereas a metric ton of subsidized BB flour was sold for LE 160. An average bakery used to lose (due to low profit margins and high operating costs) around LE 100–LE 150 for each metric ton of wheat used to produce bread, compared with a profit of LE 1,100 for wheat sold on the black market (Perry and Youssef 2013). The incentive for leakage was worsened by the weak monitoring capacity of MOSIT and the underdeveloped manual controls along the supply chain. Accordingly, an estimated 30 percent of subsidized wheat flour (for BB or for home baking) was lost to leakage in 2009, according to the HIECS (Al-Shawarby and El-Laithy 2010). MOSIT estimates the loss even higher: 40–50 percent of wheat flour was lost to leakage given the tendency of bakeries to produce underweighted BB (less than 130 grams per loaf).

Such practices dramatically reduced the amount and quality of baladi bread produced. The wheat leakage resulted in bread shortages and pushed down the national average consumption of BB below its already low level of 2.5–2.7 loaves per day. Long queues, violent protests, significant wasted time, and soaring public dissatisfaction were hallmarks of the system. MOSIT specified a wheat quota for each bakery and set a specific number of working hours for each bakery in an attempt to minimize leakage. However, the change did not alter the behavior of bakeries, which reacted by slowing their pace of production and further reducing the quality of bread.

Another key challenge involved wastage at both the supply and demand sides of the BB system. Supply-side problems occurred during the storage and warehousing of domestic wheat in open shawnas, which lost an estimated 10 percent of wheat to rodents, birds, and weather-related damage.[9] The Egyptian Holding Company for Silos and Storage (EHCSS), which was established in 2002 with the mandate of building and renovating the silos (which are used mainly for imported wheat), did not focus much attention on improving the shawnas (EHCSS 2016).

Wastage on the demand side included consumers' lack of incentives to rationalize or even stabilize their consumption of bread. The subsidized bread system failed to sustain perhaps the most effective tool that could have justified it from the public health perspective—fortification (box 3.1). On the

BOX 3.1 **Fortification Program of Baladi Bread**

According to findings of the 2005 Egypt Demographic and Health Survey, the rates of anemia doubled between 2000 and 2005 nationwide, particularly among women and young children. That trend prompted the country to prioritize the problem in the National Food and Nutrition Strategy (2007–17), which created a national program that fortified BB wheat flour with iron (ferrous sulfate) and folic acid between 2008 and 2012. The program was first piloted in Fayoum with the support of the World Health Organization between 2004 and 2005 and then rolled out nationally with the support of the Global Alliance of Improved Nutrition and the World Food Programme.

The fortification program showed some good results, despite questions about local capacity to monitor and ensure the quality of flour at the mills. Anemia rates fell nationally, and ownership of the program by MOSIT and the Ministry of Public Health and Population raised public awareness about the nutritional benefits of a good diet. MOSIT's capacity to manage the program improved, and the program continued until 2012, when funding was discontinued.

supply side, domestic wheat farmers saved significant amounts of their own production for daily baking and consumption—instead of selling it to the government (to avoid poor-quality bread and long queues).

Similar to BB, the RC system was prone to inefficiencies. Some ration card warehouses and groceries used to leak large amounts of oil and sugar to the black market, where they made a profit from the price difference. Warehouses and groceries had no incentive to sell the subsidized commodity quota to end consumers (RC holders). Also, the increasing cost of the government's imported oil subsidy created an incentive to procure low-quality oil and compromise the standards of the refining and bottling process. This decline in quality created dissatisfaction among consumers, particularly the lower middle class.

The design of ration cards also created obstacles for the poor. An average family of four was required to pay LE 40 up-front to the grocery to receive the monthly quota of food commodities, which created a financial barrier. In 2010, based on HIECS fiscal year 2008/09 data, an estimated 27 percent of the poor did not benefit from the RC system, and about 75 percent thought that the selling prices of subsidized commodities were too high.

Finally, the basket of subsidized commodities in the old RC system was characterized by calorie-dense foods.[10]

LOOKING BACK: THE EVOLUTION OF THE FSS IN EGYPT

Since the mid-1940s, when the first food subsidy program was initiated, Egypt's FSS has experienced changes in design and implementation. Those changes have progressed through five distinct phases: (a) the birth of the system (1941–55), (b) the socialist orientation during the Nasser era (1956–70),

(c) the liberalization and hobbled reforms during the Sadat era (1970–81), (d) the successful quiet reforms that dissipated with time during the Mubarak era (1981–2011), and (e) the transformational reform of the system in post-revolutionary Egypt (2011–present).

Seeds of Egypt's FSS, 1941–55

Food subsidies were first introduced after World War I (1914–18), when the government began to import large quantities of wheat and flour from Australia and to sell those products in government outlets at discounted prices (Ahmed and others 2001). The objective was to mitigate increases in international food commodity prices (Scobie 1981). During World War II, in response to high inflation and food shortages, the government introduced a ration-type subsidy to mitigate the negative impacts of the war on prices and on the availability of necessities. The objective was to ensure that a minimum level of the population's basic needs would be met as well as to reduce the cost of living for the Egyptian masses. Therefore, subsidies were originally universal and had no specifically targeted objective. Subsidized goods included, at the beginning, kerosene and textiles. Shortly thereafter, subsidies were expanded to include sugar, cooking oil, tea, and margarine.

Egypt maintained those controls even after the war ended. There was no significant fiscal burden during the decade following the war, although no official data are available about the magnitude of food subsidies. One study indicates that food subsidies totaled LE 1 million in 1941 and did not exceed a few million until the end of 1950s (Hashish 1980).[11] The small subsidy bill resulted from three main features of this period: low inflation rates, lower rates of growth of domestic consumption than of GDP, and high food self-sufficiency rates.

Nasser Era: Socialist Orientation, 1956–70

Until the mid-1960s, the main objective of the FSS continued to be to ensure social equity at a time of domestic shortfalls. As the leader of a nationalist and socialist revolution, Gamal Abdel Nasser set out to redistribute income and opportunities. Control of food marketing and prices was an important element in this plan (Baker 1978). Building on the long history of food price control in Egypt, Nasser adapted the framework of food subsidy provision, tightening the government's control over wheat prices and marketing as well as other rationed goods. The FSS was an allocative measure for social equity purposes in a centrally planned economy. To tighten its control on the food distribution system, the government established many public companies for retailing and importing.

The FSS also sought to finance industrialization by providing inexpensive food to urban consumers and ensuring a low cost of living and thereby low wages (Farrar 2000; Sachs 2012). Vocal constituencies, mainly urban, thus became a central element in the political context of food subsidies.

Having this key role in the implicit social contract, FSS assumed symbolic significance, instilling support for the regime by providing a "diffuse symbolic fulfillment of a social contract" (Hopkins 1988, 108), but also meant that any change in subsidies would call into question other elements of the social contract.

The limited available data indicate that FSS represented only 0.4 percent of GDP in 1960 (LE 9 million) and in 1970 (LE 11 million) (figure 3.4).[12] Yet the level of food subsidies increased in this period for several reasons: (a) expansion of food price controls, partly in response to Nasser's socialist ideology; (b) increase in consumption that resulted from population growth and an increase in households' disposable income, especially after agrarian reforms; and (c) availability of cheap wheat from the United States under U.S. Public Law (P.L.) 480,[13] which lasted only until 1967, when U.S. foreign assistance was suspended.[14]

Sadat Era: Economic Liberalization, Riots, and Hobbled Reforms, 1970–81

Anwar Sadat came to power in 1970 with a heritage of economic difficulties indicating that Egypt's aims had greatly exceeded its means. Within the philosophy of a centralized economy, the government set up a welfare state with guaranteed employment, free access to education and health care, and extensive price administration and subsidies.

Sadat reversed the economic and political orientation of his predecessor and moved closer to the West, hoping to attract private investment, particularly foreign investment. This goal became a key element in a series of

FIGURE 3.4

Increases in Food Subsidies in the Arab Republic of Egypt, 1970–80

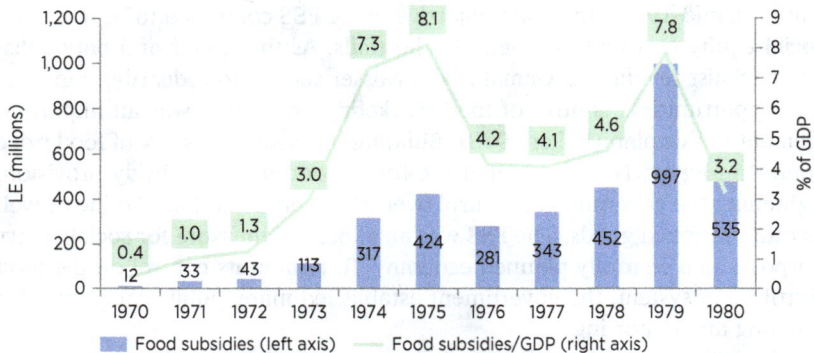

Source: El Essawi 2007.

economic reforms that took the name of *infitah* (open-door) economic policy. The infitah era was also characterized by a reduction in state intervention in the economy, marking a dramatic shift from the import substitution policy and self-sufficiency promoted under Nasser (Abdel-Khalek 1981).

Tackling the expanding FSS was one of the main strategic changes taking place in the 1970s. As in other countries covered in this volume (notably, India), food subsidies increased steadily in Egypt throughout 1970–75, from less than 0.4 to 8 percent of GDP, and fluctuated afterward around an average of 5 percent of GDP. This increase was due primarily to skyrocketing world food prices, which more than quadrupled from US$60 per ton in 1970 to nearly US$250 per ton in 1973. The cost of maintaining a stable domestic price for basic commodities resulted in ballooning GASC trading losses in 1973 (from US$28 million in 1972 to US$228 million in 1973) (Ikram 2006). Food security became a major policy issue, with Egypt becoming a net importer of several agricultural commodities, most importantly wheat.

The objective of the FSS became to insulate Egyptian consumers from inflation caused by high international prices. As such, the FSS became a major economic burden: by 1977, the cost of the 18 subsidized food commodities available on a monthly basis to all RC holders increased significantly. In 1976 the International Monetary Fund (IMF) put forward some requirements for economic reforms, centering on the budget deficit and making lower subsidies the main condition for passing a program (Ikram 2006).

In January 1977, a subsidy reform plan was announced, shortly after a focused cabinet reshuffle brought more reform-minded players into place (Feiler 2003). Subsidy reduction measures included both food and nonfood subsidies. The regulated prices of French bread, sugar, and rice were increased, and the tea subsidy was canceled.[15] The prices of BB and *shami* bread, as well as beans, cooking oil, and rationed sugar, were left untouched (Alderman 1986).

The public responded immediately with extreme opposition, even though the government kept the prices of most essential commodities unchanged. Riots and strikes spread in major cities. The government's legitimacy seemed to be at stake, and decrees mandating the subsidy cuts were eventually canceled on January 20, 1977. Efforts to contain the unrest during those few days cost the country 73 dead, around 800 injured, and 1,270 arrested. The government reportedly considered introducing a food voucher, but dismissed this idea after the assassination of Sadat.[16]

Since then, successive Egyptian governments have fallen captive to the conviction that food subsidy reforms put the country's social peace and political stability at risk. As a result, the subsidy bill rose from 4.1 percent of GDP in 1977 to 7.8 percent in 1979. Drawing on the events of early 1977, a more conservative and incremental approach to reform was adopted—focusing on "easier" subsidies and price controls and establishing wage adjustments in the

public sector as compensation. Although such reforms ignored workers in the
informal sector who are especially vulnerable to commodity price increases,
the nexus of subsidies and public wages continued to characterize Egypt's
food subsidy reforms in the following decades.

Mubarak Era: Successful Quiet Reforms, with a Very Dramatic End, 1981–2011

When Hosni Mubarak came to power in 1981, the FSS continued to expand,
with costs rising from 6.3 percent of GDP in 1981 to 8.1 percent in 1982.
Gradual reforms started afterward and succeeded in reducing the fiscal
burden of the subsidy bill while avoiding political difficulties (World Bank
2005). Spending on food subsidies declined to 3 percent of GDP in fiscal year
1986/87 and to less than 1 percent of GDP in fiscal years 1997/98 to 2000/01
(figures 3.5 and 3.6). This reduction, together with other reforms undertaken under an IMF agreement in 1987, contributed to large cuts in the
deficit. FSS reforms under the Economic Reform and Structural Adjustment
Program, which Egypt concluded with the IMF and the World Bank in 1991,
contributed to further reductions in the budget, which reached around
1 percent of GDP in the period between fiscal year 1994/95 and 1997/98.

Specifically, two types of reforms were adopted. The first type limited
eligibility for subsidies by introducing lower-valued RCs for relatively
better-off beneficiaries and freezing the registration of newcomers (children
born after 1988), with the aim being to move gradually to a better targeted
food subsidy program. The second type made cautious cost-saving changes in

FIGURE 3.5

Food Subsidy Spending and the Fiscal Deficit in the Arab Republic of Egypt, 1980–99

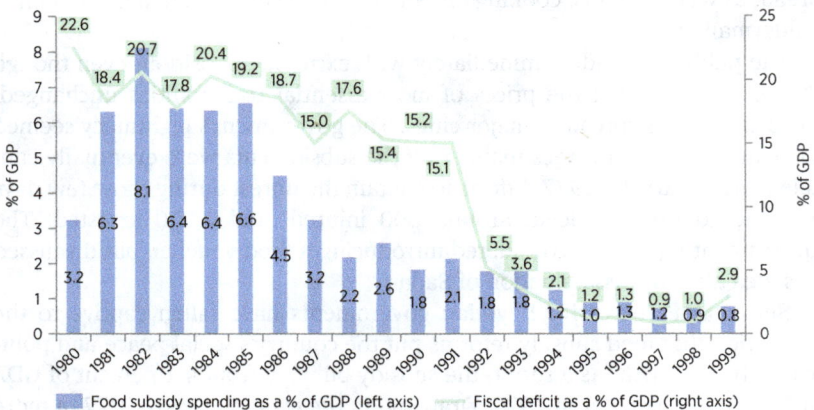

Food subsidy spending as a % of GDP (left axis)   Fiscal deficit as a % of GDP (right axis)

Source: Based on data from the Ministry of Finance and the Ministry of Supply and
Internal Trade.

FIGURE 3.6

Food Subsidy Costs in the Arab Republic of Egypt, Fiscal Years 2001/02 to 2014/15

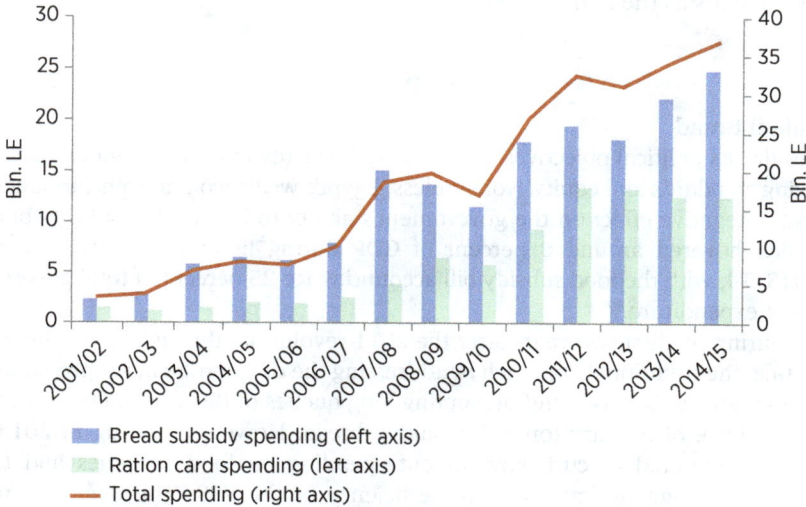

Bread subsidy spending (left axis)
Ration card spending (left axis)
Total spending (right axis)

Source: Based on data from the Ministry of Finance and the Ministry of Supply and Internal Trade.

the provision of food subsidies, such as reducing the number and weight of subsidized rationed food items, changing the weight and ingredients of BB, and incrementally raising prices. Both types of quiet reforms largely avoided social disruption similar to that of 1977. This success can also be attributed to the association of food subsidy reforms with annual wage and salary increases and to some political repression (Sachs 2012).

The downward trend in the FSS fiscal burden reversed in the 2000s, mainly because of the depreciation of the Egyptian pound. Those drops resulted in a dramatic increase in inflation rates—from about 3 percent in 2000–02 to 11.3 percent in 2004. This trend coincided with a decline in local wheat production and a sharp rise in the international prices of imported consumer commodities (including cost of freight). To mitigate the negative inflationary impact and contain public discontent about rapidly soaring prices, the government expanded the food subsidy program, increasing the number of types and quantities of items as well as the number of covered beneficiaries.

In spite of the increases in the 2000s, FSS costs never reached the alarming levels seen under Sadat, averaging 1.4 percent of GDP in that decade. In those years, about 96 percent of the poor were benefiting from the FSS, but those in the richest quintile were receiving about 12.6 percent more from food subsidies than those in the poorest quintile (Al-Shawarby and

El-Laithy 2010). The BB and cooking oil subsidies were the most regressive of all food subsidies. The only subsidized food that was progressive was baladi wheat flour, which provided the poorest quintile as much as 5.8 times the benefits as the richest.

CURRENT SIGNS OF A TRANSFORMATION

Baladi Bread

Besides its political objectives, the January 2011 revolution demanded better living standards and equity. Nonetheless, Egypt's weak economic performance had a negative effect on the government's ability to finance the subsidy bill, which hovered around 8 percent of GDP during fiscal years 2011/12 to 2013/14, with the food subsidy bill accounting for 25 percent of total government expenditure.[17]

During the first two years after the 2011 revolution, the MOSIT continued to take the traditional approach to addressing the daily problems of providing wheat flour to bakeries and preventing long queues of BB consumers, including the use of military forces for baking bread. However, starting in 2013, Egypt attempted to curb government spending on food subsidies and to reduce wastage by improving the efficiency of the FSS. The plan was to improve the control measures that were in place to manage and monitor the supply chain and eliminate intermediaries from various parts of the chain as well as to ration BB consumption through a smartcard system. The plan was commended, but stakeholders within the FSS resisted these reforms, and bakery owners threatened a nationwide bakers' strike if the government did not back down (Kamal 2015).

In February 2014, MOSIT introduced several radical changes to the structure of the BB system, carefully preparing and planning the steps of reforms and using evidence and new opportunities offered by technological advances. The reforms were motivated by and responded to high expectations following the 2011 and 2013 revolutions.

In an effort to improve the supply chain of the BB system and to enhance the system's effectiveness, in 2013 the government introduced a pilot system for BB in Port Said City (box 3.2). On the basis of the lessons learned from that pilot, the new system was modified and rolled out nationwide in fiscal year 2014/15. The new system had the following features and design parameters: (a) shifting from an input-based subsidy to an output-based subsidy, (b) capping the benefit size and consolidating the system, (c) automating the system and supporting financial inclusion, and (d) reducing wheat waste and cutting storage leakage.

Shifting from an Input-Based to an Output-Based Subsidy
The new system shifted toward output-based financing; that is, the wheat flour that is being distributed to bakeries is no longer subsidized. Instead,

BOX 3.2 **Port Said Baladi Bread Pilot**

In November 2012, the government launched its program for subsidy reform and improved targeting in several national programs. In January 2013, MOSIT began to pilot the use of smartcards to distribute bread in Port Said, installing point-of-sale (POS) readers in each bakery. The pilot's objective was to improve the supply chain and to monitor the actual consumption of each family so that the government could cap the size of benefit.

Port Said was chosen because of its small population, its well-defined boundaries, its low dependency on bread compared with other governorates (which meant less criticism in case of failure), and its having the lowest number of bakeries per capita nationwide. That is, if it was able to tackle the queuing issue in Port Said, the system could be replicated throughout the country.

After one year, MOSIT hailed the pilot as a success and rolled it out nationwide, with a few modifications, such as the capped benefit size. The system was consolidated through a point system in April 2014 as a radical move toward a system-based approach. During the Port Said pilot, MOSIT also moved from an input-based to an output-based subsidy, liberalizing the wheat flour sold to bakeries to cut leakage and minimize trading on the black market. The communication strategy behind that move, however, was strongly criticized for not being inclusive.

bakeries get the wheat flour from mills at the market price and sell BB loaves to consumers at agreed-upon prices (5 piastres). MOSIT then subsidizes the difference between the real cost (which includes the bakeries' marginal profit) and the selling price. The actual price of a BB loaf is determined on the basis of the price of wheat and the price of wheat flour. This new pricing system interrupted leakage of wheat flour to the black market, curtailed the long queues at the bakeries, and encouraged bakeries to meet certain quality standards to increase their sales and thus their profits.

In the new system, an average bakery can make a profit of LE 800–LE 1,000 per metric ton of BB loaves sold. Bakeries have turned into market competitors that have an incentive to improve their efficiency and effectiveness. Previous attempts by bakeries to reduce the weight of a bread loaf (which must be 110 grams in the new system) have declined dramatically because consumers can choose to go to any bakery in search of better-quality BB loaves. In fact, the number of reported violations by bakeries in regard to underweight loaves and loaf specifications decreased from prereform rates of 37,339 and 45,598 incidents, respectively, to 11,860 and 14,102 incidents, respectively, in 2015. Under the new system, bakeries are neither limited to any quota of wheat flour nor tied to a specific number of working hours.

Making bread available for citizens at any time of the day had a very positive social impact: it dramatically reduced queuing times for the majority of beneficiaries, who cited the new system as a tangible government reform since the 2011 revolution (annex 3B). The availability of quality bread is thought to have encouraged Egyptian farmers to sell a higher percentage of their wheat production to the government, taking into consideration the higher government procurement price of domestic versus imported wheat.[18] In fiscal year 2014/15, the share of domestic wheat procured by the government reportedly surpassed the share of imported wheat for the first time, reflecting the influence of the government strategy.

Automating the System and Supporting Financial Inclusion and Transparency
MOSIT would not have been able to modify the FSS without an automated smart system to monitor both the bakeries' financial transactions and the beneficiaries' daily consumption of BB and accrued savings points. The ministry built on the smartcard system that was developed in 2006 to monitor consumption under the RC system. Linking the BB and RC systems was relatively easy for private companies, which were able to consolidate the system, print bread cards, and roll out the model nationwide within 8–13 months, starting in Port Said (box 3.3).

Automating the system meant that all bakeries had to have POS readers to sell their goods to cardholders. To retrieve their daily bread quota, cardholders enter a personal identification number in the POS reader. All of the financial transactions between MOSIT and bakeries are now automated, and the amount of bread produced and sold is known. Moreover, the system prompted all bakeries to open a bank account for the financial settlement of sold bread.

BOX 3.3 Family Smartcard System

In 2006, as part of its efforts to integrate the social programs and consolidate the social safety net system, the Egyptian government developed and introduced a family smartcard system for food ration cards. All groceries contracting with MOSIT were equipped with POS readers, and each beneficiary household received a smartcard.

Despite some pitfalls, the system represents a successful example of a private-public partnership. The family smartcard team at MOPMAR, contracted with the private sector to develop and maintain the system, and the government plays a stewardship and financial role. Private companies invest in the hardware and software of the program and claim their profits through card use and transactions. They have a strong incentive to keep the system running smoothly to ensure the flow of their revenues. According to MOPMAR, any system bugs or POS errors are fixed within one or two hours at any governorate branch.

The system has some challenges, however. Some fake cards have been printed, and the POS machines have been manipulated to accept fake cards or to report fake transactions. MOSIT and the family smartcard team at MOPMAR are exploring options to digitize the system better and to unify the coding in a way that minimizes any possible leakages or fraud.

More than 25,000 bakeries are now financially included in the banking system and paying taxes according to their sales.

Capping the Benefit Size and Consolidating the System
The current reform seeks not only to address supply-side issues, but also to change consumer behavior and build a new social contract. MOSIT, under the new system, set a maximum of 5 BB loaves per individual per day or 10 kilograms of subsidized flour per individual per month in 13 governorates, mostly in Upper Egypt.[19] This level was based on the country's highest per capita consumption of bread (4.5 loaves in North Sinai) and was guided by the pilot in Port Said. The state's bread subsidy stands at around 30 piastres per loaf, which means a monthly subsidy of LE 45 per individual. To change consumer behavior, MOSIT introduced a system for rewarding the rationing of BB or subsidized flour (for private baking). The point-based system rewards every loaf saved with 10 piastres, which consumers can use to purchase commodities under the RC system. That is, for each loaf of bread saved, the government saves 20 piastres and the consumer gets 10 piastres, in addition to the 5 piastres saved by not buying a loaf of bread. By consolidating the BB system with the RC system, the government, for the first time in the history of the FSS, introduced an opportunity cost for bread consumption. The new system turned Egypt's subsidy beneficiaries into market consumers, who can maximize their benefits according to their needs and preferences.

The new system, which provides good-quality and readily available bread, attracts more beneficiaries. According to World Food Programme estimates and the Ministry of Finance's fiscal year 2016/17 budget assumptions, the number of beneficiaries of the BB system grew from 56.0 million in 2013 to 82.2 million in 2016 (WFP 2013). Without the new point system and at the same coverage of 82.2 million people, the BB subsidy alone would cost the government about LE 40 billion annually. By rationing the consumption of bread, the point system led to an estimated annual savings to the state of about LE 11 billion. In addition, the national annual procurement of wheat dropped below the levels of fiscal year 2013/14. The consolidation of the BB and RC programs allowed beneficiaries more choice with regard to their dietary priorities.

Analysis of the savings of the BB point system by governorate suggests questions for further assessment. The highest bread savings per household come from urban governorates, whereas the lowest savings are concentrated in governorates in Upper Egypt with the highest poverty rates and a majority rural population (figure 3.7). This result could be explained by differences in the regions' make-up of meals—BB is a major element in almost all meals in rural Upper Egypt—and reliance on subsidized flour for baking. However, the consumption of subsidized flour for home baking has dropped in the 13 governorates where this scheme is allowed (both in percentage and quantity). That is, the reliance on BB in these governorates has increased.

FIGURE 3.7

Pattern of Household Savings from the Point System in the Arab Republic of Egypt, by Governorate, January 2016

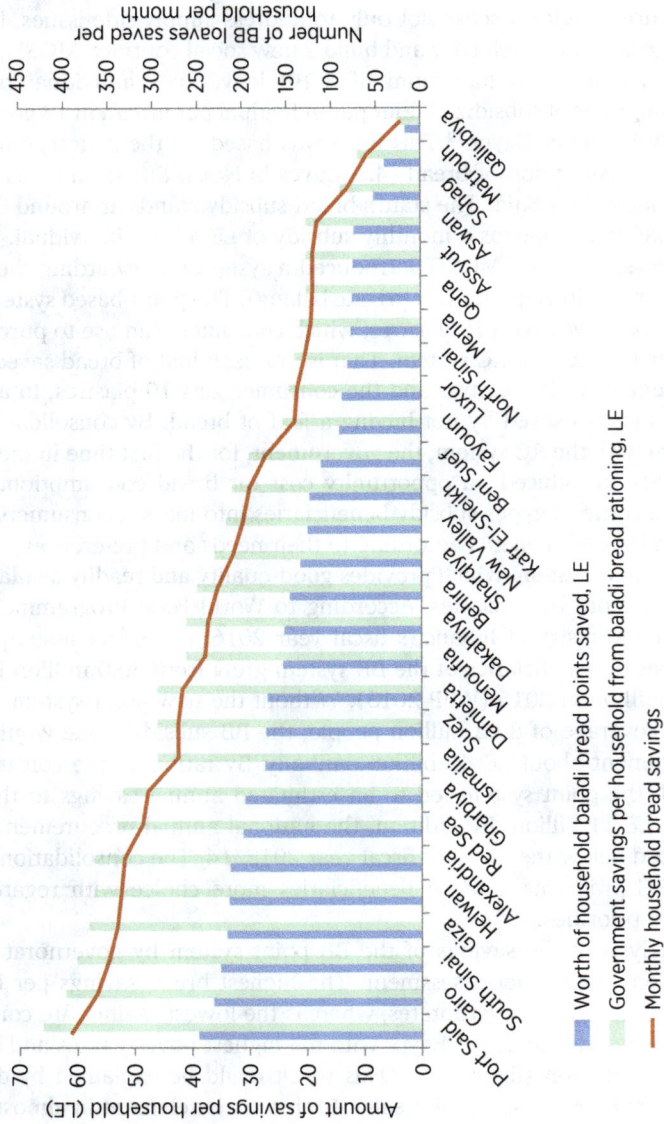

Number of BB loaves saved per household per month

Amount of savings per household (LE)

Qalubiya, Matrouh, Sohag, Aswan, Qena, Assyut, Menia, North Sinai, Luxor, Fayoum, Beni Suef, Kafr El-Sheikh, New Valley, Sharqia, Behira, Dakahliya, Menoufia, Damietta, Suez, Ismailia, Gharbiya, Red Sea, Alexandria, Helwan, Giza, South Sinai, Cairo, Port Said

■ Worth of household baladi bread points saved, LE

■ Government savings per household from baladi bread rationing, LE

— Monthly household bread savings

Source: GASC 2016.

Reducing Waste and Storage Leakage

In order to reform the BB supply chain even more, a national project to upgrade storage of local wheat was launched in 2014. About 30–40 percent of the open-land barns (*shawna torabiya*), which are estimated to have wasted 11 percent of domestic wheat, have been or are being upgraded to concrete or asphalt construction with proper ventilation and storage capacity. About 50–60 additional silos are being built across the country to increase the government's storage capacity and reduce the dependency on the shawnas. In addition, a smart tracking system is being developed to monitor the storage of wheat at silos and shawnas, minimizing any double counting (revolving shawnas).

Ration Card

The RC system sustained a paradigm shift after the issuance of Ministerial Decree 215 for 2014. Now, each RC household receives a monthly cash allotment of LE 15 per person, with no limit on the number of beneficiaries per family. This amount was decided on the basis of the nominal cost of RC subsidies per capita in fiscal year 2013/14. The new system has four main differences from the old one (detailed in table 3.2). First, the system offers consumer choice and a wider variety of food commodities. The list of commodities

TABLE 3.2 Summary of the Main Differences between the Old and New Food Subsidy System in the Arab Republic of Egypt

FEATURE	OLD FOOD SUBSIDY SYSTEM	NEW FOOD SUBSIDY SYSTEM
General features		
Consolidation	Fragmented system (no link between baladi bread and ration card programs)	Integrated and consolidated system through a point reward mechanism
Automation and database	For ration card program only	For the whole system
Cost of system (% of GDP)	1.69–1.77%[a]	1.35–1.63%[b]
Benefit size (% of poverty line adjusted per year)	LE 438 per individual per year, up to 4 per family (11.1% in 2013)[c]	LE 605 per individual per year (11.4% in 2016)[d]
Baladi bread		
Coverage (individuals)	Around 56 million beneficiaries	About 82.2 million beneficiaries
Targeting	Universal on a first-come, first-served basis	Universal with smartcard registration
Benefit size	Unlimited	5 loaves per person per day
Subsidy	Cost of loaves subsidized using an input-based subsidy for wheat flour	Beneficiaries subsidized using output-based financing for loaves of bread sold to the intended beneficiaries

table continues next page

TABLE 3.2 **Summary of the Main Differences between the Old and New Food Subsidy System in the Arab Republic of Egypt** *(continued)*

FEATURE	OLD FOOD SUBSIDY SYSTEM	NEW FOOD SUBSIDY SYSTEM
Wheat procured (domestic and imported)	Annual average of 10 million metric tons	Annual average of 10 million metric tons
Wheat leakage and wastage	Average of 15% per year	Average of 7–8% per year
Wheat flour leakage	Estimated 30–50% to the black market	Minimal or no leakage
Consumption of bread	2.5–2.7 loaves per day with a total weight of 350 grams	3.5 loaves per day, with a total weight of 350 grams
Quality of bread	Reported to be of low quality	High quality
Availability of bread	Long queues and violence	Available at most times
Waiting times	Very long waiting times, reportedly several hours in some cases	Mostly less than 15 minutes
Bakeries' profits	Losses of LE 100–LE 150 per metric ton and a flourishing black market (Perry and Youssef 2013)	Profit of LE 800–LE 1,000 per metric ton
Method of payment to bakeries	No payment received from government, only subsidized flour plus 5 piastres from consumers in cash	5 piastres in cash received from beneficiaries plus 30 piastres from government through bank transfers
Opportunity cost	No opportunity cost; beneficiaries given the incentive to overconsume	An opportunity cost through the point system, resulting in consumers saving more than 30 percent of their entitled number of loaves
RC program		
Coverage	66 million people	71 million people
Targeting	Almost universal with lax criteria	Almost universal with lax criteria
Benefit size	LE 26 worth of certain commodities[e]	LE 18.5 of any commodity
Subsidy	Commodities subsidized in-kind	Beneficiaries subsidized through a voucher-like or semicash system
Market distortions	Sale of subsidized commodities to the black market, particularly oil for frying-intense modest restaurants	Minimal market distortions except for the price difference between the RC allowance and credit saved from points

table continues next page

TABLE 3.2 **Summary of the Main Differences between the Old and New Food Subsidy System in the Arab Republic of Egypt** (continued)

FEATURE	OLD FOOD SUBSIDY SYSTEM	NEW FOOD SUBSIDY SYSTEM
Quality	Mostly inferior (oil, rice, sugar)	Mostly high quality, similar to private market products
Diversity and consumer choice	Only 3 commodities	More than 100 commodities
Private sector	Limited involvement	Open-door policy
Market competition	No competition	Highly competitive environment with different players (government companies, outlets, franchises, private suppliers)
Consumer power	Very limited power, with government choosing for beneficiaries	High consumer power due to cash allowance, with consumers choosing for themselves
Financial barrier	Payment of LE 10 per person to get the subsidy (LE 40 for four persons)	Payment of LE 2 per family to the grocer to get the subsidy (LE 2 for four persons)
Consumer preferences	Unknown	Easily tracked and could open the door for analyzing consumption trends by region or by groups
Availability of the 3 main commodities (oil, sugar, rice)	Mostly available	Sugar, available; rice and oil, some shortages

Note: MOF = Ministry of Finance.
a. Ministry of Finance financial statements for the fiscal years 2012/13 to 2013/14 budgets. Excludes subsidy to wheat farmers.
b. Ministry of Finance financial statements for the fiscal years 2014/15 to 2015/16 budgets. Excludes subsidy to wheat farmers.
c. Based on 2.7 loaves per day at a cost of 25 piastres plus LE 16 worth of commodities a month.
d. Based on 3.5 loaves per day at a cost of 30 piastres plus LE 18.5 a month.
e. Up to four members per family. Beyond this, the subsidy declines to LE 7.25 per extra family member.

available under the RC system started with 20 items and has gradually expanded to about 100 items, covering foods (including chicken, meat, fish, and dairy products) and nonfood products (for example, detergents). Many of these commodities come in more than one package size and include different brands. The RC beneficiary can now purchase any quantity of any of the items available in any grocery at any time throughout the month, up to the amount of the benefit. The quality of the basket of commodities is equal to the quality available in the private market, because the government is no longer subsidizing any particular commodity.

Second, the system encourages a more diversified diet through a wider variety of commodities, which has potentially positive nutritional effects. The new system may reduce—although not fully remove—the considerable economic incentives for the consumption of calorie-dense foods (bread, cooking oil, sugar, and rice). This change has been supported by consolidation of the BB and RC systems and the use of points-based incentives for forgoing BB. GASC data for 2016 shows an increase of 30 percent in dietary diversity under the new points model.

Third, the new system has increased market competition and stimulated commercial activities by allowing retail groceries, which used to sell only the three subsidized commodities, to sell as many commodities as they want in addition to the RC commodities. Groceries have become more efficient through economies of scale. In addition, MOSIT launched a new chain—called *Game'yeti* (My Cooperative)—with a target of 14,000 retail shops across Egypt by 2018. This franchising model enables young owners to get concessional loans to equip and stock their shops with commodities according to the specifications and price policies of MOSIT. The market-based policy has led to higher sales in Egypt's three state-owned grocery chains—Al-Ahram, Alexandria, and Nile. The three chains had total annual sales of LE 1.5 billion in 2015, compared with LE 0.8 billion in 2014 and LE 0.7 billion in 2013.

Fourth, the system has a simpler supply chain that gives MOSIT and its affiliated agencies more negotiation power in the commodity market. The Holding Company for Food Industries (HCFI), which has been under MOSIT since 2014, is authorized to manage tenders to get the needed quantities of various RC commodities. As the largest buyer in the market, with LE 1.5 billion every month, HCFI can negotiate with suppliers, leading to wholesale prices that are at least comparable with what mega retailers can obtain. This influence enables HCFI to give a large discount to grocers licensed to receive RC commodities (up to 15 percent), helping to make their business profitable.

CHALLENGES OF THE NEW FOOD SUBSIDY SYSTEM

The new FSS continues to face challenges, including shortages of some basic commodities, continued distortions in the market, poor targeting, and lack of adequacy (smaller subsidies—that is, fewer basic commodities—per beneficiary). At the current stage, the main focus of the reform efforts is to tighten up the targeting of beneficiaries, starting with cleaning the lists from duplicates and fake IDs, as noted in box 3.3. There is a continuing challenge of ensuring adequacy of benefits, both in terms of value and availability.

Over the first half of 2016, cooking oil and rice were reported to be unavailable in MOSIT-affiliated groceries. The shortages created significant dissatisfaction, particularly among persons dependent on the food subsidy: "What is the use of money in the new system if we cannot find what we need?" asked a beneficiary interviewed in a television media report. According to GASC data, the shortage of oil was equal to more than one-third of the total supply between July and December 2015, compared with the same period in 2014. The shortage of rice, however, was caused by MOSIT's late procurement of rice in relation to the planting season. The shortage led to a more than 67 percent reduction in supply and a near doubling in price. As a quick mitigating measure, MOSIT had to subsidize rice in the supply chain and import large quantities of rice to counterbalance the high prices.

Since 2014, MOSIT has set two prices for the same commodities, a lower one for the RC allowance and an upper one for the points credit. That is, beneficiaries buy 1 kilogram of rice at LE 4.5 using the LE 15 monthly allowance and 1 kilogram of rice at LE 6 using their credit from the points system. At the beginning, the difference between the two prices for all essential commodities (rice, sugar, and oil) was not enough to create any market distortions. But given the acute shortage of rice and oil, the difference became larger, and beneficiaries began to sell their quotas on the black market. MOSIT's reasons for adopting differential pricing for basic commodities are not yet clear.

Although the new system provides higher-quality products (bread and commodities) and wider consumer choice, the amount of subsidy itself is lower than it was under the old system. In 2014–16, food price inflation reduced benefits by 18 percent compared with the old system.

A survey among a random sample of beneficiaries across locations was conducted for this study in May 2016.[20] The survey was meant to measure the perceptions of beneficiaries regarding the new FSS as a whole and to compare specific aspects such as food quality, availability, and adequacy. The majority of respondents (72 percent) said that they had no difficulty obtaining a smartcard, while 25 percent had difficulties. Almost all respondents stated that the new BB system is better than the old one. For example, 91 percent claimed that the quality of the bread is better; 96.4 percent reported that the new BB system provides adequate amounts and weight of bread; 99 percent stated that BB is available most of the time; and 84 percent said they receive BB with waits of less than 15 minutes. Similar results are seen across regions and income quintiles.

Regarding the RC system, respondents reported that they mainly consume five commodities in the new system: packed sugar (99.4 percent of respondents), oil (96.2 percent), packed rice (62.6 percent), packed macaroni (33.5 percent), and tea (22.2 percent). Satisfaction with the new RC system is not as strong, with mixed results by region and income quintile. In general, 59 percent of respondents said that they favor the new RC system and the diversity of the commodities it offers over the old one. Respondents in Lower Egypt seem to prefer the new RC system more than those in Upper Egypt (67 and 55 percent, respectively) or in metropolitan governorates (47 percent). In addition, the majority of respondents from the sample's poorest quintile said they favor the old RC system (52.2 percent) and that the old system's diversity was adequate (54.9 percent).

The majority of respondents said that the main commodities such as oil, rice, sugar, macaroni, and tea are of excellent quality. This finding reflects the market competition created among public and private sector suppliers.

With respect to availability, most of the desired RC commodities were reported to be available most of the time, except for rice and oil.[21] When asked about the size of subsidy and whether it is adequate, about 53 percent of beneficiaries said that it is less adequate than it was under the old system (61.1 percent among the poorest quintile), and 40 percent thought it is the same. Furthermore, 83.0 and 84.3 percent of beneficiaries in Upper Egypt stated that the amount of oil and rice, respectively, is smaller in the new system.

The overall survey findings suggest a promising transformation in the Egyptian FSS. In the BB system, the results provide strong positive signals for quality, adequacy, availability, and waiting times. The results for the RC system indicate positive signals for quality and diversity, but mixed signals for adequacy and availability. Among beneficiaries from the poorest two quintiles, the quantity or adequacy of food commodities appears to be more important than their quality or diversity.

Beyond the FSS, perhaps the most important message for government policy makers is the striking percentage (86 percent) of respondents who reported having moderate to severe difficulty fulfilling their food needs in the past three to six months. When asked what they see as the best mitigating or compensating measure, increasing the smartcard food subsidy came first (43 percent of respondents), followed by supporting cash transfers for poor families (40 percent).

Transforming the food subsidy into a voucher-like system provided the country with a tool to adjust the size of subsidy to offset inflation or to cushion price shocks. Starting from June 1, 2016, MOSIT increased the allowance per beneficiary by 20 percent, from LE 15 to LE 18 per family member per month. In May 2017, following another spike in prices, the government increased the allocation to RC again to LE 35. The preliminary findings of the 2015 HIECS show that the FSS favors families living in rural areas with regard to coverage and the poor with regard to share of household food consumption. The new FSS is protecting about 4.2 million Egyptians from falling into poverty.

Total FSS coverage of the population was 88.6 percent in 2015. Coverage was 95.4 percent in rural areas and 80.5 percent in urban areas. The new food subsidy accounts for 6.8 percent of total household food consumption, but it accounts for 10.5 percent for the lowest decile and 4.2 percent for the richest decile. In addition, total household consumption of sugar, oil, and rice represents 73.5, 73.6, and 23.4 percent, respectively (CAPMAS, various years).

Nevertheless, the universality of the new food subsidy has allowed a substantial degree of regressivity, as evidenced by the fact that 77.4 percent of the richest decile and around 90 percent of the second- through fourth-richest deciles are benefiting from the system.

LESSONS LEARNED

Understanding Egypt's recent reforms of its FSS could provide important lessons for countries considering reforms of their own social safety net programs. The government introduced transformational reforms to a large and inefficient subsidy system during a politically sensitive time for the country. Changing the behavior of suppliers and consumers through incentives has had a positive impact on the acceptability of the reform. Several lessons could be drawn from the Egyptian experience:

- *Participatory approach and communication strategy.* In 2014, the government developed a communication strategy to account for different and often conflicting needs and expectations of stakeholders in the FSS at the central and local levels. MOSIT started by mapping stakeholders with regard to their influence, power, and importance. This step was followed by a review of stakeholders' needs, interests, and expectations, along with the extent of their involvement in the system. A communication plan was developed, with specific sequencing arrangements and customized pitching strategies for each group of stakeholders.

- *Sequencing and piloting.* Piloting the BB reforms in Port Said helped MOSIT to understand the system's challenges and improve its dynamics. MOSIT kept a day-to-day record of field monitoring of the new system in Port Said and undertook regular surveys of mills, bakeries, and consumers to understand their issues. Building on the positive signals from Port Said, the rollout of the reform was based on a sequencing strategy that moved from urban to rural areas to allow enough time for the system to mature and for private companies to develop the system in rural areas.

- *Institutional ownership.* Absorbing such a significant reform in a short period, given the complex structure of MOSIT, was not an easy task. Under MOSIT's leadership, a project team, headed by the minister, was formed to conduct a series of customized training sessions and workshops with the various departments and entities of the ministry. This training was key to familiarizing officials with the objectives and features of the consolidated system and to building their sense of ownership. That approach was also part of the institutional communication plan at the central and local levels.

- *Data-driven decisions.* The new system has a database that enables policy makers to understand consumption trends and preferences by region, beneficiary, age, and other factors. The database gives the ministry precious information, and MOSIT is preparing to automate the system's databases even further (MOPMAR is building a unified national registry for social safety net programs).

Policy makers from other countries could also learn from the history of reforms in Egypt. Political crisis and rapid changes required the use of "out of the box" solutions that modern technology has offered. Similar efforts in India, documented in chapter 2 of this volume, have led to equally impressive gains in efficiency and reduction of leakage. The political economy of reform, when dealt with properly, has also proven to be an enabler of change. The decision to replace compensation mechanisms with predictable, regular subsidies for bakeries earned the support of previous opponents to reform. Egypt made a partial transition to vouchers, offering beneficiaries wider choices and moving in the direction that the United States implemented in full (chapter 6); at the same time, inflation poses risks to the adequacy of transfers, with the experience of Sri Lanka (chapter 4) serving as a cautionary note. Clearly, indexation mechanisms (as opposed to ad hoc adjustments) are required to countervail such risks. Finally, Egypt's government-run distribution system has realized economies of scale in procurement, a factor that remains relevant to Mexico's experience (chapter 5).

The current reforms could be complemented by additional steps, pointing to policy options. From one standpoint, the FSS in Egypt is almost universal: having appropriate targeting mechanisms or differentiating the amount of support depending on need could make the system more progressive, while maintaining social cohesion. Such attempts to target FSS have occurred before, but the new opportunities provided by the ongoing process of data digitalization can make targeting more accurate and inclusive.

Technology to make smartcards even more personalized and secure, such as biometrics, has been applied successfully in some countries and could be considered. Similarly, the current supply chain has been significantly improved at the beneficiary end through the use of technology and output-based financing or a voucher-like system. The other end of the food system supply chain (procurement, warehousing, wheat milling, and distribution) needs to be addressed equally. MOSIT could capitalize on the available smart technology of logistical tracking to monitor every step of the supply chain through the end user. To avoid fluctuations, benefit size could be reviewed regularly. Given the positive results of the 2008–13 national fortification program, MOSIT may consider adopting a sustainable, budgeted national program of fortifying BB using advanced quality assurance and monitoring mechanisms at the central and local levels. Nutrition awareness on the importance of food diversity should be enshrined in the program and prioritized at the national level. Finally, recent shortages of rice and oil in the FSS reemphasized the public demand for continued engagement of the government in stabilizing prices. As in the case of wheat, MOSIT could consider creating a strategic reserve for rice and cooking oil.

Egypt's FSS has evolved from an in-kind subsidy to a voucher-like system. While preliminary signals are encouraging, a robust evaluation using data from the 2016 HIECS would shed more quantitative light on the initial results.

ACKNOWLEDGMENTS

The team wishes to express their sincere gratitude for the close cooperation and generosity in sharing information provided by Egyptian officials, in particular, Atef Oweda, head of the Minister's Office Sector at MOSIT; Ibrahim Al-Akhras, senior researcher at the Minister's Technical Office at MOSIT; Ahmed Kamal, assistant to the minister of supply and internal trade; Nermin Ali, researcher at the Minister's Technical Office; Saleh Al-Mofti, former head of the Central Department for Importing Affairs at GASC; and Kawthar Al-Salamoni, head of the Central Department for Commodity Studies.

ANNEX 3A. MILESTONES RELATED TO BALADI BREAD AND RATION CARDS

TABLE 3A.1 **Milestones Related to Baladi Bread, 1941–2014**

YEAR	MEASURE(S)	MINISTERIAL DECREE NUMBER
1941	• Controls are placed on retail prices of wheat flour and bread. • Allocation of 50% of all agricultural landholdings to wheat production is mandated. • Consumer prices of all types of bread and flour are subsidized.	n.a. (not available)
1945–55	• State control over the production and trading of wheat is gradually increased.	n.a.
1955	• The area allocation requirement for wheat production is reduced to 33%. • A compulsory delivery policy is imposed, with a specific quota of wheat (between 1 and 3 *ardeb* per *feddan*) at a fixed price lower than international prices.	n.a.
1957	• Government begins to control flour extraction and bread production.	n.a.
Early 1960s	• Government imposes strong interventions in agricultural production by area allotment and forced deliveries. • Agricultural cooperatives are created in each village to control production and marketing of major crops, including wheat. • Transport of wheat without permission from the Ministry of Supply and Internal Trade (MOSIT) is prohibited. • The government gains complete control of bread price and flour extraction rates.	n.a.
1967	• Public Law (P.L.) 480 program wheat is suspended until 1975. • Baladi bread (BB) is included in the supply commodities of the MOSIT for the first time, tying BB to *tamween* subsidy allocations because of the 1967 war.	n.a.
1970	• The area allocation requirement for wheat production is reduced to 27.5% of all agricultural landholdings. • Government tightens its control on marketing, distribution, and import of wheat.	n.a.
1975	• The General Company for Greater Cairo's Bakeries is established, to be responsible for the production, trade, and distribution of all kinds of bread.	79

table continues next page

TABLE 3A.1 **Milestones Related to Baladi Bread, 1941–2014** *(continued)*

YEAR	MEASURE(S)	MINISTERIAL DECREE NUMBER
1976	• The Principal Bank for Development and Agricultural Credit is created to work with cooperatives.	n.a.
	• Compulsory delivery of wheat is replaced by an optional delivery program.	
1977	• An unsuccessful attempt is made to increase the price of *fino*, among other regulated prices, sparking widespread riots.	n.a.
1983	• The General Organization for Mills, Silos, and Bakeries is established, with 11 companies.	459
1984	• Four types of bread are in place:	516
	– BB from 87.5% extraction flour (135 grams or 130 grams, depending on the type of bakery, for 1 piastre)	
	– BB from 82% extraction flour (160 grams or 135 grams for 2 piastres)	
	– Fino bread from 72% extraction flour (140 grams for 2 piastres or 69 grams for 1 piastre)	
	– *Shami* bread from 72% extraction flour (137 grams for 2 piastres, 90 grams for 1 piastre, and 45 grams for 0.5 piastre)	516
	• Bakeries are expected to use at least 80% of their quotas from 72% extraction flour in baking fino; other flours may be used to produce cookies and biscuits.	
1987	• Wheat production and marketing are partially liberalized; mandatory area allocations and delivery quotas are abolished; optional delivery at guaranteed floor prices is introduced.	n.a.
	• The weight of BB 87.5% is reduced to 135 grams (from 160 grams), and its price is increased to 1 piastre (from 0.5 piastres).	
	• A special 82% extraction BB is introduced for 2 piastres with a weight of 160 grams.	
	• New weights and prices are set for 72% extraction *shami* bread (big loaves: 137 grams for 2 piastres per loaf; small loaves: 45 grams for 2 piastres per 3 loaves) and for 72% extraction fino bread (big loaves: 140 grams for 2 piastres; small loaves: 69 grams for 1 piastre).	
	• A mandate is imposed on fino bakeries to use at least 80% of their flour quota in producing fino bread, leaving a maximum of 20% of the quota for the production of sweets and other special types of bread.	
	• BB with 87.5% extraction flour gradually disappears, and BB with predominantly 82% extraction flour costs 2 piastres.	

table continues next page

TABLE 3A.1 **Milestones Related to Baladi Bread, 1941–2014** *(continued)*

YEAR	MEASURE(S)	MINISTERIAL DECREE NUMBER
1988	• BB with 87.5% extraction flour is eliminated.	n.a.
	• Three types of bread are available in the market:	
	– Regular BB made from 82% extraction, which retails at 2 piastres and weighs 160 grams	
	– Crispy 82% extraction flour bread, which retails at 5 piastres and weighs 135 grams	
	– Soft 72% extraction flour bread, which retails at 5 piastres and weighs 160 grams.	
1990	• Regular BB made from 82% extraction retails at 5 piastres and weighs 160 grams.	n.a.
1990/91	• Subsidy is eliminated on 72% extraction fino flour and bread.	n.a.
	• The private sector is allowed to import, produce, and trade unsubsidized fino flour.	
	• Fino with 76% extraction flour is eliminated.	
1992/93	• All restrictions on marketing fino flour are eliminated.	n.a
	• Mills are restricted to the production of only one type of flour.	
1993/94	• Shami flour and bread are eliminated from the subsidy system, leaving just 82% extraction BB and flour subsidized.	n.a.
	• Private and public millers producing fino flour are required to use only imported wheat.	
1998	• An 80:20 ratio of wheat flour (82% extraction) and corn flour (97% extraction) is introduced in subsidized flour to reduce leakage and wastage.	591
	• The size of 82% BB is reduced to 130 grams (from 135 grams), keeping the price at 5 piastres.	
	• The size of *tabaki* 76% extraction is reduced to 110 grams (from 160 grams), and its price is increased to 10 piastres (from 5 piastres).	
	• Informal bakeries are formalized, and flour quotas are allocated to them.	
1999	• Most public holding companies are closed, and all their affiliates are transferred to the Food Industry Holding Company, which becomes the sole administrator of public sector mills for BB flour.	n.a.
2003	• Subsidized fino bread is reintroduced, and bakeries are provided additional quantities of flour to bake fino into refined bread at 10 piastres.	n.a.

table continues next page

TABLE 3A.1 **Milestones Related to Baladi Bread, 1941–2014** *(continued)*

YEAR	MEASURE(S)	MINISTERIAL DECREE NUMBER
2004	• The number of BB bakeries is increased in populated and deprived areas. • The bread subsidy is estimated at 10 piastres per loaf.	Cabinet decree 298
2006	• The sale price for flour to bakeries using 82% extraction flour is set at LE 900 per metric ton.	176
2008	• Wheat prices skyrocket following the global food price crisis. • The military intervenes to alleviate bread shortages. • BB flour is fortified with iron.	n.a.
2009	• The decree determines the required specifications for the bakeries producing tabaki bread. • The weight of a tabaki bread loaf is increased to 140 grams, and its price is increased to 20 piastres. A small tabaki loaf of 80 grams is sold for 10 piastres.	175
	• All bakeries are specified to produce *taree* (soft) bread with 76% extraction flour, with the following specifications: (a) a loaf for 20 piastres, weight of 150 grams, diameter not less than 22 centimeters, and moisture not more than 36% and (b) a loaf for 10 piastres, weight of 85 grams, diameter not less than 18 centimeters, and moisture not more than 36%.	46
2011	• The military intervenes to alleviate bread shortages after the January 25 revolution.	n.a.
2012	• The price of subsidized 80% extraction flour for licensed tabaki bakeries is increased to LE 900 per metric ton, up from LE 110 per metric ton.	n.a.
2013	• Signs of success are seen following a smartcard-based pilot project of flour and BB distribution in Port Said.	n.a.
2014	• The BB and ration card programs are newly redesigned and consolidated for the first time in Egyptian history.	10

Note: n.a. = not applicable.

TABLE 3A.2 **Milestones Related to Ration Cards, 1941–2015**

YEAR	MEASURE(S)	DECREE NUMBER
1941	• Rationing is introduced during World War II, with subsidized basic commodities including kerosene and textiles and, later, sugar, oil, tea, and ghee.	n.a.
1943	• Ministry of Supply is established.	n.a.
1945	• Issuance of a decree that has represented the basis for all ration card (RC) system laws. • Subsidized items include kerosene, sugar, cooking oil, and tea.	95

table continues next page

TABLE 3A.2 **Milestones Related to Ration Cards, 1941–2015** *(continued)*

YEAR	MEASURE(S)	DECREE NUMBER
1966	• New RCs are issued for Egyptians and foreigners residing in the country for at least one year.	112
	• Having a civil identification card is the only requirement to get an RC, probably just to ensure no duplication in the registry.	112
	• RCs provide a limited number of strictly rationed food items: sugar, cooking oil, and tea, in addition to kerosene, soap, and some cotton textiles that are provided when available.	
1967	• Most of the regulations governing the management of kerosene are abolished.	42
1970	• More items are put under the management of the General Authority for Supply Commodities (GASC). The complete list includes cereals and beans (wheat, flour, maize, lentils, beans, sesame, green beans, kidney beans); tea, coffee, and sugar; oil, grease, ghee, milk, and dairy products; cattle, sheep, meat, and poultry.	73
1973	• Specific requirements are issued for specific categories of foreigners to get RCs for the items that are available only under the RC system.	404
	• RC items for foreigners are provided at market prices.	
1979	• Foreigners are excluded from holding RCs, except for Sudanese and Palestinians.	5
	• Issuance of new RCs is forbidden starting in February, except for those who could not have theirs issued earlier for compelling reasons, and people are penalized for not notifying the government that they are holding more than one card or for traveling abroad for more than six months without temporarily suspending the RC.	6
1980	• The decree abolishes the existing RCs and replaces them with new ones that exclude certain categories of households: those with emigrants, workers abroad for more than six months, workers in international organizations, workers in investment companies (except service assistance workers), landholders (of more than 10 *feddans*), and persons subject to general revenue tax (except government and public sector employees).	22
	• More subsidized items are covered by RCs: textiles, flour, sugar, chicken, fish, and corn.	
	• Quotas are reduced.	106
	• Newborn children are added on a regular basis, starting January 7.	

table continues next page

TABLE 3A.2 **Milestones Related to Ration Cards, 1941–2015** *(continued)*

YEAR	MEASURE(S)	DECREE NUMBER
1983	• Partially subsidized red RCs are introduced and given to specified better-off categories: those mentioned in Decree 22 for 1980 and the owners of properties that yield rent higher than LE2,000 per year (the tax exemption threshold), luxury cars (with more than a three-cylinder engine), or two cars; owners of private businesses, professionals who have been members of syndicates for more than 15 years, and workers in embassies or in the Arab League.	51
	• All other Egyptians are eligible for fully subsidized green RCs.	51
	• Sudanese and Palestinians are still eligible for special RCs.	51
	• Modifications are made to the eligibility for red RCs: in addition to the categories mentioned in Decree 51 for 1983, owners of luxury cars (with more than a four-cylinder or 2000 cc engine) are eligible.	70
	• The issuance of RCs is eased by allowing the applicants for RCs to declare that the information they have provided in the form is true and correct, so they have no need for certification by another party.	534
1984	• People in better-off categories (mentioned in Decree 51 for 1983) are allowed to get green cards if their income falls below LE 2,000 a month.	419
	• The use of red and green RCs is effective starting October 1, 1984.	452
1987	• Foreigners residing in the country for more than six months are allowed to apply for special red RCs.	483
	• RC holders do not have the right to get their monthly quota in the following month and risk being excluded from the program if they do not receive their quotas for three consecutive months, unless acceptable justification is provided.	483
	• Eligibility for red RCs receives minor modification.	
1988	• Registering children born after October 1988 is stopped, and scrutiny of RCs is discontinued until 2005.	
	• The number of beneficiaries of RCs declines to 38.5 million Egyptians out of 40 million possible beneficiaries.	
1990/91	• Meat is eliminated from RC benefits.	
	• The number of households holding RCs is 84.7% of the population.	
1991/92	• Fish and tea are eliminated from RCs.	
	• The price of a 300-pack of cooking oil is set at 30 piastres for fully subsidized RCs and 50 piastres for partially subsidized RCs.	
	• The monthly quota of cooking oil is set at 500 grams per person in cities and urban areas and 300 grams per person in rural areas.	

table continues next page

TABLE 3A.2 **Milestones Related to Ration Cards, 1941–2015** *(continued)*

YEAR	MEASURE(S)	DECREE NUMBER
	• The monthly quota of domestic sugar is set at 1 kilogram per person at a price of 50 piastres for fully subsidized RCs and 75 piastres for partially subsidized RCs.	
1992/93	• Rice is eliminated from RC quotas.	
1993/94	• A review of paper RCs results in replacing RCs with two types: green (totally subsidized) and red (partially subsidized)	
	• Items (other than sugar and oil) that were of poor quality and not bought by consumers are gradually phased out.	
	• The benefits received by beneficiaries are estimated at LE 16 per household.	
1996	• For the first time, categories eligible for fully subsidized RCs are specified, allowing all other categories to apply for partially subsidized RCs.	152
	• Eligible categories include (a) government and public sector employees and pensioners; (b) recipients of social solidarity and Sadat pensions; (c) seasonal, temporary, agriculture, and irregular workers; (d) widowed and divorced of the previous categories; and (e) others who prove to be deserving.	152
1997	• 69.2% of the population hold RCs, of which 7.3 percent hold low-subsidy cards.	
	• The price of domestic sugar is increased to 60 piastres for fully subsidized RCs and to 85 piastres for partially subsidized RCs.	
1999	• All subsidized items are eliminated, except for cooking oil and sugar.	
	• The monthly quota of cooking oil is 500 grams for cities (retailed at 50 piastres for fully subsidized RCs and at 75 piastres for partially subsidized RCs) and 300 grams for villages and *markazs* (retailed at 30 piastres for fully subsidized RCs and at 50 piastres for partially subsidized RCs).	
	• Green RCs cover 8.37 million households or 36.2 million individuals, and red RCs cover 1.6 million households or 6.8 million individuals, with total coverage of almost 10 million households or 42.4 million individuals.	
	• The private sector is allowed to produce, distribute, and export food items that are under the RC system.	
2001	• The market price of sugar is 170 piastres per kilogram, and the price of cooking oil is 575 piastres per kilogram. The price of 82% extraction wheat flour is 175 piastres per kilogram.	
2002	• The list of categories eligible for fully subsidized RCs is expanded, broadening coverage to include the most vulnerable.	225

table continues next page

TABLE 3A.2 **Milestones Related to Ration Cards, 1941–2015** *(continued)*

YEAR	MEASURE(S)	DECREE NUMBER
2003	• The market price of sugar is increased to 225 piastres per kilogram, that of cooking oil is increased to 825 piastres per kilogram, and that of wheat flour is increased to 225 piastres per kilogram. • All RCs issued before 2003 are considered canceled and nonrenewable.	
2004	• Seven new items are added to the RC program: – Cooking oil (0.5 kilogram per person, maximum 2 kilograms per household, at LE 3.50 per kilogram) – Rice (1 kilogram per person, maximum 4 kilograms per household, at LE 1 per kilogram) – Pasta (1 kilogram per person, maximum 4 kilograms per household, at LE 1.5 per kilogram) – Lentils (0.5 kilogram per person, maximum 2 kilograms per household, as LE 3 per kilogram) – Beans (0.5 kilogram per person, maximum 2 kilograms per household, at 2 LE per kilogram) – Ghee (2-kilogram pack per household, at LE 9 per pack) – Tea (50 grams per person, at LE 0.65)	75
2005	• The price of subsidized cooking oil for a 500-gram pack is set at 50 piastres for fully subsidized RCs and at 75 piastres for partially subsidized RCs. • The number of beneficiaries is 8.3 million households or 39.6 million Egyptians (56% of the population). • Of all RC system beneficiaries, 19% carry red RCs. • Additional items are eliminated because of their poor quality, reducing subsidized items to sugar, oil, and rice. • RC subsidies are distributed by 36,000 *tamween* grocery stores. • The total subsidy of LE 15.6 billion equals US$2.5 billion.	
2006	• A smartcard system for RCs is implemented.	
2007	• Beneficiaries total 11.5 million households or 38.3 million individuals (51.5% of the population).	
2008	• Red RCs are canceled, and quotas and prices of subsidized items are unified among all beneficiaries.	62
	• Children born after 1988 are added to the RC system (for the first time since 1988).	7
	• Beneficiaries total 10.8 million households or 57.7 million individuals.	
	• Strikes and demonstrations occur in Mahal Kobra because of food price increases.	

table continues next page

TABLE 3A.2 **Milestones Related to Ration Cards, 1941–2015** (continued)

YEAR	MEASURE(S)	DECREE NUMBER
2009	• A detailed list of the neediest categories eligible for RCs is presented, with a new threshold of LE 400 per month household income and a maximum of four beneficiaries per household.	31
	• Changes in the categories of the neediest (first-care) groups eligible for RCs are mentioned in Decree 31 for 2009, with an increase in the threshold to LE 750 for pensioners and LE 1,000 for government and public sector employees.	84
	• Beneficiaries total 11.8 million households or 63.1 million individuals registered at 25,129 tamween groceries.	
2010	• The price of basic and additional cooking oil is set at LE 3 per kilogram and of sugar at LE 1 per kilogram starting on May 1.	20
	• The price of sugar increases to LE 1.25 per kilogram starting on July 1.	33
	• Regulations are set for dealing with the smartcard RCs.	37
	• The regulations for dealing with smart RCs are revised.	
	• All tamween supply stores are to be open 6 days of the week, for 2 time periods, for a minimum of 5 hours each period.	45
	• Beneficiaries total 12 million households or 63.4 million individuals, and 24,975 tamween groceries participate.	
2011	• Changes in the eligibility criteria increase the maximum monthly income to LE 800 for informal workers, LE 1,200 for pensioners, and LE 1,500 for formal workers.	15
	• The number of beneficiaries of RCs is limited to 4 people per household, with no addition afterwards, even in cases of death, traveling abroad, and so on.	
	• Beneficiaries total 15.8 million households or 64.7 million individuals.	
2012	• Beneficiaries total 17.7 million households or 66.7 million individuals.	
2013	• Tamween groceries are required to open 10 hours on weekdays (12 (noon–10 p.m., November through April; 1 p.m.–11 p.m., May–October).	134
	• The working hours of tamween groceries are reduced to 2 p.m.–10 p.m., 6 days a week.	447
	• The decree relieves RC beneficiaries who voluntarily notify the state about the eligibility of some members registered on the RCs (because of death, travel longer than 6 months, or duplication) from paying the price differences, if they do this before December 31, 2013.	Prime Minister Decree 1164
	• Beneficiaries total 18.5 million households or 66.7 million individuals, and 24,003 groceries participate.	

table continues next page

Milestones Related to Ration Cards, 1941–2015 *(continued)*

YEAR	MEASURE(S)	DECREE NUMBER
2014	• Relieving RC beneficiaries who voluntarily notify the state about the eligibility of some members registered on the RCs (because of death, travel longer than 6 months, or duplication), and tamween groceries that notify about the accurate number of RCs registered with them, from paying the price differences, if they do this before June 30, 2014.	Prime Minister Decree 978
	• All tamween groceries are to be open 6 days a week, 1 p.m.–11 p.m.	
	• A paradigm shift in the system replaces monthly quotas of a specific set of food items for a maximum number of 4 individuals per family with a monthly cash allotment of LE 15 per person and no limit on the number of beneficiaries per family, to buy any of a much larger set of items.	312
	• A points-based reward system is established that uses smartcards and allows beneficiaries to use savings from BB consumption for buying commodities under the RC system, thus consolidating the RC and BB programs into one new system.	
2015	• All children age 2 and older are added to the RCs of their households.	153
	• Beneficiaries total 20.6 million households or 68.9 million Egyptians, and 25,684 tamween groceries participate.	

ANNEX 3B. MAIN RESULTS OF THE BENEFICIARY SURVEY

TABLE 3B.1 Results of the Beneficiary Survey, by Region and Income Quintile, May 2016

% of respondents

ASPECT	WHOLE SAMPLE	BY REGION (%)			BY INCOME QUINTILE				
		METROPOLITAN	LOWER EGYPT	UPPER EGYPT	Q1 (POOREST)	Q2	Q3	Q4	Q5 (RICHEST)
Baladi bread system									
Quality: How do you see the quality of bread in the new versus the old system?									
Better	90.9	82	97.3	88.1	89.6	89	93.3	87.9	95.7
Worse	2.0	2.9	1.5	2	2.2	1.7	1.8	3.2	0.8
Same	7.1	15.1	1.2	9.9	8.2	9.2	4.9	8.9	3.5
Adequacy: Is the amount of bread allowed on the card adequate?									
Yes	88.3	92.7	99.1	93.9	92.9	94.5	96.9	98.1	96.9
No	3.8	7.3	0.9	6.1	7.1	5.5	3.1	1.9	3.1
Availability									
Always	32.0	46.7	16.9	42	33.3	32.8	35.3	27	34.1
Sometimes	66.9	51.2	82.7	56.5	64.7	66.2	62.9	72.3	65.5
Rarely	1.1	2.1	0.3	1.5	1.9	1	1.8	0.6	0.4
Queuing waiting times									
<15 minutes	84.0	87.7	94.8	70.5	77.5	80.8	85.2	84.9	91.4

table continues next page

TABLE 3B.1 Results of the Beneficiary Survey, by Region and Income Quintile, May 2016 *(continued)*

% of respondents

ASPECT	WHOLE SAMPLE	BY REGION (%)			BY INCOME QUINTILE				
		METROPOLITAN	LOWER EGYPT	UPPER EGYPT	Q1 (POOREST)	Q2	Q3	Q4	Q5 (RICHEST)
15–30 minutes	13.4	11.8	4.7	23.6	16.6	15.3	13.4	13.8	8.3
>30 minutes	2.6	0.4	0.5	6	6.5	3.8	3.8	1.3	0.4
Ration card system[a]									
Is the new or old system better for you and your family?									
New	58.7	47.3	67.1	55	45.9	52	60.4	33.8	75.6
Old	38.5	50.6	29.5	42.6	52.2	46.6	36.4	61.5	22.4
Do you prefer the diversity of commodities in the new system?									
Yes	59.0	50.8	69.3	51.7	43.7	52	62.7	63.4	74.1
No	39.0	47.2	27.6	47.8	54.9	46.6	35.1	34.4	23.5
Quality: How do you see the quality of commodities in the new versus the old system?									
Better	55.5	61.8	69	38.2	43.3	50.7	54.7	59.2	70.6
Some	39.5	36.6	27.6	53.5	46.3	45.2	42.2	35.7	27.1
Worse	5.0	1.6	3.4	8.3	10.4	4.1	3.1	5.1	2.4
Perceived subsidy size in the new versus the old system									
Same	39.6	37	50.1	29.6	29.1	37.1	45.3	41.4	47.5

table continues next page

TABLE 3B.1 Results of the Beneficiary Survey, by Region and Income Quintile, May 2016 (continued)

% of respondents

ASPECT	WHOLE SAMPLE	BY REGION (%)			BY INCOME QUINTILE				
		METROPOLITAN	LOWER EGYPT	UPPER EGYPT	Q1 (POOREST)	Q2	Q3	Q4	Q5 (RICHEST)
More	7.3	4.1	3.8	12.5	9.3	6.8	4.4	8.3	6.7
Less	53.1	Less 58.9	46.1	57.9	61.6	56.1	50.2	50.3	45.9
Quality of sugar in the new system									
Excellent	81.4	82.5	76.1	86.4	78.7	81.1	80.9	82.7	85.1
Good	17.7	17.1	→22.5	13.1	20.5	17.9	18.2	16.6	14.1
Low	0.9	0.4	1.4	0.6	0.7	1	0.9	0.6	0.8
Availability of sugar in the new system									
Always	69.4	65.4	63.8	77.2	65.7	68.4	71.4	69.3	74.9
Sometimes	25.6	32.1	30.3	17.6	29.1	27.1	22.3	26.2	20.4
Rarely	5.0	2.4	5.9	5.1	5.2	4.5	6.4	4.5	4.7
Quantity of sugar purchased in the new versus old system[b]									
Same	47.1	40.7	47.9	49.1	45.9	44.4	48.4	46.5	51
More	8.6	13	5.8	9.4	10.4	12.3	9.9	5.4	5.5
Less	44.4	46.3	46.2	41.5	43.7	43.3	41.7	48.1	43.5

table continues next page

TABLE 3B.1 Results of the Beneficiary Survey, by Region and Income Quintile, May 2016 (continued)

% of respondents

ASPECT	WHOLE SAMPLE	BY REGION (%)			BY INCOME QUINTILE				
		METROPOLITAN	LOWER EGYPT	UPPER EGYPT	Q1 (POOREST)	Q2	Q3	Q4	Q5 (RICHEST)
Quality of rice in the new system									
Excellent	60.9	50.2	74.7	60.7	69.7	60.9	50.3	58.9	63.2
Good	32.6	44.6	21.9	31.3	27.2	35.6	44.4	33.2	20.5
Low	6.4	5.2	3.4	8	3.1	3.5	5.3	7.9	16.2
Availability of rice in the new system									
Always	24.5	23	55.6	13.1	16.9	22.8	27.2	26.8	33.3
Sometimes	39.4	51.2	35.4	35.9	40	44.6	41.7	36.8	29.9
Rarely	36.1	25.8	9	51	43.1	32.7	31.1	36.3	36.8
Quantity of rice purchased by the new versus old system									
Same	31.1	32.1	48.6	12	20.1	29.3	36.3	33.7	37.4
More	6.7	13.4	6.4	3.7	7.1	9.3	9	5.1	3.1
Less	62.2	54.5	45	84.3	72.8	61.4	54.7	61.2	59.4
Quality of oil in the new system									
Excellent	68.7	55.2	23	23	71.0	63.2	66.5	66.9	77.5
Good	26.4	51.2	51.2	51.2	25.9	31.1	28.8	27.2	17.2
Low	5.0	25.8	25.8	25.8	3.1	5.7	4.7	5.9	5.3

table continues next page

TABLE 3B.1 **Results of the Beneficiary Survey, by Region and Income Quintile, May 2016** *(continued)*

% of respondents

ASPECT	WHOLE SAMPLE	BY REGION (%)			BY INCOME QUINTILE				
		METROPOLITAN	LOWER EGYPT	UPPER EGYPT	Q1 (POOREST)	Q2	Q3	Q4	Q5 (RICHEST)
Availability of oil									
Always	26.3	20.9	32.9	21.6	21.2	21.8	26.0	24.6	40.6
Sometimes	41.0	61.3	27.1	47.4	41.3	46.8	42.8	42.0	32.0
Rarely	32.7	17.8	40	31.1	37.5	31.4	31.2	33.4	27.5
Quantity of oil purchased by the new versus the old system									
Same	28.5	31.7	46.2	14	22	29	34.1	32.4	37.6
More	3.1	10.2	0.9	3	3.4	4.4	2.2	3.2	3.5
Less	60.3	58.1	52.9	83	74	66.6	63.7	64.4	58.8

Note: A quantitative survey was undertaken in May 2016 on a random sample of 1,500 observations from geographically representative regions. The beneficiary survey was funded by the World Bank and conducted by Heba El-Laithy, consultant and professor at Cairo University, in collaboration with EgyPol.
a. The questions were asked to assess the perceptions of beneficiaries about the new system compared to the old one.
b. The quantity dimension reflects the adequacy of the system with respect to the size of benefit and quantity of commodities.

NOTES

1. In contemporary history, food subsidies date back to the years after World War I (1914–18), when the government imported large quantities of wheat and flour and sold them in government outlets at discounted prices to mitigate high international food commodity prices (Scobie 1981). Formal rationing was introduced only in 1941, during World War II. At that time, the Egyptian government adopted a universal subsidy program as a temporary measure to alleviate the negative effects of wartime scarcities on living standards, as well as to control the supply and price of basic goods.

2. The name of the ministry responsible for food subsidies has changed several times over the past century. It started as the Ministry of Supply (MOS) and remained so for most of the years since then. Yet, in some phases, internal trade was merged into it and the name changed to the Ministry of Supply and Internal Trade (MOSIT); between 2005 and 2010 it became the Ministry of Social Solidarity (MOSS), also carrying the mandate of cash transfers. After the 2011 revolution, the name changed to the Ministry of Social Solidarity and Justice and then the Ministry of Solidarity and Internal Trade, but since 2014 the name has become MOSIT. MOS and MOSIT are used interchangeably, depending on the phase to which we are referring.

3. All the cited data and related findings in this chapter are as of June 30, 2016.

4. The amounts allocated for cash transfer programs altogether (Takaful and Karama) in the fiscal year 2016/17 budget amount to 0.4 percent of GDP. The relationship between FSS and the new cash transfer programs is not clearly articulated in the current strategy. Hitherto, the effort of MOSS was mainly focused on ensuring that all beneficiaries of Takaful and Karama (who are among the extreme poor in Egypt) also receive FSS cards, which, according to MOSS, was not always the case.

5. Calculated from the HIECS of 2012–13, conducted by the Central Agency for Public Mobilization and Statistics (CAPMAS).

6. See, for example, the Constitution of the Arab Republic of Egypt, 2014 (http://www.sis .gov.eg/Newvr/Dustor-en001.pdf), and the Sustainable Development Strategy: Egypt Vision 2030 (http://sdsegypt2030.com/?lang=en).

7. Based on the currency exchange rate in July 2014.

8. Nonmilled wheat was calculated based on the monthly data published by MOSIT.

9. Interview by M. Abdalla with head of the Minister's Office, MOSIT, 2015.

10. Egypt Demographic and Health Survey 2014 (http://microdata.worldbank.org/index .php/catalog/2269).

11. Government officials did not deny or confirm those numbers.

12. There are no data for food subsidies in the years between 1960 and 1970. The figures were taken from El Essawi (2007) and Alderman, Von Braun, and Sakr (1982).

13. P.L. 480 is another name for the U.S. Food for Peace Program, which was signed into law in 1954. The United States uses its agricultural productivity to promote U.S. foreign policy by enhancing the food security of low- and middle-income countries through agricultural commodities. U.S. food aid programs, including P.L. 480, have been consistently modified to keep pace with economic and political changes in the world.

14. There is evidence that U.S. aid to Egypt between 1955 and 1967, which was available through P.L. 480, encouraged the food subsidy apparatus as an institution, even though the food was provided unreliably (Blue and others 1983).

15. Regulated-price nonfood items included butane cooking gas (46 percent increase), gasoline (26–31 percent increase), and cigarettes.

16. Alderman and von Braun both report being shown printed versions in the office of then–Deputy Minister of Economy Ismail Badawi in 1981 (Alderman, personal communication).

17. The remaining subsidies constitute basically fuel subsidies.

18. Some critics claim that the increase in procured domestic wheat could be explained by the large difference between the prices of domestic and imported wheat, which encouraged private intermediaries to import wheat and sell it to the government.
19. The governorates are Assyut, Aswan, Behira, Fayoum, Giza, Luxor, Matrouh, New Valley, North Sinar, Qena, Red Sea, Souhag, and South Sinai.
20. The beneficiary survey was conducted by Heba El-Laithy, consultant and professor at Cairo University, in collaboration with EgyPol (El-Laithy 2016). The survey was conducted in the midst of significant media criticism over the shortage of some basic commodities (rice and oil).
21. Among the respondents from Upper Egypt, 51 percent stated that rice was hard to find, compared with metropolitan areas and Lower Egypt, which reported 25.8 and 9.0 percent availability, respectively. Oil was also reported to be hard to find in Lower Egypt by 40 percent of respondents, compared with 31 percent in Upper Egypt and 18 percent in metropolitan areas.

REFERENCES

Abdel-Khalek, Gouda. 1981. "Looking Outside or Turning Northwest? On the Meaning and External Dimension of Egypt's Infitah, 1971–1980." *Social Problems* 28 (4): 394–409.

Ahmed, Akhter U., Tamar Gutner, Hans Löfgren, and Howarth E. Bouis. 2001. "The Egyptian Food Subsidy System." Report 119, International Food Policy Research Institute, Washington, DC.

Alderman, Harold. 1986. "Food Subsidies and State Policy in Egypt." In *Food, States, and Peasants: Analyses of the Agrarian Question in the Middle East*, edited by Alan Richards. Boulder, CO: Westview Press.

Alderman, Harold, Joachim Von Braun, and Ahmed Sakr. 1982. *Egypt's Food Subsidy and Rationing System: A Description*. Washington, DC: International Food Policy Research Institute.

Al-Shawarby, Sherine, and Heba El-Laithy. 2010. "Egypt's Food Subsidies: Benefit Incidence and Leakage." Social and Economic Development Group Report 57446, World Bank, Washington, DC.

Baker, Raymond William. 1978. *Egypt's Uncertain Revolution under Nasser and Sadat.* Cambridge, MA: Harvard University Press.

Blue, Richard N., David W. Dunlop, Michael Goldman, and Lloyd S. Harbert. 1983. "PL 480 Title I: The Egyptian Case, AID Project Impact Evaluation." AID Project Impact Evaluation Report 45, U.S. Agency for International Development, Washington, DC.

CAPMAS (Central Agency for Public Mobilization and Statistics). Various years. *Household Income, Expenditure, and Consumption Expenditure Survey (HIECS)*. Cairo: CAPMAS.

EHCSS (Egyptian Holding Company for Silos and Storage). 2016. "Current and Planned National Storage Capacity of Wheat per Governorate." Unpublished report, EHCSS, Cairo.

El Essawi, Ibrahim. 2007. *The Egyptian Economy in Thirty Years: Analysis of Macroeconomic Developments since 1974 and Their Social Implications, with a Suggested Alternative Growth Model* [in Arabic]. Cairo: Academic Library.

El-Leithy, Heba. 2016. *Beneficiary Survey on the New Food Subsidy System*. Washington, DC: World Bank.

Farrar, Curt. 2000. "A Review of Food Subsidy Research at IFPRI." Impact Assessment Discussion Paper 12, International Food Policy Research Institute, Washington, DC.

Feiler, Gil. 2003. *Economic Relations between Egypt and the Gulf Oil States, 1967–2000: Petro Wealth and Patterns of Influence*. Brighton, U.K.: Sussex Academic.

GASC (General Authority for Supply Commodities). 2016. "Wheat Imports, Price, and Storage Data." Unpublished report, GASC, Cairo.

Hashish, Adel. 1980. *Commodity Subsidy and Food Security: Analytical Study of the Problems Factors in Developing Countries and the Feasibility of Economic and Financial Policies in Egypt* [in Arabic]. Alexandria, Egypt: Dar El Gameaat El Masreya.

Hopkins, Raymond F. 1988. "Political Calculations in Subsidizing Food." In *Consumer-Oriented Food Subsidies: Costs, Benefits, and Policy Options for Developing Countries*, edited by Per Pinstrup-Andersen, 107–26. Baltimore, MD: Johns Hopkins University Press.

Ikram, Khaled. 2006. *The Egyptian Economy, 1952–2000: Performance, Policies, and Issues.* Routledge Studies in Middle Eastern Economies. London: Routledge.

Kamal, Oday. 2015. *Half-Baked, the Other Side of Egypt's Baladi Bread Subsidy.* Barcelona, Spain: Center for International Affairs.

Perry, Tom, and Abdel Rahman Youssef. 2013. "Egypt's Brotherhood Turns to Flour Power." Special report, *Reuters*, June 13. http://graphics.thomsonreuters.com/13/06 /MuslimBrotherhood.pdf.

Sachs, Ram. 2012. "On Bread and Circuses: Food Subsidy Reform and Popular Opposition in Egypt." PhD thesis, Center for International Security and Cooperation, Stanford University, Stanford, CA. http://cisac.fsi.stanford.edu/sites/default/files/CISAC_Thesis _Sachs.pdf.

Scobie, Grant. 1981. "Government Policy and Food Imports: The Case of Wheat in Egypt." Research Report 29, International Food Policy Research Institute, Washington, DC.

WFP (World Food Programme). 2013. *The Status of Poverty and Food Security in Egypt: Analysis and Policy Recommendations.* Cairo: WFP.

World Bank. 2005. "Egypt Toward a More Effective Social Policy: Subsidies and Social Safety Net." Report 33550-EG, Social and Economic Development Group, Middle East and North Africa Region, World Bank, Washington DC.

CHAPTER 4

Food-Based Social Assistance Programs in Sri Lanka

EVOLUTION AND TRANSITION TO CASH TRANSFERS

Ganga Tilakaratna and Chinthani Sooriyamudali

INTRODUCTION

As illustrated in chapter 1 of this volume, at a first glance, Sri Lanka's food-oriented social assistance (FOSA) system appears to have been transformed completely over time. Its core food subsidy program went (a) from a near-universal provision of food to a more targeted voucher-like scheme, (b) then to an even more narrowly targeted combination of cash and food rations, and (c) finally to a targeted cash transfer. FOSA might look like an "ideal" case of what a designer concerned about maximizing performance would conceive. But, in fact, as this chapter shows, the evolution has been far from linear.

Each of the steps forward was accompanied by setbacks, and what was achieved even with the full transition was very far from well-performing benchmarks, especially with regard to targeting and adequacy. *Samurdhi*, the program that has emerged from this complex history, has nevertheless helped to reduce the fiscal cost of the program and become closely integrated with other social safety nets. In that, Sri Lanka fits the global pattern of transformation.

This chapter analyzes in more detail the evolution of the FOSA in Sri Lanka. FOSA was introduced in the 1940s to provide universal access to food during World War II, and its evolution has been unsteady during the past seven decades. Economic conditions and changes in the political regime have influenced the outlook for the government's social welfare policy. With liberalization of the economy in the late 1970s, the scheme changed from a universal to a targeted one, and the benefits were defined in terms of the quantity of food that could be bought for the value of a "food stamp" issued by the government.

With the introduction of *Janasaviya* in the late 1980s, the social welfare strategy shifted from ensuring food security and nutrition levels to reducing poverty via employment creation and to achieving social mobilization and empowerment. With *Samurdhi*, which supplanted Janasaviya, greater emphasis was placed on poverty alleviation, and the food stamp component was replaced by a cash grant in 2012.

The remainder of this chapter analyzes the evolution in detail, describing, in turn, the universal food ration scheme (1942–79), the food stamp scheme (1979–89), Janasaviya (1989–94), and Samurdhi (1995–2015). A final section analyzes the transition from FOSA to cash transfers and the underlying factors that led to those changes.

The chapter is based primarily on secondary sources, including published reports, complemented by a small number of interviews with subject area experts and government officials.

FOOD RATION SCHEME, 1942–79

From 1942 to 1979, the main FOSA program in Sri Lanka was universal (until 1978) and based on entitlement to a certain quantity of food. In 1979, the per capita food assistance given by the government was limited to the amount of food that could be purchased for the value of a stamp. Up to this point, the per capita entitlement was a certain quantity of food that could be purchased at a subsidized price (and, at certain points, a quantity of food provided free of charge).

Introduction of a Universal Food Ration Scheme, 1942–52

The food-rationing scheme was first introduced in 1942 as an emergency measure of public welfare during World War II (Edirisinghe 1982; Gavan and Chandrasekara 1979; Jayasuriya 2004). It was originally intended as a wartime relief measure to ensure the equitable distribution of food supplies during a time when food imports were scarce (Edirisinghe 1982).

The program was not dismantled with the end of the war and survived for nearly three decades more. Edirisinghe (1982) argues that "continuation of the rice-rationing scheme was the logical consequence" within a postwar context in which the abolition of controls, combined with repressed demand and an excess money supply, caused postwar inflation, leading to a rapid rise in the cost of living.[1] The government continued the food subsidy scheme to prevent low-income groups from being adversely affected by the higher cost of living. According to Ratnayake (2013), the food subsidy scheme was established, in part, to counteract inflation, which was, in fact, reined in somewhat via the rationed prices of food.

However, controlling inflation was not the only reason that the universal policy was promoted and continued after the war ended. A mix of social, political, and economic factors contributed to its continuation.

After World War II, most of the country's population did not pay income tax and could be considered "poor," rendering any mechanism to distinguish between eligible and noneligible households redundant. Determining eligibility would have been an "unfruitful, meaningless, as well as an administratively cumbersome exercise," especially because the international prices of food were low (Ratnayake 1998). Therefore, at its inception, this comprehensive, generous, and universal food subsidy scheme appeared to be fiscally sustainable.

The scheme was not only a reaction to certain economic and social conditions but also a result of the welfare-oriented nature of Sri Lanka's public policy. Sri Lanka has a relatively high level of welfare-oriented public policy and human development. The origins of this welfare state can be traced back to Sri Lanka's colonial past and the British influence. The social liberalism prevailing in Britain during the colonial period influenced Sri Lankan political ideology and its welfare-oriented policies, leading to the universal food-rationing scheme and its continuation for nearly three decades.

The role that food subsidies played in Sri Lankan politics also was a factor in its continuation. Over the years, the subsidy program evolved from a mere wartime welfare measure to a political tool that held considerable sway over the populace. It simply was not politically feasible to interfere with the subsidy program without risking political capital.

When the food-rationing scheme was first introduced, the food supply was divided into food in which the country was self-sufficient and food in which it was not. Initially, rationing and price controls were introduced only for foods in which the country was not self-sufficient. However, that decision created a significant increase in the demand for domestically produced rice, and the black market price of domestic rice rose drastically. Therefore, in 1943, the distinction was removed, and the country's entire population (everyone age 3 and older) was entitled to receive the ration (Edirisinghe and Poleman 1976; Gavan and Chandrasekara 1979).

Food items distributed under the ration included rice, chili, canned milk, flour, and meat (Ratnayake 2013).[2] In February 1942, all of the beneficiaries were entitled to receive 4 pounds of rice. However, in July 1942 the entitlement was reduced because of supply constraints (Edirisinghe and Poleman 1976). Until the 1950s, the weekly ration of rice per capita fluctuated between 1 and 5 pounds, depending on availability. Whenever the rice ration was reduced, the wheat subsidy was increased to compensate.[3] By the early 1950s, the age requirement for receiving rationed rice was lowered to 1 year (Gavan and Chandrasekara 1979).

The next section discusses a pivotal moment in Sri Lankan history—the food riots that took place following a government attempt to rationalize food subsidy expenditure in September 1952.

The Food Riots (Harthal) and the Aftermath, 1952–66

The universal food subsidy program in Sri Lanka was implemented because of global food scarcity. The program was affected greatly by fluctuations in the price of rice and in the availability of rice on international markets because a large portion of the Sri Lankan food supply came from imports.[4]

Global agricultural production recovered slowly after the war, and world rice production did not reach the average output of the prewar era until the early 1950s. By that time, the Sri Lankan population (as well as the global population) was growing rapidly, and the global supply of rice was not sufficient to satisfy the higher global demand. As a result, prices continued to rise, peaking in 1952 (Edirisinghe and Poleman 1976).

Additionally, the international food market was affected by the Korean War. In a report issued in 1951, the Food and Agriculture Organization of the United Nations (FAO 1951, 8) elaborated on the prevailing situation of the world food market:

> There was a marked increase in wholesale purchases: Business inventories increased rapidly, and prices advanced at extraordinary rates. The volume and composition of international trade in agricultural goods were affected, and both the domestic and international structure of agricultural prices was appreciably altered.

At that time, the selling price (that is, the ration price) should have been increased along with import costs or at least kept constant. Instead, the price was actually reduced on several occasions, and the government's food subsidy bill continued to rise (Edirisinghe and Poleman 1976).

In 1952, the government took steps to ease the burden of food subsidies. The result was the introduction of an "austerity program" to reduce the universal subsidy entitlement without changing the price charged (Edirisinghe and Poleman 1976). In July 1953, that move was followed by the government's first attempt to increase the price of rationed rice from SL Rs 0.125 to SL Rs 0.35 per pound.[5] As illustrated in table 4.1 (which charts movements in the quantity of entitlement and prices from 1952 to 1977), there was a corresponding 0.5-pound increase in the allotment of rationed rice, perhaps in compensation for the price increase.

The subsidy reforms had to be abandoned, despite the fact that, in fiscal year 1953/54, the expenditure on rice subsidy was half of what it had been

TABLE 4.1 **Changes in the Allotment and Price of Free and Paid Rice Ration and Paid Wheat Ration in Sri Lanka, 1952–77**

| | ALLOTMENT (POUNDS PER WEEK) | | | | PRICE (SL RS PER POUND) | |
| | RICE | | | WHEAT | | |
DATE OF CHANGE	FREE	PAID	TOTAL	PAID	RATION RICE	RATION WHEAT
September 1952	0	2	2	0	12.5[a]	n.a.
July 1953	0	2.5	2.5	0	35.0[a]	n.a.
October 1953	0	2.5	2.5	0	27.5[a]	n.a.
November 1954	0	4	4	0	27.5	n.a.
May 1955	0	4	4	0	25.0	n.a.
October 1955	0	4	4	0	12.5	n.a.
May 1956	0	4	4	0	20.0	n.a.
June 1958	0	4	4	0	17.5	n.a.
June 1959	0	4	4	0	12.5/22.5[b]	n.a.
April 1960	0	4	4	0	12.5	n.a.
December 1966	2	0	2	0	0.0	n.a.
September 1970	2	2	4	0	37.5	n.a.
February 1973	2	2	4	0	50.0	n.a.
October 1973[c]	1	2	3	1	100.0	70
April 1974	1	1[d]	2	0.5	115.0	70
August 1974	1	1	2	0.5[e]	110.0	110
December 1974	1	1	2	1	110.0	110
March 1975	1	1	2	0	110.0	n.a.
November 1975	1	1	2	0	100.0	n.a.
1977	1	3	4	0	100.0	n.a.

Source: Gavan and Chandrasekara 1979.
Note: n.a. = not applicable.
[a.] Infants and children received less, workers received more.
[b.] The price for the first 2 pounds was 12.5 cents and for the next 2 pounds was 22.5 cents.
[c.] Income taxpayers were no longer eligible for free rice ration.
[d.] In the urban areas of rice-deficit districts, 2 pounds of paid rice ration were issued.
[e.] The estate sector received a larger wheat flour ration of 1.5 pounds, and the wheat ration in Colombo and some other urban areas was increased to 1 pound.

the year before (Gavan and Chandrasekara 1979). The attempt to reduce the subsidies resulted in a drastic rise in the administered price of rice and other commodities and services. Those significant increases led to widespread protests and food riots (locally referred to as *Harthal*), which were led by organized urban labor.

In the immediate aftermath of the Harthal, the subsidy reforms were partially abandoned, the prime minister resigned, and the new government increased the subsidy benefits. By November 1954, ration quantities were increased to 4 pounds per person per week; the official reason given was the steady fall in world rice prices (Edirisinghe 1987; Gavan and Chandrasekara 1979).

The Harthal had a resounding and lasting impact on the shape of government food policy and proved to be an extremely politically sensitive issue. According to Edirisinghe and Poleman (1976, 60), the significance of the Harthal lies in its repercussions on the politics of rice: "Rice has always been an important political commodity but never was its political significance exhibited in such fashion as was seen in this protest. It marked the beginning of the rice issue that was to loom large in almost every major political campaign in the future years."

In the aftermath of the Harthal, politicians understood that government policy regarding food subsidies could play a key role in both attaining and retaining political power, as is evident in the election statements of all political parties until the presidential election in 1989 (Ratnayake 2013).

After the Harthal, succeeding governments were unwilling to interfere with the program at the risk of losing political capital. As illustrated in table 4.1, the weekly per capita food ration was increased to 4 pounds in November 1954, which continued through the mid-1960s. The price of ration rice was also reduced several times during that period, from SL Rs 0.35 in 1953 to SL Rs 0.125 by 1959 (with one increase in 1956). The price remained at SL Rs 0.125 from 1959 until 1966, regardless of changes in the price of imported rice during the period.

In the period following the Harthal, the changes made to the subsidy program enhanced the benefits for the consumer. Those changes were facilitated by a general decline in world rice prices (Edirisinghe and Poleman 1976). As a result of declining prices and extended coverage, the quantity of rice distributed increased steadily, and by 1965 more than 75 percent of all rice consumed passed through the public system (Gavan and Chandrasekara 1979).

A single attempt to rationalize government expenditure on food subsidies was made during that period, by the minister of finance of the government elected in 1960. To address the country's severe fiscal and balance-of-payments problems, the minister proposed curtailing the subsidy. The proposal was dismissed by the backbenchers, and the minister resigned (Edirisinghe 1987). The fact that the minister's own party refused to support the proposed measures indicates the political sensitivity of the subsidy scheme.

The Food Subsidy Scheme during the Decade Leading up to Economic Liberalization, 1966–77

The next significant change to the food subsidy scheme took place in 1966. As a response to a worldwide rice shortage (and as a necessity borne out of continued balance-of-payments difficulties), the government adopted a policy measure that Edirisinghe (1987) terms a "strategic compromise between economic logic and political feasibility." The government cut the ration quantity by half—to 2 pounds of rice per capita per week—but issued it free of charge. This change did not bring about the desired result.

According to Gavan and Chandrasekara (1979), the new policy measure reduced the proportion of domestic rice consumed by Sri Lankans that was distributed through the ration scheme. The guaranteed price scheme operated by the government also suffered from this measure because the higher demand for open-market rice led the market price of rice to rise above the guaranteed price paid under the government paddy procurement scheme. The increase in the market price, combined with a decrease in the demand for rice provided through the ration scheme, led to a sharp decline in sales to the government. Furthermore, issuing the whole ration free of charge created a loss in revenue that neutralized any gains made from halving the entitlement. Meanwhile, import and procurement prices continued to rise, causing the food subsidy bill to rise as well.

The government's decision to reduce the food subsidy was a main topic during the parliamentary election held in 1970. The opposition heavily criticized the subsidy and promised citizens to increase the rice ration if elected to power (Ratnayake 2013). Political power changed hands during the election, and rice politics played a part in this power shift.

True to its word, the new government increased the amount of subsidy benefits. In addition to the 2 pounds of rice that people had been receiving free of charge, the government decided to give 2 more pounds of rice per person per week at a rationed price. However, the price of the paid portion of rice was significantly higher than the price charged before 1966 (Gavan and Chandrasekara 1979; Ratnayake 2013).

During the 1970–72 period, the world paddy harvests were good, rice was sufficiently available, and prices were somewhat low. However, bad weather put an end to that trend in 1972 (Edirisinghe and Poleman 1976). By 1973, world rice prices were high, creating additional pressure on the government's finances. In addition, an unexpected rise in the world price of oil further strained the government's fiscal position (Ratnayake 2013).

That scenario resulted in major changes to the food ration scheme. The price of rationed rice was increased in 1973. The free portion of rationed rice was reduced by 1 pound, and the total portion of rice ration per capita per week was reduced to 3 pounds. To compensate for the 1-pound decrease in rice ration, 1 pound of wheat flour was offered at a ration price that was lower than the price of ration rice (Gavan and Chandrasekara 1979).

As an additional measure to ease the burden of the food subsidy scheme, income taxpayers—who represented only a small fraction of the population— were no longer eligible to receive free rice in 1973 (Edirisinghe 1987). Thereafter, taxpayers (that is, individuals with a monthly income more than SL Rs 1,000) had to pay for their entire ration, whereas nontaxpayers were entitled to a portion of the ration free of charge (along with the portion charged at the subsidized price). In 1973, taxpayers were entitled to 4 pounds of rice but were charged at the subsidized price (Ratnayake 2013). This policy measure continued until 1976—the quantity of ration entitlement was changed, but taxpayers continued to pay for the whole ration. In 1976, taxpayers were excluded from the food ration scheme altogether (Ratnayake 2013).

From 1973 to 1975, the government maintained a monopoly on procurement to ensure that sufficient supplies were available to distribute under the ration (Edirisinghe and Poleman 1976; Gavan and Chandrasekara 1979). That policy limited the quantity of paddy that private individuals could transport to a very small amount. However, the rapid increase in the price of paddy resulted in the legislation being annulled in 1975 (Gavan and Chandrasekara 1979).

Economic Liberalization and the Food Subsidy Scheme, 1977–79
In 1977, the Sri Lankan economy was liberalized, and the government elected that year implemented significant modifications to the food subsidy scheme.

The new government had two main objectives: to liberalize the trading system and to raise domestic savings, according to Edirisinghe (1987). That policy outlook had a decisive impact on the food subsidy program. The time had come to acknowledge that, although the universal food subsidy scheme had played a major role in improving the quality of life of Sri Lankans, the cost of providing subsidized food to the entire population was no longer fiscally viable. Additionally, the new policies had led to a considerable devaluation of the currency by early 1978, which resulted in a substantial increase in the total food subsidy bill. That situation created an additional incentive to curb the food subsidy bill (Edirisinghe 1987).

However, political concerns also had to be addressed. Since its inception, the food subsidy scheme had proven to be extremely politically sensitive. Therefore, reductions in the food subsidy were "strategically phased" to minimize adverse reactions. Changes to the program were carried out over a two-year period (Edirisinghe 1987). As the first step, a means test was conducted in January 1978, leading to a decision to restrict subsidized rice to families with a monthly income below SL Rs 300; that is, approximately 50 percent of the population was entitled to receive 1 pound of rice free of charge and 3 pounds of rice at a subsidized price (Edirisinghe 1987). The decision to replace the food ration scheme with a food stamp scheme in 1979 is discussed later in this chapter.

Agricultural Policy and the FOSA Program, 1940s to 1970s
The food ration program was created to ensure the food security of the Sri Lankan people. Therefore, it is important to discuss the government's approach to the domestic production of food and, in particular, its agricultural policies during this period.

Sri Lankan agricultural policy during the colonial era focused on producing tea for exportation, while importing rice at low prices for domestic consumption (Gavan and Chandrasekara 1979). During World War II, agricultural policy shifted to increasing domestic rice production. From independence in 1948 until the opening of the economy in 1977, the main focus was to attain self-sufficiency in the production of food, mainly rice (Gavan and Chandrasekara 1979; Sanderatne 2004). Higher domestic production was needed to ensure sufficient supplies for the universal food ration scheme.

The 1948–70 period was marked by the implementation of agricultural policies for (a) increasing the area of paddy cultivated land, (b) increasing production and productivity, and (c) developing institutions for farmers such as cultivation committees and rural banks (Henegedara 2002). The government undertook many policies emphasizing domestic production, including (a) allotting government land to landless peasants for rice cultivation, which resulted in extensive settlement of land in the dry zone; (b) providing fertilizers at highly subsidized prices; (c) providing irrigation at low cost; (d) developing and distributing high-yielding rice via an official network; and (e) distributing, via state banks, cultivation loans, most of which were never repaid because they came to be regarded as grants (Gavan and Chandrasekara 1979; Sanderatne 2004).

One of the most significant policy measures implemented to encourage domestic rice production was the guaranteed price scheme under which the government purchased paddy from farmers at a certified price. When the measure was first introduced in 1942 as the internal purchase scheme, farmers could sell either to the government or on the open market. However, during the severe rice shortage in 1944, government introduced a compulsory levy of 2–3 bushels of paddy per acre on all the cultivated lands and then purchased all paddy above farmers' consumption level. During that time, nearly all available supplies of rice were rationed. The internal purchase scheme was replaced by the guaranteed price scheme in 1948, removing the elements of compulsion and allowing farmers to sell to whomever they wished (Edirisinghe and Poleman 1976).

With such focused attention, paddy production grew rapidly during the postwar era. Between 1952 and 1972, paddy production tripled as a result of increased acreage and yield per hectare. Gavan and Chandrasekara (1979) speculate that this may have been the most remarkable record of any rice-cultivating country. Sri Lanka's food sufficiency ratio rose steadily until the 1970s, and rice imports were considerably lower in the early 1970s than they were in the 1950s, despite population growth (Gavan and Chandrasekara 1979).

In the 1970s, the growth rate of paddy production was disappointing. This slowdown has been attributed to crop losses associated with drought, shortages of fertilizer, and large decreases in the paddy-to-fertilizer price ratio in

1975 and 1976. Furthermore, the insurgency in 1971 disrupted government services and production at the farm level (Gavan and Chandrasekara 1979).

Therefore, the period of 1970–77 was marked by a protectionist regime with many interventionist policy measures, such as restricting food and agricultural inputs, regulating domestic rice production and trade (for example, greatly limiting the quantity of paddy that could be transported by individuals), and imposing ceilings on landownership (Henegedara 2002). During that period, the government imposed a monopoly on procurement for the purpose of ensuring sufficient supplies for food rations (Edirisinghe and Poleman 1976; Gavan and Chandrasekara 1979).

In 1977, the economy was liberalized and agricultural policy was reformed. The focus remained on achieving self-sufficiency in basic foods, but new policies were directed at expanding exports. Even though general tariffs were lowered as a result of trade liberalization, agriculture sector tariffs remained high, and quantitative restrictions were placed on some domestic food crops to encourage domestic production and provide protection against competition (Kelegama 2006; Sanderatne 2004).

FOOD STAMP SCHEME, 1979–89

In 1979, the food subsidy scheme was replaced by a food stamp scheme with a fixed monetary value of the stamp rather than a quantity of food entitlement. The objectives of introducing a food stamp scheme were (a) to stabilize the budget by fixing the value of food stamps and (b) to remove the government's monopoly in food supply by creating opportunities for the private sector to get involved and for beneficiaries to purchase the food items they wanted (Ratnayake 2013).

Under the food stamp scheme, the value of the stamp was fixed in nominal terms, in contrast to the food subsidy scheme, under which the quantity of commodities was fixed. Food stamps could be used to purchase a basket of commodities composed of rice, wheat flour, sugar, dried fish, milk powder, and pulses. When the food stamp scheme was initially introduced, many food items were provided at subsidized rates, but by the end of 1982, the subsidies were almost completely eliminated (Edirisinghe 1987).

The food stamp program was a targeted program. The beneficiaries were households with an annual income below SL Rs 3,600. The value of stamps received by a family depended on the size and age composition of the family. For example, every child below age 8 was entitled to a stamp worth SL Rs 25 per month, whereas children age 8–12 were entitled to stamps worth SL Rs 20 per month. The household was entitled to stamps worth SL Rs 15 per month for every member over age 12.

Each household eligible for food stamps was also issued kerosene stamps worth SL Rs 9.50 per month to provide relief from rising fuel costs. The kerosene stamps could be used to purchase specific food items, but food stamps could not be used to purchase kerosene. Households could obtain their food items from cooperative societies or authorized distributors. Unused food stamps could be deposited in the Post Office Savings Bank (Edirisinghe 1987; Ratnayake 2013).

The food stamps scheme helped the government to maintain a stable budget and reduce the fiscal burden. According to Edirisinghe (1987), the most striking characteristic of the new scheme was the allocation of a fixed nominal amount of approximately SL Rs 1.8 billion in the annual budget. However, the program had many weaknesses. The real value of stamps deteriorated over time as food prices rose, and no provision was made to change the value of the food stamps to maintain their real value (Ratnayake 2013). The program also suffered from targeting issues, primarily because the entry and exit mechanism was not implemented properly. As a result, the number of stamp recipients increased with every issue of the stamp—that is, every three months.

Furthermore, although coverage was restricted to half of households in the country, there were many exclusion and inclusion errors. In many instances, households that did not belong to the lower half of the expenditure range received benefits, while the target group (households with income below SL Rs 300)—the lowest quintile—received only 38 percent of the total expenditure on food stamps (Edirisinghe 1988). Such targeting errors resulted in the government's decision to freeze new issues temporarily in 1980.

Another shortcoming of the food stamp scheme was that, although recipients were entitled to buy any food item they wanted using the food stamps, in practice they could buy only items such as rice, sugar, flour, and milk powder that the cooperative societies and authorized distributors issued in exchange for the stamp (Ratnayake 2013).

Estate sector households were relatively more affected by the shift from rations to food stamps than were urban and rural households: 21 percent of estate sector households received the rice ration in fiscal year 1978/79, (compared with 41 percent of urban households and 59 percent of rural households) (Edirisinghe 1987). The coverage of estate sector households declined to 13 percent in fiscal year 1981/82 after the introduction of food stamps (compared with 33 percent of urban households and 57 percent of rural households).

By the mid-1980s, poor households were receiving less relief from the food stamp scheme because no provisions had been made to adjust the real value of the stamp to the consumer price index. By 1982, the real value of the food stamps had shrunk by about 50 percent (Edirisinghe 1988).

The government capped total expenditures on the food stamp scheme. For the real value of the food stamps to have been preserved while keeping within the government budget allocation limits, the number of stamp recipients in 1985 would have had to be reduced from 7.5 million to 3.5 million (Ratnayake 2013). The government needed to reevaluate stamp-recipient families and fine-tune the targeting mechanism.

To form the legal basis for this reevaluation of beneficiaries, the Poverty Alleviation Act no. 32 of 1985 was enacted. Under this act, the Poverty Alleviation Department was charged with implementing the Poverty Alleviation Food Program. Through this legal change, food stamps became poverty alleviation stamps, and the poor had to declare their poverty to become entitled to the stamps. Furthermore, to reduce the number of beneficiaries, skilled workers (carpenters, masons, motor mechanics, tractor drivers) were removed from the scheme (Ratnayake 2013).

To be eligible for food stamps, a household's monthly income had to be less than SL Rs 700. The selection process was based on the hypothesis that the nonpoor would hesitate to participate in a public selection process that was held in their area of residence because of concerns about social status (Ratnayake 2013).[6]

However, political pressure acted as a counter force in the endeavor to limit the number of beneficiaries. The Poverty Alleviation Department was instructed to refrain from displaying the lists of beneficiaries in public places, and the program, which was launched at great expense to the government, could not be implemented properly. Thus, when the new program was launched in June 1986, the number of beneficiaries who received poverty alleviation food stamps had increased from 6.8 million to 7.2 million (Ratnayake 2013).

By the late 1980s, the real value of the food stamps had eroded to such an extent that they could no longer be used as a political tool. Therefore, political attention turned to programs that could be financed by government funds and that could sway public opinion (Ratnayake 2013). From 1979 to 1989, when the food stamp scheme was in operation, the stamps were not very effective at alleviating poverty or contributing toward living expenditure. After the presidential election in 1989, the food-based safety net in Sri Lanka changed significantly with introduction of Janasaviya.

THE JANASAVIYA PROGRAM, 1989–94

Janasaviya (Strength of the People) was introduced in 1989 after the presidential elections. The objective was to shift the focus of social welfare policy from enhancing consumption and nutrition levels to alleviating poverty through employment creation and social mobilization (Stokke 1995). The program was designed in line with the new government's development framework, which was based on mobilization and participation of the poor in the development process.

Janasaviya beneficiaries were selected from the former food stamp–recipient families whose monthly income was less than SL Rs 700. Under Janasaviya, a monthly grant of SL Rs 2,500 was allocated to each identified family for a period of two years. Of this allocation, SL Rs 1,458 was a monthly grant that consisted of two components: a consumption grant of SL Rs 1,000 and a grant of SL Rs 458. The former was given in the form of coupons to purchase food and nonfood items from local cooperative stores. The latter was given in the form of cash, which beneficiaries were encouraged to save for productive purposes. The balance of SL Rs 1,042 was to be received by beneficiaries at the end of two years as a lump sum (worth SL Rs 25,000), which could be used as capital or as collateral for a loan taken for an income-generating activity.

However, given the high costs associated with the program, the government was not able to provide the SL Rs 25,000 to beneficiaries at the end of the two-year period. Instead, beneficiaries received a "certificate of entitlement," followed by a monthly grant of SL Rs 250—an amount similar to 10 percent interest on the total amount (Ratnayake 2013). In addition, beneficiaries had access to savings and credit facilities for income generation activities through community-based organizations supported by the Janasaviya Trust Fund.

In return for the benefits received, one member from each beneficiary family was expected to participate in productive work for 20 days a month (or be engaged in training). In addition, the family member was expected to contribute four days each month to community work (Stokke 1995). The labor that was mobilized under Janasaviya was managed and monitored by a community-level task force that (a) structured viable income-generating activities according to the available physical and human resources, (b) identified specific recipients for particular economic activities on the basis of their resources, and (c) provided supervision (Marasinghe 1993).

Because of the high costs involved, Janasaviya was implemented in several rounds, with each round covering about 100,000–120,000 families. Each round covered families selected from at least one district secretariat (DS) division from each district. The initial objective was to cover the poorest DS divisions in the first round and move to other divisions depending on their poverty level. Meanwhile, the food stamp scheme continued in other areas where Janasaviya was not implemented. From 1989 to 1994, the program completed four rounds. It was continuing with the fifth round when, in 1995, the new government replaced it with Samurdhi. Table 4.2 presents the number of families and the DS divisions covered by each round before Janasaviya was replaced.

Janasaviya was designed to help beneficiaries to satisfy their nutritional and consumption requirements through a monthly consumption grant, while encouraging them to save through a savings grant for future investment. Janasaviya was intended to alleviate poverty among beneficiaries within two years (by ensuring that they were given incentive to be employed or in training). However, at the end of the two years, most Janasaviya recipients were still trapped in poverty, and many of their self-employment initiatives had failed, primarily because of the poor quality of their products and the lack of marketing facilities (Ratnayake 2013). Furthermore, removal of the monthly

TABLE 4.2 **Number of Beneficiaries and District Secretariat Divisions Covered by Janasaviya in Sri Lanka, 1989–94**

ROUND AND START DATE	NUMBER OF FAMILIES	NUMBER OF DIVISIONS COVERED
Round 1: January 02, 1989	118,000	22
Round 2: December 03, 1990	104,000	22
Round 3: December 10, 1992	100,000	22
Round 4: March 14, 1993	99,000	25
Round 5: June 04, 1994	120,000	26

Source: Ratnayake 2013.

grant at the end of the two years worsened the situation of many beneficiaries. The subsequent program, Samurdhi, also sought to alleviate poverty through social mobilization, empowerment, and employment creation.

SAMURDHI (DIVINEGUMA) PROGRAM, 1995–2015

Samurdhi, 1995–2012

Samurdhi was introduced in 1995 by the People's Alliance government as its main poverty alleviation program. It was designed to protect the poor by reducing their vulnerability in the short run and by helping them to move out of poverty in the long run. The program had three key components: (a) a welfare (grant) component, which was aimed at reducing vulnerability and improving consumption and nutrition levels among beneficiaries; (b) a savings and credit component, which operated through a network of Samurdhi banks and provided low-income families with access to loans and savings facilities for income-generating activities; and (c) a community-based rural works program for infrastructure development.

Initially, the grant component was administered by the Department of Poor Relief, the savings and credit component was managed by the Samurdhi Authority of Sri Lanka (SASL), and the community-based program was operated by the Department of Commissioner General of Samurdhi (DCGS).[7]

Since its inception, the cost of the welfare component has accounted for the bulk of the annual program budget (around 80 percent). Families with a monthly income of less than SL Rs 1,000 were eligible for the monthly welfare grant. Under the welfare (grant) program, these families were entitled to a fixed monthly grant that was given in the form of several "stamps" (coupons)—food stamps (to purchase goods from the cooperative shops),[8] cash stamps (to purchase food items or to convert to cash), and savings stamps (to be used for compulsory savings and contributions to the social security fund).

The total monthly grant received depended on the number and monthly income of the family. Table 4.3 provides details of the monthly grant received by each category of family at the inception of the program. The monthly grant

TABLE 4.3 **Eligibility and Components of the Samurdhi Welfare (Grant) Program in Sri Lanka**

CATEGORY OF FAMILY	TOTAL AMOUNT RECEIVED (SL RS)	DISTRIBUTION OF COUPONS
Families with household income < SL Rs 500 and fewer than 5 members	1,000	SL Rs 400 (to purchase food items); SL Rs 380 (to buy goods or convert to cash); SL Rs 200 (to use for compulsory savings); SL Rs 20 (to use for insurance)
Families with household income < SL Rs 1,000 and 3 or more members	500	SL Rs 200 (to purchase food items); SL Rs 18: (to buy goods or convert to cash) SL Rs 100 (to use for compulsory savings); SL Rs 20 (to use for insurance)
Families with household income < SL Rs 1,000 and 2 members	200	Only to purchase food items
Families with household income < SL Rs 1,000 and 1 member	100	Only to purchase food items
Former Janasaviya recipients	250	To buy goods or convert to cash

Source: Gunatilaka and others 1997.

ranged from a minimum of SL Rs 100 per month to a maximum of SL Rs 1,000 per month (for the "poorest families," whose monthly incomes were less than SL Rs 500 and who included more than five family members). The former Janasaviya-recipient families that were entitled to SL Rs 250 per month continued to receive SL Rs 250 per month under Samurdhi. Samurdhi-recipient families were expected to exit the program when their monthly income exceeded SL Rs 2,000 for six continuous months or when at least one family member found (regular) employment (Gunatilaka and others 1997).

Families receiving the highest grant amounts (for example, SL Rs 1,000 and SL Rs 500) had to contribute SL Rs 20 per month to the social insurance fund. The fund was used to pay social claims to beneficiaries in the event of a birth, marriage, sickness, or death of a family member. Beneficiaries received SL Rs 2,000 in the event of a birth (for the first and second child), SL Rs 3,000 in the event of a marriage of a family member, and SL Rs 5,000 at the death of a family member. Moreover, in the event of a sickness or hospitalization, SL Rs 50 per day could be claimed for each day in the hospital.[9]

In addition to the contribution to the social security fund, a compulsory savings component was included for families entitled to SL Rs 1,000 or SL Rs 500 per month. Those compulsory savings were initially deposited in the beneficiary's account at state-owned banks such as the People's Bank and the Bank of Ceylon (Glinskaya 2000; Gunatilaka and others 1997). However, after the Samurdhi banks were set up in the late 1990s, the compulsory savings were deposited in them. Compulsory savings could generally be withdrawn only after age 70 (which was reduced to age 60 in 2015) and for medical or educational purposes.

The value of food stamps and cash stamps accounted for the majority of the monthly grant. Food stamps could be used to purchase food items from the local cooperative shops. Cash stamps could be used at the cooperative shops to purchase food items or be used as cash. Stamps could only be exchanged for goods at the cooperative stores. After the Samurdhi banking societies were set up in the late 1990s, cash stamps could be used at the bank either to obtain cash or to make a deposit.

The Samurdhi welfare (grant) component underwent several changes in the past two decades to improve the quality of benefits and the structure and design of the program. As shown in table 4.4, beginning in 2000, the monthly value of grants or stamps increased for the majority of beneficiaries (except for those who received SL Rs 1,000). Moreover, the families that appeared to have moved above the income threshold ("empowered families") received a minimum monthly grant of SL Rs 155.

TABLE 4.4 Changes to the Samurdhi Welfare (Grant) Program in Sri Lanka, 1995–2015

BENEFICIARY CATEGORY	AMOUNT (SL RS)
1995–2000	
Families with 1 member	100
Families with 2 members	200
Families with 3 or more members	500
Families of 5 or more, monthly income < SL Rs 500	1,000
Former Janasaviya families	250
2000–05	
Families with 1 member	250
Families with 2 members	350
Families with 3–5 members	600
Families of 6 or more members	1,000
Former Janasaviya families	400
Empowered families	155
2012–14	
Families with 1 member	100
Families with 2 members	200
Families with 3 or more members	500
Families with 5 or more members, monthly income < SL Rs 500	1,000
Former Janasaviya families	250

table continues next page

TABLE 4.4 Changes to the Samurdhi Welfare (Grant) Program in Sri Lanka, 1995–2015 *(continued)*

BENEFICIARY CATEGORY	AMOUNT (SL RS)
January–March 2015	
Families with fewer than 3 members	1,000
Families with 3 members	2,000
Families with 4 or more members	3,000
Empowered families	420
April 2015	
Families with fewer than 3 members	1,500
Families with 3 members	2,500
Families with 4 or more members	3,500
Empowered families	420

Sources: Central Bank of Sri Lanka, various years; Gunatilaka and others 1997; Institute of Policy Studies 2015; Tilakaratna, Galapattige, and Jayaweera 2013.

In 2006, the value of the grant was increased 50 percent in 141 DS divisions with the highest poverty rates. The maximum amount given was increased from SL Rs 1,000 to SL Rs 1,500, while the amount given to other categories of beneficiaries (except for empowered families) was also increased to some extent. Consequently, this policy raised the value of the food stamps as well as the cash stamps received by these families. By contrast, the monthly grant received by the beneficiaries in the other DS divisions remained largely unchanged (Institute of Policy Studies 2015; Tilakaratna, Galapattige, and Jayaweera 2013).

Changes to the Samurdhi Program since 2012

The Samurdhi welfare (grant) program underwent important reforms in 2012. These reforms included changes to the categories of beneficiary, amount of benefits, as well as the nature of the benefits. The number of beneficiary categories was reduced to four (from six) on the basis of family size, and the monthly grant amounts were increased for some categories of beneficiaries. Moreover, changes were made to the nature of benefits and the method of payment.

In 2012, food stamps (and cash stamps) were replaced by a cash transfer, and the total value of the food and cash stamps was transferred directly to the beneficiary accounts at the Samurdhi banks. This transfer was facilitated by the well-established Samurdhi banking system, which had more than 1,000 branches islandwide. The compulsory savings and social security contributions were deducted from the total monthly grant and transferred directly to the relevant fund or account.

Many reasons led to these changes in the payment and delivery method, but the primary reason was inefficiencies related to delivery (cooperative stores). Widespread inefficiencies in the delivery system included (a) long delays in the issuance of goods and uncertain delivery dates, which required beneficiaries to visit the cooperative shops on several days and adversely affected their income-earning opportunities; (b) poor quality of goods available at cooperative stores; (c) corrupt practices such as charging higher prices than those charged by other retail stores in the area; and (d) difficulty of using the cash stamps, with beneficiaries having to purchase what was available rather than what they wanted or needed (Gunatilaka and others 1997).

The changes in the method of payment and delivery were expected to address the problems of the previous system and to improve efficiency. Moreover, they were expected to promote savings and investment among the poor because the total net grant would be transferred directly to the beneficiaries' bank accounts. They were also expected to encourage beneficiaries to use financial institutions like the Samurdhi banks for their financial needs, to be more convenient for beneficiaries because the grant amount would be transferred directly to their bank accounts, and to reduce costs overall by eliminating the need to print "stamps" (Institute of Policy Studies 2015; Tilakaratna, Galapattige, and Jayaweera 2013).

In 2014, the Divineguma Department was formed to oversee Samurdhi, which was renamed *Divineguma*. Samurdhi had been administered by the DCGS and the SASL—in 2014, the DCGS and the SASL (along with the Up-Country Peasantry Rehabilitation Department, the Sri Lanka Up-Country Development Authority, and the Southern Development Authority) were integrated to form the Department of Divineguma Development (under the Divineguma Act no. 1 of 2013).

Some changes were made to the organizational structure of the program with passage of the Divineguma Act, but no major changes were made to the welfare program or to any of the other components, such as the credit and savings program. Following the general elections in August 2015 and the change of government, changing the name of the program back to Samurdhi was discussed. In 2015, changes were made to the categories of beneficiary and the amount of subsidy, with a maximum monthly amount of SL Rs 3,500 per family (and a minimum amount of SL Rs 420) beginning in April 2015.

Currently, Samurdhi/Divineguma covers nearly 1.5 million families. The number of Samurdhi-recipient families has declined over the years from nearly 2 million in 1997–2001 to around 1.47 million in 2015. The program has been widely criticized for lapses in targeting—both inclusion errors, that is, including persons who are not eligible to receive benefits, and exclusion errors, that is, excluding persons who are eligible (Glinskaya 2000; Institute of Policy Studies 2015; Tilakaratna, Galapattige, and Jayaweera 2013). As shown in table 4.5, targeting has deteriorated over the years. In 1995–96,

TABLE 4.5 **Percentage of Households Receiving Samurdhi Benefits in Sri Lanka, by Income Decile, Fiscal Years 1995/96–2012/13**

DECILE	1995/96	2006/07	2009/10	2012/13
1 (poorest)	65.6	57.74	46.58	36.5
2	61.2	48.61	37.41	28.7
3	58.0	44.19	35.30	23.1
4	50.9	34.38	27.40	20.3
5	45.0	30.68	23.75	17.6
6	38.2	23.21	21.19	13.8
7	31.3	20.15	14.38	9.4
8	22.2	13.32	10.50	6.5
9	13.4	8.89	7.58	4.9
10 (richest)	4.8	3.79	3.20	2.7
Total	39.1	28.50	22.70	16.4

Sources: Calculations based on Department of Census and Statistics 2013; Galapattige 2010; Institute of Policy Studies 2015; Tilakaratna, Galapattige, and Jayaweera 2013.

nearly two-thirds of households in the bottom two deciles were Samurdhi beneficiaries; this number declined over the years so that today only around 36 percent of households in the poorest decile are beneficiaries.[10]

In fiscal year 2012/13, 16.4 percent of households in the country were receiving Samurdhi cash transfers, with some households having multiple beneficiaries. This figure is about three times higher than the percentage of poor households in the country (5.3 percent). However, the targeting errors are substantial—14.4 percent of Samurdhi-recipient households (accounting for about 88 percent of beneficiary households) are nonpoor, and only a small share of beneficiaries are from poor households as defined by the national poverty line (Department of Census and Statistics 2016). By contrast, many poor households do not receive Samurdhi cash benefits.

For instance, only about 38 percent of poor households receive the Samurdhi cash transfer, while more than 60 percent of poor households are excluded from the program. Such inclusion and exclusion errors are observed in all of the country's districts. As shown in figure 4.1, the percentage of households receiving cash transfers under the program is higher than the percentage of poor households in the majority of districts. However, the share of Samurdhi recipients who are nonpoor is larger in all districts, and the share of households that are poor but not receiving Samurdhi benefits is significant.

The lack of clearly defined criteria for selecting beneficiaries and the lack of a systematic entry and exit mechanism are the key reasons for the persistence of targeting errors. The selection criterion for beneficiaries, at the inception of the program, was family income of less than SL Rs 1,000 a month

FIGURE 4.1

Percentage of Samurdhi-Receiving Households in Sri Lanka, by Poverty Status and District, Fiscal Year 2012/13

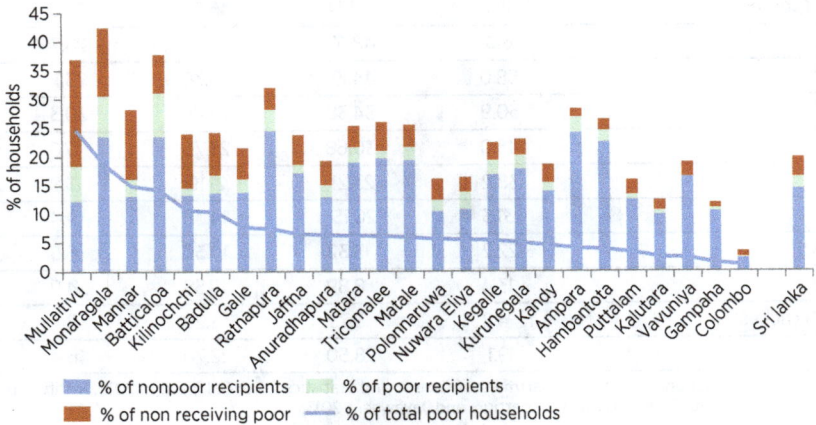

Source: Calculations based on Department of Census and Statistics 2013.

(which was later raised to SL Rs 1,500). In the mid-2000s, an attempt was made to address targeting errors by adopting a participatory methodology in which community members would select potential beneficiaries. That attempt failed for political reasons.

Currently, there are no clear eligibility criteria for selecting beneficiaries—once identified, families simply continue to receive benefits. Moreover, Samurdhi lacks an entry and exit mechanism (a) to identify the "new poor" (that is, nonpoor households that fall into poverty because of various risks and vulnerabilities) and (b) to remove households that are no longer poor.

Until recently, the new entrants were added to Samurdhi/Divineguma mostly to replace beneficiaries who voluntarily exited the program or were deceased. However, that practice has been halted since mid-2015, and the department is working to devise eligibility criteria for selecting beneficiaries and to improve targeting (Institute of Policy Studies 2015; Tilakaratna, Galapattige, and Jayaweera 2013).

Recent attempts to improve the quality of benefits by increasing the amount of cash transfer increased the cost of the program substantially in 2015 (figure 4.2). In 2015, program costs increased more than 150 percent from the 2014 level, reaching more than SL Rs 40 billion. This development under-scores the need to improve targeting by reducing the number of beneficiaries, while ensuring that the "neediest" groups receive the benefits. Such action would help to reduce the cost of the program and ensure its sustainability.

FIGURE 4.2

Expenditure of the Samurdhi Welfare Program in Sri Lanka, 2009–15

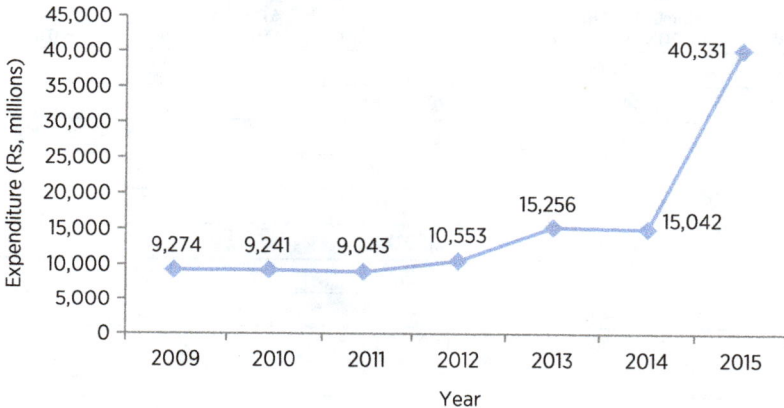

Sources: Central Bank of Sri Lanka, various years; Institute of Policy Studies 2015.

SUMMARY: THE TRANSITION FROM FOOD TO CASH TRANSFERS

As discussed in this chapter, Sri Lanka has moved from universal food-based safety net programs to targeted cash transfer programs over the years. The evolution from a universal food ration scheme to a food stamp scheme and then to a cash transfer program was driven by various factors. In this section, we discuss different stages of the transition and the underlying factors that contributed to the changes.

Food rationing was introduced in Sri Lanka to ensure social welfare during World War II. The scheme was universal and generous, and it was not abandoned when the war ended.

From 1948–70, the percentage of the population that received the food ration fluctuated, but the program always covered 70–90 percent of the population (table 4.6). Furthermore, the total number of beneficiaries grew steadily, along with total population.

Escalation of the fiscal burden of the program was inevitable, making it imperative to rein in expenditures. However, as evinced by the food riots in the mid-1950s and shifts in government power following major reductions in the subsidy benefits, it was not politically feasible to reform the food subsidy scheme until 1978, when the universal ration scheme was replaced with a targeted scheme that limited benefits to households with a monthly income below a defined level. This type of policy measure was previously politically infeasible, so it bears investigating how the modification was managed.

TABLE 4.6 Percentage of the Population Receiving Food Subsidies or Rations in Sri Lanka, 1948–70

YEAR	NUMBER OF RATION COUPON BOOKS ISSUED	TOTAL POPULATION	% OF THE POPULATION RECEIVING THE FOOD SUBSIDY OR RATION
1948	6,339,000	7,109,000	89.17
1949	6,514,000	7,321,000	88.98
1950	6,519,000	7,544,000	86.41
1951	6,780,000	7,742,000	87.57
1952	6,920,000	7,950,000	87.04
1953	6,144,000	8,150,000	75.39
1954	6,884,000	8,350,000	82.44
1955	6,140,000	8,550,000	71.81
1956	6,829,760	8,800,000	77.61
1957	7,182,269	9,165,000	78.37
1958	7,539,667	9,361,000	80.54
1959	8,060,543	9,498,000	84.87
1960	8,522,069	10,063,000	84.68
1965	10,074,992	11,232,000	89.69
1970	11,162,763	12,514,000	90.20

Source: Ratnayake 2013.

During the 1977–78 period, Sri Lanka underwent a critical political and economic transformation. The economy was liberalized in 1977. A new constitution was introduced in 1978 that changed the Sri Lankan political structure by introducing the role of executive presidency and centralizing the power structure. The opening up of the economy resulted in the rupee becoming significantly devalued, which increased the import bill and made it essential to rationalize food subsidy expenditure. The strength of the executive presidency and the majority government helped the government to introduce radical reforms to food policy, while mitigating the political complications.

Consequently, in 1978, the universal food ration was replaced by a targeted food ration that covered approximately 50 percent of the population. The next major change was the introduction of a food stamp scheme in 1979. Up to this point, the benefits received by beneficiaries were defined in terms of the quantity of food that could be bought at subsidized rates. With the introduction of the food stamp scheme, benefits were defined in terms of the amount of food that could be bought for the value of the food stamp. When that adjustment was first implemented, beneficiaries could still buy food items at subsidized rates, but those subsidies were eliminated by the end of 1982. The government took further steps to restrain the expenditures by establishing a limit on the budget allocated to food stamps.

Although those steps reduced government expenditure, they compromised the welfare objective by making no provisions to adjust the real value of the food stamps in par with inflation. The contribution of food stamps to household income was small. Furthermore, because of problems in targeting and the lack of an entry and exit mechanism, the number of beneficiaries continued to rise, prompting the government to freeze the issuance of stamps for new beneficiaries.

The significance of the food stamp program as a welfare benefit scheme declined over time, and it was replaced by Janasaviya following the presidential election in 1989. According to Stokke (1995), two interpretations of the program are possible: one view is that Janasaviya was a "massive personal propaganda show orchestrated by a populist president"; the other is that it was a "movement in civil society for the true empowerment of the poor." Regardless of the true motivations, an undeniable shift occurred in the focus from ensuring food security (via food stamps) to alleviating poverty through employment creation, social mobilization, and improved consumption.

As discussed earlier in this chapter, Janasaviya included (a) a consumption grant given in the form of coupons to purchase food and a grant to use for savings (both given on a monthly basis for 24 months) and (b) a lump sum to be received at the end of the two-year period to be used for an income generation activity. Assistance for food or consumption was only one part of the program. However, Janasaviya was implemented only in certain divisions of the country, while the food stamp scheme continued to be implemented in others.

Because of the program's high cost, the government was unable to grant the benefits that were promised at the end of two years or to ensure sustained self-employment for most families (Gunatilaka and others 1997). A new government came to power in 1994 and introduced a new poverty alleviation program, Samurdhi, in 1995.

Samurdhi followed the same principles of poverty alleviation and social mobilization. It had three key components: a welfare (grant) component, a credit and savings scheme, and a community-based program. The welfare component accounted for a major share of the program budget and consisted of a food stamp that could be used to purchase food items from the cooperative stores and a cash stamp that could be used to purchase food or obtain cash.

However, delivery through cooperative stores was inefficient, including delays in issuing goods, questionable quality of the available goods, and mismatch between the goods available and the needs of beneficiaries. The inefficiencies led to major changes in the welfare component in 2012. The food stamps (and cash stamps) were replaced by a cash transfer, and the money was transferred directly to beneficiaries' accounts at the Samurdhi banks. That transition was facilitated by the Samurdhi bank network. The shift in focus from improving consumption and nutrition levels to alleviating poverty also supported the reform because the cash grant allowed beneficiary families to have more choice in how to use the grant—for food and consumption or for investment.

As the welfare or safety net programs changed from a universal FOSA program to a targeted cash transfer scheme, the benefits, as well as the beneficiaries (proportion of population covered), also changed. Figure 4.3 depicts the approximate coverage of the population from the beginning of the universal food ration to Samurdhi in 2015.

The transition occurred over seven decades, culminating in the targeted income transfer scheme of today. First, the universal feature was removed. Then, the subsidies on the price of rationed food were discontinued. Next, a food stamp scheme was introduced, limiting the benefits to food items that could be purchased for a certain monetary limit. Later, the focus was changed to poverty alleviation in which food stamps were only one of the key components. The food stamp component was then replaced with a cash grant without stipulating how the grant should be used.

Furthermore, the significance given to ensuring food security and enhancing nutritional status diminished over time, with greater emphasis placed on creating employment opportunities and enhancing productivity. Janasaviya required beneficiaries to work (or be in training) for a stipulated time period to receive benefits. In addition to the consumption grant, Janasaviya beneficiaries received a separate grant that could be saved and used for productive activities.

FIGURE 4.3

Coverage of Food-Based Social Assistance Programs in Sri Lanka, 1942–2016

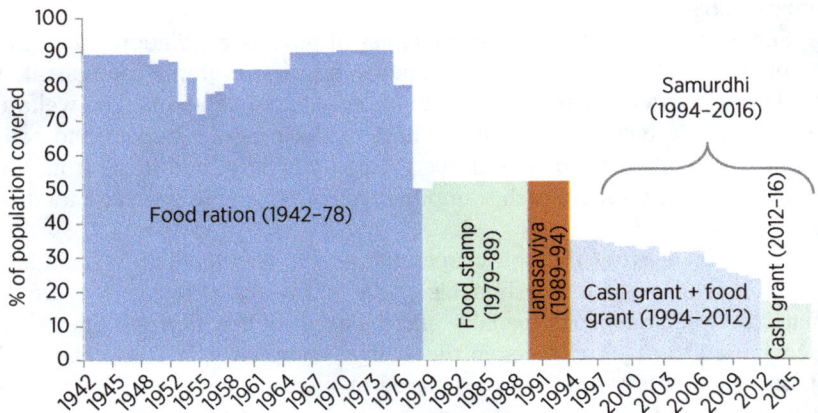

Sources: Estimates based on Edirisinghe 1987; Ratnayake 2013; estimates for number of Samurdhi/Divineguma beneficiary families based on Divineguma Department information.

This trend was amplified by the Samurdhi benefit scheme. At its inception, only 40 percent of the total amount received by the two categories of beneficiary receiving the highest benefits under Samurdhi grant was defined as a food stamp—the balance of the grant consisted of a cash transfer, a compulsory savings component, and an insurance component. In 2012, the food stamp component was eliminated and replaced by a cash transfer.

Those transformations were driven by budget constraints, problems in the prevailing scheme, and political concerns. For example, budgetary constraints led to replacement of the food ration scheme with a food stamp scheme in 1979, while problems with the delivery system led to a cash transfer program in 2012. The lack of commitment by the political parties to continuing benefits that were defined by previous regimes were also contributory factors (for example, in replacing Janasaviya with Samurdhi). Changes in the political regime were often followed by changes in welfare policies and programs.

Despite Sri Lanka's shift in focus from FOSA to cash transfers, a handful of nutrition and food-based programs have continued to operate for certain targeted groups, such as children and pregnant and lactating women. The Thriposha national food supplementation program, implemented in 1979, is carried out by the Ministry of Health and Indigenous Medicine, with the aim of improving the nutrition status of infants and children and pregnant and lactating mothers. Under this program, children ages 6–59 months, pregnant women, and lactating mothers (for the first six months after giving birth) who are identified as undernourished or underweight are given nutrition packs (containing energy, protein, and micronutrients) on a monthly basis. This program currently has more than 900,000 beneficiaries. Moreover, the Mid-day Meal and Glass of Milk programs are carried out by the nutrition unit of the State Ministry of Education to enhance the nutritional status of students in grades 1–5 in selected schools in rural areas. Thriposha, with collaboration from the World Food Programme, also provides mid-day meals to primary- and secondary-level students in selected schools. In addition to the nutrition programs for schoolchildren, a mid-day milk program is carried out for preschool children.

LESSONS LEARNED

The rich experience of Sri Lanka offers several important lessons for other countries. First, the modality of delivering assistance by itself cannot resolve key performance issues. The unsatisfactory targeting of rations and then vouchers was somewhat inherited by the cash transfer scheme.

Second, it is important to ensure that transfers are adequate once the transition to near cash or cash is undertaken. In an inflationary environment, fixing the value of transfers (with no built-in mechanism for adjusting their size) may erode their value over time, weakening their effects—a warning for the Arab Republic of Egypt and other countries that are moving toward near-cash modalities.

Granted, the erosion of benefits and enrollment procedures that limit entry to the program de facto can help to reduce fiscal costs over time, but if the program continues to perform poorly, it will be not constitute a good use of public coffers. As such, a reduction in fiscal outlays should not be confused with a deliberate strategy of reallocating funds toward better-performing programs or with efforts to improve the performance of the current scheme.

Third, it is possible to phase out the use of cooperative or public food distribution channels in the delivery of social assistance. Indonesia and Mexico, among other countries, can look to the example of Sri Lanka when addressing challenges in their delivery systems.

NOTES

1. According to Edirisinghe and Poleman (1976), import prices increased 400 percent between 1939 and 1948.
2. Under the food subsidy scheme, rice was the first commodity to be subsidized. Eventually, subsidies were extended to most other food items except sugar (Ratnayake 1998).
3. The wheat ration or subsidy started along with the rice ration and continued until the mid-1990s because the government wished to control the price of bread. Ratnayake (2013) provides a detailed account of fluctuations in the rice ration and consequent changes in the wheat ration.
4. Between 1970 and 1976, imports satisfied 30 percent of the country's rice consumption, 100 percent of its wheat consumption, and 87 percent of its sugar consumption (Gavan and Chandrasekara 1979).
5. The postal, telegraph, railway, and electricity rates were also subject to price hikes (Edirisinghe and Poleman 1976).
6. All of the applicants were called to a public place, and the names of selected recipients were publicly displayed.
7. At a later stage, the Samurdhi welfare component was also taken under the purview of the DCGS, and in 2014, the DCGS and the SASL were amalgamated to form the Department of Divineguma Development.
8. In 2012, the food stamp component was replaced with a cash transfer, and the total value of the food and cash stamps was transferred directly to the beneficiary's account at a Samurdhi bank.
9. These amounts have been increased over the years. At present, the allowance for a birth is SL Rs 5,000; for a marriage is SL Rs 5,000; for a death is SL Rs 10,000; and for a hospitalization is SL Rs 200 per day.
10. In the Samurdhi/Divineguma cash transfer program, the unit considered is the family, and some households can have multiple families.

REFERENCES

Central Bank of Sri Lanka. Various years. *Annual Report*. Colombo: Central Bank. http://www.cbsl.gov.lk/htm/english/10_pub/p_1.html.

Department of Census and Statistics. 2013. *Household Income and Expenditure Survey 2012/13 Micro-Data*. Colombo: Department of Census and Statistics.

———. 2016. *District Official Poverty Lines*. Colombo: Department of Census and Statistics. http://www.statistics.gov.lk/poverty/monthly_poverty/index.htm.

Edirisinghe, Neville. 1982. "Food Security in Sri Lanka: The Historical Record." In *Food Security: Theory, Policy, and Perspectives from Asia and the Pacific Rim*, edited by Anthony H. Chisholm and Rodney Tyers. Lexington, MA: Lexington Books.

———. 1987. *The Food Stamp Scheme in Sri Lanka: Costs, Benefits, and Options for Modification*. 1st ed. Washington, DC: International Food Policy Research Institute. https://www.ifpri.org/publication/food-stamp-scheme-sri-lanka.

———. 1988. "Recent Targeting Attempts in Sri Lanka's Food Stamp Scheme." *Food Policy* 13 (4): 401–02. http://www.sciencedirect.com/science/journal/03069192/13.

Edirisinghe, Neville, and Thomas Poleman. 1976. "Implications of Government Intervention in the Rice Economy of Sri Lanka." Department of Agricultural Economics, Cornell University, Ithaca, NY.

FAO (Food and Agriculture Organization of the United Nations). 1951. *The State of Food and Agriculture: Review and Outlook 1951*. Rome: FAO. http://www.fao.org/docrep/016/ap639e/ap639e.pdf.

Galapattige, Ayodya. 2010. "Better Targeting of Transfers: Samurdhi Programme." *Talking Economics* (blog), July 12. http://www.ips.lk/talkingeconomics/2010/07/12/better-targeting-of-transfers-samurdhi-programme/.

Gavan, James, and Indrani Sri Chandrasekara. 1979. "The Impact of Public Foodgrain Distribution on Food Consumption and Welfare in Sri Lanka." Research Report 13, International Food Policy Research Institute, Washington, DC. https://www.ifpri.org/publication/impact-public-foodgrain-distribution-food-consumption-and-welfare-sri-lanka.

Glinskaya, Elena. 2000. "An Empirical Evaluation of Samurdhi Program." Background paper for Sri Lanka Poverty Assessment Report 22-535-CE, World Bank, Washington, DC. http://siteresources.worldbank.org/INTDECINEQ/Resources/SamurdhiJune042003.pdf.

Gunatilaka, R., R. Perera, R. Saliah, and C. de Silva. 1997. *The Samurdhi Programme: A Preliminary Evaluation*. Colombo: Institute of Policy Studies.

Henegedara, G. M. 2002. "Agricultural Policy Reforms in the Paddy Sector in Sri Lanka: An Overview." *Sri Lanka Journal of Agrarian Studies* 10 (1): 1–25.

Institute of Policy Studies. 2015. *Sri Lanka State of the Economy 2015 Report*. Colombo: Institute of Policy Studies.

Jayasuriya, Laksiri. 2004. "The Colonial Lineages of the Welfare State." In *Economic Policy in Sri Lanka: Issues and Debates*, edited by Saman Kelegama, 411. New Delhi: Sage Publications.

Kelegama, Saman. 2006. *Development under Stress: Sri Lankan Economy in Transition*. New Delhi: Sage.

Marasinghe, M. L. 1993. "Poverty Elimination through Poverty Alleviation: The Janasaviya Programme of Sri Lanka for National Development." *Third World Legal Studies* 12 (2): 13–42.

Ratnayake, R. M. K. 1998. "Poverty in Sri Lanka: Incidence and Poverty Reduction Strategies." In *Fifty Years of Sri Lanka's Independence: A Socio-Economic Review*, edited by A. D. V. de S. Indreratne, 577–99. Colombo: Sri Lanka Institute of Social and Economic Studies.

———. 2013. *Food Subsidies and State Welfare* [in Sinhala]. Nugegoda: Kanchana Printers.

Sanderatne, Nimal. 2004. "Agricultural Development: Controversial Issues." In *Economic Policy in Sri Lanka: Issues and Debates*, edited by Saman Kelegama, 195–212. New Delhi: Sage.

Stokke, Kristian. 1995. "Poverty as Politics: The Janasaviya Poverty Alleviation Programme in Sri Lanka." *Norsk Geografisk Tidsskrift—Norwegian Journal of Geography* 49 (3): 123–35.

Tilakaratna, G., A. Galapattige, and R. Jayaweera. 2013. "Safety Nets in Sri Lanka: An Overview." Unpublished report prepared for the World Bank, Colombo.

CHAPTER 5

From Food Subsidies to Targeted Transfers in Mexico

John Scott and Citlalli Hernández

INTRODUCTION

Mexico has a long history of food-oriented social assistance (FOSA) programs going back to the 1930s. Over the past two decades, the country has undertaken a deep and broad process of reforming those interventions. As discussed in chapter 1 of this volume, Mexico famously streamlined a complex system of in-kind assistance and price subsidies by introducing a targeted conditional cash transfer (CCT) program, originally named *Progresa*.

In particular, reforms centered on reallocating benefits from urban beneficiaries (especially concentrated in Mexico City) to the extreme poor in rural areas; they also shifted instruments from mostly generalized subsidies to targeted cash transfers combined with services designed to address basic nutrition, education, and health. Noteworthy, the government used evidence from a range of robust impact evaluations to design the CCT and inform its scale-up. The program was sustained over four federal political administrations, with gradual expansion in coverage and scope. Its name was changed, becoming *Oportunidades* in 2002 and *Prospera* in 2014. For simplicity, this chapter mostly refers to the program as *Prospera*. Throughout those reforms, the program incorporated new components, while maintaining its original objectives, intervention model, and target population. While much has been documented about Prospera and its predecessors, this chapter discusses the universe of FOSA interventions that preceded Prospera, their reform, and the reasons why some interventions still coexist alongside the flagship cash-based program. In this context, we examine one particular intervention, *Programa de Apoyo Alimentario* (PAL, Food Support Program), which itself evolved in various ways and was implemented in areas where Prospera could not be implemented. Indeed, Prospera benefits were provided only where basic health and education services were available, excluding some of the poorest and most vulnerable households living in remote rural areas. PAL was introduced in 2003 as a complement to Prospera, with the aim of reaching those unattended populations.

Until 2008, the resources allocated to PAL were minimal compared with those allocated to Prospera (1 percent on average between 2003 and 2008), but over the following seven years, PAL grew significantly, representing 7 percent of Prospera's budget in 2015. In 2009 PAL coverage expanded to include cash transfers alongside food commodities, in 2010 its institutional home moved to the *Coordinación Nacional de Prospera* (NCP, National Coordination of Prospera), and in 2013 the *Cruzada Nacional contra el Hambre* (CNCH, National Crusade against Hunger) was created. In addition to maintaining unconditional cash transfers (UCTs), called PAL-Monetary, the in-kind food component was replaced by a voucher, called PAL–*Sin Hambre* (PAL–Without Hunger). By early 2016, PAL was fully fused with Prospera as an "unconditional scheme of benefits." However, its two modalities, PAL-Monetary and PAL–Sin Hambre, coexist with the conditional scheme of Prospera benefits.[1]

Mexico's subsidy reforms are interesting within the context of the country's social policy and as a case study of the political economy of food subsidy reform. As this chapter shows, the reforms improved the efficiency and equity of public resources allocated to food-related support, despite formidable institutional and political constraints. The overall decline in public spending on FOSAs was more than compensated by the improved targeting and operational efficiency of the new programs, and the benefits reaching the poor increased fivefold between 1997 and 2015.

What made the reforms possible? Why did highly inefficient food subsidies and transfers persist over many decades? Why do some of the older targeted food transfers persist despite their limitations? Why does Mexico still sustain a generalized food subsidy of 1 percent of gross domestic product (GDP) that exempts food from the value added tax (VAT)? Why have those exemptions proved politically challenging to eliminate despite multiple fiscal reforms? Finally, why are generalized food subsidies and transfers in the style of the *Compañía Nacional de Subsistencias Populares* (CONASUPO, National Company of Popular Subsistence) still the norm in many of the countries represented in this volume—even at a much larger scale than in Mexico and in countries with even older histories—for example, India and Indonesia?

The remainder of this chapter is structured as follows. First, it presents the economic, social, and broader policy context of the reforms, followed by a discussion of the evolution of food subsidies in Mexico over the 20th and 21st centuries, focusing on the transition to targeted transfers through both Prospera and PAL. The chapter then discusses the introduction and expansion of cash transfers, recent developments, and distribution and efficiency. It concludes with lessons learned and policy implications.

ECONOMIC, SOCIAL, AND POLICY CONTEXT

Since the 1930s and up to the early 1990s, the core public policies pursuing FOSA-related objectives were land redistribution and agrarian reform, investments in irrigation and storage infrastructure, market price support policies, and generalized consumer subsidies (Scott, forthcoming). On the supply side, those policies led to rapid agricultural growth in the first half of the 20th century, but gains were concentrated in large-scale agricultural producers, mainly in the northern states, which also received most of the public investments. By contrast, subsistence and small-scale farmers—the great majority of agricultural producers to this day—had minimal land assets and little access to markets (land sales or rents were prohibited under the *ejido* system of communal landownership, before it was reformed in 1992) and were excluded from market price and most input supports. This led to both persistent regional and household inequalities in the rural sector and stagnant agricultural growth and productivity after the 1960s.

Agricultural policy was radically adjusted and reformed in the 1980s and 1990s. First, in response to the 1982–83 debt crisis, public spending on agricultural support fell from more than 2.0 percent of GDP in the early 1980s to 0.5 percent by 1992, remaining close to that level ever since. Second, in anticipation of the gradual opening up of the agriculture sector under the North American Free Trade Agreement after 1994, an ambitious constitutional reform of the *ejido* land tenure system was implemented in 1992. Mexico's second agrarian reform, as this broad reform effort has been described (Gordillo, De Janvry, and Sadulet 1999), was accompanied by reforms in agricultural support instruments. The most relevant of these reforms was creation of the *Programa de Apoyos Directos al Campo* (Procampo, Direct Support for Farmers Program), a per-hectare cash transfer program decoupled from production and commercialization, which was introduced in 1994. Procampo was revolutionary in its efficiency as well as equity. By decoupling transfers from the amount produced or marketed—in contrast to traditional market price support and input and output support policies—the program aimed both to minimize distortions in productive decisions and to reach subsistence farmers. Although it had a regressive element, Procampo was the least regressive of the larger agricultural support programs, and it was certainly the first major agricultural program with wide coverage of small producers, transferring significant resources to poor rural households.

More than two decades after the introduction of these agrarian land and support policy reforms, rural poverty remains persistently high and agriculture constitutes a smaller source of income for rural households, suggesting that the reforms failed to achieve the expected improvements in the integration, productivity, and equity of the agriculture sector. This failure was similar to that of the first agrarian reform: both programs failed to improve the access of small producers to productive inputs and markets, which would have allowed them to benefit from the pro-market reforms, and both concentrated their support on larger producers. This failure was aggravated by a drastic decline in spending on agricultural investment and public goods. Public goods accounted for the bulk of public spending in agriculture over most of the 20th century up to the 1970s, but the decline in overall agricultural support spending in the 1980s and 1990s was characterized by a shift from investment in public goods to the provision of market price support and cash and in-kind transfers.

EVOLUTION OF FOOD SUBSIDIES

The principal FOSA policy implemented during the 20th century consisted of generalized subsidies on basic food staples. Such subsidies can be traced back to the Lázaro Cárdenas government, which created the Regulatory Committee for the Basic Goods Market in 1938 and began regulating the price of basic staples. CONASUPO was the core agency implementing those policies between 1965 and 1999, with the dual objective of protecting producers through minimum guaranteed prices and shielding consumers through low food prices. The largest of those subsidies was the subsidy on tortillas (maize), followed by a subsidy on bread (wheat); other subsidized commodities included oil, rice, sorghum, soybeans, sugar, and milk.

Figure 5.1 presents the evolution of the principal FOSA instruments in Mexico from 1970 to 2015. In addition to budgetary (tax-financed) transfers, the figure also shows the ratio of transfers to consumers and producers through market price support policies for 1986–2014 (light green line). Public spending on FOSAs expanded to 1.2 percent of GDP in 1984, its highest level (of the period and of the century), although this estimate also includes subsidies to producers through CONASUPO.

As the gap between international prices and domestic producer and consumer prices widened in the 1980s, the CONASUPO subsidies became increasingly unsustainable and were gradually reduced and eventually eliminated in 1999. By 1991, with the producer price of corn 70 percent above international prices, the subsidy was insufficient to compensate consumers for the difference (Levy and van Wijnbergen 1993).

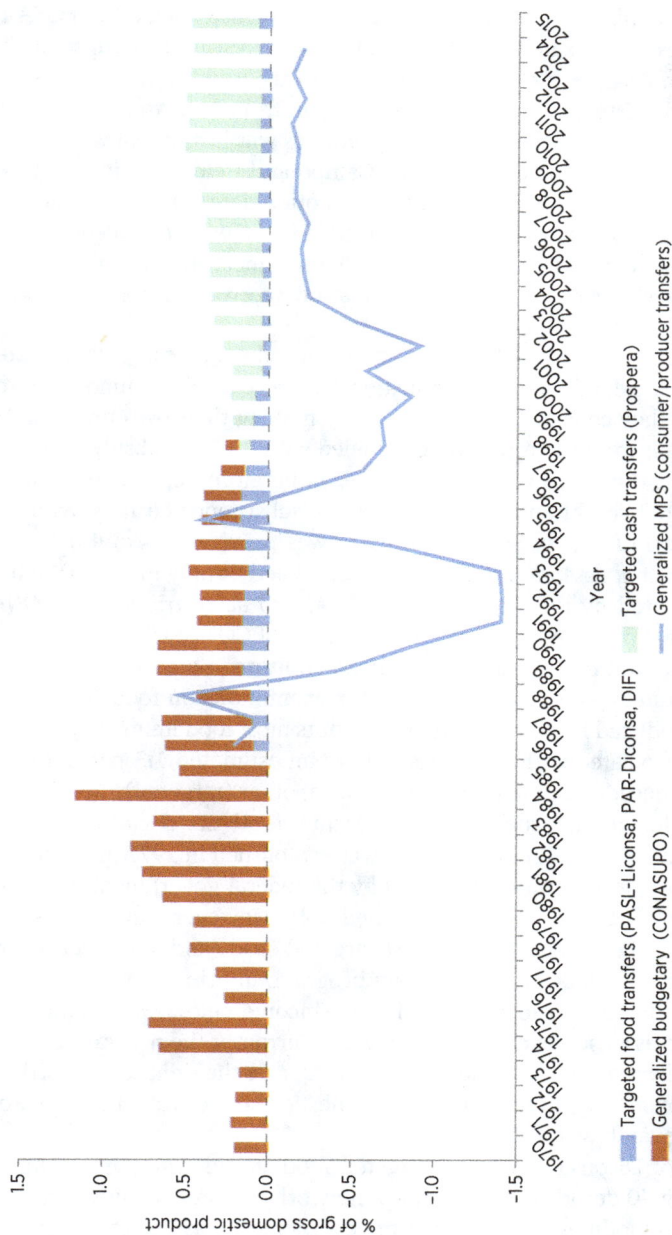

FIGURE 5.1

Evolution of Resources and Instruments for Food Assistance in Mexico, 1970–2015

Legend:
- Targeted food transfers (PASL-Liconsa, PAR-Diconsa, DIF)
- Generalized budgetary (CONASUPO)
- Targeted cash transfers (Prospera)
- Generalized MPS (consumer/producer transfers)

y-axis: % of gross domestic product

x-axis: Year

Sources: Based on the statistical annex in Poder Ejecutivo Federal, various years; OECD, various years.
Note: PASL = Social Milk Supply Program; PAR = Rural Food Supply Program; DIF = National System for Integral Family Development; CONASUPO = National Company of Popular Subsistence; MPS = market price supports.

The CONASUPO subsidies were notoriously opaque, making an evaluation of the program challenging; the program's design and implementation also made it a highly inefficient and inequitable instrument for FOSA-related objectives. For example, 20 percent of CONASUPO's food stock had an unknown destiny, and another 30 percent was used for animal consumption. If one adds irregularities in the distribution from mills to *tortillerías* (tortilla bakeries), the number of beneficiary families was just half of what the distributed resources implied (Martín del Campo and Calderón Tinoco 1992). The location of CONASUPO warehouses was often determined by political rather than economic factors and was correlated not with prevalence of poverty but with the density of private stores. For instance, Hill (1984) estimates that the poorest 50 percent of the population received just 16 percent of the subsidies.

Rural households—the population with the highest poverty rates and highest incidence of undernutrition—were excluded almost by design. Because they consume maize directly by making their own tortillas, they did not benefit from the tortillería-channeled subsidy. The subsidy to agricultural producers through a price floor on maize, therefore, represented a significant tax on poor rural households and even on subsistence farmers, who were net consumers of maize. Subsidized maize was provided in rural areas through the *Programa de Abasto Rural* (PAR, Rural Food Supply Program), which was implemented by the *Sistema Social de Abasto de Distribuidoras CONASUPO* (Diconsa, Social Supply Distribution System of CONASUPO).

In addition to CONASUPO, fiscal expenditures—another form of generalized subsidies—are associated with tax exemptions on food. The VAT, which was introduced in Mexico in 1980, exempts most food items. The fiscal expenditure associated with this measure was an estimated 1.3 percent of GDP in the past decade. Although not generalized, other (targeted) subsidy programs have older origins, such as the *Programa de Abasto Social de Leche* (PASL, Social Milk Supply Program). PASL was established in 1972 and implemented by Liconsa, a parastatal subsidized by the federal government and under the Ministry of Social Development (Sedesol). However, earlier versions date back to 1944, making it the oldest targeted food (and antipoverty) program in Mexico. PASL began as an urban program, in principle targeted to poorer neighborhoods and to households with income below two minimum wages and with at least one child under age 12. Currently, the program covers urban and rural areas, where beneficiary families have the right to buy fortified milk at approximately 50 percent of the domestic market price (in some areas, the price is even lower).

PAR of Diconsa is another targeted food subsidy program with a history spanning 40 decades. It consists of a network of stores (mainly rural) that sell basic commodities at subsidized prices. Diconsa was created in 1972 and is still operating under an expanded network of Diconsa community stores. The number of stores increased from 1,500 in 1976 to more than 27,000 in 2015.

Although Levy and Rodríguez (2005) classify PAR as a generalized food intervention because it does not restrict access to its stores, we classify it as a targeted program because it applies geographic targeting in two ways. First, it locates its stores in rural and (recently) periurban areas (between 200 and 14,999 inhabitants), and, second, it targets poor and isolated localities within rural areas. Evidence shows that at least until the 1990s, the latter type of targeting was not effective, with 40 percent of stores located in nonpoor localities and only 30 percent located in very poor localities (Levy and Dávila 1999; Levy and Rodríguez 2005). More recent data show that Diconsa's capacity to reach the poorest population has improved in the past decade, and PAR has become one of the most effectively targeted programs operating in Mexico today. However, an important concern is whether PAR undermines local production and commercial activities (box 5.1).

A third targeted FOSA program is the *Sistema Nacional para el Desarrollo Integral de la Familia* (DIF, National System for Integral Family Development), which operates a large program of school breakfasts, food baskets, and community kitchens. DIF was established in 1977, but its school breakfast program originated with creation of the Instituto Nacional de Protección a la Infancia (National Institute for the Protection of Children) in 1961. The program has a large presence in rural as well as urban areas. In 1998, it was decentralized through the *Fondo de Aportaciones Múltiples* (FAM, Multiple

---

BOX 5.1 Diconsa and the Rural Food Supply Program

Diconsa was established to extend CONASUPO's distribution network throughout the country by regulating the urban market of basic foodstuffs and by creating an institutional distribution channel. In 1979, the *Coordinación General del Plan Nacional de Zonas Deprimidas y Grupos Marginados* (COPLAMAR, General Coordination of the National Plan of Depressed Zones and Marginal Groups) was created to reduce inequalities between agriculture and industry and to combat the loss of food self-sufficiency in rural areas. Four years later, this program was transferred to Diconsa, becoming the CONASUPO Rural Program and later named the Rural Food Supply Program; in the 1980s, it was inserted into Sedesol.

After CONASUPO disappeared in 1999, Diconsa adopted a more entrepreneurial vision, consolidating itself as a competitive company. Moreover, under the Vicente Fox administration (2000–06), the Diconsa stores gradually began to offer additional products and services (at present, 90 percent of stores have become "community service units"). In 2013, Diconsa strengthened its social approach, taking action to reduce the purchase of products from trading companies and to increase the purchase of products directly from (local) producers. During the Enrique Peña Nieto administration, Diconsa has also reinforced its links with other social programs, assuming a strategic role as the operational arm for the distribution of beneficiary support; PAR is still Diconsa's main program, with a budget for 2016 of US$108.3 million, representing 2.4 percent of the social development sector budget (0.01 percent of GDP).

box continues next page

BOX 5.1 **Diconsa and the Rural Food Supply Program** *(continued)*

PAR's main objective is to guarantee the social right of access to food by facilitating physical and economic access to foodstuffs for the population living in localities of high or very high rates of marginalization. The program provides Diconsa stores with a supply of basic commodities (17 food items and 5 products like soap, toilet paper, and toothpaste) and complementary commodities (health, hygiene, and other products), at preferential prices that are at least 15 percent lower than prices in the local market. At present, savings offered by Diconsa stores range between 20.5 and 28.8 percent. Diconsa sells commodities to its network of stores at subsidized prices, so these savings are not the result of marketing efficiencies.

This program was highly innovative because it established a scheme of mutual responsibility between the government and the community, with the community a key factor in the operation and sustainability of PAR. Access to PAR support is driven by community demand (once the eligibility requirements are met). Once approved, the community owns and operates the Diconsa store (including the store premises). A store manager is democratically elected by a community assembly, and Diconsa repays him or her with 5 percent of total sales of products in the store. For a store to begin operations, Diconsa first assigns it with "working capital" (an initial credit) sufficient to cover at least 21 days of sales. Once the store has capitalized, the manager submits a request to the Diconsa warehouse for the items needed to restock the store. Therefore, the quality of the service provided to PAR beneficiary communities depends on the manager's management and service capabilities.

A Diconsa store represents the only option for food provision in 10 percent of rural localities, and the stores generally have wide acceptance, as beneficiaries associate them with social value. However, recent evaluations and monitoring studies have found that Diconsa needs to (a) ensure the optimum supply at the stores, (b) guarantee that prices are lower than those in the local market, and (c) inform the mechanisms through which beneficiaries can submit suggestions, requests regarding poor-quality products, or complaints about the manager's service. There is no evidence regarding the impacts of this program on food and nutrition.

Sources: CONEVAL 2012; Diconsa 2015; Flores, Muñoz, and Colorado 2015; Shamah and others 2014; Soto 2014.

Contributions Fund), which is part of a set of large decentralized funds that forms part of the federal budget. The funds generally ensure stable financing as well as transparent rules for the distribution of resources at the state level. However, the decentralization process has limited the transparency and accountability of the DIF program, because it is administered separately in the 32 states, and reporting and accountability responsibilities between the states and federal government tend to be ill defined. This may explain why, in contrast to the other long-standing food programs, the DIF programs have survived and expanded despite limited information about their actual impacts.

Another targeted food subsidy program that replaced generalized subsidies was the *Programa Maíz-Tortilla* (Maize-Tortilla Program), which was introduced in 1984. This program became the *Programa de Subsidio al*

Consumo de la Tortilla (Tortilla sin Costo, Tortilla Subsidy Program) in 1990 and was replaced in 1992 with the *Fideicomiso para la Liquidación del Subsidio a la Tortilla* (Fidelist, Trust to Eliminate the Tortilla Subsidy). The targeted subsidy was first implemented through the direct distribution of subsidized tortillas in the Diconsa community stores, with tortillas sold at 50 percent below the generalized price ceiling (1984–86). In 1986–90, the program was implemented through food vouchers (*tortibonos*), which were replaced in 1990 by vouchers that allowed consumers to obtain 1 kilo of free tortillas per day. In 1991, an electronic card was introduced to implement the program, which was better designed to monitor compensation to torti-llerías. The program was gradually reduced in the late 1990s and eventually eliminated in 2003.

In practice, compared with generalized subsidies, both the Fidelist and PASL programs were not effective in reaching the poor. Although programs were targeted to households with an income below two minimum wages, no credible means test was available to identify household income directly for targeting purposes (and none is available to date in Mexico, which explains why Prospera introduced a proxy means test), except through self-reporting and house visits. The application of the targeting mechanisms is opaque and subject to manipulation (Martín del Campo and Calderón Tinoco 1992). Also, the concentration of PASL and Fidelist in Mexico City did not reduce, and probably aggravated, the urban bias of food subsidies. Finally, in the case of the PASL implemented by Liconsa, operational costs were extremely high, on the order of 28.5 percent (Grosh 1994) to 36.0 percent (World Bank 1991).

Spending on targeted FOSA increased significantly over the 1980s and 1990s as food subsidies partially replaced declining generalized subsidies. The substitution was only partial, however, as total FOSA spending fell signifi-cantly during the period, before recuperating with the introduction of the Prospera CCT in 1997 and its rapid expansion over the following decade. As discussed later in this chapter, the decline in public spending on FOSAs was more than compensated by the increase in the targeting and operational effi-ciency of the instruments, so the benefits reaching the poor actually increased fivefold between 1997 and 2015.

Figure 5.2 presents the evolution of key FOSA and Prospera transfers as a percentage of GDP. For Liconsa and Fidelist, the value reported in the figure does not represent public spending; rather, it is the estimated value of the transfer to beneficiaries. For Fidelist, this is a good approximation of public spending (minus operational costs), but for Liconsa, for which public spend-ing data are also reported for comparison, the two series are very different (official estimates of the value of Liconsa transfers stopped in 2000, so the series after that year reports public spending). The difference is largely due to Liconsa's access to heavily subsidized milk imported from abroad. As a result, despite high operational costs—for distributing through a network of stores

FIGURE 5.2

Evolution of the Value of Targeted Food and Cash Transfers in Mexico, 1980–2015

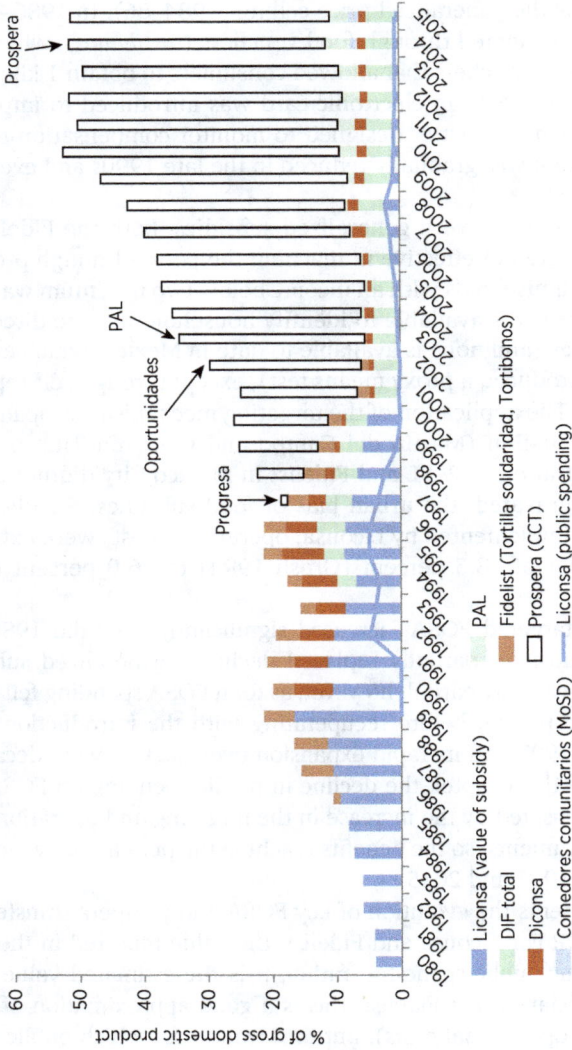

Legend:
- Liconsa (value of subsidy)
- DIF total
- Diconsa
- Comedores comunitarios (MoSD)
- PAL
- Fidelist (Tortilla solidaridad, Tortibonos)
- Prospera (CCT)
- Liconsa (public spending)

X-axis: years 1980–2015
Y-axis: % of gross domestic product (0 to 60)

Labels on chart: Prospera, PAL, Oportunidades, Progresa

Sources: Based on Poder Ejecutivo Federal, various years; SHCP, various years; OECD, various years.
Note: Liconsa (value of subsidy) refers to the estimated value of the benefit received by beneficiaries, calculated as the price paid for Liconsa milk minus the commercial price of milk times the amount of milk; Liconsa (public spending) refers to the budgetary cost of the Liconsa transfers. PAL = Food Support Program; CCT = conditional cash transfer; DIF = National System for Integral Family Development; MoSD = Ministry of Social Development (Sedesol).

and for transforming powdered into liquid milk—the program could still offer milk at half the domestic commercial price, with marginal or even zero fiscal costs (1989–90, 2000–02).

Even at their historical maximum (1989–96), the combined targeted FOSAs represented only 0.2 percent of GDP. Except for DIF, targeted subsidy programs declined significantly with the expansion of the Prospera cash transfers. Two new FOSA programs have been introduced since 2003: PAL in 2003 and *Comedores Comunitarios* (Community Kitchens) in 2014.

THE INTRODUCTION AND EXPANSION OF CASH TRANSFERS

The transition from generalized subsidies to targeted food transfers over the mid-1980s to mid-1990s was followed by a transition to targeted cash transfers. The introduction of Prospera in 1997 coincided with the elimination of CONASUPO in 1999, the phasing out of Fidelist in 2003, and the reduction of the other major targeted food transfers, except DIF (which was instead decentralized in 1998). Prospera was originally financed with the resources made available from reallocated food subsidies—in particular, from CONASUPO.

Prospera was intended to reduce the intergenerational transmission of poverty through basic human capital investments using CCTs. Prospera's target population consists of extremely poor households, originally in the poorest rural areas, although coverage has expanded into urban areas and higher education levels. The most recent reforms aimed to connect Prospera beneficiaries to financial services and productive activities.

The educational component of Prospera consists of scholarships designed to cover the opportunity cost of every child's participation in basic education, lower-secondary education, and upper-secondary education in lieu of their participation in the workforce. The scholarships have risen progressively and are slightly higher for girls than for boys after basic education. In addition, an economic incentive is provided to every child who completes high school before age 22. The food component of the program is a fixed per-household monetary transfer, which, during the 2009 financial crisis, was complemented with an additional per-household food transfer. Two life-cycle transfers were added during the federal administrations of 2000–06 and 2006–12: a basic old-age pension and a child support transfer for every child from birth to age 9, respectively. Finally, the health component includes basic preventive health services (including educational health sessions) and in-kind food transfers: nutritional supplements for pregnant or lactating mothers and for children under age 5.[2]

PAL was introduced in 2003 as a complement to Prospera. Although introduced as a separate program, PAL can be considered an extension of the Prospera food component for three reasons. First, and most important, PAL was introduced to reach the extreme poor who live in small and remote rural localities where the conditional design of Prospera cannot operate because these communities lack the required education and health services. PAL offered the food component to eligible households in such localities as a UCT. Later, this objective was broadened to include any eligible beneficiaries who could not be incorporated into Prospera for lack of access to the required services, regardless of whether lack of access was due to overstretched clinics in urban areas or scarcity of services in remote areas. Second, though PAL was initially operated by Diconsa, Prospera's coordination entity (NCP) assumed responsibility for PAL's operation in 2010. Third, in 2016 the program was formally integrated within Prospera as an unconditional scheme of benefits that coexists with the original conditional scheme of benefits.

Figure 5.3 shows the distribution of Prospera transfers between its three main components—and the ministries to which relevant resources are budgeted—including PAL. A large fraction of resources in the health component finance the food supplements, but that component also includes costs associated with health talks. (Neither the health nor the education component includes the actual cost of services, which is budgeted as part of the overall supply of these services by the relevant ministries.) The in-kind food transfers of Prospera currently represent about 7 percent of total Prospera transfers. The share of the education component increased slightly in 2000–03, reflecting the program's expansion to upper-secondary education, but in 2006–11 the participation of the transfer component (Prospera cash transfers and PAL)

FIGURE 5.3

Spending on Prospera Components and PAL as a Share of Total Prospera and PAL Spending in Mexico, 2000–15

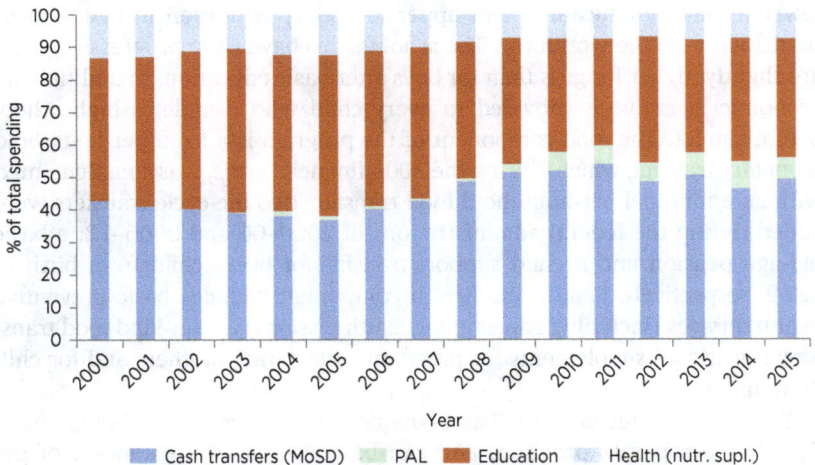

Sources: Based on Poder Ejecutivo Federal, various years; SHCP, various years.
Note: MoSD = Ministry of Social Development (Sedesol); PAL = Food Support Program; nutr. supl. = nutritional supplements.

BOX 5.2 **Evolution of PAL**

PAL emerged in 2003 as part of the *Programa Microrregiones* (Microregions Program) formerly called *Te Nutre* (Feeds You), which was implemented by Sedesol. PAL provided households with a food basket (beans, rice, maize flour, vegetable oil, powdered milk, pasta soup, canned tuna or sardines, tomato puree, lentils, and canned or dried chilies) every two weeks. The food basket was valued at US$3.75 and reached households that Prospera could not reach because the health and education ministries lacked institutional capacity in rural areas.

In 2004, Te Nutre was formally renamed PAL, and implementation was transferred to Diconsa. PAL's support was granted monthly in two forms: either in-kind support or cash transfers. The former consisted of a food basket valued at US$7.50; the latter consisted of the delivery of a cash transfer of US$7.50 per household.

In 2009, PAL began to provide two basic types of benefits: cash transfers per household and in-kind support in the form of nutritional supplements targeted to children under age 5 and to pregnant or lactating women within the beneficiary households. PAL coverage also expanded to urban areas.

In 2010, the institutional management and operation of PAL moved from Diconsa to Prospera (the NCP entity), while still providing both cash and in-kind (food) transfers. The shift was intended to address challenges in institutional and implementation coordination (for example, the synchronization of processes and the delivery of nutritional supplements without the intervention of the Ministry of Health), as well as to improve the alignment of targeting criteria and methodology, benefit size, and others.

In 2013, two major changes occurred: first, in-kind transfers were discontinued, and vouchers were added (PAL–Sin Hambre), representing an extra benefit of US$4.60 per household (that is, in addition to the original cash component valued at US$25 per household plus US$6.30, which is provided for each child under age 9). The vouchers can be used to access 19 nonperishable commodities (except eggs) available at Diconsa stores.

In 2016, PAL was fully integrated into Prospera, offering three types of benefits: conditional cash transfers, currently reaching 6.1 million beneficiary households (90 percent of the program), unconditional cash transfers (137,000 households), and vouchers (579,000 households).

increased from 40 to 60 percent, reflecting the introduction of old-age and child support transfers as well as the expansion of PAL (box 5.2 summarizes the evolution of the latter).

A large body of literature is available on the impacts of Prospera, probably one of the largest impact evaluation literatures available for any program in the world. Parker and Todd (2015) present a comprehensive survey of this literature. This section focuses on the role that the program has played in transforming food transfers in Mexico. The introduction of Progresa in 1997 and its expansion since then radically redefined food support and antipoverty policy in Mexico, with innovations in four main areas: conception and design, instruments, targeting, and institutional design.

Conception and Design

The design of Prospera reflects the recognition that effective investment in human capital cannot be achieved by providing food to poor households that lack basic education and health services. Rather, it occurs only through the simultaneous, coordinated provision of early nutritional support, basic education, basic health services, and sufficient household income to support adequate food consumption. Such transfers are targeted at the critical stages in the child's life cycle to ensure the necessary accumulation of human capital: maternal and early infant health and nutrition as well as education at the elementary, lower-secondary, and (after 2000) upper-secondary levels. CCTs were designed to finance current food consumption, to cover educational opportunity costs, and to provide incentives to access preventive health services. Furthermore, concentrating these resources in small poor communities ensures that the resources contribute to local economic development (for a review of the evidence, see Parker and Todd 2015).

Instruments: Cash and Food Transfers

Prospera replaced generalized and targeted food transfers with direct cash transfers (CTs) to households. Although the program includes in-kind food transfers, cash transfers are the principal instrument. Under a narrow, instrument-based definition of food subsidies, this transition could be interpreted as a shift from food support to income support, but, in reality, CTs were assumed to be more effective than food support (Levy and Rodríguez 2005).

This conclusion may be argued on multiple points. First, contrary to what is commonly assumed, the value of food transfers was below the food spending of beneficiary households (overall and in the specific foods subsidized, except milk), so the food transfers worked, in effect, as pure CTs, liberating resources for general purchases. Second, although a pure cash transfer is, by definition, not conditional on food spending, the program's effective targeting to the extreme poor and its allocation to mothers or female caregivers in the household ensure that most of this transfer is spent on food, as has been confirmed in evaluations of the program (Parker and Todd 2015). Third, the operational costs of transferring cash are significantly lower than the costs of distributing food (for example, 5 percent for Prospera compared with 28 percent for Liconsa). Fourth, while the indirect flow of resources involved in food transfers creates many opportunities for diverting resources away from the intended beneficiaries, direct CTs do not allow such leakage and are more transparent (the household—and any accounting agency—knows exactly the value of the transfer received). These points present a strong argument for the comparative effectiveness of CTs versus food transfers as instruments for food support.

The survival of food transfers suggests that they still serve a purpose. Alderman (2016, 2) reviews the evidence on the effectiveness of CTs versus food transfers and concludes, "UCTs as well as CCTs virtually always augment household food consumption, diet diversity, and participation in preventive health care . . . [but they] have not delivered improvements in nutrition commensurate with their success in addressing poverty." In the case of Mexico, a review of the accumulated evidence suggests that Prospera "supports significant and positive health impacts for children" (Parker and Todd 2015, 36). Although disentangling the effects of Prospera's components is difficult, two studies use the program's variations in treatment to estimate the nutritional impacts of food supplements and CTs separately. The results are somewhat ambiguous. Behrman and Hoddinott (2005) find a positive effect of food supplements, but not of the program overall, whereas Fernald, Gertler, and Neufeld (2008, 2009) find a strong positive effect of income transfers on nutrition. The contrast between the success of CTs in delivering nutritional inputs and their failure in achieving nutritional outcomes is surprising and requires further analysis.

The comparison of interest regarding Mexico's food support reforms is both between the in-kind and income components of Prospera, and between the older in-kind transfers and Prospera. An important test for the innovations in conception, design, and instruments was a large pilot program implemented in 1995 in three localities in the state of Campeche—the *Programa de Canasta Básica Alimentaria para el Bienestar de la Familia* (Basic Food Basket for Family Welfare Program; Levy and Rodríguez 2005). The program substituted the milk and tortilla subsidies for all beneficiaries in the three localities with a cash transfer of equivalent value in the form of a debit card acceptable in selected stores (including tortillerías). The pilot made these transfers conditional on attendance at health clinics by pregnant and lactating mothers and children under age 5, where they also received nutritional supplements. The evaluation confirmed that almost all beneficiaries preferred cash to in-kind transfers and that local economies gained positive effects, with no reduction in the sale in Fidelist tortillerías. It also revealed that the conditional design entailed institutional challenges in intersectoral coordination. Thus, the pilot was a way station on the path to Prospera.

Targeting

In addition to its concentration in rural areas (exclusively until 2001), Prospera applies a double targeting mechanism to identify and reach the poorest households. First, it identifies the poorer localities (or neighborhoods in urban settings) using census data, and second, it applies a proxy means test to identify poor households within those localities using the observable (and ideally nonmanipulable) household characteristics best correlated with income poverty. In rural settings, the program applies these tests as a census to the whole population in each eligible locality. In urban settings, that approach is not feasible, and the program sets up application modules (self-targeting of the eligible population).

Although geographic targeting has many antecedents in Mexico's social policy, Prospera was the first program to implement an effective administrative targeting mechanism at the household level. As discussed later in this section, survey evidence suggests that Prospera is among the most effectively targeted programs operating in Mexico, although it is not free from targeting errors. The exclusion error, in which the poor population that would be eligible (by the proxy means test) is left out of the program, falls into two main categories: (a) poor households in rural localities that lack the required health and educational services and (b) poor households in urban localities who either fail to identify themselves to the program or that cannot be included because of constraints associated with Prospera's budget or with the locality's lack of capacity to provide services to program beneficiaries. The second population is by far the largest, but the first involves the poorest of the poor. Although PAL was set up in 2003 initially to address the first challenge, it has also been leveraged in the context of the second challenge.

Institutional Arrangements

The institutional design of Prospera responded to two important failures of previous social programs: lack of effective interagency coordination and lack of accountability. Many social programs before and since Prospera began have been inspired by the idea that coordinating different ministries and programs within ministries can address a social problem more effectively than taking isolated actions, but these efforts have generally failed in the face of Mexico's strongly vertical ministerial cultures and power structures. Prospera has been unique in the history of social policy in Mexico in that it has successfully integrated the actions of three major ministries: Sedesol, the Ministry of Education, and the Ministry of Health. That integration has been possible because Prospera was set up as part of a centralized coordinating entity, the NCP, within Sedesol. The responsibilities of each ministry were clearly defined and formalized in operational rules from the beginning (Prospera was a pioneer in publishing its rules). Sedesol operates the delivery of CTs, and the ministries of health and education oversee the provision of services and the certification of beneficiaries' fulfillment of co-responsibilities. A specific category was created under each ministry's budget to specify the budget allocated to Prospera's implementation and to CTs. This coordination was facilitated by the fact that the program was introduced with strong political commitment from the president and the treasury.

The second institutional advantage of Prospera, ensuring accountability, was important in the aftermath of the *Programa Nacional de Solidaridad* (Pronasol, National Solidarity Program). This flagship antipoverty program of the Carlos Salinas administration (1988–94) was highly opaque in its allocation, ineffectively targeted, and widely suspected of being manipulated for electoral purposes. In that context, Prospera made its allocation criteria (except for the specific weights in the formula to avoid manipulation of the proxy means test), beneficiaries list, and actual allocations fully transparent. The program also incorporated—from its inception and for the first time in Mexico—an ambitious external and fully public long-term impact evaluation project. That design has played an important role in the construction of evaluation practices and institutions in Mexico in the past two decades.

RECENT DEVELOPMENTS

The most recent change in Mexico's food-oriented policy, introduced by the Enrique Peña Nieto administration, has been the adoption of a broad antipoverty strategy. The CNCH was originally inspired by the Zero Hunger Challenge promoted by the United Nations. Despite its origin and name, the CNCH is a broad coordination and targeting strategy involving a large set of programs from multiple ministries that is designed to reduce Mexico's multidimensional poverty index. This index measures income poverty together with poverty gaps in six social dimensions: education, health, social security, housing quality, housing services, and food security. The population targeted by the CNCH is the subset of the extreme poor who suffer food insecurity, as measured by this poverty index.

The CNCH has introduced only one new program, Comedores Comunitarios, which is implemented by Sedesol. This initiative was first implemented as a response to the effects of natural disasters in Guerrero State and then adopted as a federal program under the CNCH, substantially increasing its coverage. This program has three components: one-time provision of equipment to set up a kitchen; monthly provision of nonperishable inputs; and, for eligible communities, one-time support for the installation of a backyard garden to produce vegetables and poultry. In 2015, 7,937 kitchens were operating, around three-quarters of them in rural localities. The program operates only in localities with more than 200 inhabitants, because the nonperishable inputs are provided by the distribution chain of Diconsa, which only operates in such communities.

The Peña Nieto administration also introduced PAL–Sin Hambre, in which households incorporated into PAL after 2013 received the food component as an in-kind transfer in the form of a prepaid card, which could only be used to buy from a predefined list of food items in Diconsa stores (box 5.3). The introduction of these two new food transfers—Comedores Comunitarios and PAL–Sin Hambre—suggests that the present administration has a renewed interest in in-kind food transfers, but such transfers represent only a marginal increase in existing food transfers in comparison with Prospera's cash transfers (figure 5.2),[3] an increase from 0.06 percent of GDP to 0.08 percent between 2012 and 2015. However, if one considers the conclusions obtained in evaluations of the CNCH (CONEVAL 2016), from a food security perspective, the strategy used by Prospera and PAL is still fragmented, and relevant long-term interventions are missing, notably those aimed at addressing urban poverty. Overall coverage of PAL is laid out in figure 5.4.

BOX 5.3 **Delivery of Voucher Benefits**

PAL–Sin Hambre entails two steps. First, beneficiaries are directed to the temporary transfers delivery centers of the *Banco del Ahorro Nacional y Servicios Financieros* (BANSEFI, National Bank of Financial Services), a public institution, in order to have their transfers deposited in their prepaid card, as determined in their transfers delivery schedule. In some cases, BANSEFI hires Diconsa stores to undertake this step. After-wards, beneficiaries can freely decide when to go to the Diconsa store to redeem all of their benefits (although, in practice, beneficiaries attend the same day that their trans-fers are deposited). Diconsa stores may be either fixed or mobile stores or centers set up to provide services to PAL–Sin Hambre beneficiaries.

According to monitoring reports, beneficiaries often need to attend the Diconsa store two or three times because they cannot find all of the products they want or need to buy on the first visit. These extra trips impose higher costs on them in terms of time and cash spent (given that some beneficiaries have to pay a taxi or hire local transpor-tation for the trip). They do not receive CTs, and so they need to cover this expenditure with their own resources.

To improve the consumption patterns of beneficiaries, Diconsa, jointly with Pospera, also provides nutritional information at the Diconsa stores (including printed materials, which have been developed by an expert institution). In Mexico State, beneficiaries of programs that promote family backyard gardens sell their surplus of perishables in a sort of farmer's market set up outside the Diconsa stores during the payment days. This project benefits the local economy and encourages the consumption of healthy, nutritional products, since the food basket does not include perishable items other than eggs.

Source: Based on fieldwork conducted by the authors in 2016.

FIGURE 5.4

Coverage of PAL in Mexico, by Geographic Location, 2010–15

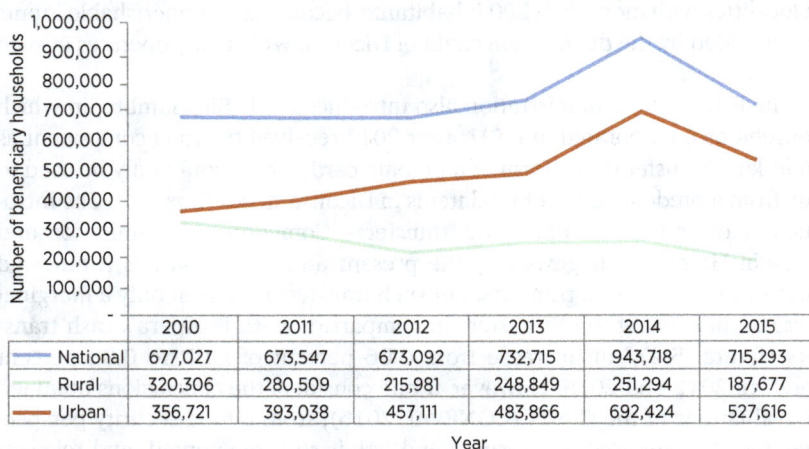

	2010	2011	2012	2013	2014	2015
National	677,027	673,547	673,092	732,715	943,718	715,293
Rural	320,306	280,509	215,981	248,849	251,294	187,677
Urban	356,721	393,038	457,111	483,866	692,424	527,616

Year

Source: Based on internal administrative information provided by Prospera staff in 2016.

DISTRIBUTION AND EFFICIENCY

The revolutionary impact of these reforms is clear, considering the distribution of food support benefits in Mexico before and after the reforms. This section presents estimates of the distribution of benefits at the regional and household levels. The estimates are based on household nutrition and income surveys conducted by Mexico's *Instituto Nacional de Estadísticas y Geografía* (National Institute of Statistics and Geography)—the National Nutrition Survey, National Health and Nutrition Survey, and National Household Income and Expenditure Survey—that report the number of beneficiaries and the amount of benefits received for the principal food programs.

As reported earlier in this chapter, the incidence of child undernutrition and extreme poverty has historically been higher in rural areas of Mexico than in urban areas and higher in the southern than in the northern states and Mexico City, although such regional inequalities are smaller than in previous decades. Examining the regional distribution of food support transfers and of undernourished children (children under age 5 who are stunted) reveals a strong antirural and antisouth bias in the allocation of food transfers that favors urban localities and Mexico City particularly. In 1994, the rural sector accounted for half of the nation's chronically undernourished children, but rural areas received only 22 percent of all food transfers (including CONASUPO), and the south accounted for 51 percent of undernourished children, but received only 8.6 percent of targeted food transfers. At the other extreme, Mexico City accounted for 7.3 percent of undernourished children but received almost 70 percent of targeted food transfers. This distribution changed dramatically after the introduction and early expansion of Progresa beginning in 1993. By 2000, the rural sector received 63.6 percent of food support transfers, and the southern states received 54 percent. By 2000, the regional allocation of such transfers coincided with the distribution of chronic undernutrition. This reallocation of transfers was achieved mainly through the rural concentration and geographic targeting of Prospera (Progresa at the time), but also through the reallocation of other programs from urban and metropolitan areas to the rural sector and southern and central states of Mexico. By 2010–12, the rural share of transfers had declined slightly, to 59 percent, but the rural share of undernourished children had declined to 38 percent, so food support is now rurally biased by this measure.

A more detailed geographic analysis of food assistance can be performed using administrative records and poverty estimates at the state and municipal levels. As shown in figure 5.5, the allocation of DIF—Mexico's largest in-kind food transfer today—is regressive at the state level in relation to the distribution of extreme poverty. The poorest states (Chiapas, Guerrero, Oaxaca) receive the lowest transfers per poor person, representing just one-sixth of the transfers received by the two states with the lowest poverty rates

FIGURE 5.5

Geographic Distribution of DIF Spending on Food Assistance in Mexico, by Amount of Transfer per Extreme Poor, 2015

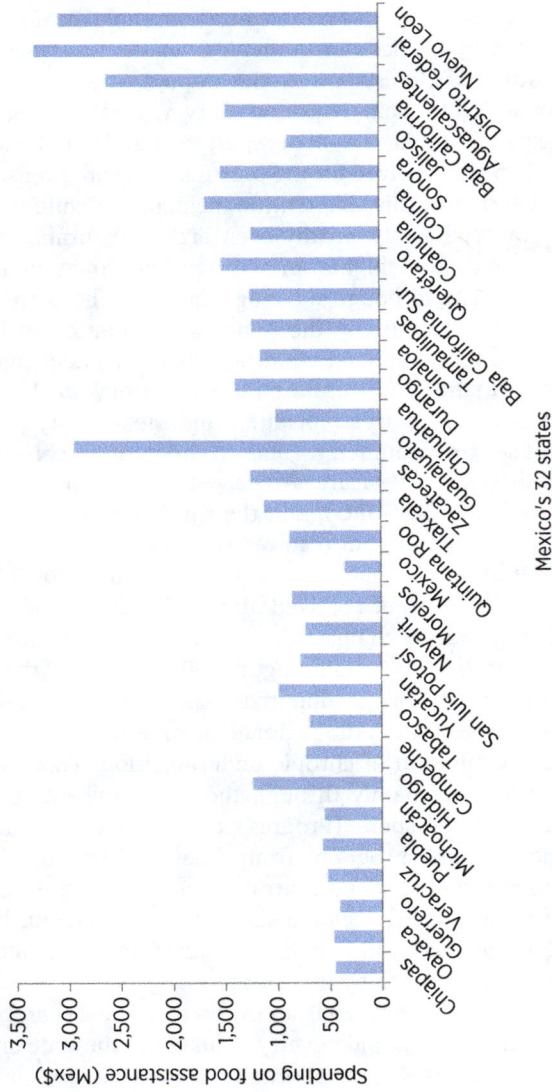

Sources: Based on the 2015 distribution of FAM social assistance (*Diario Oficial de la Federación*, January 29, 2015) and poverty estimates from CONEVAL 2015.
Note: States are ranked by extreme poverty rate, with Chiapas being the poorest state. FAM = Multiple Contributions Fund; DIF = National System for Integral Family Development.

(Mexico City, Nuevo León). The southern region's share of total program spending fell from 46 to 40 percent between 2000 and 2015.

The distribution of benefits can be estimated more precisely at the household level. This estimate confirms a similar transformation in the distribution of benefits after the introduction of Prospera. As shown in figure 5.6,

FIGURE 5.6

Public Spending on Food-Oriented Social Assistance (FOSA) in Mexico, by Population Decile, 1990s–2010

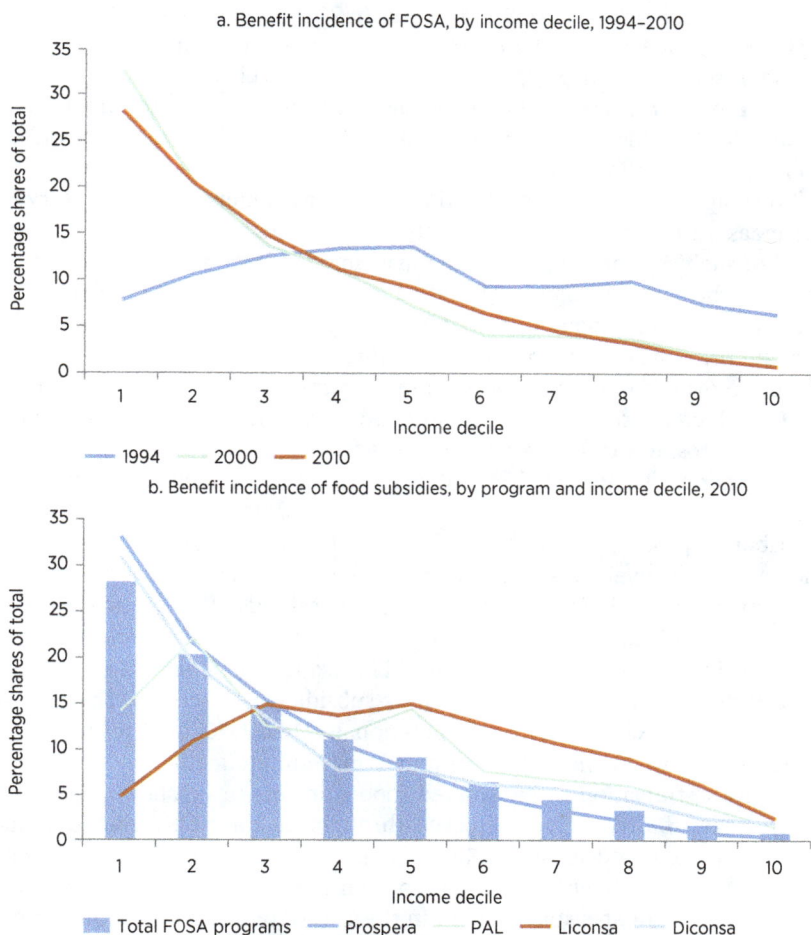

a. Benefit incidence of FOSA, by income decile, 1994–2010

b. Benefit incidence of food subsidies, by program and income decile, 2010

Sources: Based on data from the National Nutrition Survey for 1999, the National Health and Nutrition Survey for 2006, the National Household Income and Expenditure Survey for 2010, as well as from SHCP, various years, for 2010.
Note: FOSA = food-oriented social assistance; PAL = Food Support Program.

panel a, the global distribution of food support (including the generalized tortilla subsidy) was fairly flat in 1994, but became highly pro-poor by 1999–2000, when the share of food subsidies received by the poorest decile rose from 7 to 33 percent. The distribution of food subsidies was very similar for 2000 and 2010, and over that decade the level of undernutrition in the poorest half of the distribution fell significantly (from 48 to 31 percent in the first income decile and from 41 to 19 percent in the second income decile between 1999 and 2006). This decline implies that, as in the regional analysis, the current allocation of benefits corresponds closely with the distribution of undernutrition and poverty, as measured by this indicator. Considering the principal FOSA programs in 2010, Prospera and Diconsa are highly pro-poor, PAL is less effective than Prospera in reaching households in the poorest decile,[4] DIF programs are somewhat less effective in reaching the first quintile, and Liconsa has very low rates of participation among the poorest households and is concentrated in the middle of the income distribution (figure 5.6. panel b).

To compare the efficiency of various FOSA instruments, it is necessary to (a) measure the instruments' capacity to reach the households in greatest need of such support; (b) assess the instruments' targeting efficiency, measured as the share of transfers received by the target population divided by the share of that population in the total population; and (c) take into account the costs of the programs, including both operational costs incurred by the government and participation costs incurred by beneficiaries. Table 5.1 compares generalized and targeted milk and tortilla subsidies with the Prospera transfers and an average for targeted food programs in Latin America. Generalized subsidies are, in principle, cheap to operate, but, as in the case of tortillas, provide many opportunities for leakage in the distribution process before the food reaches the final consumers; by design, they are ineffectively targeted. The estimates show that, for every Mexican peso spent on food support, the poorest households (the lowest quintile) receive, net of costs, almost 60 percent of Prospera transfers, but only 17 percent of Fidelist and 8 percent of Liconsa transfers, and 11 and 4 percent of the generalized tortilla and milk subsidies, respectively. The cost of transferring Mex$1.00 to this population is Mex$1.70 for Prospera, but Mex$11.70 for Liconsa. The gains in targeting effectiveness achieved through the transition from targeted food transfers to Prospera have been much larger than the gains achieved through the transition from generalized to targeted food subsidies. Table 5.2 presents estimates of indicators of redistributive effectiveness for total food transfers implemented in 1990 and 2000. These estimates suggest that, in the 1990s, with the shift from generalized and targeted food subsidies to Prospera, the redistributive efficiency (percentage reduction in the Gini coefficient per transfer as a percentage of market income) doubled, and the share of the poorest quintile in the transfers tripled.

TABLE 5.1 Comparisons of Redistributive Cost-Effectiveness of Various Subsidies in Mexico

INDICATOR AND TARGET POPULATION (TP)	PROSPERA	MILK SUBSIDY		TORTILLA SUBSIDY		AVERAGE LATIN AMERICA[a]
		TARGETED (PASL)	GENERAL	TARGETED (FIDELIST)	GENERAL	
% of transfers received by TP (F)						
Poorest 20%	64.9	12.2	4.3	20.0	12.3	—
Poorest 40%	89.0	35.4	15.7	62.4	33.6	72.0
Targeting efficiency (F/%TP in total population)						
Poorest 20%	3.24	0.61	0.22	1.00	0.62	—
Poorest 40%	2.23	0.89	0.39	1.56	0.84	1.80
% of transfers benefiting TP (B)						
Poorest 20%	58.3	8.5	4.1	17.3	11.7	—
Poorest 40%	80.1	24.8	14.9	53.8	31.9	64.2
Cost per amount transferred (Mex$)						
Poorest 20%	1.70	11.70	24.50	5.80	8.60	—
Poorest 40%	1.20	4.00	6.70	1.90	3.1	1.60
Operational costs (CO) (% of total)	8.2[a]	28.5[b]	5.0	12.0[a]	5.0	9.0
Participation costs (CP) (% of total)	2.0[b]	2.0	0.0	2.0	0.0	2.0

Sources: Based on data from the Social Module of the National Household Income and Expenditure Survey for 2002.

Note: Numbers from variables in bold are imputed. Household deciles are ordered by per capita market income. PASL = Social Milk Supply Program; — = not available.

a. Cost data are from Grosh 1994.
b. Cost data are from Coady 2000.

TABLE 5.2 **Estimated Effectiveness of Total Food Subsidies in Mexico, 1990–2000**

INDICATOR	TARGET POPULATION	1990	2000
Operational costs (% of total)	n.a.	13.1	10.5
Participation costs (% of total)	n.a.	1.0	2.1
Redistributive efficiency[a] (after costs)	n.a.	−0.74	−1.50
% of beneficiaries in poverty	Bottom 20%	11.9	32.0
Beneficiaries in poverty as % of total beneficiaries	Bottom 40%	29.9	53.8
% of benefits received by poor	Bottom 20%	10.3	27.9
Benefits received by poor as a % of spending	Bottom 40%	25.7	47.0
Cost per Mex$1 transferred	Bottom 40%	3.90	2.10

Sources: Based on data presented in table 5.1; figures 5.6 and 5.7.
Note: n.a. = not applicable.
[a]. % reduction in the Gini coefficient divided by the transfer as a % of market income.

Figure 5.7 shows the evolution of food support resources actually reaching the target population (defined as the poorest quintile), after costs and leakage to nonpoor food consumers. (The figure overestimates CONASUPO benefits to the poor because it does not show leakage to nonconsumers.) The evolution of food support in figure 5.7 looks very different from the evolution of public spending shown in figure 5.6. The food support resources effectively reaching the poor are a fraction of public spending on those programs (0.14 percent of GDP at the height of CONASUPO spending, when it reached 1.20 percent of GDP). Also, the drastic reduction in food support transfers between 1984 and 1999 was reversed through the Prospera transfers, resulting in a fivefold increase in food transfers reaching the poor, from an average of 0.05 percent of GDP over CONASUPO's history to 0.23–0.25 percent of GDP in the present decade.

LESSONS LEARNED

The impact of cash transfer programs on human capital investments as well as their costs are well documented. The role of food within the larger social protection system is, arguably, less explored. As documented in this chapter, the transition from generalized food subsidies to targeted food transfers and then to targeted vouchers and cash led to a dramatic reallocation of food assistance in Mexico. This reallocation includes shifts from households in urban areas and richer regions, such as Mexico City, to households in rural settings and disadvantaged southern states. Those reforms have aligned resource allocations with the spatial and household distribution of needs—measured in

FIGURE 5.7

Total Spending on Food Support and Benefits Reaching Households in the Poorest Quintile (Net of Operational Costs) in Mexico, 1970–2015

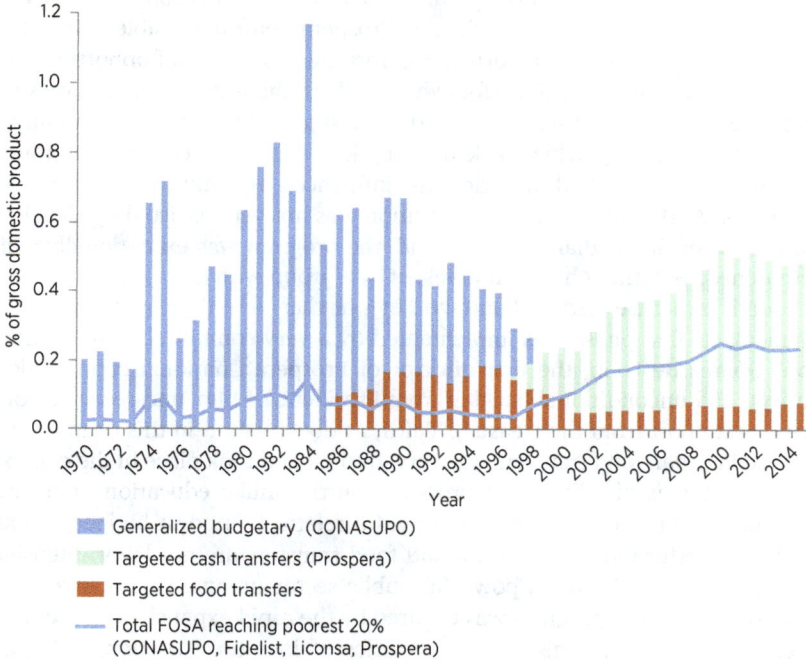

Legend:
- Generalized budgetary (CONASUPO)
- Targeted cash transfers (Prospera)
- Targeted food transfers
- Total FOSA reaching poorest 20% (CONASUPO, Fidelist, Liconsa, Prospera)

Sources: Based on data presented in figures 5.1, 5.2, and 5.6 and table 5.2.
Note: The share benefiting the poorest 20% of the population (the extreme poor) is based on the main programs (CONASUPO, Fidelist, Liconsa, Prospera), but does not include DIF and Diconsa. GDP = gross domestic product; FOSA = food-oriented social assistance.

terms of the incidence of child undernutrition, income poverty, or multidimensional poverty—while reducing operational costs and leakage and enhancing the efficiency and impact of domestic food-oriented assistance interventions.

The concentration of the older generation of generalized and targeted food subsidies in Mexico City and other urban areas may be explained largely by the limited institutional capacities of the state. Those capacities might have been sufficient to transfer resources to a relatively small number of urban mills and tortillerías and to produce and distribute perishable liquid milk through a network of stores mainly in Mexico City. They were not sufficient to support direct transfers to millions of dispersed rural households lacking access to the banking system. Similarly, VAT exemptions protect the poor's food-purchasing capacity at very high cost in leakage to the nonpoor, but without requiring an administrative mechanism to identify and distribute transfers to those households.

In terms of political economy, the fact that Prospera implemented a radical reallocation of resources from Mexico City to remote rural households with such speed and permanence—despite a long history of urban food subsidies—appears to contradict the predictions of the political economy of targeting. Several circumstances made the Prospera reform possible. First, the reform was introduced in a narrow, but fortunate, window of opportunity in Mexico's democratic transition following Carlos Salinas de Gortari's contested 1988 election. The introduction occurred during the Ernesto Zedillo administration (1994–2000), which lacked strong loyalties to the corporatist groups and networks that had traditionally influenced the allocation of public resources. At the same time, the transition was not yet restricted by the electoral force of the median voter. Second, the program was exceptionally well researched, well thought out, and tested by a group with highly technical and academic expertise (led by Santiago Levy, at that time the vice minister for finance). Its first phase was implemented by a very committed team (led by José Gómez de León, the first director of Prospera's national coordination entity), had unconditional backing from President Zedillo, and received continuous support from the treasury. Third, as documented in this chapter, the decline in urban food transfers was very gradual and took place in the context of a broader fiscal adjustment process. Fourth, unlike education or health reforms, the Prospera reform reallocated a relatively modest budget; unlike health and education services, in-kind food transfers are not labor intensive and do not affect Mexico's powerful public sector unions. Finally, the long-term survival of the program was ensured by the rapid expansion of its coverage, along with a promise to beneficiaries of long-term support, a highly successful independent and rigorous evaluation process, and international dissemination of the program's impacts.

With regard to the thorny question of why apparently suboptimal food transfers are still in place, the following factors play a role: institutional capacities geared to implementing those programs, political equilibrium, food insecurity coupled with market failures, information and behavioral constraints, accountability constraints and possible rent capture, and inertia. Under common economic circumstances, it is reasonable to assume that cash should be preferred to in-kind food transfers of equivalent monetary value: cash provides choice, but this might not be the case when markets fail to provide economic access to products. Such cases occur when inflation erodes the value of the transfer, or when provision of the desired food products to very remote and dispersed rural populations is too costly to be viable. But those are exceptional circumstances, which often can be easily resolved in more efficient forms than through in-kind food transfers. For example, in the first case, the problem could be resolved by simply indexing the transfers to inflation (something that Prospera used to do for its conditional cash arm).

The fact that in-kind transfers still represent a substantial share of national budgets worldwide shows that governments and societies value transfers in certain merit goods and services—such as education, health, or food—much more than income transfers to promote income equality. Such preferences assume that households may not always spend in their best interests because of informational or behavioral constraints. The renewed interest in Sedesol's in-kind food transfers may reflect a concern for the nutritional quality of food consumed in the context of Mexico's obesity and diabetes epidemic. However, the nutritional contribution of the food basket that the government is able to provide (due to Diconsa's operational constraints) requires further analysis. The complex and indirect flow of resources from the state to the target population, which inevitably results from in-kind food transfers, creates multiple opportunities for intermediaries to divert the program's resources. Such opportunities can create stakeholders with strong interests in the continuity of those transfers.

NOTES

1. As of 2017, PAL–Sin Hambre was eliminated, and beneficiaries were transited (whenever possible) to either the conditional or the unconditional scheme of Prospera benefits.
2. For a detailed description of Prospera's design and implementation, see Dávila (2016).
3. This holds, in particular, for Prospera because, after 2014, most PAL beneficiaries participated in the PAL–Sin Hambre scheme.
4. After 2010, PAL adopted the same targeting methodology and criteria as Prospera.

REFERENCES

Alderman, Harold. 2016. "Leveraging Social Protection Programs for Improved Nutrition." World Bank, Washington DC.
Behrman, Jere, and John Hoddinott. 2005. "Programme Evaluation with Unobserved Heterogeneity and Selective Implementation: The Mexican Progresa Impact on Child Nutrition." *Oxford Bulletin of Economics and Statistics* 67 (4): 547–69.
Coady, David. 2000. "The Application of Social Cost-Benefit Analysis to the Evaluation of Progresa." Working Paper, International Food Policy Research Institute, Washington, DC.
CONEVAL (Consejo Nacional de Evaluación de la Política de Desarrollo Social). 2012. "Programa de Abasto Rural a cargo de Diconsa S.A de C.V. Informe de la evaluación específica de desempeño 2012–2013." CONEVAL, Mexico City. http://www.coneval.gob .mx/Informes/Evaluacion/Especificas_Desempeno2012/SEDESOL/20_S053/20_S053 _Completo.pdf.
———. 2015. "Medición de la pobreza en México y en las entidades federativas 2014." Presentation developed by CONEVAL, Mexico City. http://www.coneval.org.mx/Medicion /Documents/Pobreza%202014_Coneval_web.pdf.
———. 2016. "Balance de la Cruzada Nacional Contra el Hambre 2013–2016." Report, CONEVAL, Mexico City. http://www.coneval.org.mx/Evaluacion/ECNCH/Documents /Balance_Cruzada_2013_2016.pdf.
Dávila, Laura. 2016. "¿Cómo funciona Prospera? Mejores prácticas en la implementación de programas de transferencias monetarias condicionadas en América Latina y el Caribe." Nota Técnica IDB-TN-971, Inter-American Development Bank, Washington, DC.
Diconsa (Sistema Social de Abasto de Distribuidoras CONASUPO). 2015. *Reglas de operación del programa de abasto rural a cargo de Diconsa S.A. de C.V. para el ejercicio fiscal 2016.*

Operating rules. Mexico City: Disconsa. http://www.diconsa.gob.mx/images/swfs/paayar/mpar/ReglasOperacion/Reglas_de_Operaci%C3%B3n_del_PAR_Diconsa ,Ejercicio_Fiscal%202016.pdf.

Fernald, Lia C. H., Paul J. Gertler, and Lynnette M. Neufeld. 2008. "Role of Cash in Conditional Cash Transfer Programmes for Child Health, Growth, and Development: An Analysis of Mexico's Oportunidades." *The Lancet* 371 (9615): 828–37. http://www.thelancet.com /journals/lancet/article/PIIS0140-6736(08)60382-7/fulltext.

———. 2009. "10-Year Effect of Oportunidades, Mexico's Conditional Cash Transfer Programme, on Child Growth, Cognition, Language, and Behavior: A Longitudinal Follow-Up Study." *The Lancet* 374 (9706): 1997–2005. http://www.thelancet.com /journals/lancet/article/PIIS0140-6736(09)61676-7/fulltex.t

Flores, José, Jair Muñoz, and Jorge Antonio Colorado. 2015. *Estudio de seguimiento físico y operativo del programa de abasto rural a cargo de Diconsa, S.A de C.V.* Mexico City: Instituto Nacional de Administración Pública and Diconsa. http://www.diconsa.gob.mx /images/swfs/transparencia/Focalizada/Informe%20Final%20Estudio%20Segui%20 F%C3%ADsico%20INAP%202015.pdf.

Gordillo, Gustavo, Alain De Janvry, and Elisabeth Sadulet. 1999. *La segunda reforma agraria de México: Respuestas de familias y comunidades, 1990–1994.* Mexico City: Fondo de Cultura Económica.

Grosh, Margaret. 1994. *Administering Targeted Social Programs in Latin America: From Platitudes to Practice.* Washington, DC: World Bank.

Hill, Raymond. 1984. "State Enterprise and Income Distribution in Mexico." In *The Political Economy of Income Distribution in Mexico*, edited by Pedro Aspe and Paul E. Sigmund. New York: Holmes and Meier.

Levy, Santiago, and Enrique Dávila. 1999. "Dispersión poblacional y pobreza." In *La seguridad social en México*, edited by Fernando Solís and Alejandro Villagómez. Mexico City: Fondo de Cultura Económica.

Levy, Santiago, and Evelyn Rodríguez. 2005. *Sin herencia de pobreza: El Programa Progresa-Oportunidades de México.* Washington, DC: Inter-American Development Bank.

Levy, Santiago, and Sweder van Wijnbergen. 1993. "Mercados de trabajo, migración y bienestar: La agricultura en el tratado de libre comercio entre México y los Estados Unidos." *El Trimestre Económico* 60 (238): 371–411.

Martín del Campo, Antonio, and Rosendo Calderón Tinoco. 1992. "Reestructuración de los subsidios a productos básicos y la modernización de CONASUPO." In *Mexico: Auge, crisis y ajuste*, edited by Carlos Bazdresch, Nisso Bucay, Soledad Loaeza, and Nora Lustig. Mexico City: Fondo de Cultura Económica.

OECD (Organisation for Economic Co-operation and Development). Various years. Consumer and Producer Support Estimates database. Paris: OECD. http://www.oecd.org/tad /agricultural-policies/ForDistribution___MEX.xls.

Parker, Susan, and Petra E. Todd. 2015. "Conditional Cash Transfers: The Case of Progresa/ Oportunidades." Revised draft, prepared for the *Journal of Economic Literature*, May. https://www.researchgate.net/publication/315477299_Conditional_Cash_Transfers _The_case_of_ProgresaOportunidades.

Poder Ejecutivo Federal. Various years. *Informe de gobierno.* Mexico City: Poder Ejecutivo Federal.

Scott, John. Forthcoming. *Economía política de la desigualdad en México.* Mexico City: Editorial CIDE.

Shamah, Teresa, María Morales, Alejandra Jiménez, Rebeca Uribe, Araceli Salazar, Ignacio Méndez, Martza Alejandra Amaya, and Danae Gabriela Valenzuela. 2014. *Estudio de satisfacción de los beneficiarios y operadores del Programa PAL–Sin Hambre y variedad de la dieta de los beneficiarios del Programa PAL en sus dos esquemas de apoyo.* Cuernavaca,

Mexico: Instituto Nacional de Salud Pública. http://www.diconsa.gob.mx/images/swfs/transparencia/Focalizada/Diconsa%20satisfacc%20PAL%20-SINHAMBRE.pdf.

SHCP (Secretaría de Hacienda y Crédito Público). 2015. "Presupuesto de egresos de la federación para el ejercicio fiscal 2010–2015." Online access to budget. SHCP, Mexico City. http://www.apartados.hacienda.gob.mx/presupuesto/temas/pef/2015/index.html.

———. Various years. *Cuenta pública federal.* Mexico City: SHCP.

Soto, Jorge, ed. 2014. *Estudio de la cobertura, comercialización y financiamiento de Programa de Abasto Rural a cargo de Diconsa, S.A de C.V.* Mexico City: Universidad Intercultural del Estado de México and Sedesol. http://www.gob.mx/cms/uploads/attachment/file/28377/PAR_CCF_InformeFinal.pdf.

World Bank. 1991. "Mexico—Malnutrition and Nutrition Programs: An Overview." World Bank, Washington, DC. August.

CHAPTER 6

Evolution and Implementation of the Supplemental Nutrition Assistance Program in the United States

Victor Oliveira, Laura Tiehen, Mark Prell, and David Smallwood

INTRODUCTION

The Supplemental Nutrition Assistance Program (SNAP)—formerly the Food Stamp Program—is the first line of defense against hunger in the United States, providing monthly benefits to low-income households for purchasing food. By increasing their food-purchasing power, the program also provides participants the opportunity to improve the quality of their diet, thereby improving their nutrition and health. Compared with other case studies presented in this volume, the experience of SNAP is relatively coherent. As with the other programs discussed in this volume, SNAP has evolved over time, particularly with elimination of the purchase requirement and transformation of the program into an entitlement in the mid-1970s. Since the late 1970s, it has not been subject to drastic overhauls, nor has its role been recast dramatically. SNAP, instead, has been subject to a relatively steady and increasingly nuanced set of technical and institutional improvements that are making it one of the most effective social assistance programs globally.

The program touches the lives of many Americans: an average of 45.8 million people residing in 22.5 million households participated in the program per month in fiscal year 2014/15 or about 14 percent of the nation's population (USDA 2015a).[1] Almost half (49 percent) of all American children reside in a household that will participate in SNAP at some point during their childhood (Rank and Hirschl 2009).

Program Overview

SNAP participants receive an electronic benefit transfer (EBT) card that can be redeemed for most types of food in more than 261,000 authorized commercial retail (that is, private sector) food stores across the nation (USDA 2015c) (box 6.1). Benefits, which increase with household size and decrease with income, were worth a monthly average of US$258 per household or US$127 per person in fiscal year 2014/15 (USDA 2015a) (table 6.1).[2] In 2010, SNAP benefits accounted for more than 10 percent of all U.S. spending for food-at-home purchases (Wilde 2013b).

BOX 6.1 **Implications of the Form of Benefit**

SNAP benefits lie midway on the continuum of possible forms of benefit, between one extreme of limited in-kind benefits (for example, a fixed bundle of specific commodities) and the other extreme of cash benefits.

SNAP provides recipients with more choices than those provided by a package of specified commodities. Under SNAP, there is likely to be less participant stigma, lower administrative costs, and fewer burdens on retail stores than with a program where food choices are more restricted. For example, participants who face restricted food choices may inadvertently attempt to purchase ineligible foods or brands. However, a prescribed set of foods could potentially be a more effective means of improving nutrition and health, although recipients may prefer more choice. In this way, a more prescribed set of foods may discourage participation and reduce the effectiveness of the program on the whole.

Because SNAP benefits are food targeted, SNAP is a more effective tool than cash benefits for increasing food expenditures, thereby benefiting the agriculture sector and potentially increasing the nutritional benefits of the program. Because it provides food instead of cash to recipients, SNAP may also be viewed as an antihunger program more than an income support program; therefore, it may enjoy more political support than a cash-based program (Besharov 2015). However, participant stigma, administrative costs, and the burden on retail stores are likely to be greater than if benefits were in the form of cash. Restricting SNAP recipients to purchasing food with their benefits may encourage illegal behavior—for example, selling benefits for cash or nonfood items (Ohls and Beebout 1993). Also, in-kind programs such as SNAP may be vulnerable to brokering by providers of the in-kind benefit (such as food producers and retailers), who gain from growth of the program (Andrews and Clancy 1993).

TABLE 6.1 **Selected Features and Key Research Findings for SNAP**

INDICATOR	DETAILS
Selected feature	
Target population	Low-income households
Year permanently authorized	1964
Federal cost	US$73.9 billion (fiscal year 2014/15)
Form of benefit	Electronic benefit card used to purchase food
Benefits as a % of federal program costs	94% (fiscal year 2014/15)
Number of participants	Average 45.8 million per month (fiscal year 2014/15)
Participants as a % of U.S. population	14.3% in a typical month (fiscal year 2014/15)
Participants as a % of the eligible population	85% in a typical month (2013)
Average benefit per person	US$126.83 per month (fiscal year 2014/15)
Benefits structure	Decreases with income, increases with household size
Financial eligibility criteria	Gross income, net income, and asset tests
Nonfinancial eligibility criteria	Employment and immigrant requirements
Asset limit per household	US$2,250 (US$3,250, if elderly member)
Certification payment error rate	3.42% (fiscal year 2011/12)
Key research findings	
Marginal propensity to spend on food out of SNAP benefits	0.17–0.47[a]
Increase in U.S. GDP for every US$1 billion in SNAP benefits (when underused resources are available)	US$1.79 billion
Reduction in U.S. poverty rate when SNAP benefits are counted as family income	4.9 percentage points

Note: SNAP = Supplemental Nutrition Assistance Program; GDP = gross domestic product.
[a.] This range is based on estimates from a majority of studies. The studies find that, for each dollar of SNAP benefits that a typical household receives, food spending rises US$0.17–US$0.47, which is less than a full dollar because some out-of-pocket food spending is saved.

SNAP is available to most financially needy households (Eslami, Filion, and Strayer 2011), and eligibility is based primarily on a household's income, size, and assets. Some individuals are also subject to certain work and immigration status requirements. SNAP serves the country's most vulnerable populations: in fiscal year 2013/14, 76 percent of all SNAP households included a child, an elderly person (age 60 or older), or a disabled nonelderly person (Gray and Kochhar 2015). Those households received 82 percent of all program benefits. Most SNAP households (83 percent) had monthly income below the federal poverty line and 43 percent had monthly income less than or equal to 50 percent of the poverty line. SNAP also provides support for the working poor: 31 percent of SNAP households had some earned income (that is, income received from working).

USDA's Array of Food Assistance Programs

About one in four Americans participates in at least 1 of 15 domestic food assistance programs of the U.S. Department of Agriculture (USDA) at some point during the year (Oliveira 2016). This array of programs—which vary by target population, form of benefit, number of participants, and cost—was developed because of the difficulties associated with serving diverse populations through a single program (Smallwood, Prell, and Andrews 2002).[3] SNAP is the cornerstone of this network of food assistance programs, accounting for almost US$74 billion or 71 percent of all federal food assistance spending in fiscal year 2014/15 (October 1, 2014, to September 30, 2015). In contrast to SNAP, the other food assistance programs provide benefits targeted to special populations, dietary needs, and delivery settings (USDA 2015g). With limited exceptions, participation in SNAP does not prevent participation in other food assistance programs. Multiprogram participation increases access to a healthy diet for low-income people (Institute of Medicine and National Research Council 2013).

SNAP and the U.S. Safety Net

SNAP is one of several programs that provide cash, in-kind benefits, or refundable tax credits to low-income Americans. In 2012, federal spending on the 10 major means-tested programs that directly target assistance toward low-income people totaled US$588 billion or about one-sixth of federal spending and almost 4 percent of gross domestic product (GDP) (Congressional Budget Office 2013). Programs providing in-kind (or noncash) benefits accounted for three-quarters of federal spending on these programs. Medicaid is the largest means-tested transfer program (US$251 billion), providing health insurance to low-income families, the elderly, and the disabled (figure 6.1). SNAP is the second largest, with expenditures of US$80 billion in 2012. The federal government provided in-kind benefits to low-income families in the form of housing assistance (US$36 billion), either through housing vouchers in the private housing market or through subsidized rent in specified public or private housing. Pell Grants, which help to fund tuition and expenses for postsecondary students from low-income families, accounted for another US$34 billion in federal spending. Other major in-kind programs include the low-income subsidy (Part D) of Medicare that provides prescription drug benefits, which accounted for US$21 billion, and USDA's child nutrition programs (including the National School Lunch Program and the School Breakfast Program), which accounted for US$18 million.[4]

FIGURE 6.1

Overview of Major U.S. Means-Tested Programs, 2012

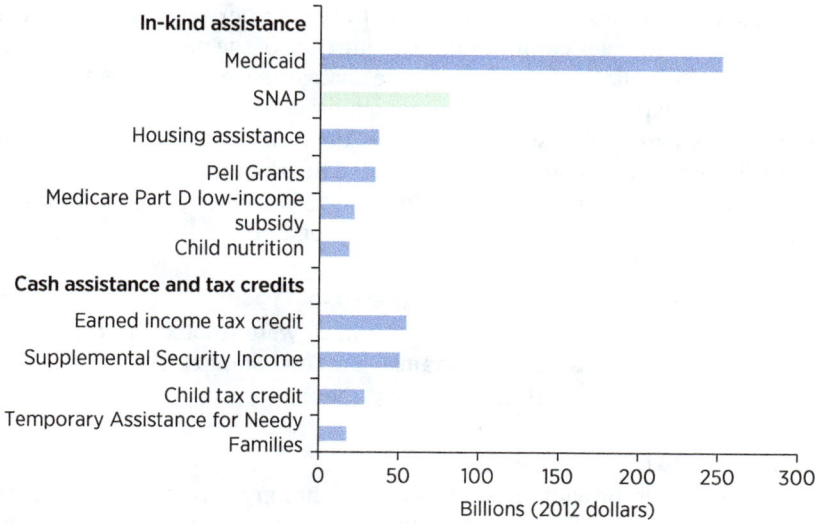

Source: Congressional Budget Office 2013.
Note: SNAP = Supplemental Nutrition Assistance Program.

Cash assistance safety net programs in the United States are targeted primarily to working families and to individuals who are considered unable to work, such as the elderly and disabled. The earned income tax credit (EITC), which provides a refundable tax credit based on family size and earnings, is the largest cash assistance program and the third largest means-tested program overall, with expenditures of US$54 billion. The next largest program is Supplemental Security Income (SSI) (US$50 billion), which provides cash benefits to low-income elderly, blind, and disabled individuals. Other major cash assistance programs include the child tax credit (US$28 billion), which allows families to claim a tax credit for children, and the Temporary Assistance for Needy Families (TANF) (US$17 billion), which provides cash and other forms of assistance to families with little or no income.

Organization of this Chapter

This chapter examines the evolution of SNAP, highlighting the major changes that have shaped the program over time, and describes how SNAP works, including a discussion of the program's impacts. A final section examines lessons learned.

EVOLUTION OF SNAP

SNAP's origins go back more than 80 years. Over its history, the program has undergone numerous changes as it has evolved from programs designed primarily to reduce agricultural surpluses into one of the major social protection programs in the United States. Those changes have been driven primarily by policy changes as well as by economy-related factors that reflect the need for assistance. This section examines the history of SNAP, focusing on major changes to the program, factors behind the changes, and their implications. The discussion proceeds chronologically through five periods or phases, each characterized by major changes in the program.

Precursors to the Food Stamp Program, 1930s–1940s

The first national food assistance programs were rooted in the Great Depression. One of those early programs—the Food Stamp Plan—would later serve as the prototype for the modern-day SNAP.

Federal Food Assistance Origins

Before the 1930s, providing assistance to the hungry was the responsibility of the states and local communities—not the federal government (Poppendieck 1986). Federally administered domestic food assistance programs originated during the Great Depression in the late 1920s and 1930s. During that time period, when the overproduction of agricultural commodities reduced food prices and lowered farm incomes, the country was experiencing widespread unemployment, hunger, and malnutrition—a situation referred to as "the paradox of want amid plenty" (Poppendieck 1986). In response, the federal government purchased surplus food under the premise that removing those price-depressing foods from normal marketing channels would help to limit commercial supply, thereby increasing prices along with farm incomes (Shields 2014). In the early 1930s, the federal government began making those surplus foods available to organizations such as the Red Cross to distribute to the needy (Gold, Hoffman, and Waugh 1940; Poppendieck 1986).

In 1935, the U.S. Congress passed the Agricultural Act of 1935.[5] Section 32 of the act provided the USDA with an annual source of funding—30 percent of the import duties collected from U.S. customs receipts—to encourage the domestic consumption of certain foods, usually in surplus, by diverting them from normal channels of trade. The belief was that providing surplus foods to low-income families would "supplement, not displace, normal food purchases by these recipients" (Shields 2014, 4).

The Commodity Distribution Program was established in 1936 to distribute the surplus commodities acquired by Section 32 funding to low-income families and school lunch programs. Thus, the ongoing program of purchases and distribution of surplus commodities was not dependent on annual appropriations from Congress. Whereas the primary purpose was to reduce farm surpluses, the program simultaneously helped needy people. Large distribution systems were established by state and local governments to dispense the surplus food to needy families, schools, and charitable organizations (Congressional Budget Office 1977). However, the program did little to increase the total demand for food; recipients largely substituted the free surplus food that they received for food that they normally would have purchased from their own funds (Berry 1984).

The Food Stamp Plan
The first coupon-based food assistance program was established by the USDA (and financed with Section 32 funds) during the tail end of the Great Depression in 1939. The Food Stamp Plan provided participating families with stamps (similar to postage stamps in design) that they could exchange for food in any retail food establishment that would accept them (Federal Surplus Commodities Corporation 1939). Eligibility standards were set locally rather than nationally. The change from a commodity distribution program to a coupon or food stamp program was driven by several factors, including (a) an attempt to assure that the government benefit would be used to increase food consumption rather than to replace previous food expenditures; (b) the desire to improve the match between the types and amounts of available foods and people's actual needs; and (c) a belief that it was more advantageous to use existing commercial food distribution channels than to develop a separate distribution system (U.S. Senate 1985). Grocery trade officials and local retailers had expressed concern that the Commodity Distribution Program, which operated outside commercial distribution networks, resulted in fewer sales—and therefore less revenue—for retail food stores (Maney 1989).

To control the types of foods that recipients could obtain, the program was based on a two-color system of stamps—orange and blue—that participants could exchange for food in participating retail food stores (U.S. Senate 1985). Program participants would buy orange stamps with cash and could use them to purchase an equal value of most types of food. They would also receive a free bonus amount of blue stamps worth half of the value of the orange stamps. The blue stamps, which represented the participants' increase in purchasing power, could only be used to buy surplus commodities as designated by the USDA.

The program was carefully designed to increase a household's food purchases and not to encourage households to substitute food purchased with the coupons for food purchased from their own funds. To purchase orange stamps, participating families were required to spend an amount of money that represented their estimated normal food expenditures (U.S. Senate 1985). Therefore, the food purchased with the blue stamps was intended to be a net increase in participants' food consumption. The program was meant to be a nutrition program more than an income transfer program. That goal differentiated the Food Stamp Plan from the Commodity Distribution Program, in which the surplus foods the recipients received for free could be substituted for foods they previously purchased out-of-pocket, thereby resulting in little or no net increase in household food consumption.

At its peak in August 1942, the program operated in areas containing about two-thirds of the U.S. population (U.S. Senate 1985). Although studies found that the Food Stamp Plan increased food consumption levels among participants (U.S. Senate 1985), the program had several drawbacks. First, requiring that households purchase food stamps with their own money significantly reduced access to the program, particularly among very poor households that may have had limited cash on hand (Ohls and Beebout 1993). Second, the program was complicated to administer. The USDA would designate the surplus foods that could be purchased with blue stamps on a monthly basis. Consequently, retailers and their staff, along with program participants, would have to be informed each month about changes in the surplus foods that could be purchased (U.S. Senate 1985). Third, reports of fraud and abuse plagued the program. An estimated 25 percent of all benefits were misused (U.S. Senate 1985). In particular, it was thought that a large number of smaller, family-owned stores yielded to pressure from long-term customers to give them cash for their blue stamps or to exchange blue stamps for foods not on the list of allowable foods (Berry 1984).

The Food Stamp Plan was discontinued in 1943 when wartime conditions reduced unemployment and decreased agricultural surpluses (U.S. Senate 1964). After World War II, food assistance was once again provided through the Commodity Distribution Program, although at lower levels than before (Andrews and Clancy 1993). Whereas the Food Stamp Plan existed for only a relatively brief period, several of its features would set the stage for the future Food Stamp Program or SNAP. For example, it used the existing, efficient commercial food distribution system to distribute the foods by requiring that participants obtain their foods at participating retail food stores. In this way, retailers, wholesalers, and food distributors benefited economically from the program via increased sales. It also provided the needy with more autonomy. Participants could choose which types of foods to purchase (at least with the orange stamps) rather than simply accept a set of available commodities.

Establishment of the Food Stamp Program, 1961–67
The Food Stamp Program was created by the USDA as a pilot program in the early 1960s. Congress permanently authorized the program in 1964.

The Pilot Food Stamp Program
The United States was in the midst of an economic downturn in the early 1960s, and concern about America's poor grew. In his first executive order as president, John F. Kennedy in January 1961 stated, "One of the most

important and urgent problems confronting this nation today is the development of a positive food and nutrition program for all Americans" (Kennedy 1961). Noting that many needy people were not participating in the Commodity Distribution Program, which provided food of limited variety and inadequate nutritional content, President Kennedy directed the USDA to "take immediate steps to expand and improve the program of food distribution throughout the United States" and to make available "to all needy families a greater variety and quantity of food out of our agricultural abundance."

Later that year, the USDA began an experimental pilot program that became the basis for the Food Stamp Program. The pilot program operated in eight economically depressed areas and was once again financed from Section 32 funds, with the USDA paying 100 percent of the program's costs. Participating families were provided with stamps that they could exchange for food in any retail food establishment, but the pilot program eliminated the two-color coupon system and no longer required that some portion of the stamps be used to purchase surplus foods (USDA 2014b). Thus, the primary focus of the program began to shift away from reducing agricultural surpluses and toward improving the nutritional status and well-being of low-income people.

The goal of serving as a nutritional safety net for low-income people was not completely decoupled from that of supporting agriculture. The designers of the pilot program thought that by letting participants purchase nearly whatever foods they wanted, the increased purchasing power would increase overall demand for food, which would, in turn, reduce surplus commodities (Berry 1984). Furthermore, the pilot projects targeted domestic foods—thus, benefiting U.S. farmers—because participants could use the stamps to purchase any food or food product for human consumption, except coffee, tea, cocoa, alcoholic beverages, tobacco, and products clearly identified on the package as being imported from foreign sources (Agricultural Marketing Service 1961). Food stamps could only be redeemed for food at approved retail food stores; those food stores then redeemed the coupons through the commercial banking system (U.S. Senate 1985).

Eligibility was determined at the state or local level, usually using the applicable welfare eligibility guidelines for that area (U.S. Senate 1985). The pilot program retained the requirement that households purchase their food stamps. Families exchanged the amount of money that a family of that size would normally spend for food—based on averages derived from the USDA household food consumption survey data (Richardson 1979)—and would receive food coupons of a higher monetary value. The difference between what a household paid for the stamps (the purchase requirement, PR) and the value of stamps received (the allotment, A) was the federal contribution (the bonus, B), where $B = A - PR$. The bonus was the amount of the subsidy for participants and represented the increase in participants' purchasing power.

The basis of the allotment was the Economy Food Plan, developed by the USDA in 1961 as a low-cost, nutritionally adequate diet for short-term or emergency use (Carlson and others 2007). Unlike in the earlier Food Stamp Plan, the allotments were based on a sliding scale. Counterintuitively, families with higher incomes received the full value of the economy food plan, while lower-income families received less than the full value (Berry 1984). The rationale for providing lower-income families an allotment that might not be sufficient for them to purchase a nutritious diet was to discourage the illegal trading of stamps. That is, if the value of the stamps was greater than what they normally spent for food, the low-income families might sell some of the stamps for cash on the black market. The designers of the pilot program believed that a scandal related to cheating and fraud could jeopardize the program's existence (Berry 1984). Thus, a link between the amount of the allotment and a nutritionally adequate diet was established for some, but not all, recipients.

The purchase requirement was also based on a sliding scale, with families paying "an amount roughly equal to what they usually spent on food" (Berry 1984). Thus, higher-income families paid more for stamps. Having families pay what they usually spent on food minimized the substitution of stamps for food normally spent out-of-pocket. "Income" meant that portion of gross income after certain deductions (U.S. Senate 1985). The deductions were instituted as a way of compensating for the higher living costs associated with some areas (Berry 1984). The main deduction was a shelter deduction whereby combined expenses for rent or mortgage, electricity, and heat that were above 30 percent of families' income were deducted from their income before determining their purchase price for food stamps.

Permanent Authorization of the Food Stamp Program
By 1964, 43 areas in 22 states had pilot food stamp projects (U.S. Senate 1985). The pilots proved to be effective in expanding farm markets, improving food consumption and nutrition among participants, and increasing retail food store sales. In August 1964, President Lyndon B. Johnson signed the Food Stamp Act of 1964, stating that the program "will be one of our most valuable weapons for the war on poverty" (Johnson 1964).[6] The act made the program permanent, and funding (from the U.S. Treasury) would then be provided by Congress rather than through Section 32 funds within the USDA (USDA 2014b). Congress determined the size of the program, while the USDA was charged with administering it (box 6.2).

Each state was responsible for selling and issuing food stamps and for determining the eligibility of applicants, including establishing maximum income limits using standards consistent with those used by each state in its federally aided public assistance programs. States were also to establish a limit on allowable household assets in recognition that some households

BOX 6.2 **Who Makes SNAP Policy?**

The pilot Food Stamp Program and the earlier Food Stamp Plan were developed and managed by the USDA with minimal input from Congress. The enactment of the Food Stamp Act of 1964 made the program permanent and brought it under increased congressional oversight. Since that time, Congress has appropriated necessary funds and, through legislation, created statutes (that is, laws) establishing how SNAP operates. Congress made the USDA responsible for administering the program at the national level. Statutes typically do not address all of the details necessary for administering a program as large and complex as the Food Stamp Program. Through procedures that Congress created for executive branch departments of the federal government, the USDA has the power to issue regulations to address operational details not addressed by Congress. Such regulations are legally binding on participants in the program and on agencies administering the program at the state level. Congress also delegates certain policy decisions to the states. Such policies are often referred to as "options" to emphasize that states also have a role in establishing some sets of policies.

Approximately every five years, the legislative and executive branches propose changes to SNAP policies in the context of a farm bill (the most recent farm bill is referred to as the Agricultural Act of 2014). Farm bills reauthorize programs and set policies for SNAP and other food and farm programs (SNAP-related legislation can also be enacted outside of a farm bill). Observers have hypothesized that linking agriculture and food assistance together in one bill has created an informal alliance of lawmakers who support agricultural interests (including legislators in rural areas) and those who support food assistance programs (including legislators representing urban areas) that has helped to protect food assistance programs such as SNAP (Abbott 2016; Andrews and Clancy 1993).

with low or no income may have substantial resources on which to draw (U.S. Senate 1964). As a result of differing income and asset criteria, eligibility standards varied widely across states.

The federal government continued to pay 100 percent of the food stamp benefit costs and all federal administrative costs (including the printing of stamps). However, unlike the earlier pilot program, states now shared some of the costs of administering the program, including costs associated with determining eligibility and distributing the stamps (Richardson 1979; U.S. Senate 1985). The federal government paid about 30 percent of the states' administrative costs, and states paid the remaining 70 percent. Congress debated the issue of states and the federal government sharing of administrative costs. On the one hand, requiring states to share expenses raised concern that, because a state's participation in the program was voluntary, some states would choose not to participate in it. On the other hand, not requiring them to share costs raised concern that the states, without a direct financial stake in the program, would have little or no incentive to be "diligent in administration of a program financed entirely by the federal government" (U.S. Senate 1985). If states did not incur any of the costs of the program, this would result in a moral hazard whereby states might behave differently—that is, be less attentive in verifying that all program participants are actually eligible for the program.

Allotments at that time—determined by the USDA—were still based on a sliding scale that had families with higher incomes receiving larger allotments (Andrews and Clancy 1993; Congressional Budget Office 1977; Reese, Feaster, and Perkins 1974). As in the pilot program, the bonus represented the difference between the monthly allotment and the purchase requirement. Essentially, the bonus, when added to a household's normal expenditures for food, provided the household with an opportunity to "more nearly" obtain a low-cost nutritionally adequate diet. The value of the allotment was intended to be low enough that recipients would be restricted to basic foods and discouraged from purchasing luxury foods. The purchase requirement, which varied by household size and income, represented an amount equal to normal food expenditures as determined by consumption surveys (U.S. Senate 1985).

Participants could use their food stamps to purchase any food in authorized retail stores that sold food for home consumption (except alcohol, tobacco, and certain imported foods). As in the earlier Food Stamp Plan and pilot program—and continuing to the present—the Food Stamp Program made use of the existing system of commercial food distribution (box 6.3).

The Food Stamp Act also addressed accountability issues related to retail food stores, individuals, and states. For example, the act allowed approved retail food stores to be disqualified from further participation in the program if they violated provisions of the act. It also established fines and possible imprisonment for people who use, acquire, transfer, or process food stamps in an unauthorized manner. Financial penalties for states were established for gross negligence or fraud on the part of the state agency in the certification of applicant households.

States had the option of establishing the program, and those that chose to implement it could do so in all or part of the state. However, states were prohibited from operating the Food Stamp Program in areas that operated the Commodity Distribution Program. Total participation in the program increased gradually throughout the rest of the 1960s, as the program replaced the Commodity Distribution Program in many areas (figure 6.2).[7] At that time, the Food Stamp Program's rate of growth was limited by its budget, which was determined by congressional appropriations.

Nationwide Expansion, 1968–80

Participation in the Food Stamp Program grew rapidly through most of the 1968–80 period as the program expanded nationwide. Two of the most important developments in the history of the program—the transition of food

BOX 6.3 **Implications of Operating through Normal Channels of Trade**

By operating through normal channels of trade, SNAP makes use of the existing commercial food distribution system. Because of the large number of stores authorized by SNAP, most participating households can continue to shop and to use their SNAP electronic benefit transfer card at their usual food stores—not at a less conveniently located store. SNAP recipients are not restricted in terms of when or how often they shop for food. Use of the retail food delivery system also provides recipients with access to the wide variety of nutritious foods found in commercial food stores.

The flexibility provided to diverse households by increasing their food-purchasing power (rather than providing them with specific commodities) is one of the strengths of the program. Households make their own decisions regarding what foods to acquire with SNAP benefits on the basis of their food preferences and dietary needs as well as the price of foods. Because SNAP benefits are for a fixed dollar amount, participants have an incentive to seek out the best value across items and retailers.

Although SNAP increases the overall demand for food, it has a relatively small price-distorting effect on any individual food product because recipients have an almost limitless number of foods to choose from and SNAP benefits do not account for a large portion of any single product's sales. That is, the effect of the increase in total food demand is distributed across a wide spectrum of foods. Because SNAP-authorized food stores operate in a highly competitive retail food environment, they have a profit incentive to keep costs and prices low. In the absence of such competition, government-owned shops might not be as cost-effective as private retail stores, and their use might result in inefficiencies in the delivery system.

stamps into an entitlement and the elimination of the purchase requirement—occurred during this period.

Growing Public Awareness of the Poor
In the late 1960s, the issue of hunger and malnutrition among low-income Americans began to receive increased national attention. For example, in 1968, a series of events, including the Poor People's March on Washington, the television documentary "Hunger in America," and the report *Hunger, U.S.A.* (Citizens' Board of Inquiry into Hunger and Malnutrition in the United States 1968), raised the public's awareness of the problem. Around that time, public interest groups advocating on behalf of low-income citizens also began to form (Berry 1984).

Recession, Improving Access, and Standardization
To increase participation in the program, the USDA announced in late 1969 (the start of a recession) that, as of 1970, all participating households of a particular size would receive the same total allotment of stamps regardless of household income (Congressional Budget Office 1977). In 1971, Congress

FIGURE 6.2

Food Stamp Participation and the Unemployment Rate in the United States, 1962–2014

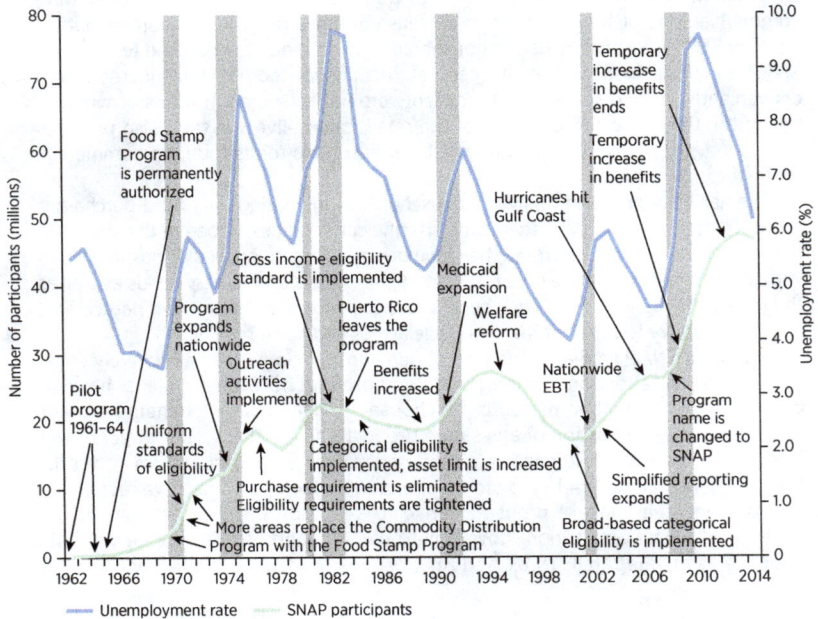

Note: Gray vertical bars indicate recessions. EBT = electronic benefit transfer; SNAP = Supplemental Nutrition Assistance Program.

endorsed those changes by incorporating them into amendments to the Food Stamp Act of 1964 (P.L. 91-671).[8] Allotments were set at the level of the USDA's Economy Food Plan, which established monthly dollar amounts that were enough "to purchase a minimally nutritious diet" (Berry 1984, 64). Thus, for the first time, all households participating in the Food Stamp Program, regardless of income, theoretically received an allotment sufficient to purchase a nutritionally adequate diet (Berry 1984).

Public Law (P.L.) 91-671 also directed the USDA to establish uniform national standards of eligibility on the basis of income and asset limits (previously, each state was responsible for setting eligibility standards). The USDA determined that eligibility was to be based on (a) a household's net income after certain stipulated deductions (shelter, medical, educational, and others) and (b) a household's assets after excluding several basic categories of assets (home, one car, furnishings, and so on) (Food and Nutrition Service 1971; President's Task Force on Food Assistance 1984). The net income limit was set at about 10–15 percent above the federal poverty guidelines

(Berry 1984; Richardson 1979). The act also imposed work requirements on able-bodied adults age 18–65 as a condition of participation. That provision—the origin of work requirements in the program—was intended to ensure that only the truly deserving would be able to participate (U.S. House of Representatives 1970).

The same 1971 legislation made several substantial changes to the program's benefit structure. For example, purchase requirements were limited to no more than 30 percent of household income. That is, a household's food stamp benefits were reduced by US$0.30 for every dollar of net income (or, stated another way, households were able to keep US$0.70 for every additional dollar earned), thereby encouraging additional work effort and making the program more attractive to the working poor than if participants kept a lower proportion of their net income (Andrews and Clancy 1993). In addition, allotments were to be adjusted annually to keep pace with food price inflation. Before that provision, a household's food stamp allotment remained constant over time (changing only when there was a change in household size or income), even as inflation reduced the purchasing power of the benefits. As a result of the changes in allotment levels and purchase requirements, average benefit levels increased.

P.L. 91-671 also authorized people 60 years of age and older who were unable to prepare all of their meals adequately to use food stamps to purchase home-delivered meals from government or nonprofit organizations. This allowance sought to reach needy elderly who did not have cooking facilities or who could not prepare meals due to illness or physical disability (U.S. Senate 1985). That accommodation for the elderly was one of the first initiatives tailored to a special population (Maney 1989).

The various policy changes and a weak economy together increased the demand for the program. As congressional funding increased, more states entered the program, and the number of participants rose sharply through the early 1970s (Richardson 1979) (figure 6.2). The program's rapid expansion was further bolstered by the Agriculture and Consumer Protection Act,[9] passed in the recessionary year 1973, which required states to expand the program to every political jurisdiction by June 30, 1974 (U.S. Senate 1985). The act also amended the definition of food to mean any food or food product for home consumption except alcoholic beverages and tobacco (USDA 2014a). Thus, for the first time, recipients were not prohibited from purchasing imported foods, further shifting the primary goal of the program toward helping the needy and away from helping American farmers. The same law increased the federal share of state and local administrative costs to about 50 percent, making it less financially burdensome for states and localities to participate (Richardson 1979). By 1974—11 years after the program was made permanent—the Food Stamp Program had expanded to all 50 states and territories. The following year, the U.S. territory of Puerto Rico entered the program.

Participation in the program continued through 1976 in response to the increased benefit levels in the early 1970s, a recession in 1973–75, and double-digit food price inflation that reduced consumers' purchasing power (MacDonald 1977) (figure 6.2). In 1976, an alternative to the Food Stamp Program—the Food Distribution Program on Indian Reservations (FDPIR)—also was implemented (box 6.4).

Food Stamps as an Entitlement Program

Since the mid-1970s, the Food Stamp Program (and its successor) has essentially operated as an entitlement program: "Congress has always fully funded the program as if it were an entitlement" (U.S. Senate 1985, 175). In other words, no eligible person is denied benefits due to lack of funds. Making the Food Stamp Program a de facto entitlement program had several important consequences. First, because the program does not limit the number of eligible applicants who can participate, economic conditions can influence the number of participants. That is, because eligibility is based primarily on the financial situation of applicants and participants are required to recertify at regular intervals to continue receiving benefits (their financial situation is reassessed periodically), program participation is countercyclical—expanding during economic downturns (when the number of unemployed and poor

---

BOX 6.4 **FDPIR—An Alternative to the Food Stamp Program**

The Food Distribution Program on Indian Reservations provides supplemental foods as an alternative to SNAP for low-income households living on Indian reservations and to American Indians living near reservations. Congress established the program in 1976 out of concern that the Food Stamp Program might not adequately meet the food assistance needs of American Indians. The remote location of many reservations makes it difficult for some American Indians to participate in the program because they live a long distance from a food stamp office and authorized retail food stores (Usher, Shanklin, and Wildfire 1990). Instead of food coupons to be exchanged for food in retail food stores, participants are provided with a monthly package of various foods. Participants may select from more than 70 food products. The USDA purchases and ships the foods to local agencies that store and distribute them. Households on or near reservations can choose whether to participate in SNAP or the FDPIR, but cannot participate in both programs in the same month.

In fiscal year 2014/15, the FDPIR served almost 89,000 people in an average month, annual program expenditures totaled almost US$119 million or less than 1 percent of SNAP expenditures (USDA 2015a), and average monthly food costs per person (US$65.22) were almost half those in SNAP (US$126.83). Administrative and other nonfood costs were a higher proportion of program costs in the FDPIR, accounting for about 41 percent of costs in fiscal year 2014/15 compared with 6 percent in SNAP (based on Economic Research Service calculations of USDA data; USDA 2015a).

people rises and incomes decline) and contracting during periods of economic growth.[10] Second, because program costs—which are ultimately borne by U.S. taxpayers—are closely tied to the number of participants, program costs rise during economic downturns if there is no corresponding decrease in benefit levels per participant.[11] Third, the take-up rate—the proportion of people eligible for benefits who actually participate—is no longer limited by congressional appropriations.

Elimination of the Purchase Requirement
Another change in the program with long-term implications—elimination of the purchase requirement—occurred with enactment of the Food Stamp Act of 1977.[12] Before the act, households were required to spend up to 30 percent of their income to purchase food stamps. Removal of the last major barrier to participation for low-income people had been urged by the antihunger public interest groups that had formed in the late 1960s and early 1970s as well as by the administration of President Jimmy Carter (Berry 1984; U.S. Senate 1985). After 1979—when that act was implemented—all participants received food stamps for free. However, households were still expected to supplement food stamp benefits with their own income. The size of the food stamp benefit (B) was determined by deducting 30 percent of the household's net income (I) from the cost of the Thrifty Food Plan (TFP) for that household size, that is, $B = TFP - 0.3(I)$ (USDA 2014a). Thus, the benefit reduction rate—the rate at which the SNAP benefit is reduced per dollar of net income—was set at 30 percent. Very low-income households received food stamps for free in amounts that were equal in value to the full cost of the Thrifty Food Plan for the size of the household.

Proponents of eliminating the purchase requirement argued that it served as a barrier to participation for many low-income families, in particular, the elderly and those living in poverty, who could not afford the purchase requirement (U.S. Senate 1985). They also argued that removing the purchase requirement would streamline the program by eliminating the administrative costs associated with selling coupons to recipients, would reduce fraud among vendors selling coupons, and would increase the autonomy of recipients.

Opponents of the change argued that, by eliminating the purchase requirement, the program would become an income support program, not a nutrition program: it would free up or divert grocery money to be spent on nonfood items and services (or food away from home) and thereby reduce the program's nutritional effectiveness (Salathe 1980; U.S. Senate 1985). Previously, all participants received the maximum allotment equal to a low-cost nutritionally adequate diet (that is, the Thrifty Food Plan). With elimination of the purchase requirement, most food stamp participants were compelled to pay about 30 percent of their net income at the grocery store to obtain a nutritionally adequate diet (Richardson 1979). Other arguments for keeping the purchase requirement were that having participants contribute some of their own funds to purchase food stamps reduced fraud and abuse (U.S. Senate 1985), encouraged personal financial responsibility (U.S. Senate 1985), and provided some dignity to recipients (Berry 1984).

Opponents further argued that increasing program access by eliminating the purchase requirement would increase participation, which would increase the cost of the program, holding other factors constant. Therefore, to minimize the cost increase, the act contained provisions that tightened eligibility requirements. Those provisions included lowering the net income eligibility standards to 100 percent of the federal poverty guidelines, allowing fewer deductions, and making other deductions more restrictive (U.S. Senate 1985). The medical deduction that was established by the USDA in 1971 was eliminated. However, in response to concerns about the loss of benefits to some households, amendments enacted in 1979 established deductions for excess medical expense, dependent care, and excess shelter expense for households with an elderly or disabled member (U.S. Senate 1985).[13]

In 1977 and 1978, the number of people participating in the program fell. The decrease—the first in the program's history—coincided with growth in the nation's economy that reduced the need for food stamps (Richardson 1979). Improving economic conditions can be expected to reduce the number of participants of an entitlement program, holding other factors constant. But the demand for food stamps rose once again after 1978, a situation that was attributed to a weak economy (including recessions in 1980 and in 1981–82) as well as elimination of the purchase requirement (President's Task Force on Food Assistance 1984).[14] As a fully funded program, whereby all eligible applicants are able to participate, funding grew to meet the increase in demand (Maney 1989).

Cutbacks in the Program, 1981–2000
Participation in the program fluctuated widely during 1981–2000, reflecting changes in policy and the economy. Congress enacted several acts with the specific intent of decreasing program caseloads and program costs. Participation at the end of the period was lower than at the start.

A New Eligibility Criterion
The late 1970s and early 1980s was a period of deteriorating economic conditions and rapidly increasing numbers of participants (figure 6.2). The program had come under criticism that too many people were participating because of (a) overly generous eligibility standards, which, for instance, permitted undeserving high-income participants to qualify because their large deductions resulted in low net incomes, and (b) alleged widespread cheating and fraud (Berry 1984). Before 1981, income eligibility was determined solely by a family's net income, that is, gross income after certain deductions.

As a result, it was possible for households with relatively high incomes but large deductions to be eligible for food stamps (Urban Institute 1985). As part of a plan to reduce program growth, P.L. 97-35, enacted in 1981, added a gross income standard to the eligibility requirements for households (Urban Institute 1985; U.S. Senate 1985). Most participants had to have gross income (that is, income before deductions) at or below 130 percent of poverty to be eligible to participate, so some higher-income households were blocked from participating. Recognizing the special needs of some subgroups of the vulnerable population, the new gross income test did not apply to households with elderly or disabled members.

The legislation also replaced the Food Stamp Program in the U.S. territory of Puerto Rico with a block grant effective in 1982. That change was the second instance (after the FDPIR) of a food assistance program being established in lieu of SNAP (box 6.5).

BOX 6.5 **The Nutrition Assistance Program in Puerto Rico**

Puerto Rico, a territory of the United States, was authorized to participate in the Food Stamp Program in 1971, and the program began operations in 1974. By fiscal year 1980/81, approximately 56 percent of Puerto Rico's population participated in the program, and the territory accounted for 8 percent of total food stamp expenditures in the United States (USDA 1983). To reduce spending and simplify program operations, Congress replaced the Food Stamp Program in Puerto Rico with an annual block grant for nutrition assistance (Trippe and others 2015). In July 1982, Puerto Rico implemented the Nutrition Assistance Program (NAP) with funds from the block grant. Funding was originally capped at US$825 million; however, since 1986, the NAP block grant has been indexed to inflation. Unlike SNAP, which operates as an entitlement program, the number of people who can participate in Puerto Rico may be limited by the funding levels established by Congress.

Puerto Rico was given broad flexibility to establish a program designed to meet the needs of its residents, while controlling costs to the U.S. government (Peterson and others 2010). To reduce administrative costs and simplify program operations, NAP recipients received checks that could be fully redeemed for cash (Trippe and others 2015). As a result, recipients were able to purchase ineligible foods or even nonfood items with their cash benefits. However, in 2001, Puerto Rico mandated that 75 percent of participants' benefits be used to purchase food via electronic benefit transfer (Peterson and others 2010). The purpose of the change to more targeted benefits was to align the program more closely with SNAP regulations that require SNAP benefits to be used only to acquire food (Trippe and others 2015). The remaining 25 percent of the benefit was provided in cash to be spent on food at uncertified retailers (although use of the cash component of the benefit was not monitored). That provision helped (a) to ensure that program recipients who lived in remote areas (or who faced other mobility or transportation barriers) would be able to purchase basic food items from their most easily accessed retailers, regardless of whether the retailers were certified for participation in the NAP, and (b) to allow retailers in remote areas to serve NAP participants, even if they did not have access to EBT.

Program Contraction in the 1980s
Despite the poor economic conditions, caseloads declined after 1981 (figure 6.2). The decrease in participation from 1981 to 1982, a period that included a recession from July 1981 to November 1982, remains the only instance of program participation declining during a recessionary period. The policy changes resulting from legislation that tightened eligibility rules (including the new gross income eligibility criteria) and reduced actual benefits offset the influence of the weak economy on participation.[15]

The decline in participation continued into the mid-1980s. In response, the Food Security Act of 1985 made it easier for households to participate in the Food Stamp Program.[16] For example, the act made households categorically (or automatically) eligible for SNAP if all members participated in certain specified cash assistance programs for low-income people, such as Aid to Families with Dependent Children (AFDC) and SSI. That is, households were eligible for food stamps, without consideration of their income or assets, as long as they met all nonfinancial eligibility criteria. Categorical eligibility was intended to simplify the application process because those other programs had their own income and resource tests that were often stricter than food stamp tests. Therefore, "subjecting a household to a separate set of income and resource tests for food stamps could be seen as redundant and inefficient" (Falk and Aussenberg 2014). The 1985 legislation also raised the asset limit from US$1,500 to US$2,000 for households with no elderly members (thereby making more households eligible to participate) and authorized a simplified application for households in which at least one member received AFDC, SSI, or Medicaid. The act also required all states to implement an employment and training (E&T) program to assist food stamp recipients in obtaining employment. E&T programs were funded by the federal government, but states could contribute their own funds, which would be matched with federal funds.

In a cost-saving move in 1982, the maximum benefit level was cut from 100 percent to 99 percent of the Thrifty Food Plan.[17] In 1988, the Hunger Prevention Act reversed direction by establishing incremental increases to benefits over a three-year period so that, by 1991, maximum benefits were 103 percent of the cost of the Thrifty Food Plan.[18] The law was enacted to account for the time lag in adjusting food stamp allotments for changes in food prices. Program benefits were adjusted each year to reflect increases in the cost of the Thrifty Food Plan. Because benefits for the fiscal year were based on the cost of the Thrifty Food Plan in June of the prior fiscal year, "benefits are based on lagged data that are 4 months old at the beginning of the fiscal year and 15 months out of date by the end of the fiscal year" (Rosenbaum 2008).

Program Expansion in the Early 1990s
After seven consecutive years of decline (1982–88), participation began to rise, a result attributed in part to the increase in benefit levels and in part to

the expansion of Medicaid, a program often run by the same state office (McConnell 1991). Participation in Medicaid—a federal and state program that assists low-income families and individuals with medical costs—had an indirect effect on participation in SNAP. In the 1980s, concerns about the infant mortality rate and inadequate prenatal and newborn care for low-income women and infants prompted several changes in the Medicaid program, including raising the income eligibility threshold for children and pregnant women, introducing more aggressive outreach programs, and streamlining application procedures. Those changes resulted in an increase in participation in Medicaid, which led to an increase in participation in SNAP for two reasons: (a) Medicaid workers informed their clients about SNAP and (b) for people already applying for Medicaid, the additional time and effort to apply for food stamps was low (some states had joint application forms) (McConnell 1991).

Participation increased rapidly in the late 1980s and early 1990s, reflecting not only the legislative changes and Medicaid expansion but also declining economic conditions. A recession occurred in 1990–91. Even after unemployment started to fall after 1992, participation continued to rise before reaching what was at that time a record high of 27.5 million people per month, on average, in fiscal year 1993/94.

Welfare Reform Reduces Participation
The next major development in the Food Stamp Program was the Personal Responsibility and Work Opportunities Reconciliation Act of 1996 (PRWORA).[19] The act, commonly known as the Welfare Reform Act, transformed the U.S. welfare system by replacing AFDC, an entitlement program, with a block grant to states for administering the TANF program. Built on the premise that a permanent guarantee of benefits contributes to welfare dependency, PRWORA was designed to limit the length of welfare spells, while "preserving the role of welfare as a safety net for families experiencing temporary financial problems" (U.S. House of Representatives 1996). PRWORA made several changes to the program, including (a) eliminating the eligibility of most legal immigrants to food stamps, (b) placing a time limit—the first in the program's history—on the receipt of food stamps for able-bodied adults without dependents (ABAWDs), age 18–50, who are not working at least 20 hours a week or participating in a work program, to only 3 out of 36 months, and (c) reducing maximum allotments from 103 to 100 percent of the cost of the Thrifty Food Plan (USDA 2014b).

Subsequent legislation diminished some of the act's impacts on the Food Stamp Program by restoring eligibility for some elderly, people with disabilities, and child immigrants and for individuals who had been living in the United States for at least five years (USDA 2014b). Many states were also granted waivers from the ABAWD time limits. States could request that the USDA waive time limits for ABAWDs who lived in an area with either an unemployment rate over 10 percent or with an insufficient number of jobs. Legislation enacted in 1997 permitted states to exempt up to 15 percent of the state caseload that was ineligible because of the ABAWD time limits.[20]

Starting in the mid-1990s, the program entered another extended period of contraction. From fiscal year 1994/95 to fiscal year 1998/99, participation declined almost 32 percent (figure 6.2). That decline was due to the effect of welfare reform as well as to the strong economy—both unemployment and poverty fell during the period, reducing the number of people in need of assistance.

Economic Downturn and SNAP as a Fiscal Stimulus, 2001–15
SNAP participation more than doubled between fiscal years 2000/01 and 2012/13. That increase was the result of a combination of factors that included the Great Recession, policy changes that increased accessibility and expanded states' flexibility in determining the eligibility of applicants, and a large temporary increase in SNAP allotment levels.

Increased Accessibility and Policy Devolution
Following the rapid decline in participation in the late 1990s, starting in 2000 states were given greater flexibility to simplify and streamline their programs to make participation less burdensome and to increase accessibility. For example, in 2000, Congress gave states an array of options that allowed them more liberal means for establishing the asset value of vehicles that were used in determining a household's eligibility for food stamps (Super and Dean 2001).[21] That same year, the USDA issued regulations allowing states to convey categorical eligibility on the basis of receipt of a noncash or in-kind TANF benefit (Food and Nutrition Service 2000; Trippe and Gillooly 2010). This expansion was referred to as broad-based categorical eligibility. These noncash benefits included transportation and child care benefits. They could also include receipt of an informational pamphlet or provision of an 800-number on how to obtain public assistance, making this type of noncash benefit available to a broader range of households and at higher levels of income than were TANF cash assistance benefits. However, as of July 2014, no state had a gross income limit above 200 percent of federal poverty guidelines (Falk and Aussenberg 2014). Many states used the broad-based categorical eligibility option to eliminate the asset test (U.S. Government Accountability Office 2012).

The United States experienced another recession in 2001. That same year, the USDA gave states the option to implement "simplified reporting" for households with earnings. In 2002, Congress expanded the option, allowing states to cover almost all households—including those without earnings.[22] Before the simplified reporting option, most states had three-month certification periods for many food stamp recipients, and recipients were required to report financial changes periodically or within a certain time frame (typically within 10 days) after the change occurred (USDA 2010c). Simplified reporting was implemented to streamline paperwork and increase access, especially for the working poor, who were most likely to experience changes in income (Isaacs 2008). It allowed states to lengthen certification periods and reduce the information that food stamp recipients must provide to the food stamp office between recertification. Simplified reporting offered clients more stability and reduced reporting and recertification requirements, while offering states less work (fewer time-consuming recertifications) and reducing administrative errors by having longer certification periods.

Nationwide EBT

A major technological change marked the end of the traditional paper coupon in the Food Stamp Program. Beginning in 2004, all states used EBT to issue program benefits (USDA 2004).[23] EBT allowed recipients to obtain their SNAP benefits electronically using an EBT card, which is similar in design to a credit or debit card. EBT creates an electronic record of each food stamp transaction, making it easier to identify and document instances in which SNAP benefits are exchanged for cash, drugs, or other illegal goods (USDA 2014b). EBT also reduces the administrative costs associated with printing, distributing, and redeeming paper coupons. At checkout in a retail food store, the use of an EBT card makes it more difficult for someone to be identified as receiving public assistance than the use of a SNAP paper coupon did, thereby reducing stigma, making the program more attractive to eligible people, and increasing their likelihood of participating.

The transition to EBT did have an unintended negative consequence. Farmers markets—multiple-stall markets at which farmers sell agricultural products directly to the general public—increase participants' access to nutritious foods, particularly fresh fruits and vegetables. However, with the implementation of EBT, food stamp and SNAP redemptions at farmers markets initially declined. Unlike most other authorized SNAP retailers, farmers markets do not always operate in areas with electricity (to operate the point-of-sale terminal) and landline phone connections (to check funds in participants' accounts) (USDA 2010b). As a result of switching from paper vouchers to EBT, the real value of SNAP benefits redeemed at farmers markets fell 71 percent between 1994 and 2008 (Briggs and others 2010). However, coinciding with USDA efforts supporting the use of EBT at farmers markets, including the use of support grants to markets needing administrative help in implementing and managing EBT service and customer outreach, the number of farmers markets accepting SNAP EBT has increased eightfold since 2010 (USDA 2015f).

New Name for the Program

The Food, Conservation, and Energy Act of 2008 changed the name of the Food Stamp Program to SNAP beginning in October 2008 (states had the option to give the program a different name) (USDA 2014b).[24] The new name reflected the transition from paper coupons to EBT cards. It also emphasized that SNAP benefits were designed to supplement a household's food expenditures financed from its own income. To increase participation, the law expanded eligibility by indexing asset limits to inflation.

Stimulus Legislation

The program began a long expansionary phase in fiscal year 2000/01 as legislative changes made participation less burdensome and the economy experienced a short recession. Participation increased in 12 of the next 13 years. Only in fiscal year 2006/07, when participation dipped slightly after a period of improved economic conditions, was the expansion interrupted. The dip was also due, at least in part, to the temporary increase in participation that occurred in fiscal year 2005/06 as a result of a series of hurricanes (including Hurricane Katrina) that devastated large areas along portions of the U.S. Gulf Coast (Hanson and Oliveira 2007) (box 6.6).

The increase in participation was especially sharp during and immediately after the Great Recession, which lasted from December 2007 to June 2009. Between 2007 and 2010, the unemployment rate in the United States more than doubled, from 4.6 to 9.6 percent.[25] To help people affected by the Great Recession and to stimulate the economy's recovery, the American Recovery and Reinvestment Act of 2009 (ARRA)—also known as the Stimulus Act[26]—temporarily increased SNAP benefit levels.

Passage of this act was the first time that the program was explicitly used as a fiscal stimulus (box 6.7). It was estimated that US$20 billion in increased SNAP benefits would create US$36.8 billion in economic activity over

---

BOX 6.6 The Disaster Supplemental Nutrition Assistance Program

SNAP responds quickly to increased need in disaster situations. During disasters, the USDA uses two different methods to deliver emergency food. Initially, emergency food is provided to shelters, mass feeding sites, and households when normal commercial food distribution is disrupted. Once grocery stores and other food retailers are operating again, emergency food stamps are issued through the Disaster Supplemental Nutrition Assistance Program (D-SNAP), an extension of the regular SNAP program. Under D-SNAP, eligible households can receive short-term benefits when the U.S. president declares a major disaster (USDA 2013a). Eligible households receive one month of benefits that are equivalent to the maximum amount of benefits normally available to a SNAP household of that size. D-SNAP benefits may be provided to current participants as well as to people who might ordinarily be ineligible for SNAP if they have disaster-related expenses such as loss of income, property damage, relocation expenses, and, in some cases, loss of food due to power outages.

BOX 6.7 **SNAP Impacts on the Macroeconomy**

SNAP benefits help to stabilize the economy, expanding during economic downturns when resources are idle or unemployed and contracting during economic expansions (Hanson and Golan 2002). Some households that lose some or all of their income during a recession can become eligible for and participate in SNAP. Moreover, SNAP benefits increase for households that were already participating if their income falls. SNAP benefits support a household's spending, which in turn augments the income and spending of others, which in turn affects still others. Thus, SNAP benefits start a multiplier process that supports macroeconomic spending and production. Once in place, SNAP participation and benefits can automatically expand during weaker economic conditions and contract during stronger economic conditions, without the need for discretionary legislation. Research estimates a multiplier of SNAP benefits on GDP of 1.73 to 1.79—that is, an increase of US$1 billion in SNAP benefits results in an increase in GDP of US$1.73 billion to US$1.79 billion (Hanson 2010; Zandi 2008) and an increase in full-time-equivalent jobs of 8,900 to 17,900 (Hanson 2010).

five years (USDA 2010a). Furthermore, because SNAP benefits are spent very quickly—97 percent are redeemed within 30 days of issuance—the effect on the economy occurs quickly.

Beginning in April 2009, average monthly benefits increased 15 percent (USDA 2015d). Benefits were to remain at the new higher level until SNAP's maximum benefits adjusted for food price inflation caught up with the maximum benefits set by the ARRA. However, inflation was less than anticipated, and Congress established a sunset, then advanced it to November 1, 2013 (the beginning of fiscal year 2013/14).[27] At that time, the maximum SNAP allotment for a family of four decreased 5.4 percent.

From fiscal year 2007/08 to 2012/13, SNAP caseloads increased 81 percent, the result of a combination of the economic downturn during the Great Recession, policy changes such as the temporary increase in SNAP benefits due to the ARRA, and expanded use of broad-based categorical eligibility. Few states implemented broad-based categorical eligibility policies when they became available in 2001. However, once the economic downturn began later that decade and the number of households applying for SNAP benefits began to rise sharply, the USDA encouraged states to adopt these policies to streamline the eligibility process (U.S. Government Accountability Office 2012). Before 2007, only 11 states had implemented broad-based categorical eligibility; from 2007 to 2011, 29 additional states implemented it.

During the debate leading up to the Agricultural Act of 2014[28]—the 2014 farm bill—concerns were raised that the broad-based categorical eligibility option had allowed SNAP participation to expand beyond the poorest Americans. Despite early proposals to eliminate it, states retained the broad-based categorical eligibility option in the final legislation. The 2014

Agricultural Act did not include major changes to SNAP; however, it did provide additional funding to enhance employment and training activities and to expand antifraud efforts.

SNAP participation reached an all-time high of more than 47 million individuals in fiscal year 2012/13 (figure 6.2). It decreased about 2 percent in both fiscal year 2013/14 and fiscal year 2014/15, as the temporary increase in SNAP benefits ended and the unemployment rate fell for the fifth consecutive year.

CURRENT SNAP IMPLEMENTATION

SNAP is a complex program with multiple eligibility requirements, including both gross and net income limits, an asset test, and work and immigrant eligibility requirements.[29] Benefit levels vary by a household's size and income, taking into account numerous exclusions and deductions, and are reassessed periodically for changes in household circumstances.[30] The federal government operates SNAP in partnership with states and local governments. Researchers have assessed the impact of the Food Stamp Program and SNAP on both nutrition and related outcomes. As a result of that assessment, several policy changes have been proposed to improve recipients' nutrition and health.

Eligibility Requirements

SNAP operates as an entitlement program, meaning that it is available to every household that meets the eligibility requirements. Federal guidelines require that, to be eligible to participate in SNAP, households must meet two income tests, an asset test, and certain nonfinancial tests.

Gross Income Test
Total household income (that is, monthly income before any deductions) must be at or below 130 percent of the monthly federal poverty guidelines, which are based on the number of people in the household and are adjusted annually for inflation.[31] Household income includes earnings from the wages and salaries of household members as well as unearned income, such as public assistance benefits, unemployment benefits, child support, and pensions. Exclusions that do not count as income include in-kind income, loans, income earned by children younger than 18 years of age, allowable self-employment business expenses, federal energy assistance, and certain types of educational benefits. Households with an elderly person (60 years of age or older) or a disabled person are excluded from the gross income test, but they must still pass the net income test.

Net Income Test
Net income—that is, gross income minus allowable deductions—takes into account the expenses for necessities that reduce the funds available to

purchase a nutritious and palatable diet. To meet the net income test, a household's net income must be at or below 100 percent of the federal poverty guidelines. As of 2016, allowable deductions consist of the following:

- A standard deduction of US$155 for households with one to three people and US$165 for households with four people (higher for some larger households)

- A 20 percent deduction from earned income

- A dependent care deduction when needed for work, training, or education

- Medical expenses for elderly or disabled members that are more than US$35 for the month if they are not paid by insurance or someone else

- Legally owed child support payments

- Excess shelter costs that are more than half of a household's income after the other deductions. Allowable costs include the cost of fuel to heat and cook with, electricity, water, the basic fee for one telephone, rent or mortgage payments, and taxes on the home.[32]

The standard deduction recognizes that most households have some nondiscretionary expenditures other than those considered in the other deductions, such as tuition, alimony, and unusual expenses due to disasters (Ohls and Beebout 1993). Other deductions encourage certain behaviors such as working (the earned income and dependent care deductions) or paying child support (the child support payment deduction) (USDA 2012a).

Asset Test
Assets, like income, are a measure of a household's available resources for obtaining food. Households with large assets, even if their current income is low, can potentially draw on their assets (the ease of which is determined by their liquidity) to meet their basic needs. Historically, under the asset test, households may have up to US$2,250 in countable resources, such as a bank account, or US$3,250 in countable resources if at least one person is 60 years of age or older or is disabled. However, certain resources are not counted, such as a home and lot, most retirement (pension) plans, and the resources of people who receive SSI or TANF. States have the option to relax or eliminate the asset limit for most households using broad-based categorical eligibility, and many have chosen to do so.

Additional Eligibility Criteria
Households must meet the following eligibility criteria in addition to the income and asset tests:

- *Employment requirements.* Able-bodied adults age 16 through 59 must register for work, accept suitable employment, or take part in an employment and training program to which they are referred by the local office. Exemptions are allowed for persons who are disabled, working, attending school, taking care of a young child or incapacitated person, participating in a drug or alcohol treatment program, or complying with the work-related requirements of another assistance program. Generally, able-bodied adults age 18–49 who do not have dependents can receive SNAP benefits for only 3 months in a 36-month period if they do not work or participate in a workfare or employment and training program other than job search. That requirement can be waived in locations where the unemployment rate is high.

- *Immigrant eligibility requirements.* Undocumented noncitizens are not eligible for SNAP. Most legal immigrants are eligible if they have lived in the country for five years, are receiving disability-related assistance or benefits, or are under age 18. Certain noncitizens, such as those admitted for humanitarian reasons and those admitted for permanent residence, may be eligible for the program. States are allowed to expand immigrant eligibility beyond federal limits if they fund the expansion with nonfederal dollars.

Some households are categorically eligible for SNAP if they participate in other approved programs. That is, households whose members all receive TANF, SSI, or, in some places, general assistance do not have to meet the gross and net income eligibility standards or the asset limits test (although they must meet the employment and immigrant eligibility requirements). SNAP's categorical eligibility helps to align SNAP with other state-run assistance programs, facilitates participation, and streamlines the application process. Categorically eligible applicants do not have to provide documentation of income when they apply for SNAP because the other program already conducted means testing. In recent years, states have been granted more flexibility regarding program access, and many states have responded by relaxing some of the eligibility criteria (discussed in the section on state policy options).

Certification periods—the length of time a household is authorized to receive SNAP benefits before eligibility is reevaluated—may not exceed 12 months (24 months if all adult members are elderly or disabled). During the certification period, most households are required to report changes in income or other household circumstances that would make them ineligible. State agencies have varying rules on how often and whether households are required to report changes that would affect the amount of benefits.

Program Benefits
SNAP benefits are provided to recipients on a monthly basis. They can be redeemed for most types of food but cannot be used to purchase tobacco, alcohol, hot foods, or foods to be eaten in the store (except by people who

cannot cook for themselves). The dollar value of SNAP benefits that a household receives per month is the household's allotment. SNAP allotments are not intended to cover all of a household's food needs unless a household has zero net income, in which case the household receives the maximum allotment. The maximum allotment increases with household size. SNAP households are expected to contribute about 30 percent of their net income to food, a figure reflected in the SNAP benefit formula (for a household of any given size): household allotment = maximum allotment − (0.30 × net income). Thus, a household's allotment is reduced by US$0.30 for every dollar of net income the household receives. A household's maximum allotment is based on the cost of the USDA's Thrifty Food Plan in June of the previous year.[33] The Thrifty Food Plan is a minimal-cost meal plan, consisting of bundles of foods, that shows how a nutritious and palatable diet may be achieved with limited resources (the plan assumes that all purchased food is consumed at home) (Carlson and others 2007). The cost of the Thrifty Food Plan is adjusted for household size and indexed annually for food price inflation.

Benefit Delivery System

A household applies for SNAP benefits at its state or local SNAP office or by completing an online application. The state or local SNAP office determines whether the applicant is eligible to participate in the program and issues SNAP benefits to eligible households through an EBT system.[34] Each state operates its own EBT system. However, EBT cards are portable—an EBT card issued in one state can be used in any other state. In most states, participants can also use the card to obtain benefits from other cash assistance programs such as the TANF program administered by the U.S. Department of Health and Human Services, thereby taking advantage of common operational platforms. Benefits are deposited electronically into the household's account each month and can be used to purchase groceries at a SNAP-authorized food store (only stores authorized by SNAP may accept SNAP EBT cards). SNAP participants do not pay sales tax on SNAP purchases. Unused SNAP benefits are carried over to the next month.

SNAP-authorized retail food stores sell food to the general public and to SNAP recipients. To be eligible, a store must sell food for home preparation and consumption and meet one of two criteria:

1. Offer for sale, on a continuous basis, at least three varieties of qualifying foods in each of the following four staple food groups, with perishable foods in at least two of the four categories: meat, poultry, or fish; bread or cereal; vegetables or fruits; and dairy products.

2. More than half of the total dollar amount of all retail sales (food, non-food, gas, and services) sold in the store must be from the sale of eligible staple foods.

In fiscal year 2013/14, there were 261,150 outlets authorized to accept SNAP, including specialty stores, farmers markets, direct marketing farmers, providers of meals to the homeless, treatment centers, group homes, and others (USDA 2015c). Two types of stores—super stores (that is, large stores containing a large variety of goods, including both food and nonfood items) and supermarkets—accounted for only 14 percent of all SNAP-authorized stores but more than 80 percent of all redemptions (figure 6.3).

Retailers participate in SNAP on a voluntary basis. All stores that apply for authorization and meet the eligibility criteria are able to redeem SNAP benefits; there is no limit on the number of stores that can participate. The USDA monitors stores for compliance; statistical monitoring is based on the store's characteristics and volume of SNAP sales (Mantovani, Williams, and Pflieger 2013). Participating stores are reimbursed by the federal government for the full value of the food purchased through SNAP.

Take-Up Rates and SNAP Dynamics
The take-up rate is the percentage of eligible people who participate in the program. It provides a measure of how effectively the program reaches its target population (box 6.8). Among all people estimated to be eligible in an

FIGURE 6.3

SNAP Redemptions in the United States, by Type of Store, Fiscal Year 2013/14

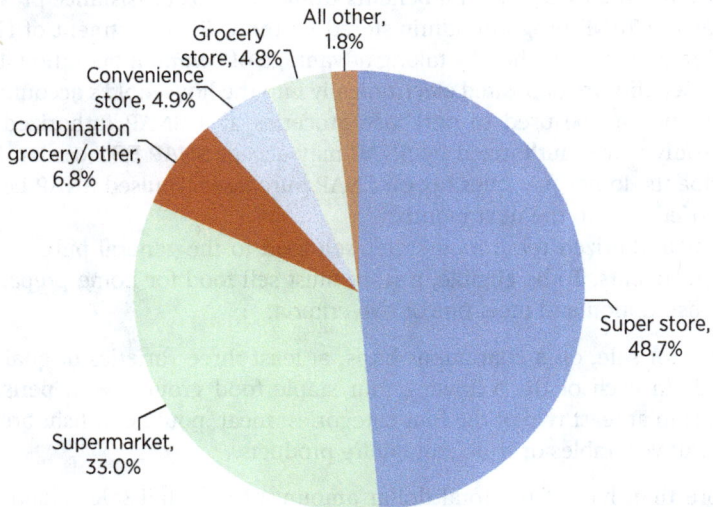

Source: USDA 2015c.
Note: Combination grocery-other are stores whose primary business is the sale of general merchandise but that also serve a variety of food products (Mantovani and Wilson 2011).

BOX 6.8 **Influencing the Take-Up Rate**

Various factors can affect the take-up rate (also referred to as the participation rate or coverage rate), including changes in policy and administrative practices. Changes that likely increased take-up include those that reduced the financial cost of partic-ipation (for example, eliminating the purchase requirement) as well as those that reduced the burden on participants (for example, implementing categorical eligibil-ity, simplified reporting, and online application) or those that reduced participant stigma (for example, switching from paper coupons to electronic benefit transfer). Take-up rates have also been affected by policies that affected benefit levels, including those that (a) changed the ratio of the maximum allotment to the cost of the Thrifty Food Plan; (b) adjusted the frequency of inflation-related adjustments that affect the real value of benefits; and (c) made changes in the allowable deduc-tions from gross income (more deductions translate into higher SNAP benefits because deductions are subtracted from gross income to determine a household's net income, which is used to determine a household's monthly allotments). Through its outreach efforts, the USDA provides information about the nutritional benefits of SNAP to eligible people who are not currently participating in the program to help them to make an informed decision regarding participation. Some state SNAP agencies have worked with community- and faith-based organizations to promote SNAP and provide services, including sign-up promotions, application assistance, and prescreening for eligibility.

Some factors influencing take-up rates are outside the control of SNAP. For exam-ple, expansion of Medicaid in the 1980s likely increased take-up rates because Medicaid workers told their clients about food stamps (both programs are often administered by the same state office). Economic conditions may also affect the take-up rate by influ-encing eligible people's decisions on whether to participate in the program. For exam-ple, an expanding economy may create expectations of future increases in income, which may make eligible households less likely to participate in the program (Hanson and Gundersen 2002). Conversely, during a weakening economy, eligible households may be uncertain about their future financial prospects and thus be more likely to participate. In general, take-up rates follow the trend in total participation, suggesting that changes in caseloads during periods of economic growth and decline are due to changes in the number of eligible people as well as to changes in the take-up rate (Hanson and Oliveira 2012).

average month in 2013, approximately 85 percent participated in SNAP (Eslami 2015b). Those people eligible for higher benefits were more likely to participate than those eligible for lower benefits. Participation was concen-trated among the most economically disadvantaged.

Take-up rates differ from the national average of 85 percent for various demographic groups. On the one hand, take-up rates for children and people living in poverty are higher than the national average, at 99 percent (Eslami 2015b). On the other hand, take-up rates for elderly individuals (41 per-cent), individuals living in households with incomes above the poverty line (42 percent), and individuals in households with earnings (74 percent) are lower than the national average.[35]

The SNAP caseload is dynamic; each month, some people enter the program, while others exit. Among people who entered the program from 2008 to 2012 (a period of relatively high unemployment and poverty), one-third exited within 6 months, half exited within 12 months, and two-thirds exited within 24 months (Leftin and others 2014). The median SNAP "spell"—the continuous period of time that an individual spends on one instance of SNAP participation—for people who entered the program during that period lasted about one year. For most SNAP participants, there are no limits on the number of times they can participate in the program or the total length of time they can participate (subject to meeting eligibility requirements). Many participants who exit the program reenter at a later date, cycling on and off the program.

Activation Features

A household's SNAP benefit is highest when it has no net income and is reduced by US$0.30 for every dollar of net income the household receives. The decline in benefits as earned income increases can be considered an implicit marginal tax on earnings and may reduce the incentive for a SNAP recipient to work compared with a zero marginal tax rate whereby households keep 100 percent of their benefits. Two deductions from gross income in the SNAP benefit formula have been established to reduce the work disincentive: (a) a 20 percent deduction for earned income and (b) a deduction for dependent care.

Several program features have been designed to increase the labor force participation of SNAP recipients and to make the program more accessible to working households. Some of those features are in the form of work requirements and participation restrictions for nonworking adults. As noted previously, SNAP recipients who are able-bodied and without dependents are required to register for work and accept a suitable job if offered one. ABAWDs are subject to strict time limits on the SNAP benefits they receive if they do not work or participate in a training program. Many SNAP recipients—84 percent in fiscal year 2012/13—are exempt from SNAP work registration and training requirements because of their age or disability status or because they are working, in school, taking care of a young child or incapacitated person, taking part in a drug or alcohol treatment program, or complying with the work-related requirements of another assistance program (Gray and Kochhar 2015). SNAP recipients who do not qualify for the work registration exemption are required to participate in a SNAP Employment and Training (SNAP E&T) program if mandated by the state.

SNAP E&T was established with the goal of helping recipients to gain the skills, training, or experience needed to find employment. Each state is required to operate a SNAP E&T program under a federally approved plan, but each state has flexibility in the design.[36] Services may include job search training, workfare, work training or retraining programs for the recently unemployed, basic education, and English-as-a-second-language classes (USDA 2013b). In fiscal year 2014/15, federal SNAP E&T expenditures totaled US$281 million, representing about 0.3 percent of total federal program expenditures (USDA 2015a).

SNAP-Ed
States provide nutrition education to participants through the SNAP-Ed program. The goals of SNAP-Ed are to increase the likelihood that people eligible for SNAP will make healthful food choices within the constraints of a limited budget and will choose a physically active lifestyle. SNAP nutrition education must include obesity prevention services. State agencies can submit a nutrition education plan to the USDA, which may include a variety of approaches to delivering nutrition education and obesity prevention activities. Once a state plan is approved, the state receives federal funding, which is allocated among states on the basis of the state's historical SNAP-Ed spending and current SNAP caseload (Food and Nutrition Service 2013).

Program Administration
The USDA operates the program in partnership with state and local governments. Within the USDA, the Food and Nutrition Service is responsible for administering the program at the federal level. The USDA issues regulations and is responsible for establishing benefit levels and eligibility criteria (with some policy options on eligibility delegated to the states), defining eligible foods, authorizing and monitoring food stores, and ensuring that states administer the program in compliance with program rules (table 6.2).

State agencies administer the program through local offices. In some states, the program is administered directly by local office staff employed by the state, whereas in other states, the program is administered by local governments under state supervision (Ohls and Beebout 1993). Local offices determine applicants' eligibility, certify participants, determine participants' benefit levels, issue EBT cards, and provide supplemental services such as nutrition education and E&T programs. The federal government pays 100 percent of the program benefits and federal administrative costs, whereas the state and federal governments share state administrative costs equally.

SNAP operates similarly across geographic areas, with the exception of income eligibility thresholds and benefit levels in Alaska and Hawaii, which are adjusted to account for higher food prices in those states. However, states do have some flexibility in how they operate the program.

State Policy Options
Legislative and regulatory changes since the late 1990s gave states increased flexibility to simplify program administration and increase program access, especially for low-income working families. However, those changes decreased national uniformity. States have used the flexibility to align eligibility criteria

TABLE 6.2 **Federal versus State SNAP Responsibilities and Costs in the United States**

LEVEL OF GOVERNMENT	RESPONSIBILITY	COSTS
Federal	Issues regulations	Pays 100% of program benefits
	Establishes benefit levels	Pays 100% of federal administrative costs
	Establishes eligibility criteria	Pays about 50% of state administrative costs
	Defines eligible foods	
	Authorizes and monitors participating food stores	
	Monitors state compliance with program rules	
	Overseas quality control measures	
State	Administers the program locally	Pays about 50% of state administrative costs
	Interacts with applicants and participants	
	Determines applicants' eligibility	
	Certifies participants	
	Determines participants' benefit level	
	Issues electronic benefit transfer cards and benefits	
	Provides nutrition education and employment and training programs	

for gross income and assets with their guidelines for other state-run safety net programs. Through the "broad-based categorical eligibility" policy option, almost all states have either removed the federal asset test for most SNAP households or have at least exempted the value of all vehicles from the asset test. In addition, a majority of states have raised the gross income limit above 130 percent of the poverty guidelines (although the limit cannot exceed 200 percent).

States have also implemented some program changes to simplify the process of applying for and remaining on SNAP (U.S. General Accounting Office 2002). States have lengthened recertification periods—the number of months that can elapse before a SNAP household has to recertify eligibility—thereby reducing the transaction costs of participation, particularly for working households that may need to take off from work to complete the recertification process. Between eligibility certifications, households who receive SNAP must report changes in circumstances that may affect their eligibility or monthly benefit. Since 2000, all states have had the option to allow SNAP recipients with earned income to report income changes on a semiannual basis, rather than each month or each time a change in circumstances occurs (U.S. General Accounting Office 2002). Semiannual, or "simplified," reporting decreases the reporting burden on SNAP recipients because it requires households to declare changes in their financial circumstances within reporting periods only if the changes would make them ineligible for the program. By 2014, all but one state had adopted the simplified reporting option (USDA 2015b).

Program Integrity

A central challenge in the design of any assistance program is to balance the goals of making program benefits accessible to eligible households and screening out ineligible households. In the case of SNAP, in which states administer the program, while the federal government pays benefits, federal oversight is needed to monitor how states distribute the federal benefit. The USDA established the quality control system in 1977 to monitor the accuracy of determinations of eligibility and benefits by state agencies. Each state is required to conduct periodic reviews of a sample of its SNAP case files. State quality control auditors reexamine the case files, reinterview recipients, and recheck documentation. Federal staff workers then recheck a sample of the state audit sample. Both overpayments and underpayments are tracked. In fiscal year 2013/14, less than 3 percent of SNAP benefits were deemed overpayments and less than 1 percent were underpayments (USDA 2015e). The quality control system forms the basis for providing monetary bonuses to states for high or improved accuracy of payments and terminations and for timely processing of applications.

SNAP OUTCOMES

Hunger and malnutrition—in the form of undernutrition—were serious problems when the Food Stamp Program was established in the 1960s. In a message to Congress in 1969, President Richard M. Nixon stated, "In the past few years we have awakened to the distressing fact that despite our material abundance and agricultural wealth, many Americans suffer from malnutrition. Precise factual descriptions of its extent are not presently available, but there can be no doubt that hunger and malnutrition exist in America and that some millions may be affected" (Nixon 1969). Over time, the prevalence of undernutrition in the United States has diminished significantly. A landmark assessment of poverty-related programs in 1997 stated, "Evidence of severe malnutrition-related health problems has almost disappeared in this country. The primary reason is Food Stamps" (Blank 1997, 163).

Today, the focus of SNAP outcomes extends beyond hunger and undernutrition. Because of the significance of SNAP to both program participants and U.S. taxpayers, it is important to evaluate the program's effects. Researchers have assessed the impact of the Food Stamp Program and SNAP on various outcomes, including economic well-being, food spending, food security, nutrition and health, and the prevalence of overweight and obesity.

Economic Well-Being

A household's economic well-being is often measured by its poverty status. Moreover, other outcomes such as food insecurity, poor health, and reduced earnings potential are associated with poverty (Tiehen, Jolliffe, and Smeeding 2016). Official U.S. estimates of poverty omit in-kind benefits from family income. As a result, those estimates understate the resources of families that receive SNAP benefits. When benefits are counted as part of family income to obtain an "inclusive-of-SNAP" measure of poverty, SNAP lifted 4.7 million people, including 2.1 million children, out of poverty in 2014 (Short 2015).

The *depth* of poverty and the *severity* of poverty are two additional measures that capture how SNAP increases income among poor families, even if it does not lift them out of poverty.[37] The severity measure is particularly sensitive to how effectively program benefits reach the poorest of the poor. Because SNAP provides more benefits to persons with lower incomes, SNAP leads to relatively larger decreases in the depth and severity of poverty than in the poverty rate (Tiehen, Jolliffe, and Gundersen 2012; Tiehen, Jolliffe, and Smeeding 2016). For example, while SNAP benefits lowered the poverty rate an average of 4.9 percent during 2000–11, they lowered the depth and severity of poverty 11.0 and 14.0 percent, respectively (Tiehen, Jolliffe, and Smeeding 2016).

Poverty among children is especially lessened by SNAP benefits. Children in the United States experience significantly higher rates of poverty than the overall population and account for almost half of total SNAP benefits. During 2000–11, SNAP benefits reduced the depth of child poverty 16.4 percent and the severity of child poverty 22.3 percent (Tiehen, Jolliffe, and Smeeding 2016).

Food Spending

By increasing spending on food, SNAP is expected to increase households' nutrient availability and, in turn, the nutrient intake of individuals in those households (Fox, Hamilton, and Lin 2004). Therefore, the extent to which SNAP increases food security and improves diet quality and nutrition depends on the degree to which SNAP benefits augment a household's food expenditures that are financed from cash income. SNAP benefits are redeemable only for food. However, when receiving SNAP benefits, a household can partially or fully reduce its cash-based food expenditures.

The marginal propensity to spend (on food) out of SNAP benefits (MPS_{SB}) represents the net increase in total food expenditures that results from a US\$1 increase in SNAP benefits. For example, an MPS_{SB} of 0.25 means that a US\$1 increase in SNAP benefits increases total food expenditures by US\$0.25. A review of 17 studies found that most estimates range from 0.17 to 0.47 (Fraker 1990).[38] Four more recent studies reported estimates of 0.26, 0.35, 0.40, and 0.69 (Fox, Hamilton, and Lin 2004). Following the ARRA, which temporarily increased benefits to all SNAP households, Beatty and Tuttle (2015) estimated the MPS_{SB} to be 0.48. Thus, the research consistently indicates that, for each dollar of SNAP benefits a typical household receives, food spending rises (but by less than a full dollar), and, in most studies, the rise is as great as or greater than for a comparable increase in cash.[39]

Providing assistance in the form of food-targeted benefits—paper coupons or EBT cards—increases the administrative complexity and cost of a program, raising the issue of whether food-targeted benefits increase food expenditures by *more* than an equal increment of cash. A review concluded that studies "strongly suggest that coupons would be more effective than cash food assistance at increasing food expenditures" (Fraker 1990, 77). Most estimates of the marginal propensity to spend (on food) out of a dollar of cash lie between 0.05 and 0.10—that is, less than estimates of the MPS_{SB}.[40]

Food Security
The terms *food security* and *food insecurity* have different definitions and connotations around the globe because countries exhibit marked differences in their average and their distribution of household income, food consumption, and nutrient intakes. The USDA defines a household as food secure when all members of the household have access at all times to enough food for an active, healthy life.[41] Food-insecure households are those that, at some point during the year, have difficulty providing enough food for all their members because of a lack of resources. A subgroup of food-insecure households exhibits the more severe condition of very low food security—the eating pattern of one (or more) household member is disrupted and food intake is reduced at some point during the year—because they cannot afford enough food.

Reliable monitoring of food security contributes to the effective operation of federal and private food assistance programs.[42] In 2014, 86.0 percent of U.S. households were food secure throughout the year. Food insecurity was evident at least some time during the year in the remaining 14.0 percent of households, of which 5.6 percent had very low food security (Coleman-Jensen and others 2015).

Recent studies based on different research designs provide strong evidence that SNAP decreases food insecurity. A 2011–12 study measured food insecurity for a sample of households at the time of entering SNAP and again after six months of SNAP participation. The study found that food insecurity among the households fell 10.6 percentage points (Mabli and others 2013). Another study found that, after the ARRA increased SNAP benefits and expanded SNAP eligibility for jobless adults without children, food insecurity among lower-income households fell 2.2 percentage points, while food insecurity increased 0.16 percentage point among households with annual incomes 150–250 percent of the poverty thresholds that were likely to be ineligible to participate in SNAP (Nord and Prell 2011). Another study found that, from 2009 to 2011, when the real value of SNAP benefits declined because of inflation in food prices, the estimated number of SNAP-recipient households with very low food security increased (Nord 2013).

Nutrition and Health

SNAP attempts to improve the diet quality of participants by increasing their purchasing power, allowing them to purchase more and higher-quality foods. However, higher food expenditures do not necessarily result in purchases of more nutritious foods. Instead, SNAP recipients can purchase more of the same foods or purchase higher-priced, more convenient, but not necessarily more nutritious foods.

Research findings on the nutritional effects of SNAP participation are mixed. A comprehensive 2004 review of 14 studies on the availability of household nutrients concluded, "Overall, the literature strongly suggests that the FSP [Food Stamp Program] has little to no impact on individual dietary intake" (Fox, Hamilton, and Lin 2004, 62). A 2013 analysis of SNAP's effect on the nutritional quality of participants' diets found inconclusive results, with SNAP participants showing improvement on some components of a healthy diet, but slightly lower diet quality as a whole and for many dietary components (Gregory and others 2013).

However, results from other recent studies suggest that SNAP does have positive effects on health and other outcomes. For example, Almond, Hoynes, and Schanzenbach (2011) found that in counties in which the Food Stamp Program was operating during 1968–77, pregnancies tended to be associated with increased birthweight, the largest gains were at the lowest birthweights, and birthweight effects were larger in high-poverty areas where SNAP participation was most common. Hoynes, Schanzenbach, and Almond (2016) examined the period of Food Stamp Program rollout across counties between 1961 and 1975 and found that children with access to the program had, on reaching adulthood, a lower metabolic syndrome index (an aggregate of health conditions such as obesity, high blood pressure, and diabetes) and that women with access to the program had greater economic self-sufficiency (an aggregate of socioeconomic conditions such as high school graduation, employment, and earnings) compared with similar groups in counties that had not yet implemented the program. A 2015 report by the President's Council of Economic Advisers reviewed recent studies and concluded, "SNAP's benefits are especially evident and wide-ranging for those who receive food assistance as children; they extend beyond the immediate goal of alleviating hunger and include improvements in short-run health and academic performance as well as in long-run health, educational attainment, and economic self-sufficiency" (Furman, Muñoz, and Black 2015, 2).

Overweight and Obesity

As SNAP has evolved over time, so too have nutritional concerns. In recent decades, the prevalence of overweight and obesity—which are correlated with excess morbidity and mortality (National Center for Health Statistics 2015)—has increased. An emerging issue involves the potential paradox that a program that contributed to the disappearance of severe undernutrition may be contributing to malnutrition in the form of overweight or obesity.[43] That is, does increasing the purchasing power of SNAP participants lead to more food purchased and more calories consumed or to a more nutrient-dense diet with the same calories?

A USDA review of the literature found that for most participants—children, nonelderly men, and the elderly—use of SNAP benefits is not associated with either an increase in body mass index or the likelihood of being overweight or obese (Ver Ploeg and Ralston 2008). However, for nonelderly women, some evidence suggests that participation in SNAP may increase body mass index and the probability of obesity. The different results for age and sex subgroups remain unexplained. A review by DeBono, Ross, and Berrang-Ford (2012), which includes studies published since 2008, found results that are generally consistent with the findings of Ver Ploeg and Ralston (2008). A more recent study organized a review of the literature by whether a study found a positive effect, a negative effect, or no effect of SNAP on obesity and concluded, "There is very little evidence that SNAP is associated with higher probabilities of obesity among participants in comparison to eligible nonparticipants" (Gundersen 2016, 177).

PROPOSALS TO IMPROVE SNAP RECIPIENTS' NUTRITION AND HEALTH

Improving the nutrition and health of SNAP participants is challenging (box 6.9). For example, the SNAP-Ed program is the primary means by which SNAP attempts to influence the food choices of program participants (Condon and others 2015). Although SNAP-Ed funding has increased substantially in recent decades, federal expenditures for nutrition education totaled about US$350 million or only 0.5 percent of total federal program costs in fiscal year 2014/15 (USDA 2015a). Expenditures for SNAP-Ed are far exceeded by spending on advertising for food, beverages, and restaurants (Guthrie and Variyam 2007).

BOX 6.9 **Focusing on Nutrition: SNAP versus WIC**

SNAP differs in several ways from the Special Supplemental Nutrition Program for Women, Infants, and Children (WIC), which is widely recognized as one of the most successful nutrition programs in the United States. WIC currently serves more than half of all infants and more than one-quarter of pregnant and postpartum women, as well as children age 1–4 (Oliveira and Frazão 2015). An estimated 53 percent of WIC participants also participate in SNAP (USDA 2012b).

WIC was established in 1974, when it was generally acknowledged that the other available food assistance programs, including the Food Stamp Program, were not meeting the special needs of infants and pregnant women. Drawing on the premise that early intervention during critical times of growth and development can help to prevent future medical and developmental problems, WIC is targeted at nutritionally at-risk, low-income pregnant and postpartum women; infants; and children age 1–4. WIC is not intended to be the primary source of food or general food assistance. Rather, it supplies participants with a free set of prescribed types and quantities of specific foods that provide supplemental amounts of specific nutrients known to be lacking in the diets of target populations. The amount of food provided to recipients does not vary with household income. Moreover, the authorized maximum monthly allowances for all WIC foods must be made available to participants if medically and nutritionally warranted.

WIC offers more nutrition- and health-related services to participants than does SNAP. For example, in addition to offering nutrition education and counseling to all participants, WIC provides breastfeeding promotion and support; health risk assessment; and referrals to other health, welfare, and social services. As a result, food benefits accounted for only 68 percent of WIC's total program costs in fiscal year 2014/15 compared with 94 percent of total SNAP costs (percentages are based on data from USDA 2015a).

Some changes to the program have been proposed to improve the diet quality of SNAP participants. Throughout the program's history, some have argued that recipients should not be allowed to use their SNAP benefits to purchase "unhealthy" foods—usually defined as foods high in calories, fats, or sugars. In recent years, attempts to restrict what recipients can purchase with SNAP have become more frequent. For example,

• In 2004, the state of Minnesota sought to prohibit the use of SNAP benefits to purchase candy and soft drinks (Guthrie and others 2007).

• In 2010, the mayor of New York City proposed prohibiting SNAP recipients from using SNAP benefits to purchase soft drinks (Hartocollis 2010).

• In 2015, the state of Maine requested a waiver from the USDA that would allow a ban on the use of SNAP benefits to purchase foods with little or no nutritional value (Maine Legislature 2015).

The USDA has not approved any request by states and localities to restrict SNAP purchases. In a review of policy issues, the Food and Nutrition Service noted that prohibition policies would be administratively complex and, even if implemented, might have limited effectiveness (USDA 2007). The complexity arises, in part, when identifying thresholds for calories, fats, or sugars that would disqualify a food item from SNAP—especially if that same item contains desirable nutrients. No less burdensome would be applying any standard to the hundreds of thousands of food products on the market as well as requiring stores (especially small stores) to keep track of which items are allowable and which are disqualified from SNAP.

Prohibition policies may also have limited effectiveness. SNAP participants might use their own cash to purchase an item that is disqualified from SNAP (about 70 percent of SNAP participants receive less than the maximum allotment and presumably use cash to supplement SNAP benefits).

Finally, the Food and Nutrition Service review states, "There is no strong research-based evidence to support restricting food stamp benefits. Food stamp recipients are no more likely than higher-income consumers to choose foods with little nutritional values; thus the basis for singling out low-income food stamp recipients and restricting their food choices is not clear" (USDA 2007, 1). Restricting the types of food that can be purchased through SNAP could also discourage participation in the program.

Pricing Strategies
Low-income households spend a larger share of their income on food than higher-income households, suggesting that price manipulation could be an effective incentive for improving the eating habits of SNAP households (Lin and Guthrie 2007). In 2011–12, SNAP conducted a pilot in western Massachusetts, known as the Healthy Incentives Pilot, that provided a treatment group of randomly assigned SNAP-participating households a price incentive that increased SNAP benefits by US$0.30 for every dollar spent on targeted fruits and vegetables using SNAP benefits, while a control group of SNAP households received no price incentive. The price incentive essentially lowered the effective price of fruits and vegetables by 30 percent. The price incentive increased the estimated average daily consumption for adults by about one-quarter-cup equivalent of targeted fruits and vegetables, which represented an increase in consumption of about 26 percent compared with the control group (Bartlett and others 2014). That result suggests that a price incentive could change the purchase and consumption behaviors of SNAP participants.

A related strategy for promoting fruits and vegetables is being used at some farmers markets across the country. Many farmers markets offer a "match" or "bonus" to SNAP recipients who purchase foods—typically, fruits and vegetables—at the market. A dollar-for-dollar match is common (up to some specified limit such as US$20) and essentially acts as a 50 percent discount on the effective price of fruits and vegetables. Such programs have received funding from private foundations, nonprofit organizations, and local governments, while complying with SNAP rules and regulations and informing the Food and Nutrition Service (King and others 2014). Research has found evidence that incentives bring SNAP consumers to farmers markets (Dimitri and others 2015; King and others 2014). However, research about the effects of incentives on the consumption of fruits and vegetables is impeded by the relatively large expense of collecting dietary recall data.

Dispersing SNAP Allotments More Frequently

Currently, each SNAP household's entire allotment of monthly benefits is electronically loaded onto the household's EBT card in a lump sum once each month. Previous research suggests that households spend more of their benefits soon after benefit disbursement and therefore have less to spend later in the month (Wilde and Ranney 2000). This "monthly food stamp cycle" of food purchases can help SNAP households, giving them the flexibility to spend benefits at the times and places they choose and potentially allowing them to obtain lower food prices by buying some food items in bulk.

There is evidence, however, that, for some households, the up-and-down cycle of food purchases can result in a second "monthly food stamp cycle" of caloric intake. Wilde and Ranney (2000) found that, for households that shopped infrequently, food energy declined significantly between the first and fourth week of the food stamp month. Shapiro (2005) found that the average caloric intake for members of food stamp households fell 10–15 percent over the food stamp month. The implication is that, toward the end of the SNAP month, after benefits have run out, some recipients have less to eat or may have to stretch their SNAP benefits (or their own cash) by purchasing cheaper foods that may be less nutritious. Thus, dispersing SNAP benefits just once each month may have negative consequences for food security, nutrition, and weight status for some recipients.

One policy proposal is to distribute a household's allotment of SNAP benefits more frequently than once a month (Wilde and Ranney 2000). For example, households could receive half their allotment at the beginning of the month and the remaining portion halfway through the month. Arguments have been raised that this policy is overly paternalistic, reduces choices for recipients, and makes it more difficult for recipients to take advantage of bulk discounts. However, Wilde (2007) points out that having a twice-monthly delivery of benefits does not necessarily prevent people from shopping once a month: "A family that prefers to shop once monthly is still welcome to do so, on the occasion of the second benefit credit each month." Wilde (2013a) suggests pilot testing a twice-monthly benefit delivery to determine its effect on recipients. A related option is to allow households some choice over their frequency of receipt in place of a uniform policy of either monthly or biweekly dispersal for all (Wilde 2007).

Benefit Adequacy

Two recent studies summarize several concerns that have been raised regarding the adequacy of SNAP allotments (Institute of Medicine and National Research Council 2013; Ziliak 2016). These concerns include geographic variation in food prices, cost variations associated with the age and nutrient requirements of household members, and the costs of time in food preparation. Currently, the cost of the Thrifty Food Plan, on which SNAP allotments are based, is calculated using national average food prices and therefore does not account for geographic differences in the price of food (with exceptions for Alaska and Hawaii). Leibtag (2007) estimated that, during 1998–2003, average prices within four U.S. regions for a representative mix of foods were 8.0 and 11.1 percent greater than the national average in the East and West, respectively, and 7.0 and 5.2 percent less than the national average in the South and Midwest, respectively. As a result of regional variations in food prices, the nutritional benefits of the SNAP allotment may vary across geographic areas. Regarding household composition, the basic allotment of SNAP benefits assumes a household composed of two adults and two children under age 12 and makes simple adjustments for household size. The adjustments do not reflect that households with teenagers (who need more nutrients than younger children) have a more difficult time purchasing adequate foods with their SNAP benefits. Lastly, the Thrifty Food Plan assumes that low-income households can spend an unlimited amount of time preparing meals. However, societal norms in food preparation have changed greatly since the Thrifty Food Plan was first constructed. The average household now buys more convenience food, such as packaged vegetables and ready-to-cook foods, which save time in preparation but can cost an additional 20 percent or more. Addressing these concerns could result in substantial increases in benefit and administrative costs.

LESSONS LEARNED

SNAP offers a wealth of lessons of global relevance. For instance, it is clearly integrated with the economic cycles and the poverty outcomes that ensue. As such, SNAP's flexibility to expand and contract makes it a highly countercyclical social assistance program. SNAP also offers insights on transparency and accountability, including investments in verifying eligibility and in combating fraud and corruption. Its integration with the private retail sector illustrates the potential for a social assistance program to create sizable economic multipliers.

Based, in part, on a program originating during the Great Depression, the Food Stamp Program—now SNAP—began as a small pilot program established by the USDA in 1961. Permanently authorized by Congress in 1964, SNAP has grown to become the cornerstone of the nutritional safety net for low-income Americans, benefiting about one in seven Americans during 2015. The longevity of the program, across periods of a changing American political climate, is evidence that the program has support from a variety of influential (and dissimilar) stakeholder groups, including advocates for the poor, food retailers, and agricultural producers. By increasing food expenditures at the retail level, SNAP increases the purchasing power of program recipients and has upstream effects that support farmers and others involved in the agriculture sector. SNAP's 83 percent take-up rate among those eligible in fiscal year 2011/12 suggests a high level of acceptance by the program's target population. The program's low error rate indicates strong program integrity and efficiency, which are important factors for maintaining the confidence of the American public, who ultimately fund the program.

SNAP is constantly evolving. Although some of the fundamental features of today's program were established at the program's onset—including using the commercial food system to distribute foods and giving recipients a wide choice of foods to purchase—many other program features were established later on. One of the most important changes occurred in the late 1970s, when Congress began to fund the program fully. As an entitlement, the program responds quickly to changing economic conditions, increasing during economic downturns and decreasing as the economy improves without the need for legislative intervention. Policy changes have also affected the program over its history. Major changes included (a) establishing nationwide eligibility standards and benefit levels in the early 1970s, (b) eliminating the purchase requirement in 1977, (c) using technological improvements in the form of EBT to issue benefits (effective nationwide by 2002), and (d) implementing a large, but temporary, increase in benefit levels as a means to stimulate the economy in the wake of the Great Recession. Numerous other policy changes have been enacted on a smaller scale, often affecting eligibility standards or benefit levels.

In terms of effectiveness, research has shown that participation in SNAP increases food expenditures, decreases food insecurity, and helps to reduce the rate, depth, and severity of poverty in participating households (box 6.10). By responding quickly and automatically to changes in need, SNAP also functions as an automatic stabilizer during economic cycles. Despite those successes, challenges remain. Recent research provides mixed results on whether and how much SNAP improves various aspects of diet quality for program participants—problems that affect both the rich and the poor to varying degrees. Various policy changes to improve recipients' nutrition and health have been proposed. The extent to which those proposals are adopted will reflect the balancing of competing goals, including health promotion, consumer sovereignty of individual food choices, and program costs.

As one of the country's most important—and expensive—social programs, SNAP is closely scrutinized by the U.S. Congress and others. Because the two major SNAP policy makers—USDA officials (who answer to the president)

BOX 6.10 **SNAP Monitoring and Research**

Program monitoring and research are deliberate and legislated components of SNAP that assess program performance and effectiveness and inform policy decisions. SNAP has benefited from an extensive and transparent system of program monitoring and evaluation that regularly reports on measures such as participation levels, take-up rates among key groups, participant characteristics, program costs, and payment errors. Many of these activities make direct use of administrative records, while others make use of special surveys to capture information on food expenditures, nutrition, health, and food security outcomes. The resulting information and analysis are valued by a range of stakeholders, including policy officials, program managers, and the general public. Debate and decisions benefit from a shared base of objective evidence.

In the United States, monitoring and research activities are performed by government, academic, and independent research institutions. Within the U.S. Department of Agriculture, a program agency (the Food and Nutrition Service) and a federal statistical agency (the Economic Research Service) cooperate in ongoing studies of SNAP and other USDA food assistance programs. With funding from the USDA and others, researchers in universities and independent research institutions also contribute to a body of knowledge about the programs. Making government data publicly available when confidentiality restrictions permit also encourages academic research. Whether the evidence has been positive, negative, or mixed, monitoring and research have contributed to SNAP's ongoing success by providing key evidence-based information to the program's stakeholders.

and Congress (who are elected representatives)—are responsive to political forces, the political environment along with the economy will continue to shape the program in ways both large and small.

NOTES

1. Because people enter and exit SNAP throughout the year, the number of people participating in SNAP over the course of the year is greater than the number of people participating in an average month. In fiscal year 2011/12, the number of people who participated in the program at some time during the year was estimated to be about 28 percent greater than participation in an average month (Prell, Newman, and Scherpf 2015).
2. Benefits accounted for almost US$70 billion or 94 percent of federal SNAP costs in fiscal year 2014/15. Remaining costs covered administration, nutrition education, employment and training programs, and program evaluation (USDA 2015a).
3. Information on individual programs that compose USDA's array of domestic food assistance programs can be found at http://www.fns.usda.gov/.
4. Medicare is a health insurance program for people age 65 and older and for younger people with certain disabilities.
5. Agricultural Act of 1935, P.L. no. 74-320, 49 Stat. 773 (1935).
6. Food Stamp Act of 1964, P.L. no. 88-525, 78 Stat. 703 (1964).
7. In those areas that switched from the Commodity Distribution Program to the Food Stamp Program, the decrease in participation in the Commodity Distribution Program

(in which recipients did not have to pay to receive the program's food benefits) exceeded the increase in participation in the Food Stamp Program (in which recipients had to purchase their food benefits) (Berry 1984).

8. Amendments to the Food Stamp Act of 1964, P.L. no. 91-671, 84 Stat. 2048 (1971).

9. The Agriculture and Consumer Protection Act of 1973, P.L. no. 93-86, 87 Stat. 221 (1973).

10. Furthermore, when incomes fall, households qualify for higher benefits, thereby making participation in SNAP more attractive (participants may also stay in the program longer as they try to find employment). In terms of federal programs that are most responsive to economic downturns, SNAP is second to the Unemployment Insurance Program, which provides unemployment benefits to eligible workers who are unemployed through no fault of their own (Center on Budget and Policy Priorities 2015).

11. The correlation between the number of SNAP participants and real (that is, adjusted for inflation) program expenditures is extremely strong, at 0.99, using annual data for the period from fiscal year 1964/65 to fiscal year 2013/14.

12. Food and Agricultural Act of 1977, P.L. no. 95-113, 91 Stat. 913 (1977).

13. Food Stamp Act Amendments of 1979, P.L. no. 96-58, 93 Stat. 389 (1979).

14. The legislation that eliminated the purchase requirement was enacted near the end of 1977, and states were given a year to implement the changes. Therefore, the impact of the legislation on participation would not have been felt until 1979 (Hanson and Oliveira 2012).

15. Omnibus Budget Reconciliation Act of 1981, P.L. no. 97-35, 95 Stat. 357 (1981).

16. Food Security Act of 1985, P.L. no. 99-198, 99 Stat. 1354 (1985).

17. Omnibus Reconciliation Act of 1982, P.L. no. 97-253, 96 Stat. 763 (1982).

18. Hunger Prevention Act of 1988, P.L. no. 100-435, 102 Stat. 1645 (1988).

19. Personal Responsibility and Work Opportunity Reconciliation Act of 1996, P.L. no. 104-193, 110 Stat. 2105 (1996).

20. Balanced Budget Act of 1997, P.L. no. 105-33, 111 Stat. 251 (1997).

21. Agriculture, Rural Development, Food and Drug Administration, and Related Agencies Appropriations Act of 2001, P.L. no. 106-387, 114 Stat. 1549 (2000). Before 2000, low-income households with cars that were worth relatively more (often reflecting that they were newer and more dependable) were penalized more than households with cars that were worth less. According to Super and Dean (2001, 34), the liberalization of vehicle asset limits was "partly motivated by the broader policy goal of supporting asset accumulation to assist low-income recipients attain long-term goals of self-sufficiency. But it also probably reflects state administrators' judgment that the administrative burden of calculating car values was not worth the potential benefit of targeting benefits more tightly by excluding families with expensive or even moderately valuable cars or trucks."

22. Farm Security and Rural Investment Act of 2002, P.L. no. 107-171, 116 Stat. 134 (2002).

23. The USDA began implementing EBT demonstration projects in 1984 (USDA 2004). The 1990 farm bill (P.L. no. 101-624, 104 Stat. 3359) permitted states—with the approval of USDA—to implement EBT.

24. Food, Conservation, and Energy Act of 2008, P.L. no. 110-234, 122 Stat. 923 (2008).

25. See the Bureau of Labor Statistics, Labor Force Statistics from the Current Population Survey (http://www.bls.gov/cps/cpsaat01.htm).

26. American Recovery and Reinvestment Act of 2009, P.L. no. 111-5, 123 Stat. 115. (2009).

27. Healthy, Hunger-Free Kids Act of 2010, P.L. no. 111-296, 124 Stat. 3183 (2010).

28. Agricultural Act of 2014, P.L. no. 113-79, 128 Stat. 649 (2014).

29. Much of the material on SNAP operations in this section is based on information from the USDA Food and Nutrition Service's website as of January 2016. See http://www.fns .usda.gov/snap/supplemental-nutrition-assistance-program-snap.

30. A SNAP household—the program's basic recipient or beneficiary unit—is a group of individuals who live together and customarily purchase food and prepare meals together, an individual who lives alone, or an individual who, while living with others, customarily purchases food and prepares meals apart from the others (Food and Nutrition Act of 2008, as amended). The concept of household is an important issue in determining eligibility as well as benefits. Because SNAP "benefits are issued based on economies of scale, smaller households receive larger per person benefits than do larger households" (U.S. Senate 1985, 187).

31. Under policies involving "broad-based categorical eligibility," states are allowed to adopt options that have the effect of raising the limit on a household's gross income above 130 percent of the official poverty line, often to match the income-to-poverty limit of another assistance program such as Medicaid. Those options also have the effect of eliminating the asset test. The options streamline the determination of eligibility across multiple programs, saving states' administrative costs. They also increase the number of eligible households and participants in SNAP and increase program costs.

32. For most households, the allowable deduction is limited to US$504 (as of February 2016), but all shelter costs that are more than half of a household's income may be deducted for households with an elderly or disabled member.

33. The maximum allotment was US$649 for a household with four members in fiscal year 2015/16 (USDA 2014c). Maximum allotments increase with household size, but at a decreasing rate to account for economies of scale in the purchase and preparation of food. The minimum monthly SNAP benefit per person was US$16 in fiscal year 2015/16.

34. Eligibility of a SNAP applicant is determined, in part, using information provided by the applicant, along with supporting documentation such as a driver's license, rent or mortgage receipts, check stubs from an employer, and bank statements. Some types of information are obtained or verified through sources other than documentation. The Agricultural Act of 2014 requires states to verify applicant employment data through the National Directory of New Hires (Food and Nutrition Service 2016).

35. The relatively low SNAP take-up among the elderly is partly explained by their relatively higher incomes, which means that they qualify for relatively lower SNAP benefits. In 2011, almost half of SNAP-eligible elderly qualified for only the minimum benefit of US$10 per month (Eslami 2015a). Evidence also indicates that the elderly nonparticipants may be relatively less disadvantaged, exhibiting lower rates of food insecurity and material hardship than the nonelderly population (Coleman-Jensen and others 2015; Haider, Jacknowitz, and Schoeni 2003). However, SNAP take-up rates are much lower among the elderly than among the nonelderly even among those eligible for a benefit of at least US$150 per month (USDA 2002).

36. A state agency can partner with local agencies to provide E&T services or, in some cases, to operate a substantial portion of the E&T program. States have created partnerships with educational institutions, such as community colleges and vocational training centers, as well as community-based organizations and local workforce development agencies (USDA 2013b).

37. The poverty-gap index measures the depth of poverty and is defined by the mean distance below the poverty threshold, where the mean is formed over the entire population (the nonpoor are counted as having zero poverty gap). The squared-poverty-gap index, which provides a measure of the severity of poverty, is defined as the mean of the squared proportionate poverty gaps.

38. Three studies that used data collected after elimination of the purchase requirement provided estimates of 0.23, 0.26, and 0.29 (Fraker 1990).

39. In related research on spending propensities within a specific low-income subpopulation, the USDA conducted the Summer Electronic Benefits Transfer for Children demonstration in 2011–13 to study alternative approaches to providing food assistance to

children in the summer months when school meals are not operating. Some households received an EBT card that enabled them to purchase any foods allowed by SNAP. The marginal propensity to spend on food was estimated to be US$0.57 for each dollar of benefits (Collins and others 2013).

40. Additional evidence comes from four cash-out demonstrations conducted in the 1970s (Fraker 1993).

41. An expert panel tasked with reviewing the USDA's measurement of food insecurity and hunger concluded, "Hunger is a concept distinct from food insecurity, which is an indicator and possible consequence of food insecurity, that can be useful in characterizing severity of food insecurity. Hunger is an important concept, but it should be measured at the individual level distinct from, but in the context of, food insecurity" (National Research Council 2006, 48).

42. Since 1995, the USDA has monitored the extent and severity of food insecurity in U.S. households through an annual, nationally representative survey conducted by the U.S. Census Bureau and sponsored and analyzed by USDA's Economic Research Service. The 2014 food security survey covered 43,253 households comprising a representative sample of the U.S. civilian population of 124 million households (Coleman-Jensen and others 2015). The food security survey asked one adult respondent in each household a series of questions about experiences and behaviors of household members that indicate food insecurity, such as being unable to afford balanced meals, cutting the size of meals because of having too little money for food, or being hungry because of having too little money for food. The food security status of the household was assigned using the number of food-insecure conditions reported. Hunger, in the sense of an individual-level physiological condition, is not measured by USDA's food security survey.

43. SNAP has provided obesity prevention services as part of its nutrition education since 2010.

REFERENCES

Abbott, Chuck. 2016. "Farm Bill Coalition Prepares for a Fight." *Successful Farming*, April 25. http://www.agriculture.com/content/farm-bill-coalition-prepares-for-a-fight.

Agricultural Marketing Service. 1961. "Pilot Food Stamp Projects." *Federal Register* 26 (4137): 3409–15.

Almond, Douglas, Hilary W. Hoynes, and Diane W. Schanzenbach. 2011. "Inside the War on Poverty: The Impact of Food Stamps on Birth Outcomes." *Review of Economics and Statistics* 93 (2): 387–403. http://www.mitpressjournals.org/doi/abs/10.1162/REST_a_00089#.V7maBZgrLIU.

Andrews, Margaret S., and Katherine L. Clancy. 1993. "The Political Economy of the Food Stamp Program in the United States." In *The Political Economy of Food and Nutrition Policies*, edited by Per Pinstrup-Andersen. Baltimore, MD: Johns Hopkins University Press.

Bartlett, Susan, Jacob Klerman, Lauren Olsho, Christopher Logan, Michelle Blocklin, Marianne Beauregard, and Ayesha Enver. 2014. *Evaluation of the Healthy Incentives Pilot (HIP): Final Report*. Washington, DC: Food and Nutrition Service, U.S. Department of Agriculture.

Beatty, Timothy K. M., and Charlotte J. Tuttle. 2015. "Expenditure Response to Increases in In-Kind Transfers: Evidence from the Supplement Nutrition Assistance Program." *American Journal of Agricultural Economics* 97 (2): 390–404.

Berry, Jeffrey M. 1984. *Feeding Hungry People: Rulemaking in the Food Stamp Program*. New Brunswick, NJ: Rutgers University Press.

Besharov, Douglas J. 2015. "Testimony before the Committee on Agriculture, Public Hearing: Review of the SNAP Program." U.S. House of Representatives, 114th Cong., 1st sess., February 25.

Blank, Rebecca M. 1997. *It Takes a Nation: A New Agenda for Fighting Poverty*. Princeton, NJ: Princeton University Press.

Briggs, Suzanne, Andy Fisher, Megan Lott, Stacy Miller, and Nell Tessman. 2010. *Real Food, Real Choice: Connecting SNAP Recipients with Farmers Markets*. Portland, OR: Community Food Security Coalition and the Farmers Market Coalition.

Carlson, Andrea, Mark Lino, Wen Yen Juan, Kenneth Hanson, and P. Peter Basiotis. 2007. *Thrifty Food Plan, 2006*. Center for Nutrition Policy and Promotion Report CNPP-19, Washington, DC: U.S. Department of Agriculture.

Center on Budget and Policy Priorities. 2015. "Policy Basics: Introduction to the Supplemental Nutrition Assistance Program (SNAP)." Policy Basics Brief, updated January 8, Center on Budget and Policy Priorities, Washington, DC.

Citizens' Board of Inquiry into Hunger and Malnutrition in the United States. 1968. *Hunger, U.S.A.* Washington, DC: New Community Press.

Coleman-Jensen, Alisha, Matthew P. Rabbitt, Christian Gregory, and Anita Singh. 2015. "Household Food Security in the United States in 2014." Economic Research Report ERR-194, Economic Research Service, U.S. Department of Agriculture, Washington, DC.

Collins, Ann M., Ronette Briefel, Jacob A. Klerman, Gretchen Rowe, Anne Wolf, and Christopher W. Logan. 2013. *Summer Electronic Benefits Transfer for Children (SEBTC) Demonstration: Evaluation Findings for the Full Implementation Year*. Washington, DC: U.S. Department of Agriculture.

Condon, Elizabeth, Susan Drilea, Keri Jowers, Carolyn Lichtenstein, James Mabli, Emily Madden, and Katherine Niland. 2015. *Diet Quality of Americans by SNAP Participation Status: Data from the National Health and Nutrition Examination Survey, 2007–2010*. Washington, DC: U.S. Department of Agriculture.

Congressional Budget Office. 1977. *The Food Stamp Program: Income or Food Supplementation?* Washington, DC: Congressional Budget Office.

———. 2013. *Growth in Means-Tested Programs and Tax Credits for Low-Income Households*. CBO Publication 4504. Washington, DC: Congressional Budget Office.

DeBono, Nathaniel L., Nancy A. Ross, and Lea Berrang-Ford. 2012. "Does the Food Stamp Program Cause Obesity? A Realist Review and a Call for Place-Based Research." *Health and Place* 18 (4): 747–56.

Dimitri, Carolyn, Lydia Oberholtzer, Michelle Zive, and Cristina Sandolo. 2015. "Enhancing Food Security of Low-Income Consumers: An Investigation of Financial Incentives for Use at Farmers Markets." *Food Policy* 52 (April): 64–70.

Eslami, Esa. 2015a. *State Trends in Supplemental Nutrition Assistance Program Eligibility and Participation among Elderly Individuals, Fiscal Year 2008 to Fiscal Year 2013*. Mathematica Policy Research report. Washington, DC: U.S. Department of Agriculture.

———. 2015b. *Trends in Supplemental Nutrition Assistance Program Participation Rates: Fiscal Year 2010 to Fiscal Year 2013*. Washington, DC: U.S. Department of Agriculture.

Eslami, Esa, Kai Filion, and Mark Strayer. 2011. *Characteristics of Supplemental Nutrition Assistance Program Households: Fiscal Year 2010*. Nutrition Assistance Program Report SNAP-11-CHAR. Washington, DC: U.S. Department of Agriculture.

Falk, Gene, and Randy A. Aussenberg. 2014. "The Supplemental Nutrition Assistance Program (SNAP): Categorical Eligibility." CBO Report R42054, Congressional Research Service, Washington, DC.

Federal Surplus Commodities Corporation, U.S. Department of Agriculture. 1939. "Regulations and Conditions Governing Issuance of Food Order Stamps." *Federal Register* 4: 1683.

Food and Nutrition Service, U.S. Department of Agriculture. 1971. "Food Stamp Program." *Federal Register* 36: 14107.

————. 2000. "Food Stamp Program: Noncitizen Eligibility, and Certification Provisions of Pub. L. 104-193, as Amended by Public Laws 104-208, 105-33, and 105-185." *Federal Register* 65: 70134–212.

————. 2013. "Supplemental Nutrition Assistance Program: Nutrition Education and Obesity Prevention Grant Program." *Federal Register* 78: 20411–22.

————. 2016. "SNAP Requirement for National Directory of New Hires Employment Verification and Annual Program Activity Reporting." *Federal Register* 81 (16): 4159–63.

Fox, Mary K., William Hamilton, and Biing-Hwan Lin, eds. 2004. *Effects of Food Assistance and Nutrition Programs on Nutrition and Health.* Vol. 3: *Literature Review*. Food Assistance and Nutrition Research Report 19-3. Washington, DC: Economic Research Service, U.S. Department of Agriculture.

Fraker, Thomas. 1990. *The Effects of Food Stamps on Food Consumption: A Review of the Literature.* Washington, DC: U.S. Department of Agriculture.

————. 1993. *The Effects of Food Stamps on Food Consumption: An Assessment of Findings from Four Evaluations.* Washington, DC: U.S. Department of Agriculture.

Furman, Jason, Cecilia Muñoz, and Sandra Black. 2015. "Long-Term Benefits of the Supplemental Nutrition Assistance Program." Executive Office of the President, Council of Economic Advisers, Washington, DC.

Gold, Norman L., A. C. Hoffman, and Frederick V. Waugh. 1940. "Economic Analysis of the Food Stamp Program, A Special Report." Bureau of Agricultural Economics and the Surplus Marketing Administration, U.S. Department of Agriculture, Washington, DC.

Gray, Kelsey F., and Shivani Kochhar. 2015. *Characteristics of Supplemental Nutrition Assistance Program Households: Fiscal Year 2014.* Nutrition Assistance Program Report SNAP-15-CHAR. Washington, DC: U.S. Department of Agriculture.

Gregory, Christian, Michele Ver Ploeg, Margaret Andrews, and Alisha Coleman-Jensen. 2013. "Supplemental Nutrition Assistance Program (SNAP) Participation Leads to Modest Changes in Diet Quality." Economic Research Report ERR-147, Economic Research Service, U.S. Department of Agriculture, Washington, DC.

Gundersen, Craig. 2016. "SNAP and Obesity." In *SNAP Matters: How Food Stamps Affect Health and Well-Being,* edited by Judith Bartfeld, Craig Gundersen, Timothy Smeeding, and James Ziliak. Stanford, CA: Stanford University Press.

Guthrie, Joanne F., Elizabeth Frazão, Margaret Andrews, and David Smallwood. 2007. "Improving Food Choices—Can Food Stamps Do More?" *Amber Waves* 5 (2): n.p. http://www.ers.usda.gov/amber-waves/2007-april/improving-food-choices%E2%80%94can-food-stamps-do-more.aspx#.V5KD5BiSCKx.

Guthrie, Joanne F., and Jayachandran N. Variyam. 2007. "Can Food Stamps Do More to Improve Food Choices? An Economic Perspective—Nutrition Information: Can It Improve the Diets of Low-Income Households?" Economic Information Bulletin 29-6, Economic Research Service, U.S. Department of Agriculture, Washington, DC. http://www.ers.usda.gov/media/1155896/eib29-6pdf0¢r_h___.pdf.

Haider, Steven J., Alison Jacknowitz, and Robert F. Schoeni. 2003. "Food Stamps and the Elderly: Why Is Participation So Low?" *Journal of Human Resources* 38 (Suppl): 1080–111.

Hanson, Kenneth. 2010. *The Food Assistance National Input-Output Multiplier (FANIOM) Model and Stimulus Effects of SNAP.* Economic Research Report ERR-103, Economic Research Service, U.S. Department of Agriculture, Washington, DC.

Hanson, Kenneth, and Elise Golan. 2002. "Effects of Changes in Food Stamp Expenditures across the U.S. Economy." Food Assistance and Nutrition Research Report FANRR 26-6, Economic Research Service, U.S. Department of Agriculture, Washington, DC.

Hanson, Kenneth, and Craig Gundersen. 2002. "Issues in Food Assistance—How Unemployment Affects the Food Stamp Program." Food Assistance and Nutrition

Research Report FANRR 26-7, Economic Research Service, U.S. Department of Agriculture, Washington, DC.

Hanson, Kenneth, and Victor Oliveira. 2007. "The 2005 Gulf Coast Hurricanes' Effect on Food Stamp Program Caseloads and Benefits Issued." Economic Research Report ERR-37, Economic Research Service, U.S. Department of Agriculture, Washington, DC.

———. 2012. "How Economic Conditions Affect Participation in USDA Nutrition Assistance Programs." Economic Information Bulletin 100, Economic Research Service, U.S. Department of Agriculture, Washington, DC.

Hartocollis, Anemona. 2010. "New York Asks to Bar Use of Food Stamps to Buy Sodas." *New York Times*, October 6.

Hoynes, Hilary, Diane W. Schanzenbach, and Douglas Almond. 2016. "Long-Run Impacts of Childhood Access to the Safety Net." *American Economic Review* 106 (4): 903–34.

Institute of Medicine and National Research Council. 2013. *Supplemental Nutrition Assistance Program: Examining the Evidence to Define Benefit Adequacy*, edited by Julie A. Caswell and Ann L. Yaktine. Washington, DC: National Academies Press.

Isaacs, Julia. 2008. "The Costs of Benefit Delivery in the Food Stamp Program: Lessons from a Cross-Program Analysis." Contractor and Cooperator Report CCR-39, Economic Research Service, U.S. Department of Agriculture, Washington, DC.

Johnson, Lyndon B. 1964. "Remarks upon Signing the Food Stamp Act." August 31. The American Presidency Project. http://www.presidency.ucsb.edu/ws/?pid=26472.

Kennedy, John F. 1961. "Providing for an Expanded Program of Food Distribution to Needy Families." Executive Order 10914, January 21. The American Presidency Project. http://www.presidency.ucsb.edu/ws/?pid=58853.

King, Melissa, Sujata Dixit-Joshi, Keith MacAllum, Michael Steketee, and Stephen Leard. 2014. *Farmers Market Incentive Provider Study*. Washington, DC: U.S. Department of Agriculture.

Leftin, Joshua, Nancy Wemmerus, James Mabli, Thomas Godfrey, and Stephen Tordella. 2014. *Dynamics of Supplemental Nutrition Assistance Program Participation from 2008 to 2012*. Washington, DC: U.S. Department of Agriculture.

Leibtag, Ephraim. 2007. "Can Food Stamps Do More to Improve Food Choices? An Economic Perspective—Stretching the Food Stamp Dollar: Regional Price Differences Affect Affordability of Food." Economic Information Bulletin 29-2, Economic Research Service, U.S. Department of Agriculture, Washington, DC.

Lin, Biing-Hwan, and Joanne Guthrie. 2007. "Can Food Stamps Do More to Improve Food Choices? An Economic Perspective—How Do Low-Income Households Respond to Food Prices?" Economic Information Bulletin 29-5, Economic Research Service, U.S. Department of Agriculture, Washington, DC.

Mabli, James, Jim Ohls, Lisa Dragoset, Laura Castner, and Betsy Santos. 2013. "Measuring the Effect of Supplemental Nutrition Assistance Program (SNAP) Participation on Food Security." Mathematica Policy Research report. Washington, DC: U.S. Department of Agriculture.

MacDonald, Maurice. 1977. *Food, Stamps, and Income Maintenance*. New York: Academic Press.

Maine Legislature. 2015. "Resolve, to Require the Department of Health and Human Services to Request a Waiver to Prohibit the Use of Food Supplement Benefits for the Purchase of Taxable Food Items." 127th Maine Legislature, 1st regular sess. in 2015, Legislative Document 526, February 26. http://www.arkleg.state.ar.us/assembly/2015/Meeting%20Attachments/770/I14435/Exhibit-D2_Maine-Legislation.pdf.

Maney, Ardith. L. 1989. *Still Hungry after All These Years: Food Assistance Policy from Kennedy to Reagan*. Westport, CT: Greenwood Press.

Mantovani, Richard, Eric Sean Williams, and Jacqueline Pflieger. 2013. "The Extent of Trafficking in the Supplemental Nutrition Assistance Program: 2009–2011." ICF International report for the U.S. Department of Agriculture, Washington, DC.

Mantovani, Richard, and Hoke Wilson. 2011. "The Extent of Trafficking in the Supplemental Nutrition Assistance Program: 2006–2008." ICF Macro report for the U.S. Department of Agriculture, Washington, DC.

McConnell, Sheena. 1991. *The Increase in Food Stamp Program Participation between 1989 and 1990: A Report to Congress.* Washington, DC: U.S. Department of Agriculture.

National Center for Health Statistics. 2015. *Health, United States, 2014: With Special Feature on Adults Aged 55–64.* Department of Health and Human Services Publication 2015-1232. Hyattsville, MD: National Center for Health Statistics.

National Research Council. 2006. *Food Insecurity and Hunger in the United States: An Assessment of the Measure,* edited by Gooloo S. Wunderlich and Janet L. Norwood. Washington, DC: National Academies Press.

Nixon, Richard. 1969. "Special Message to the Congress Recommending a Program to End Hunger in America." May 6. The American Presidency Project. http://www.presidency.ucsb.edu/ws/?pid=2038.

Nord, Mark. 2013. "Effects of the Decline in the Real Value of SNAP Benefits from 2009 to 2011." Economic Research Report ERR-151, Economic Research Service, U.S. Department of Agriculture, Washington, DC.

Nord, Mark, and Mark Prell. 2011. "Food Security Improved Following the 2009 ARRA Increase in SNAP Benefits." Economic Research Report ERR-116, Economic Research Service, U.S. Department of Agriculture, Washington, DC.

Ohls, James C., and Harold Beebout. 1993. *The Food Stamp Program: Design Tradeoffs, Policy, and Impacts.* Washington, DC: Urban Institute Press.

Oliveira, Victor. 2016. *The Food Assistance Landscape: FY 2015 Annual Report.* Economic Information Bulletin EIB-150, Economic Research Service, U.S. Department of Agriculture, Washington, DC. http://www.ers.usda.gov/media/2031346/eib150.pdf.

Oliveira, Victor, and Elizabeth Frazão. 2015. "The WIC Program: Background, Trends, and Economic Issues, 2015 Edition." Economic Research Service, U.S. Department of Agriculture, Washington, DC. http://www.ers.usda.gov/publications/eib-economic-information-bulletin/eib134.aspx.

Peterson, Anne, Bryan Johnson, Benjamin E. Moulton, Emily O. Smith, Alexandra Suchman, Claire Wilson, Shiara Francisquini Oquendo, Jacqueline Kauff, Jonathan Ladinsky, and Laura Castner. 2010. *Implementing SNAP in Puerto Rico: A Feasibility Study.* Washington, DC: U.S. Department of Agriculture.

Poppendieck, Janet. 1986. *Breadlines Knee-Deep in Wheat: Food Assistance in the Great Depression.* New Brunswick, NJ: Rutgers University Press.

Prell, Mark, Constance Newman, and Erik Scherpf. 2015. "Annual and Monthly SNAP Participation Rates." Economic Research Report ERR-192, Economic Research Service, U.S. Department of Agriculture, Washington, DC.

President's Task Force on Food Assistance. 1984. *Report of the President's Task Force on Food Assistance.* Washington, DC: President's Task Force on Food Assistance.

Rank, Mark R., and Thomas A. Hirschl. 2009. "Estimating the Risk of Food Stamp Use and Impoverishment during Childhood." *Archives of Pediatrics and Adolescent Medicine* 163 (11): 994–99.

Reese, Robert B., J. Gerald Feaster, and Garey B. Perkins. 1974. "Bonus Food Stamps and Cash Income Supplements: Their Effectiveness in Expanding Demand for Food." Marketing Research Report 1034, Economic Research Service, U.S. Department of Agriculture, Washington, DC.

Richardson, Joe. 1979. "A Concise History of the Food Stamp Program." CRS Report 79-244, Congressional Research Service, Washington, DC.

Rosenbaum, Dorothy. 2008. "Food Stamp Benefits Falling Further behind Rising Food Prices." Center on Budget and Policy Priorities, Washington, DC.

Salathe, Larry E. 1980. "The Food Stamp Program and Low-Income Households' Food Purchases." *Agricultural Economics Research* 32 (4): 33–41.

Shapiro, Jesse. 2005. "Is There a Daily Discount Rate? Evidence from the Food Stamp Nutrition Cycle." *Journal of Public Economics* 89 (2–3): 303–25.

Shields, Dennis A. 2014. "Farm and Food Support under USDA's Section 32 Program." CRS Report RL34081, Congressional Research Service, Washington, DC. https://www.fas .org/sgp/crs/misc/RL34081.pdf.

Short, Kathleen. 2015. "The Supplemental Poverty Measure: 2014." Current Population Reports P60-254, U.S. Census Bureau, Washington, DC.

Smallwood, David, Mark Prell, and Margaret Andrews. 2002. "Income Volatility and the Implications for Food Assistance Programs." *Focus* 22 (2): 56–60.

Super, David, and Stacy Dean. 2001. "New State Options to Improve the Food Stamp Vehicle Rule." Center on Budget and Policy Priorities, Washington, DC.

Tiehen, Laura, Dean Jolliffe, and Craig Gundersen. 2012. "Alleviating Poverty in the United States: The Critical Role of SNAP Benefits." Economic Research Report ERR-132, Economic Research Service, U.S. Department of Agriculture, Washington, DC.

Tiehen, Laura, Dean Jolliffe, and Timothy M. Smeeding. 2016. "The Effect of SNAP on Poverty." In *SNAP Matters: How Food Stamps Affect Health and Well-Being*, edited by Judith Bartfeld, Craig Gundersen, Timothy M. Smeeding, and James P. Ziliak. Stanford, CA: Stanford University Press.

Trippe, Carole, Rachel Gaddes, Alexandra Suchman, Kate Place, James Mabli, Chrystine Tadler, Teresa DeAtley, and Brian Estes. 2015. *Examination of Cash Nutrition Assistance Program Benefits in Puerto Rico*. Washington, DC: U.S. Department of Agriculture.

Trippe, Carole, and Jessica Gillooly. 2010. "Non-Cash Categorical Eligibility for SNAP: State Policies and the Number and Characteristics of SNAP Households Categorically Eligible through Those Policies." Final memo developed by Mathematica Policy Research for the U.S. Department of Agriculture, Washington, DC.

Urban Institute. 1985. *The Effects of Legislative Changes in 1981 and 1982 on the Food Stamp Program*. Vol. 1. Washington, DC: Urban Institute.

U.S. Department of Agriculture. 1983. "Evaluation of the Puerto Rico Nutrition Assistance Program." Food and Nutrition Service, U.S. Department of Agriculture, Washington, DC.

———. 2002. "Elderly Participation and the Minimum Benefit." Food and Nutrition Service, U.S. Department of Agriculture, Washington, DC. http://www.fns.usda.gov/sites /default/files/ElderlyPartRates.pdf.

———. 2004. "Veneman Announces Full Implementation of Food Stamp Program Electronic Benefits Transfer System—Reports National Error Rate Is at Historic Low." News Release 0251.04, U.S. Department of Agriculture, Washington, DC, June 22.

———. 2007. "Implications of Restricting the Use of Food Stamp Benefits." Food and Nutrition Service, U.S. Department of Agriculture, Washington, DC. http://www.fns .usda.gov/sites/default/files/arra/FSPFoodRestrictions.pdf.

———. 2010a. "Supplemental Nutrition Assistance Program (SNAP) American Recovery and Reinvestment Act Plan Update." Food and Nutrition Service, U.S. Department of Agriculture, Washington, DC, June 23. http://www.fns.usda.gov/sites/default/files /SNAP_ARRA-Plan.pdf.

———. 2010b. *Supplemental Nutrition Assistance Program: Feasibility of Implementing Electronic Benefit Transfer Systems in Farmers' Markets*. Report to Congress, Food and Nutrition Service, U.S. Department of Agriculture, Washington, DC.

———. 2010c. *Supplemental Nutrition Assistance Program, State Options Report, Ninth Edition*. Food and Nutrition Service, U.S. Department of Agriculture, Washington, DC. http://www.fns.usda.gov/sites/default/files/9-State_Options.pdf.

————. 2012a. "Building a Healthy America: A Profile of the Supplemental Nutrition Assistance Program." Food and Nutrition Service, U.S. Department of Agriculture, Washington, DC. http://www.fns.usda.gov/sites/default/files/BuildingHealthyAmerica .pdf.

————. 2012b. *National Survey of WIC Participants II*. Vol. 1: *Participant Characteristics Report*. Report CN-10-NSWP2-R2. Washington, DC: U.S. Department of Agriculture, Food and Nutrition Service, Office of Research and Analysis.

————. 2013a. "Disaster Supplemental Nutrition Assistance Program (D-SNAP)." Food and Nutrition Service, Office of Emergency Management, U.S. Department of Agriculture, Washington, DC. http://www.fns.usda.gov/sites/default/files/D-SNAP_Disaster.pdf.

————. 2013b. "Supplemental Nutrition Assistance Program Employment and Training Toolkit." Food and Nutrition Service, U.S. Department of Agriculture, Washington, DC.

————. 2014a. *From Food Stamps to the Supplemental Nutrition Assistance Program: Legislative Timeline*. Food and Nutrition Service, U.S. Department of Agriculture, Washington, DC. http://www.fns.usda.gov/sites/default/files/timeline.pdf.

————. 2014b. "A Short History of SNAP." Food and Nutrition Service, U.S. Department of Agriculture, Washington, DC. http://www.fns.usda.gov/sites/default/files/History_of _SNAP.pdf.

————. 2014c. "SNAP Fiscal Year 2015 Cost-of-Living Adjustments." Food and Nutrition Service, U.S. Department of Agriculture, Washington, DC.

————. 2015a. "Program Information Report (Keydata): U.S. Summary, FY 2014–FY 2015, September 2015." Food and Nutrition Service, U.S. Department of Agriculture, Washington, DC. http://www.fns.usda.gov/sites/default/files/datastatistics/keydata -september-2015.pdf.

————. 2015b. "Simplified Reporting—Conversations with States." Memo, Food and Nutrition Service, U.S. Department of Agriculture, Washington, DC. http://www.fns .usda.gov/sites/default/files/a-sr-report.pdf.

————. 2015c. *SNAP Retailer Management 2014 Annual Report*. Washington, DC: U.S. Department of Agriculture, Food and Nutrition Service.

————. 2015d. "Supplemental Nutrition Assistance Program: ARRA." Economic Research Service, U.S. Department of Agriculture, Washington, DC. http://www.ers.usda.gov /topics/food-nutrition-assistance/supplemental-nutrition-assistance-program -%28snap%29/arra.aspx.

————. 2015e. "Supplemental Nutrition Assistance Program: Payment Error Rates FY 2014." Food and Nutrition Service, U.S. Department of Agriculture, Washington, DC.

————. 2015f. "USDA Announces Grants to Enable More Farmers Markets to Serve Low-Income Families." News Release 0123.15, U.S. Department of Agriculture, Washington, DC, May 5.

————. 2015g. "2015 USDA Budget Explanatory Notes for Committee on Appropriations, Food and Nutrition Services." Office of Budget and Program Analysis, U.S. Department of Agriculture, Washington, DC. http://www.obpa.usda.gov/32fns2015notes.pdf.

U.S. General Accounting Office. 2002. "Food Stamp Program: States' Use of Options and Waivers to Improve Program Administration and Promote Access." Report to the ranking minority member, Committee on Agriculture, Nutrition, and Forestry, U.S. Senate, GAO -02-409, U.S. General Accounting Office, Washington, DC. http://www.gao.gov/assets /240/233683.pdf.

————. 2012. "Supplemental Nutrition Assistance Program: Improved Oversight of State Eligibility Expansions Needed." Report to congressional requesters, GAO-12-670, U.S. Government Accountability Office, Washington, DC. http://www.gao.gov/assets/600 /593070.pdf.

Usher, Charles L., David S. Shanklin, and Judith B. Wildfire. 1990. *Evaluation of the Food Distribution Program on Indian Reservations (FDPIR)*. Vol. 1: *Final Report*. Report by the

Research Triangle Institute for the Food and Nutrition Service. Washington, DC: U.S. Department of Agriculture. https://naldc.nal.usda.gov/naldc/download.xhtml?id=CAT 93996877&content=PDF.

U.S. House of Representatives. 1970. "House Report No. 91-1402 (Food Stamp Act—Amendments, Legislative History)." Agriculture Committee, Washington, DC, August 10.

———. 1996. "Summary of Welfare Reforms Made by Public Law 104-193, The Personal Responsibility and Work Opportunity Reconciliation Act and Associated Legislation." 104th Cong., 2nd sess., WMCP 104-15, Committee on Ways and Means, Government Printing Office, Washington, DC.

U.S. Senate. 1964. "Senate Report No. 1124 (Food Stamp Act of 1964, Legislative History)." Committee on Agriculture, Nutrition, and Forestry, Washington, DC, June 29.

———. 1985. *The Food Stamp Program: History, Description, Issues, and Options.* Prepared by the staff of the Committee on Agriculture, Nutrition, and Forestry. Washington, DC: Government Printing Office.

Ver Ploeg, Michele, and Katherine Ralston. 2008. "Food Stamps and Obesity: What Do We Know?" Economic Information Bulletin EIB-34, Economic Research Service, U.S. Department of Agriculture, Washington, DC.

Wilde, Parke. 2007. "Food Stamps Twice Monthly?" *U.S. Food Policy* (blog), November 3. http://usfoodpolicy.blogspot.com.

———. 2013a. "Food Stamp Cycle in the Washington Post." *U.S. Food Policy* (blog), March 18. http://usfoodpolicy.blogspot.com.

———. 2013b. "The New Normal: The Supplemental Nutrition Assistance Program (SNAP)." *American Journal of Agricultural Economics* 95 (2): 325–31.

Wilde, Parke E., and Christine K. Ranney. 2000. "The Monthly Food Stamp Cycle: Shopping Frequency and Food Intake Decisions in an Endogenous Switching Regression Framework." *American Journal of Agricultural Economics* 82 (1): 200–13.

Zandi, Mark M. 2008. "Assessing the Macro Economic Impact of Fiscal Stimulus 2008." Moody's Economy.com. https://www.economy.com/mark-zandi/documents/Stimulus-Impact-2008.pdf.

Ziliak, James P. 2016. "Modernizing SNAP Benefits." The Hamilton Project, Policy Proposal 2016-06, Brookings Institution, Washington, DC.

CHAPTER 7

Evolution and Implementation of the Rastra Program in Indonesia

Peter Timmer, Hastuti, and Sudarno Sumarto

INTRODUCTION

Among the countries reviewed in this volume, only Indonesia has not engaged in major reforms of its food subsidy program, at least until recently. Its flagship food subsidy program *Rastra*, formerly *Raskin* (Rice for the Poor),[1] has made some improvements in delivery, but its overall performance continues to be limited. As such, some rethinking of the business model as well as the form of transfers provided is overdue.

Meanwhile, Indonesia has achieved significant progress in building and scaling up its cash transfer programs. Reflecting the progress achieved, the government recently took important steps toward reforming and modernizing Rastra. As this chapter shows, these steps are in line with global trends in the evolution of food-based social assistance. However, the international experience also suggests that such transitions will take time, will need to be sustained politically, will need to go beyond Rastra itself, and will require revisiting both the role of actors in different sectors and the objectives.

This chapter explores the history, design, implementation, and impact of Indonesia's experience with food-based social safety nets. That experience started well before the implementation of Rastra—a program introduced after the Asian financial crisis in 1997–98 that distributes rice directly to poor households at heavily subsidized prices. The chapter examines that history (a) for insights into the rationale behind the broad concern in Indonesia for providing basic food security to its citizens and the specific role of rice in it and (b) for clues that reveal the underlying political economy of the programs' design and implementation.

As illustrated in chapter 1 of this volume, until recently the nature and design of Rastra had changed relatively little over time, but the program was, and largely still is, woven into a broader set of agricultural and price management objectives. Indonesia's approach to food security is remarkably well studied and documented, from Dutch colonial days to the present. However, the rich historical record, full of repeated food crises linked to institutional learning, provides only limited insights into the future of food-based safety nets in the country. Indonesia is attempting a radical reform of Rastra, including cashing out its benefits everywhere that food (rice) markets are working reasonably effectively and leaving only isolated areas, mostly in Eastern Indonesia, where the direct delivery of rice remains a cost-effective means of providing food security to poor households.

Even in those circumstances, Rastra needs to be seen as part of a much broader array of social safety nets. It has been understood for several decades that effective food policy—one that is successful in reducing poverty and hunger to low levels within a generation—needs to employ all the levers of economic development, not just those available to ministries of health or agriculture.

The chapter reviews the history of Indonesia's approach to food security for its citizens. It focuses particularly on three basic ways to achieve that goal: (a) stabilizing rice prices, especially in urban markets; (b) generating a widespread process of pro-poor growth that pulls the rural poor into a rapidly expanding economy; and (c) providing direct food subsidies to poor households, which it has pursued since 1998 through Rastra. The first half of the chapter lays out the historical and political economy perspective; the second half reviews the design, implementation, and impact of Rastra as of early 2017 and discusses briefly the most recent pilots to reform it. A final section discusses the lessons learned.

THE HISTORICAL ORIGINS OF RASTRA

Guaranteeing that food is available on a reliable and regular basis to all citizens is part of the "mandate of heaven" under which all Asian rulers are empowered, whether democratic or authoritarian.[2] Indonesia is no exception. Its rulers have tried to maintain ready access to affordable rice since at least the 17th century. For most of the nation's history, the main social safety net in Indonesia has been a public guarantee that rice would be available in urban markets at affordable (and stable) prices. If some citizens were too poor to buy this market-priced rice, they suffered, or they were helped by local community organizations. When the state failed in this obligation, it often lost power.

That pattern is centuries old throughout Asia, but it would have resulted in food security for only a minority of urban households unless further steps were taken. Several possible approaches could extend the paradigm of food security in Asia. One approach is to achieve widespread, inclusive economic growth that brings the great mass of the population above a meaningful poverty line, so that stable rice prices in key urban markets really do guarantee food security for an increasing share of the population (as many rural workers move to urban jobs). Two reinforcing factors would eliminate rural poverty: people would migrate to urban opportunities, and the state would stimulate farm incomes for the remaining rural population by maintaining higher commodity prices. That approach is widespread in all high-income countries and is a popular political strategy that has uniformly been rewarded by electoral success for parties that follow it. To work, however, the approach needs (a) a reasonably wealthy urban middle class that willingly pays higher food prices and (b) a progressively smaller and more productive agricultural workforce.

A second approach is to protect agriculture much earlier in the historical process of structural transformation, when farmers (especially, in Asia, rice farmers) become a very potent voting bloc in newly formed democratic societies. Many poor households remain—in both rural and urban areas—but they are not numerous enough to outvote a coalition of urban middle-class households, which want to guarantee supplies of rice in their local markets, and of farmers, who want higher rice prices to compensate for the loss of economic competitiveness in the production of labor-intensive crops (especially rice). This is the Indonesian story, but it also resonates in Malaysia, Thailand, and even China.

How can politicians reconcile rice prices that are high enough to ensure food security through increased rice production with the existence of a substantial proportion of households that are unable to afford that rice? The answer is obvious, both politically and logistically. Distributing rice directly to poor households (despite how ineffective the actual delivery system might be) is a political winner. And for the food logistics agency, previously charged with stabilizing rice prices around long-run trends in world prices, the reality of high domestic rice prices sharply reduces the need for those services. A new mandate—to procure rice at high prices from farmers and deliver it at subsidized prices to poor households—gives that agency a new lease on life.

This approach, established for the last decades as the political norm in Indonesia, was an innovation when viewed through the lens of Indonesia's long history of repeated food crises and government responses. A slightly arbitrary list of 10 food crises over several centuries is presented here. These crises have come from both too little and too much rice, and stability has been the dominant policy goal, sometimes sacrificing the short-run welfare of farmers in favor of the welfare of consumers and sometimes the opposite. In all the crises, however, institutional learning occurred, as coping mechanisms developed to keep governments in power. The following 10 crises shaped Indonesia's approach to food security.

First, the Indonesian sultanates rule with a "mandate from heaven," known as "rice for the people." Sultan Amangkurat I prohibited the exportation of rice from Java in 1655 in response to a drought that sent rice prices up by 300 percent.

Second, the Dutch took over the rice economy of the Netherlands East Indies in March 1933, in response to collapsing rice prices in the region. Rice milling, inter-island and international trade in rice, and price formation were all tightly controlled by government agencies, most of them newly formed for the task (Boeke 1946). The Dutch effort at government control of the rice economy resonates to this day.

Third, the collapse of the Sukarno government in 1966, after a decade of spiraling inflation, increased poverty, and repeated shortages of rice in urban markets, gave the new Suharto government a mandate for stability—a mandate it eagerly sought in the wake of widespread violence and turmoil during the transition. *Badan Urusan Logistik* (BULOG, the State Logistics Board) is a food logistics agency established to control rice prices, with an agency head who reported directly to the president and with a line of credit at subsidized interest rates from the central bank.

Fourth, the world food crisis in 1972–73 caught the Indonesian government—and BULOG—unprepared. After several years of price stability, rice prices spiraled out of control, and the government quickly tried to arrange emergency imports from a world rice market that disappeared for nearly a year. The response, once control was regained late in 1973, was to formulate plans for paying greater attention to agricultural development, increasing productivity of the rice sector, and keeping rice prices stable (Timmer 1975).

The fifth food crisis followed the collapse of commodity prices in world markets in the mid-1980s, including for rice, and again caught BULOG unprepared. As the Dutch learned during the Great Depression in the 1930s, surpluses are just as hard to manage as shortages. A major reevaluation of how to define and maintain food security in Indonesia was commissioned.[3] A new focus on poverty came to the fore with the realization that surplus rice could be distributed as part of a social safety net. By 1991, BULOG had implemented a trial of *Operasi Pasar Khusus* (OPK, Special Market Operations) to deliver rice directly to drought-stricken villages as a poverty-relief effort (Timmer and others 1992).

In the sixth crisis, BULOG's focus on disposing of rice surpluses caused it to lose track of its actual stock in mid-1994. A drought caused rice production to fall, but BULOG did not respond when stocks were depleted early in 1995, before the new rice harvest started in March. A rice crisis was in the making. President Suharto replaced the head of BULOG, and the new head ordered emergency imports that arrived just in time to keep rice prices from getting out of control. Knowing what to do makes all the difference, but business as usual was a failure. Still, by August 1996, it was possible for the *Jakarta Post* to report a story (based on an interview with Timmer) that headlined "BULOG to limit itself to poverty alleviation," a recognition of the changing dynamics in the rice economy.

Seventh, the Asian financial crisis in 1997–98 caused Indonesia to lose control of its macroeconomy. Again, an important lesson was learned: it is impossible to stabilize rice prices when the macroeconomy and exchange rate are out of control. A new OPK emerged out of the macroeconomic and political chaos. This program almost immediately became the largest element in the country's shift to targeted social safety nets (Tabor and Sawit 2001).

Eighth, with the emergence of democracy in 1998, the political economy of food security took an entirely new direction. The dominant approach was to impose high rice prices as a political policy choice in 2004–06, which had a significant impact on the poor. Rastra, which was the OPK program relabeled, became the political answer to the problems of food insecurity caused by high rice prices. Although rice self-sufficiency had long been a key objective of Indonesia's drive for food security, stable rice prices had always trumped the desire to restrict imports (Timmer 2003). That political calculus changed in the first half of the 2000s.

Ninth, Indonesia was quite successful in getting through the 2007–08 world food crisis, partly because its domestic prices were already high. When the minister of trade announced a ban on rice exports early in 2008, the world rice market took little notice because Indonesia had never been a significant rice exporter. But domestic consumers and traders were reassured that ample supplies were available, so there was no panicked hoarding of the sort seen in the Philippines and even in urban markets in Vietnam. Stable domestic prices, even if very high, were a political winner for Susilo Bambang Yudhoyono's second presidential campaign in 2009.

Tenth, BULOG faced rice shortages in 2015–16, the worst El Niño year on record. Some officials in the new Jokowi government tried to order imports in a timely fashion, even recalling publicly the fall of the Suharto government over spiraling rice prices during the previously worst El Niño on record in 1997–98, when imports also were delayed. Many contracts were delayed or canceled (although nearly 1 million tons of imported rice did arrive before the end of February 2016). Rice prices spiraled, BULOG had to cut back deliveries to Rastra recipients, and once again the country learned that rice self-sufficiency is not food security. Nascent efforts to reform Rastra, even to convert it to cash or vouchers in urban settings and rural areas with good market infrastructure, were generally delayed, although they are now being tested in several cities.

Crises focus the mind and political action. Perhaps more important, they shape the expectations—among the citizenry and policy makers alike—about appropriate public actions and private responses in a highly volatile food system. Interpreting the long-run impact of these repeated food crises over nearly four centuries of Indonesian history is a matter of judgment, of course, but at least three phases are visible in the evolution of policy approaches to food security.

First, stabilizing rice prices in urban markets has long been the political touchstone of legitimacy: a reasonably stable food economy seems to be an essential ingredient of sustainable economic growth. Second, a strategy of pro-poor growth, building on the potential to improve rural labor productivity through broad-based agricultural development, brought the rural poor into the political calculus of food security (and their participation made food more available and accessible). And third, perhaps prematurely, the country moved explicitly to a targeted, food-based social safety net—implemented through Rastra—as the offset to a political strategy of wooing the political loyalty of rice farmers by keeping rice prices high. These issues are hereafter discussed.

Rice Price Stabilization in Indonesia

Why did Indonesia attempt to stabilize rice prices for extended periods of time? No one in Indonesia—policy makers, academics, journalists, or the "man in the street"—has ever doubted that stable rice prices are essential to political stability and economic growth. During the chaotic and often violent transfer of power from Sukarno to Suharto in the mid-1960s, rice was, as the influential student newspaper *Harian KAMI* put it on September 14, 1967, "the barometer of the economy."

The Motivation for Rice Price Stabilization in Indonesia: A Brief Overview
Food security as a political concept requires an operational definition.[4] In most Asian countries the definition has taken the form of stable domestic prices relative to world prices, thus requiring state control over trade flows in rice. To minimize the need to resort to trade at all and to avoid the uncertainties in the international price of rice, self-sufficiency has also become a popular objective. It has become more important as countries have become rich enough to implement policies that achieve greater degrees of self-sufficiency.

A further impetus toward greater domestic rice production has been the fear of food shortages in urban areas, which evoke a universal and visceral reaction. Governments are held accountable for provisioning cities at reasonable costs, and citizens have repeatedly demonstrated their capacity to bring down governments that fail in this obligation.[5] Acute food shortages—not the average level of food prices—are what induce antigovernment panic, however. Sharp price rises are simply the mirror image of food shortages.

Indonesia provides a particularly vivid case study of policy initiatives that are designed specifically to stabilize the domestic price of rice—using imports or domestic production to avoid food shortages—with a careful analytical debate paralleling the policy actions. The role of trade versus domestic production as the basis for food security has been analyzed and discussed in a surprisingly open and articulate manner since the beginning of the Suharto government in 1966.

The proximate definition of food security in Indonesia has always revolved around price stability, especially for the price of rice, the country's primary food staple. The analysis that underpinned this approach never focused only on the static and partial equilibrium consequences of changes in rice prices. Instead, an effort was made, even well before computable general equilibrium models became a standard tool of policy analysis, to consider the dynamic and economywide ramifications of price policy, the distributional consequences for farmers and consumers, and the role of other commodities in the rice stabilization program.

The Role of Self-Sufficiency in Rice in Ensuring Food Security
Self-sufficiency in rice and other foodstuffs such as sugar and soybeans has been a consistent (if often rhetorical) objective of Indonesian agricultural policy since the beginning of the New Order regime of President Suharto in 1967 (Timmer 1975). Historical and production cost data based on farm surveys suggest that self-sufficiency in rice has often been less costly (on average and over the long run) than large-scale rice imports from the world market, at least when the green revolution in rice production technology was spreading rapidly. Because of fluctuations due to weather (especially El Niño events), diseases, and pests, however, rice production in Indonesia is unstable, and productivity growth has slowed. In mosт years, Indonesia's rice production is below the normal level of rice consumption.

To stabilize the rice economy, BULOG was charged with operating a floor and ceiling price policy using domestic buffer stocks to smooth out year-to-year fluctuations in production and consumption. The goal was to keep rice consumption on a smooth trend despite unstable production. The primary policy instrument for stabilizing rice *consumption* is the stabilization of rice *prices*, which has been BULOG's most important task.[6]

Successful stabilization of rice prices between policy-determined floor and ceiling prices requires an active and ongoing analytical capacity—to determine annually the appropriate levels—that is linked directly to the political (and budgetary) decision-making process. Indonesia developed this capacity gradually through the early 1970s and 1980s. Much of that analytical effort is now in the public record.[7]

From the late 1960s until the early 1980s, BULOG routinely used imports and open-market sales of rice to balance supply and demand in its defense of a floor and ceiling price for rice. The world food crisis in 1972–73 stimulated serious efforts to increase rice production, and the long-sought goal of rice self-sufficiency was achieved in the mid-1980s. The balancing role of international trade was superseded by the problems of managing domestic buffer stocks as the sole mechanism for smoothing seasonal and annual differences between production and consumption (Timmer 1996).[8]

For the 10 years of the fourth and fifth five-year development plans (Repelita IV and V), fiscal years 1983/84 to 1993/94, Indonesia was almost exactly self-sufficient in rice, on average, and per capita availability (consumption) increased smoothly in all years but two. In none of the individual years, however, was domestic production exactly equal to consumption. In some years—for example, 1984, 1989, and 1992—production was higher than consumption, and BULOG stocks increased. In other years—for example, 1985 and 1993—production also exceeded consumption, but, with BULOG warehouses full, the surplus was exported. In 1986, 1987, 1990, and 1991, consumption was slightly higher than production, and BULOG stocks were drawn down. In 1988, 1992, and 1994, production was again less than the desired consumption level. With BULOG stocks low, external supplies were called on to provide stability to Indonesia's rice markets.

The overall picture is one of stable growth in per capita rice consumption, relative stability in Indonesia's rice market, and, perhaps most important from a political perspective, the achievement of self-sufficiency in rice (on average) for two consecutive five-year plan periods. Figure 7.1 shows clearly that BULOG was quite successful in stabilizing rice prices from late 1973, when it regained control of domestic prices after a good harvest, until the Asian financial crisis in late 1997. Table 7.1 presents the comparative evidence by time period using the coefficient of variation (CV), which is the standard deviation of monthly prices divided by the mean of prices. The reference for stability of domestic prices is what is happening to world prices.

As table 7.1 shows, domestic rice prices have been somewhat more stable than world prices, but the relative stability is especially striking for the Suharto era from January 1969 to right before the Asian financial crisis in July 1997. During that period, when BULOG was most successful in its logistical operations, the domestic CV is less than a third of the world CV. The comparison would be even more striking if it ran from late 1973, after BULOG regained control of the Indonesian rice economy (and learned its lesson), until mid-1997. Since 1998 (and the establishment of democracy), BULOG has not been very successful at stabilizing rice prices, but keeping rice prices high seems to be the political objective rather than achieving stable or efficient prices. Also worth pointing out is a sharp spike in 1998 in world rice prices as measured in real rupiah, a spike that does not appear when world rice prices are measured in U.S. dollars. The difference, of course, is that the Asian financial crisis caused the Indonesian rupiah to collapse. It is impossible to stabilize domestic rice prices in the middle of a meltdown of the economy and political system.

Source: Data and graphics provided by David Dawe, Food and Agriculture Organization of the United Nations, Bangkok.

FIGURE 7.1

Real Prices of Domestic and Imported Rice in Indonesia, 1969–2014

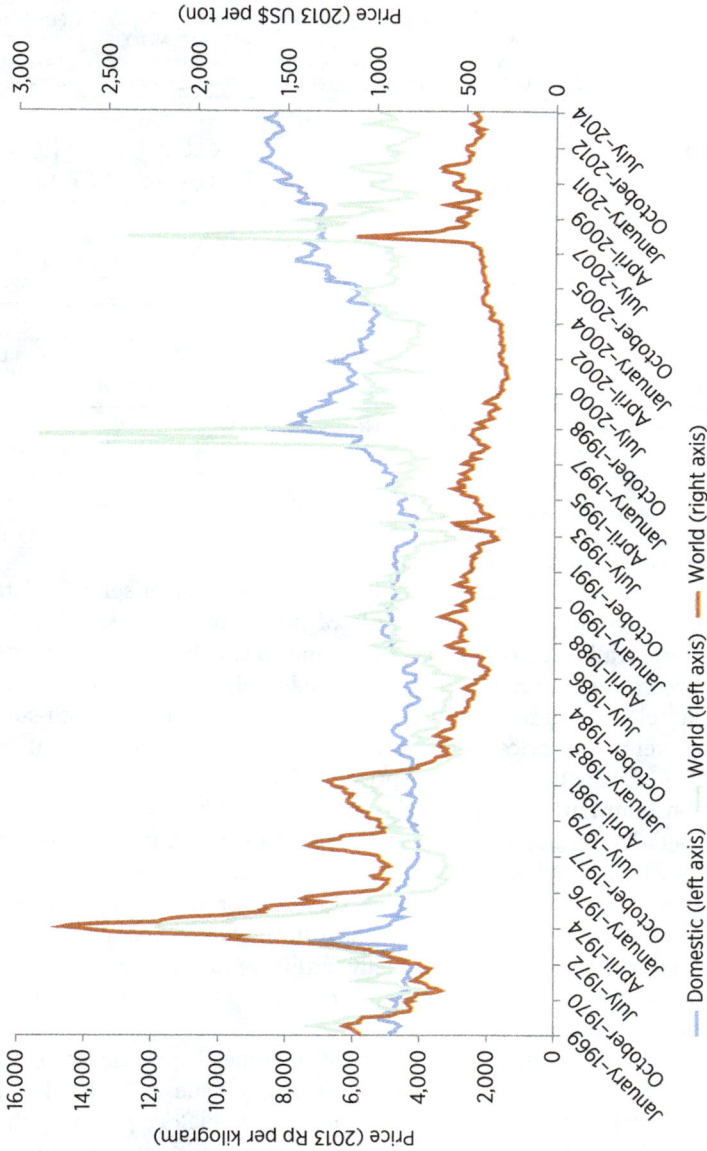

TABLE 7.1 **Real Prices of Rice in Indonesia, by Regime, 1969–2014**

Rp per kilogram

INDICATOR	WHOLE PERIOD, JANUARY 1969–JULY 2014	SUHARTO PRE-1998 ASIAN FINANCIAL CRISIS, JANUARY 1969–JULY 1997	POST-SUHARTO, JANUARY 1999–JULY 2014	POST-2007/98 FOOD PRICE CRISIS, NOVEMBER 2008–JULY 2014
Mean				
Domestic	5,132.91	4,303.20	6,562.17	7,490.28
World	4,760.10	4,452.22	4,988.76	4,928.22
Standard deviation				
Domestic	1,263.43	410.94	943.61	563.05
World	1,591.70	1,448.70	1,042.13	684.18
Coefficient of variation				
Domestic	0.25	0.10	0.14	0.08
World	0.33	0.33	0.21	0.14

Source: Data provided by Peter Warr, Australian National University.

Lessons from Indonesian Experience

Increasing rice production was only part of the story of self-sufficiency and rising consumption of rice. The role of prices and price stability was also important in allowing consumers to maintain a smooth trend in rice consumption, even though production varied considerably from year to year.

A key element of the government's involvement in reaching self-sufficiency is the level of rice prices maintained in the domestic economy. Other things being equal, a higher level of rice prices will increase rice production, decrease rice consumption, and make self-sufficiency easier to achieve. It has often been said that Indonesia can always be self-sufficient in rice at some price; the issue is whether consumers can maintain satisfactory levels of rice consumption as well. But domestic rice prices do not exist in a vacuum. In particular, their level relative to the trend of prices in the world market and relative to the costs of farmers' inputs (especially fertilizer prices) strongly influences the efficiency with which consumers and producers allocate the scarce economic resources of the society.

Stabilization itself is also an element in domestic production and its contribution to food security. The short-run policy issue is the level of BULOG stocks considered appropriate for maintaining stable rice prices. With infinite stocks, prices can be kept completely stable, but both economic theory and experience dictate that a finite level of stock cannot defend price stability under all circumstances.[9] Accordingly, an important trade-off exists. Larger buffer stocks permit a longer period of stable prices, but at costs that rise exponentially with the size of the buffer stock. Smaller stocks cause prices to fluctuate more, but with substantial cost savings. The only escape from this apparent dilemma is to add a degree of freedom to the system by permitting supplies to move into or out of the country, once stocks are drawn down or warehouses are filled up. As noted, a rigid definition of self-sufficiency removed the operational role for imports for several years. Still, this experience of trying to understand the value of additional stocks in the Indonesian context was valuable, because, after the world food crisis in 2007–08, it helped with understanding the value of additional stocks at a global level (which must be self-sufficient by definition).[10]

Three elements of government policy interact to create the economic environment for self-sufficiency in rice and its subsequent role in food security: (a) public investments in rice production to maintain it on the trend of rice consumption—mostly in rice research and extension, irrigation facilities, and rural roads; (b) the establishment of a domestic level of rice (and fertilizer) prices that reflects their long-run opportunity costs in world markets (a substantial, marketwide fertilizer subsidy in the mid-1980s was a major factor in boosting rice production to self-sufficiency, and the debate over fertilizer subsidies continues even today); and (c) the stabilization of domestic rice prices through market interventions using buffer stocks and imports, when politically feasible, as a balance wheel.

Each of those policy elements has powerful effects on efficiency individually, as well as direct effects on the state budget, and these effects make each component a separate, important policy issue. But the interconnections among the three elements make it impossible to set policy for one without having a substantial impact on the others. Consistency among all three elements is essential in the long run if substantial resources are not to be wasted. Achieving this consistency is clearly the most difficult aspect of designing a policy to ensure food security at the macroeconomic level.

The New Policy Debate: Price Stability at What Price?
Price stabilization has remained an important policy objective during surpluses and deficits, but the financial costs,[11] feasible level of prices, and general policy thrust with respect to the agriculture sector differ sharply—that is, (a) when the rice economy is in surplus and the main political problem is maintaining the floor price for rice farmers and (b) when the rice economy is in deficit and urban prices are rising. Because of the high costs of storing rice in the tropics, the finite size of stocks, and the sharply limited role for imports for political reasons, wider margins between the floor price and ceiling price have become a de facto balance wheel as well, but these wider margins call into question the implicit assumption that food security and price stability are synonymous.

In 2004, Indonesia made a policy decision to raise domestic rice prices significantly above world prices (by preventing imports). In December 2004, the price of domestic rice was at parity with the price of equivalent rice imports (figure 7.1). By February 2006, however, the price of domestic rice had risen 25 percent in real terms, whereas the price of equivalent rice on the world market had fallen 11 percent, an increase of more than a third in the relative price. In March 2007, the Statistics Indonesia National Socioeconomic Survey (Susenas) on poverty in Indonesia reported a significant increase in the poverty headcount ratio, despite fairly rapid economic growth nationwide (BPS 2002–14).

In 2006, a vigorous debate developed in Indonesia over the causes of the increase in poverty, which included the reduction in the fuel subsidy in 2005 and the use of cash transfers to compensate poor households. The role of high rice prices and the import ban were hotly contested.[12] Calls to allow rice imports went unheeded, and by March 2007, domestic rice prices were 57 percent higher than world prices. Poverty rates stayed high, and the number of near poor rose significantly.

The vigorous and open debate late in 2006 over the impact of the rice import ban led to discussions of how to arrange imports in a timely fashion to prevent further price increases and harm to the poor. By December 5, 2006, the *Jakarta Post* ran a headline story by Urip Hudiono in which Timmer was quoted as saying, "Banning rice imports [is] 'not the right option.'" Options for managing the impending rice crisis by arranging emergency rice imports were prepared for the minister of trade, who immediately requested presidential permission to start the import process. A presidential decree was issued on December 9, 2006, authorizing imports. Unfortunately, there was enough political and bureaucratic opposition to prevent rice imports from arriving until late February, which was far too late to prevent a sharp spike in rice prices in December 2006–February 2007. The high poverty rates were directly caused by the decision to restrict rice imports and to keep domestic rice prices well above world prices (Warr 2011).

Similar opposition to rice imports materialized late in 2015 and early in 2016, as the El Niño drought put pressure on domestic supplies and BULOG's ability to procure rice domestically. Making the stabilization of rice prices the foundation of Indonesia's food-based social safety net is clearly a thing of the past.

Pro-Poor Growth and Food Security: The Inclusion of Rural Households in a Food-Based Social Safety Net

Only 60 years ago, Indonesia was one of the poorest countries in Asia.[13] The story of its poverty and poverty reduction is a story of the political and economic eras that determined the nation's development trajectory: colonial rule and exploitation; authoritarian rule, coupled with sustained growth and then dramatic collapse; and, most recently, democracy accompanied by economic flux and tentative stabilization. At Indonesia's independence, in 1945, the vast majority of its population was impoverished. By 1993, however, with poverty reduced to 14 percent of the population and annual economic growth at more than 7 percent, Indonesia was ranked, along with a handful of other East Asian countries, as a high-performing Asian economy (World Bank 1993) and lauded for its astonishing transformation. To understand this remarkable turnaround, it is necessary to understand the key factors that drove the change in livelihoods of some 100 million Indonesians.[14]

History has much to teach Indonesia as it struggles to reestablish economic growth and reconnect that growth to its remaining poor. Because Indonesia has experienced such sharp swings in its development path, a multitude of successes and also many failures are available to examine. Drawing on the vast historical literature in this area (Hofman, Rodrick-Jones, and Thee 2004; MacIntyre 2003; Temple 2001; Timmer 2003), this section briefly sets out that history. It begins with the unfavorable starting point, focuses on the policies of the Suharto government that brought about the structural transformation in the livelihoods of the poor, and then reflects on the causes and effects of the greatest economic crisis in Indonesian history. The story of three decades of sustained pro-poor growth, juxtaposed with the story of rapid collapse and recovery, provides useful insights for future policy making.

Troubled History and Chronic Poverty

For the duration of the 350-year period of Dutch colonial rule, the trade and tax regime favored Dutch extraction of income, with dire consequences for the Indonesian population. Analysis provided by Van der Eng and interpreted by Timmer enables an examination of growth, the severity of poverty through a comparison of annual food energy intake measured in kilocalories, and income elasticity of consumption over the past century (table 7.2). During the 19th century, growth in consumption was negative, estimated at −0.34 kilocalories per year, while the index of pro-poor growth (IPPG) was only a fraction of the long-term average,[15] illustrating the severe disconnect between the situation of the poor and the modest economic growth that occurred during this period.

At the beginning of the 20th century, when Dutch public opinion influenced the management of the colonies, a more developmental approach, known as "ethical policy," was implemented briefly. The policy brought significant benefits both to the economy (growth reached 1.63 percent per year) and to the poor (food intake increased an annual average of 1.39 kilocalories). But this investment in the country lasted for only a brief period. The collapse of world prices for export commodities in the 1920s and the abysmal economic management of Indonesia during the Great Depression[16] resulted in the lowest rate of growth and pro-poor growth in any period before independence.

By the 1930s, the colonial authorities had built a significant network of irrigation and transport facilities, but there was very little investment in educating the nation's population. Poverty increased significantly during World

TABLE 7.2 **Long-Term Patterns of Pro-Poor Growth in Indonesia, 1880–1990**

TIME PERIOD	ANNUAL GROWTH IN INCOME PER CAPITA (% PER YEAR)	ANNUAL GROWTH IN CALORIC CONSUMPTION (% PER YEAR)	INCOME ELASTICITY OF CALORIC CONSUMPTION	INDEX OF PRO-POOR GROWTH (IPPG)
Dutch colonial exploitation, 1880–1905	0.33	−0.34	0.051	0.05
Ethical Policy under the Dutch, 1905–25	1.63	1.39	0.878	4.57
Depression, Pacific War, and fight for independence, 1925–50	−2.42	−0.78	0.333	−2.57
The Sukarno era, including the Guided Economy, 1950–66	1.46	0.68	0.509	2.37
The New Order regime of Suharto, 1966–90	3.45	2.10	0.595	6.56
Long-term averages, 1880–1990	0.89	0.22	0.313	0.89

Source: Timmer 2005.
Note: See text and endnote 15 for the definition of IPPG and an explanation of how it is calculated and interpreted. Details of the regressions are provided in Timmer (2005), along with a full explanation of the analytical relationship between the overall incidence of poverty and the average income elasticity of demand for food energy.

War II and the subsequent struggle for independence, which reached closure only with final acceptance by the Dutch in 1949. The tumultuous global period spanning the Great Depression, the Pacific War, and the fight for independence (1925–50) saw a marked deterioration in rates of per capita income growth (−2.42 percent) and a negative rate of pro-poor growth (−2.57 percent).

By the early 1960s, as in other postindependence states, poverty had fallen in the postwar recovery, and Indonesia was muddling along with modest growth and weak but quasi-democratic governance. After Sukarno imposed "guided democracy" in 1959, however, the situation deteriorated sharply. By adopting an inward-looking development policy and severely neglecting agriculture, Indonesia was "a prime exemplar of the dangerously degenerative consequences of weak governance and a sickly economy" (MacIntyre 2003, 1). Incomes fell dramatically, and the hyperinflation of 1965–66 had an adverse effect on the entire population, as the poverty rate increased rapidly and the economy collapsed.[17] An estimated 70 percent of the population was absolutely poor by 1966. Hunger was widespread (Timmer 2003). In 1968, with no hint of the future, Gunnar Myrdal observed, "No economist holds out any hope for Indonesia" (Myrdal 1968).

A Period of Growth and Rapid Poverty Reduction

The trajectory of growth and poverty transformed dramatically under the New Order government of President Suharto. Starting in 1968, for three remarkable decades, Indonesia's gross domestic product (GDP) grew an average of 7.4 percent annually. As a result, in 1997 Indonesia's per capita income reached US$906, more than quadruple the 1968 level.[18] When compared with previous periods in Indonesian history, the quarter century from 1965 to 1990 saw an annual growth in caloric intake of 2.1 percent a year, 50 percent higher than the next best period in 1905–25 and almost 10 times the long-term average. The IPPG reached 6.56 for the period 1965–90—the highest in Indonesian history—seven times the long-term average and nearly half again as large as the next best period in 1905–25 (table 7.2).

As the export economy boomed in the late 1980s and early 1990s and overall GDP grew nearly 7 percent annually, roughly half of that growth was made up of nontradable goods and services, where most of the poor make a living (Timmer 1997, 2002, 2004). The structure of economic growth during this period led to a remarkably high growth elasticity of poverty (table 7.3).

Sound macroeconomic management was strongly supported by investment in sectors that benefited the poor—education, health, family planning, and infrastructure—enabling the poor to benefit from the country's oil windfall at the household level. The windfall also supported the development of widespread and large-scale investment in infrastructure assets, significantly lowering transaction costs.

The government's success in reinstating macroeconomic stability and, through the exchange rate, bringing down the relative price of rice, was

TABLE 7.3 **Growth Elasticity of Poverty in Indonesia, 1967–2002**

TIME PERIOD	ANNUAL % CHANGE		GROWTH ELASTICITY OF POVERTY
	PER CAPITA INCOME	POVERTY INDEX	
1967–76	5.48	−6.0	−1.09
1976–80	6.37	−8.1	−1.27
1980–84	4.23	−6.8	−1.61
1984–87	2.69	0.7	−2.60
1987–90	6.66	−4.6	−0.81
1990–93	5.41	−4.6	−0.85
1993–96	5.23	−6.2	−1.19
1996–99	3.25	9.9	−3.05 (+)
1999–2002	2.49	−8.2	−3.29

Source: Timmer 2005.
Note: The growth elasticity of poverty is calculated as the ratio of the percentage reduction in the poverty headcount index relative to the percentage change in per capita income (in US$ purchasing power parity) from the World Bank database on pro-poor growth.

critical to Indonesia's rapid reduction of the poverty rate from its crisis spike of 23.4 percent in 1999 to 18.2 percent in 2002. The fall in the relative price of rice (index of rice prices over all food prices) from 1.43 to 1.08 over the period from September 1998 to September 2000 was a key factor driving the decline in poverty over that period. Although the poverty headcount rates declined to precrisis levels, studies also suggest that the crisis had lasting impacts. Ravallion and Lokshin (2005) estimate that the poverty headcount index would have been about half what it was in 2002 had the crisis not taken place.

The crisis and recovery showed that the price of rice is the most important determinant of poverty at the household level in Indonesia. Macroeconomic price stability matters to the poor (Timmer 2004). Rice prices are important for poverty alleviation, not only because higher or lower prices have direct, short-term benefits on the poorest quintiles but also because they play a key role in the structural transformation of the agriculture sector and economy as a whole. In agriculture, low rice prices encourage farmers to diversify crops and to plant less rice by making rice less valuable to farmers at the market. The result is a move toward crops that give the poor higher profit margins. In Indonesia, artificially high rice prices have slowed the crop diversification process as well as investments in nonfarm rural activities (Timmer 2004).

During the severe economic contraction in 1998–99, the government developed and extended several formal safety net programs. The *Jaring Pengaman Sosial* (JPS) social safety net programs, known until then for their patchy record, were extended to protect the chronically and transitory poor from the impacts of the crisis. Initially, these crash programs were directed to urban areas throughout the country, but they were also intended to reach rural areas where harvest failures were causing significant hardship. The JPS programs had four goals: (a) to ensure that the poor could obtain food at affordable prices, (b) to create employment, (c) to preserve access to social services such as health and education, and (d) to sustain local economic activity through regional block grants and small-scale credit programs (Sumarto, Suryahadi, and Pritchett 2001). Evidence highlights the mixed effectiveness of the various programs (Sumarto, Suryahadi, and Widyanti 2004). Although the scholarship program helped to keep children in school and the health card program improved access of the poor to public health facilities, the Rastra program saw higher levels of capture by upper quintiles. The next section analyzes the performance of Rastra.

FROM PRICE STABILITY TO FOOD ACCESS: THE RASTRA PROGRAM

The previous sections have highlighted the role played by price stability at the aggregate level. Yet stability does not mean affordability for net food consumers, especially when prices are stable at exceptionally high levels. This disconnect, as pointed out, led the government to provide subsidized rice for poor households. In the following sections, the chapter moves from a historical macro-level perspective to a more micro-level perspective on design and implementation matters related to Rastra.

Rice accounts for nearly a quarter of the total average monthly expenditures among poor households, consuming 34 and 26 percent of the rural and urban poverty budgets, respectively. This finding suggests that the issue of food security—particularly in regard to rice as a staple food—still requires serious attention.

The adequacy of food in terms of quality and quantity is important for Indonesian development because several nutritional indicators still need attention. In terms of quantity, the proportion of people who consume less than the required daily intake of 1,400 or 2,000 calories remains quite high, at 8.5 and 35.3 percent, respectively, in 2013. In terms of nutritional quality, between 2007 and 2013, the nutritional status of children under five stagnated or even worsened, the prevalence of underweight children increased from 18.4 to 19.6 percent, stunting increased from 36.8 to 37.2 percent, and the prevalence of central obesity (accumulation of belly fat) rose from 18.8 to 26.6 percent. Only the prevalence of wasting improved slightly, falling from 13.6 percent in 2007 to 12.1 percent in 2013 (Isdijoso and others 2014).

The government has made efforts to increase food security and adequacy, together with reducing poverty, through social protection and poverty alleviation programs. To ensure sufficient food, especially for low-income groups, the government has introduced food subsidies, primarily in the form of rice. Essentially, Rastra is a continuation of the OPK program, which was undertaken by the government during the 1997–98 economic crisis. It commenced in July 1998 as part of a broader social safety net (JPS), with the aim of reducing the expenditure burden on households by fulfilling basic needs with rice. Since January 2002, Rastra was broadened in scope, shifting from a project focused on responding to crisis situations through food subsidies to become a program aimed at social protection for the poor.

Rastra is the most well-funded social assistance program in Indonesia. In 2007, the total allocation for the program was Rp 6.6 trillion or around 43.1 percent of the total budget for social protection programs, and it covered as many as 15.7 million target households. In 2016, the total budget allocation for Rastra increased threefold, to Rp 21 trillion, with coverage of 15.5 million households. The allocation for each household is 15 kilograms of rice per month at a price of Rp 1,600 per kilogram at the distribution point. Rastra now accounts for more than half of total social assistance expenditure.

Throughout its implementation, Rastra has undergone changes in relation to its institutionalization, coverage, frequency of distribution, quantity of rice allocations, price of rice, and implementation mechanisms. Several of those changes were made to align the program with changes in budget allocations, poverty conditions, and rising costs. Others changes were made to improve the program's effectiveness or to accommodate recommendations from various sources.

Institutionalization

Rastra cuts across sectors vertically and horizontally, and it engages many institutions at all levels of government. Nationally, the responsibility for implementation rests with the Coordinating Ministry for Human Development and Culture (Menko PMK). Furthermore, each government leader at the provincial, district, subdistrict, and village levels is responsible for implementing Rastra in the respective region. Those leaders are also responsible for creating the Rastra coordination team in their region. At the village level,[19] the coordination team is called the distribution team.

The membership of Rastra coordination teams cuts across sectors. At the central level, membership comprises representatives from Menko PMK, the Coordinating Ministry for the Economy, the Ministry of National Development Planning, the Ministry of Finance, the Ministry of Home Affairs, the Ministry of Social Affairs, Statistics Indonesia (BPS), and BULOG. At the provincial and lower levels, membership is also taken from agencies at the relevant level of government with responsibilities similar to those at the national level. In general, Rastra coordination teams are tasked with coordinating and managing policy formulation, planning, quota determination, public socialization, complaint handling, monitoring and evaluation, and reporting.

The organizational structure of Rastra has been subject to several adjustments, and the role of BULOG has tended to decline. When OPK was first implemented, program coordination was the responsibility of the Ministry for Food and Horticulture. That ministry was dissolved at the end of 1999, and BULOG took responsibility for coordinating OPK. In 2007, Menko PMK, which before October 2014 had been called the Coordinating Ministry for Social Welfare, became the program coordinator. The agency with authority over budget expenditure also has changed. The power to authorize the budget was held by BULOG in 2005–07 and again in 2010–11, by the Coordinating Ministry for Community Welfare in 2008–09, and since 2012 by the Ministry of Social Affairs. Since the beginning of the program, BULOG has been responsible for the provision and distribution of rice from acquisition (from BULOG warehouses) through to the distribution point.

In theory, the institutionalization of Rastra is geographically sufficient and comprehensive, because it involves many cross-sectoral agencies at all levels of government. Each agency at the central level tends to carry out its own specific function, such as the Ministry of Social Affairs for budget expenditure, BPS for the provision of data, and BULOG for the distribution of rice. Meanwhile, interagency cooperation, which determines the program's effectiveness, remains weak. Coordination between levels of government, from the central to the district level, is also weak. Weak coordination is largely due to the implementation of decentralization in Indonesia since 2001.

Regional governments are responsible for implementation in their region, for their coordination teams, and for the delivery of rice from the distribution point to beneficiaries. Local governments are expected to allocate funds to the regional budget for Rastra, at least for the transport of rice from distribution points to recipient households. Regions with larger budgets can allocate funds for further development; for example, they can provide funding to expand the provision of rice to additional households beyond the initial quota, add a subsidy that lowers the buying price for beneficiaries, empower the community through the *Padat Karya Rastra* (Rastra for Work) program, and distribute Rastra through more accessible locations such as local stalls and through community groups.

The role of regional governments in implementation, especially for budget provision, varies. Districts vary in the level of funding from their own budget for Rastra implementation, but most districts do not provide any funding at all (Hastuti and others 2008, 28). Some regional governments have a negative attitude toward the program, seeing Rastra as a central government program that does little good for regions; some governments refuse to implement it altogether (TNP2K 2015, 41). Some areas refuse to implement Rastra because the high administrative costs to local governments outweigh the benefits of the small amount of rice received (Hastuti and Maxwell 2003, 15). Furthermore, regional governments may be concerned that targeted social assistance programs will exacerbate preexisting social conflicts. However, the number of regional governments that pay attention to Rastra has grown over the past few years. Some districts have even decided to make Rastra free. These districts have not only available funds, but also a political desire to lower poverty rates. They also may be responding to awareness-raising efforts and encouragement from provincial governments.

Rastra program management is regulated by implementation guidelines that are created and published each year by the coordination teams at several levels. The Central Rastra Coordination Team creates the general Rastra handbook as a policy directive for nationwide implementation. Each provincial implementation team creates implementation instructions, and each district coordination team creates a technical guide. The implementation instructions and technical guides are based on the general guidelines but can be adapted for the local conditions and situations of each area. According to Hastuti and others (2008, 6), only a few local governments have prepared instructions for the program's implementation. Even when such instructions have been prepared, the contents are merely a copy of the general guidelines, without any further detailed stipulations. Rastra institutionalization is also subject to a control system that is conducted through oversight, reporting, monitoring and evaluation, and complaint handling. Those activities are carried out in stages at all levels of government at assigned periods.

Rastra is part of the broader poverty alleviation agenda of the central government and is implemented in coordination with other poverty alleviation programs. The institutions for poverty alleviation at the central level include the *Tim Nasional Percepatan Penanggulangan Kemiskinan* (TNP2K, National Team for the Acceleration of Poverty Reduction), which is headed by the vice president. Before TNP2K was established in 2010, the *Tim Koordinasi Penanggulangan Kemiskinan* (TKPK, National Team for Poverty Reduction) operated at the national level. Similar bodies operate at the provincial and district levels and are under the authority of the head of the district or province. Those teams, made up of a cross-section of sectoral and stakeholder representatives, are tasked with coordinating and managing poverty alleviation programs, including Rastra.

TKPKs at the provincial and district levels are designed to bridge poverty alleviation programs, but in actual implementation they are often not functional. In several districts, stakeholders told researchers that they were unaware of the existence of the team. According to Sumarto, Vothknecht, and Wijaya (2014), TKPK plays a significant role in reducing poverty. In districts that have had a TKPK office for at least one year, poverty was found to be more than 1 percentage point lower than in districts where a TKPK office had not yet been established. In addition, in districts that have had a TKPK office for at least three years, poverty incidence was found to be nearly 4 percentage points lower than in a district with no TKPK office.

Distribution Mechanisms

Rastra distribution involves two bodies: BULOG and the regional governments. BULOG is responsible for transport from the storage warehouse to the distribution point, and regional governments are responsible for transport from the distribution point to each target household (figure 7.2). The distribution of Rastra commences when the district government issues a request for allocation to the BULOG branch of that region. BULOG then issues a delivery order to the storehouse to release the rice to the appointed work unit (*satker*). The work unit then sends the rice to the agreed-upon distribution point, in accordance with the target households.

Since 2012, local governments have four options for distributing goods from the distribution point to households. In practice, almost all use the same method, which involves work teams consisting of village officials or heads of neighborhood subdivisions—RTs (groups of neighborhood households), RWs (groups of RTs), and hamlets.[20] The work team takes the rice that has been delivered by BULOG to the distribution point and transports it to local distribution centers, except when distribution points also serve as local distribution centers. Distribution points are usually located in a village office. In some regions, primarily outside of Java, local distribution centers are located at a subdistrict office or are merged with other village distribution points because of transportation limitations. Moreover, distribution centers in some villages

FIGURE 7.2

Rastra Distribution Channels

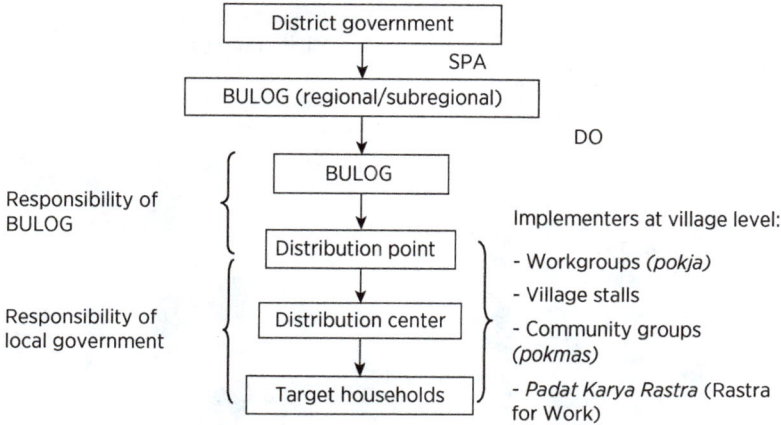

Note: DO = delivery order; SPA= Surat Permintaan Alokasi (allocation request document); BULOG = State Logistics Board.

may spread across several locations, such as in homes of neighborhood leaders (of the RT or RW) or hamlet leaders. Once the rice arrives, the work team advises households to pick up their allocation of rice at the distribution center, using both loudspeakers located at places of worship and word of mouth.

The total amount of time needed for one distribution usually does not exceed one week. On the day the allocation request document is received from the regional government, the regional BULOG submits a distribution order to the warehouse, which then delivers rice to the distribution point. From the distribution point, the rice is distributed to local distribution centers or directly to households. The length of time from when the rice is received at the distribution center to the completion of distribution to households is usually one to three days.

Cost of Subsidies

Through Rastra, the government has provided increasingly large subsidies for rice (figure 7.3). In 2005, the subsidy amounted to Rp 2,494 per kilogram, which rose each subsequent year and in 2015 was worth Rp 6,725 per kilogram. This increase occurred because the government's purchase price increased, although the prices paid by households remained relatively steady. The government's purchase price increased in line with shifts in the market price of rice, from Rp 3,494 per kilogram in 2005 to Rp 8,825 per kilogram in 2015, a 2.5-fold increase over 10 years. At the same time, the subsidized price for target households at distribution points remained Rp 1,000 per kilogram

FIGURE 7.3

The Price of Rastra Rice and Cost of Government Subsidies in Indonesia, 2002–16

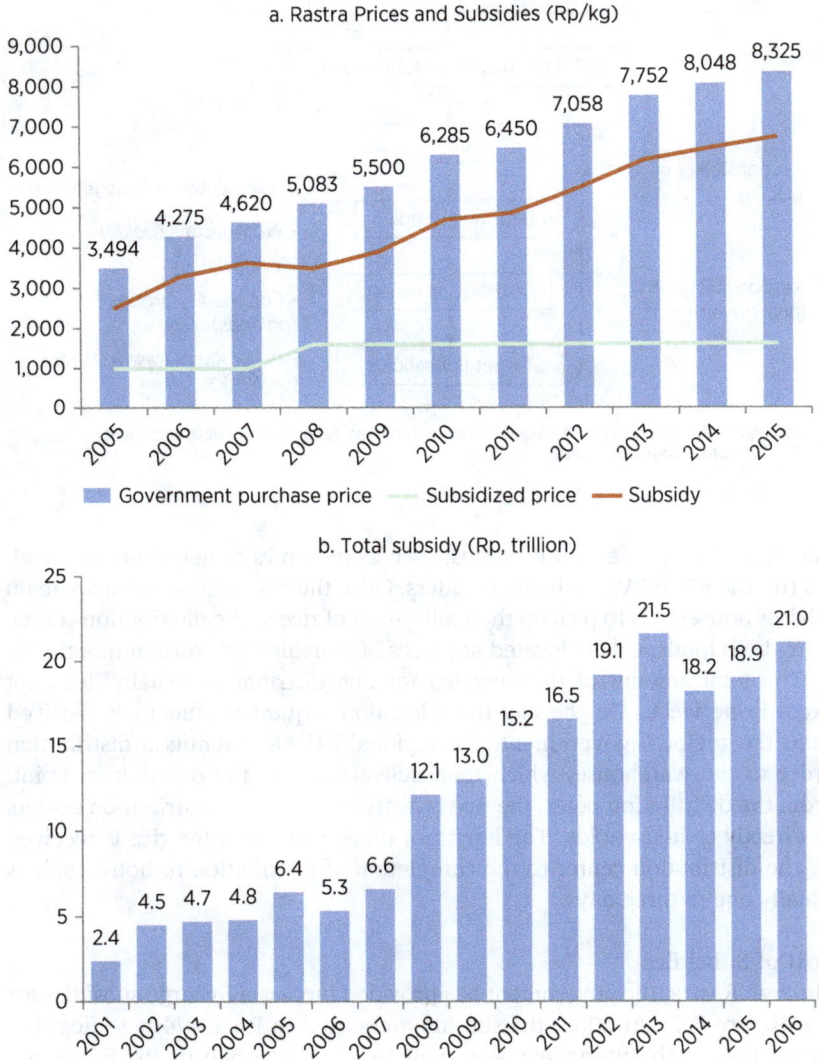

a. Rastra Prices and Subsidies (Rp/kg)

b. Total subsidy (Rp, trillion)

Source: Government of Indonesia 2004–16.
Note: Subsidy figures for 2015 and 2016 are budget figures.

from the start of the program to 2007 and only increased once, in 2008, to Rp 1,600 per kilogram, which still applies today.

The national budget funds Rastra through to the delivery of rice at each distribution point. The cost of Rastra subsidies has risen significantly along with increases in the government's purchase price, the number of target households, the frequency of distribution, and the costs of distribution and storage. Those increases were significant over the 2007–13 period. Despite a decrease in the number of target households since 2010, the frequency of distribution has increased, with 15 distributions in 2013. In 2014, the total cost of the subsidy declined because there was no increase in the frequency of distribution (which had increased from 13 deliveries per year in 2010–12 to 15 per year in 2013), but in 2016 the distribution cost rose again to Rp 21 trillion.

The Rastra subsidy is used to fund three main activities: procurement, storage, and distribution of rice to the distribution points. During 2002–07, most of the subsidy was spent on procurement (41–80 percent). Other cost components included repayment of interest (7–13 percent), operational costs (5–11 percent), management fees (3–6 percent), bank fees (1–2 percent), and packaging costs (1–3 percent). Until 2004, costs for historical stock carry-over accounted for 22–43 percent.

Target Households

Rastra targets are poor and vulnerable households; however, depending on the data sources used, target criteria have changed several times. Until 2005, Rastra used *Badan Koordinasi Keluarga Berencana Nasional* (BKKBN, National Family Planning Coordination Board) data, which at that time were the only national-level data that provided family-level information. Target households were classified as *keluarga pre-sejahtera* (pre-prosperous family) and *keluarga sejahtera 1* (prosperous family 1), the two lowest classifications on a five-point scale of family economic welfare. However, for the first two years of implementation, families experiencing food insecurity were also included, on the advice of regional governments. After BPS conducted a survey of very poor, poor, and near-poor households through the socioeconomic survey of 2005, Rastra used these data over the period 2006–09.[21] From 2010 to 2012, data from the 2008 Social Protection Program Census (PPLS) were used, and since July 2012, the *Basis Data Terpadu* (BDT, Unified Database), a national database for social protection programs (managed by the TNP2K), which is sourced from the 2011 PPLS, has been used. The target groups of the final two surveys conducted by BPS are poor and vulnerable households.

The number of target recipients of Rastra has changed in line with the levels of poverty and budget allocations. The total rose yearly and peaked in 2008, before falling slightly. These figures do not necessarily reflect the total number of poor and vulnerable people, because, except for 2008–12, Rastra targets did not include all poor and vulnerable groups or households recorded in the database for social assistance. Since 2013, Rastra targets have totaled 15.5 million households (figure 7.4). That number includes 62 percent of households in the BDT and around 24 percent of all households in Indonesia.

Data on the total number of target recipients are used to establish quota allocations from the national down to the village level. Allocations are made at different levels. First, the government, together with the parliament, determines the national allocation. Second, Menko PMK determines the allocations for each province. Third, provincial governors determine the allocations for districts and cities. Fourth, the mayor determines the allocations for subdistricts and villages. In determining the quota for regional allowances, governors and mayors must refer to the quota determined by Menko PMK. However, they can increase the total number of target households with funding from their own regional budget. The quota for villages cannot be reallocated to other villages unless doing so is discussed at the district level, at the request of two villages. Targeting accuracy, an important aspect of achieving program goals, has been a primary weakness of the program. The eventual number of recipient households far outweighs the number of target households. Recipient households are not all from poor or vulnerable backgrounds; they also include households with adequate levels of welfare. Nationally, data from the Susenas,

FIGURE 7.4

Total Number of Poor Households and Rastra Target Households in Indonesia, 1998–2015

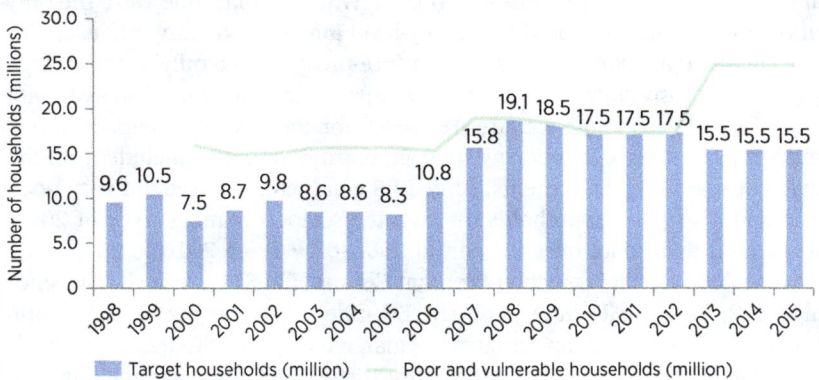

Source: Kemenko Kesra 2015. In particular, data for target and total poor households in 1998 and 2000–10 are from BULOG 2011 (BULOG provided the authors with a table containing Rastra characteristics); data for target households in 1999 are from Tabor and Sawit 2001; data for target households in 2011–15 are from Kemenko Kesra 2015; data for total poor in 2011–12 are the same as for total poor in 2010 (2008 Social Protection Program Census data). *Note:* Data on target households in 1998 and 1999 are the highest number of targets. Target households are those that the government intended to support. Actual recipients are higher in number due to de facto redistribution at the village level.

the BPS socioeconomic survey, shows that the number of recipient households is around twice as large as the number of target households. When the number of target households increased significantly in 2007 and 2008, the gap between the number of recipients and targets decreased somewhat before rising again to a twofold difference in 2013. In 2014, target households amounted to only 15.5 million, but recipient households totaled 33.4 million (figure 7.5).

Half of the households in Indonesia purchase Rastra rice. Figure 7.5 shows a relatively steady increase in the number of recipients or households that purchase subsidized rice. In 2002, when the total number of households was around 55 million, the number of Rastra-recipient households was around 21 million or 38 percent of the total. Since 2007, that proportion has reached more than 50 percent, and in 2014—when the total number of households was 65 million—households receiving Rastra rice constituted 52 percent of the total.

Results of data analysis based on expenditure deciles show both inclusion and exclusion errors (figure 7.6). In the first error, Rastra recipients are not only from the lower deciles; those in high-expenditure deciles are also included, although the higher the decile, the lower the proportion of households receiving Rastra. The rate of leakage is quite high. In 2002–14, target households—the first three deciles of expenditure—amounted to between 15 and 33 percent of the total number of households. However, in the same period, between 51 and 57 percent of recipients were outside these target deciles.

FIGURE 7.5

Total Number of Rastra Target and Recipient Households in Indonesia, 2002–14

Recipient households (million)   — Target Households (million)

Source: BPS 2002–14 (raw data).

FIGURE 7.6

Benefit Incidence in Indonesia, by Expenditure Decile, 2002 and 2014

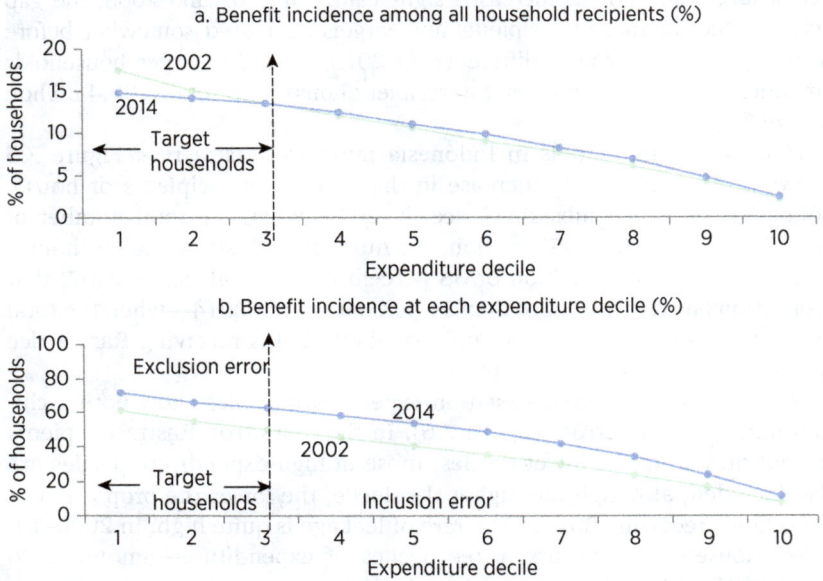

a. Benefit incidence among all household recipients (%)

b. Benefit incidence at each expenditure decile (%)

Source: BPS 2002–14.
Note: Deciles are divided on the basis of expenditure categories. The higher the decile, the higher the level of household expenditure or welfare.

The exclusion error is seen in the proportion of recipients in the lowest three deciles, which demonstrates that some poor and vulnerable households do not receive Rastra. However, the proportion of recipients is higher in the lower deciles than in the upper, showing that the poorest groups have the greatest access to Rastra. There was some improvement in 2002–14, with those in the bottom 30 percent receiving a greater share of total Rastra benefits. In 2014, the proportion of households in the lowest three deciles receiving Rastra was 72, 66, and 63 percent, respectively.

Field research has produced the same findings: inaccurate targeting is the key weakness of the program because not all poor households receive Rastra rice, while many nonpoor households do (Hastuti and others 2008, 14). Moreover, Rastra rice tends to be distributed evenly across all households in the village—that is, it is distributed to more than the targeted households. A field report in 2014 found that most of the 10 villages studied practiced even distribution (Hastuti and others 2014b). Although the central implementation team makes available the list of target households (the beneficiary list), the lists generally are not used at the village level to identify recipient households. Instead, they are used only to determine overall allocations of rice for each area. Implementers in villages, smaller neighborhood units (RT or RW), or hamlets generally determine the recipients.

The even distribution of Rastra rice is usually related to the social and political context and the limitations of information available to program implementers. Implementers at the local level consider rice to be a basic need for all levels of society. Aside from this expectation, local implementers also believe that because cooperative community projects (*gotong royong*) or events to collect donations expect everyone to contribute, when assistance is available, the whole community is entitled to benefit. Otherwise, they are concerned that community harmony would be disrupted and that community members would no longer be willing to assist with community projects. By maintaining a fair attitude toward all sections of the community, village implementers, who are usually local leaders, feel assured that they will receive support from all sections of society, support that is particularly important leading up to elections.

The other factor affecting the even or uneven distribution of rice is insufficient or inaccurate data. Regional governments have the opportunity to review and update recipient data at the start of each year on the basis of consultations with villages. However, a field study in 2014 found that almost all of the villages visited had not updated their household data (Hastuti and others 2014b). In 6 out of 10 villages that did not enact even distribution, the factors that influenced the decision included program socialization, public announcement of the list of target households, and use of the social protection card.[22]

In several field visits, researchers also found that some poor households did not buy Rastra rice when it was available. Usually those households were eligible to buy rice, but they did not have enough money at the time that rice was distributed. Other reasons were that they did not receive information about the distribution, were not in the area at the time, or arrived late, after all of the available rice had run out.

Frequency of Distribution

Rastra rice is distributed approximately 12 times a year except in 2006, 2007, and 2010–13. In 2006 and 2007, it was distributed 10 and 11 times, respectively. In 2010–13, one to three extra distributions were added annually, to minimize the impact of increasing fuel prices and drought and in anticipation of rice price volatility. In 2014 and 2015, the number of distributions returned to 12 annually.

Basically, Rastra rice is distributed each month, and frequency is regulated by agreements between BULOG and district-level coordination teams. If the frequency of distribution increases because of a central government decision, more than one distribution will occur within a given month. Conversely, if the decision is made by the regional government, or obstacles such as geographic location, weather, or transport affect distribution, distribution may occur less than once a month. Where the distribution schedule coincides with the rice harvest, distributions may be merged, because the poor tend to have a larger supply of rice, especially those who are employed as harvest workers.

According to an analysis of secondary data and field visits (Hastuti and others 2008), Rastra rice is not always distributed monthly. The 2012 TNP2K monitoring study (TNP2K 2015, 20) produced the same finding: of 220 villages studied, only 46 percent distributed rice monthly. In 2011, the *Badan Pengawasan Keuangan dan Pembangunan* (BPKP, the Finance and Development Supervisory Agency) found that eligible households in 15 provinces did not receive rice monthly. A field study conducted in 2014 also found that half of the 20 study villages received Rastra rice each month (Hastuti and others 2014a). The other half received rice once every two to four months. The reasons for the difference included insufficient allocations, long travel times from the BULOG storehouse to the distribution point, the cost savings of having fewer trips from the distribution point to local distribution centers, the reduced burden on village distributors, and late payments by villages or subdistricts for the previous shipment.

The frequency at which Rastra rice is delivered to distribution points is not always the same as the frequency at which rice is received by households. Recipient households are not always able to purchase Rastra rice each time it arrives in the village because distributions are based on a rotation system. In such systems, households that received rice in the previous distribution cannot receive rice in the following distribution. In that system, half of the 20 villages in the field study received Rastra rice only once every two to four months, not every month.

Quantity of Rice Distributed and Received by Households

The household allocation has changed several times because of changes in the state government's budget allocation. The allocation has varied between 10 and 20 kilograms per household per month, although the amount is usually between 15 and 20 kilograms (table 7.4). Since about 2006, the allocation has been fixed at 15 kilograms. At this quantity, and with the frequency described, in any one year each family receives between 150 and 240 kilograms, excluding the first year of implementation. In total, between 1.6 million and 3.5 million tons of Rastra rice are distributed annually.

In 2013, the BPS estimated that annual rice consumption reached 102 kilograms per capita, while the Ministry of Agriculture put this figure at 130 kilograms. Assuming that the average household consists of four people, one household requires 408–520 kilograms of rice annually or 34–43 kilograms a month. Through Rastra, the government hopes to reduce the expenditure burden of poor households and increase their ability to meet their staple food needs. If target households receive 15 kilograms of rice per month as stipulated, then the program will fulfill approximately one-third to half of their rice needs.

TABLE 7.4 **Allocation of Rastra Rice in Indonesia, 1998–2014**

YEAR	ALLOCATION PER TARGET HOUSEHOLD (KILOGRAMS)		TOTAL ALLOCATION (TONS)[a]
	PER DISTRIBUTION	PER YEAR[a]	
1998	10 or 20[b]	20–70[c]	455,843
1999	20	240	2,506,960[d]
2000	20	240	1,800,000
2001	15	180	1,566,000
2002	20	240	2,349,600
2003	20	240	2,059,275
2004	20	240	2,061,793
2005	20	240	1,992,000
2006	15	150	1,624,500
2007	15	165	2,604,011
2008	10 or 15[e]	175	3,342,500
2009	15	180	3,329,514
2010	13 or 15[f]	185	3,235,281
2011	15	195	3,410,161
2012	15	195	3,410,161
2013	15	225	3,494,452
2014	15	180	2,795,561
2015	15	180	2,795,561

Sources: Government of Indonesia 2004–16 (financial notes); BULOG (raw data); BPS 2002–14 (treated); 1999 recipient data from Tabor and Sawit 2001.
[a.] Treated data.
[b.] In 1998, the allocations were 10 kilograms from July to November and 20 kilograms in December.
[c.] In 1998, the number of target recipients grew each month, from 141,655 households at the start of the year, to 9,588,857 at the end of the year.
[d.] The figure is based on three distributions, in March, June, and December 1999 (the number of households was not the same for each distribution, but ranged from 9.6 million to 10.5 million households).
[e.] In 2008, the allocation of 10 kilograms applied only in January.
[f.] In 2010, the allocation was 13 kilograms from January to May.

Estimates of the number of recipient households and the amount of rice distributed show that, over the course of 2002–13, recipient households received only 59–108 kilograms of Rastra rice annually. Compared with the stipulated allocations of 150–240 kilograms per household annually, the amount of rice purchased reached only 36–61 percent of the amount allocated (table 7.5). This finding weakens the program's ability to meet its objectives, as only 11–26 percent of household rice needs are being met.

Analyzing the amount of rice purchased by households at the time of the most recent distribution (2008–12) and in the past month (2013–14) also shows that the amount of rice purchased is lower than stipulated (almost the

TABLE 7.5 **Amount of Rice Allocated to and Received by Households Annually in Indonesia, 2002–13**

| YEAR | TOTAL RECIPIENT HOUSEHOLDS | TOTAL RICE DISTRIBUTED (TONS) | ANNUAL AMOUNT OF RICE FOR HOUSEHOLDS | | |
			AMOUNT ALLOCATED (KILOGRAMS)	AMOUNT RECEIVED (KILOGRAMS)	% OF ALLOCATION RECEIVED
2002	20,943,085	2,235,141	240	107	44.47
2003	22,519,131	2,023,664	240	90	37.44
2004	19,537,271	2,060,198	240	105	43.94
2005	22,939,778	1,991,131	240	87	36.17
2006	24,545,069	1,624,089	150	66	44.11
2007	29,412,414	1,731,805	165	59	35.68
2008	30,542,384	3,236,644	175	106	60.56
2009	30,171,692	3,254,103	180	108	59.92
2010	31,021,803	3,234,538	185	104	56.36
2011	32,615,580	3,410,161	195	105	53.62
2012	33,163,914	3,372,818	195	102	52.15
2013	32,849,522	3,431,615	225	104	46.43

Sources: Based on BPS 2015 (treated); Government of Indonesia 2004–16.

same as the results of yearly calculations presented in table 7.5), that is, only 39–61 percent. The difference between the actual amount purchased and the stipulated amount became more pronounced in 2013 and 2014 because the national allocation of Rastra rice fell, while the number of recipient households remained stable (figure 7.7). In some cases, target households could not buy the full allocation because their portion was being redistributed (thus became smaller) so that all households (not just targeted households) could receive a share of rice. Moreover, not having enough money to buy the rice or missing the time of distribution also constrained the purchase of the full allocation.

Field research has also found that recipient households receive less than the stipulated amount, even less than the estimated calculations, with variation between regions (Hastuti, Mawardi, and Sulaksono 2012, 6; Hastuti and Maxwell 2003, 26; Hastuti and others 2008, 21; Hastuti and others 2014b, 37–38). Recipient households receive, on average, only 5 kilograms per distribution, varying between 1.8 and 15 kilograms per distribution. The amount received each month is less because distribution does not occur each month or because the system rotates recipients. Variation occurs not only between villages, but also between subvillage units (hamlets, RTs, and RWs), because implementers have the full authority to make decisions about how Rastra rice is divided. Some improvement is evident in the application of stipulated

FIGURE 7.7
Estimated Amount of Rice Allocated to and Purchased by Households in One Distribution in Indonesia, 2008–14

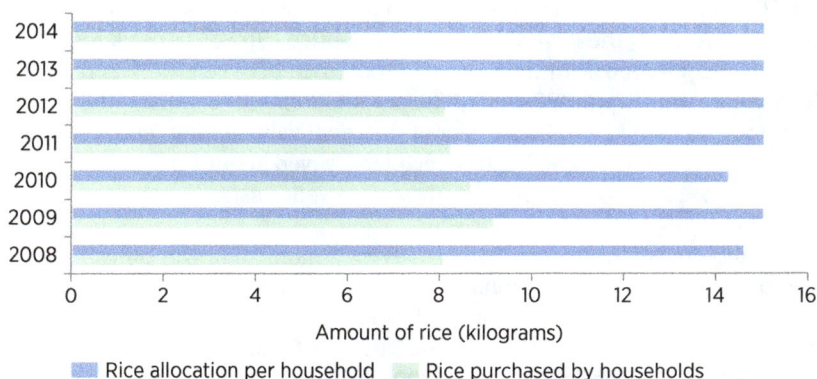

Amount of rice (kilograms)

Rice allocation per household   Rice purchased by households

Sources: Based on data from BPS 2002–14; Government of Indonesia 2004–16.
Note: In some distributions between 2008 and 2010, the stipulated allocation amounted to less than 15 kilograms per household.

TABLE 7.6 **Unpurchased (Missing) Rastra Rice in Indonesia, 2012–13**

PERIOD	OFFICIAL BENEFIT (KILOGRAMS PER HOUSEHOLD)	AMOUNT OF RICE (KILOGRAMS, MILLIONS)				MISSING RICE AS A % OF RICE PURCHASED
		PROCURED	DISTRIBUTED	PURCHASED	MISSING	
December 2012– February 2013	45	697.5	684.945	419.62	265.325	38.7
June– August 2013	75	1,162.5	1,141.575	591.45	550.125	48.2

Source: BPS data (treated) in World Bank 2015.
Note: Missing rice refers to the difference between the amount of rice distributed and the amount purchased by households.

distribution procedures at the village level, but the number of such villages remains limited.

The World Bank (2015) has noted the existence of fraud or missing rice in the implementation of Rastra. During two periods in 2012–13, not all of the available Rastra rice was purchased by households, and it is estimated that Rastra lost 38.7 and 48.2 percent of the total rice allocation, respectively (table 7.6). In the second period, the estimated amount of missing rice was greater, possibly because additional distributions over that period were not well promoted among beneficiary households and local implementers.

Prices Paid by Households

The government sets the price for Rastra rice at an amount far lower than its own purchase price and retail prices: Rp 1,000 per kilogram until 2007, and Rp 1,600 per kilogram since 2008. In 2015–16, the subsidized price did not reach 20 percent of the government purchase price (Rp 8,325 per kilogram). Even when compared with the average retail price between 2011 and 2014, which went up to Rp 8,090–Rp 9,730 per kilogram (BPS 2015), the subsidized price was only 16 to 20 percent of the retail value. Using retail prices as an approximate benchmark, in 2014 recipients saved about Rp 8,130 per kilogram or Rp 122,000 a month if they received Rastra in line with the regulations.

In reality, recipient households usually pay more than the official subsidized price of Rastra rice. Nationally, during 2004–14, households paid 15 to 34 percent more than the stipulated price (figure 7.8). The percentage increased year to year; however, the rate of increase tended to slow. In 2004–07, when the subsidized price was Rp 1,000, the purchase rice rose by about 4 percent annually, whereas in 2008–14, when the official subsidized price was Rp 1,600, the price rose only 2 percent annually.

A large proportion of households pay more for Rastra rice than the official subsidized price. Some studies found payments in line with the official price, but this holds true in a small number of areas and households. TNP2K reported that, of 220 villages studied, only 29 percent sold Rastra rice at the prescribed rate (Hastuti, Mawardi, and Sulaksono 2012). Hastuti and others (2014a) found that only 2 of 20 villages studied applied the stipulated price. The other villages applied higher prices, in some cases Rp 3,000 per kilogram, almost twice the official amount. Prices are decided at the village level, and, in some

FIGURE 7.8

Average Stipulated Price of Rastra Rice and Price Paid by Households in Indonesia, 2004–14

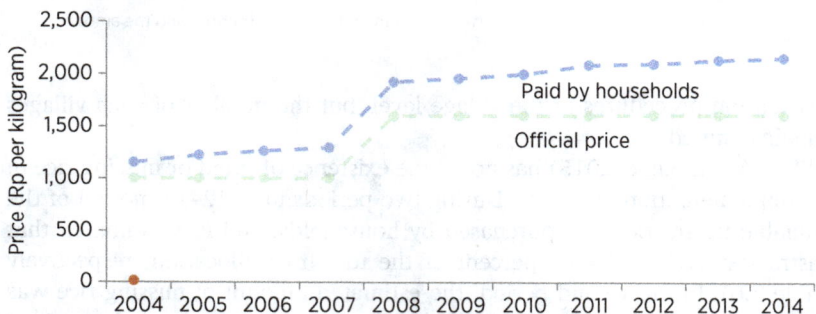

Source: BPS 2002–14 (treated).

areas, prices are changed by the RT, RW, or hamlet heads who distribute the rice. Consequently, the price of Rastra rice can vary within a village.

Increases in the official price of Rastra rice are primarily the result of recipient households having to pay for the transport of rice from the distribution point to the local distribution center. Where this occurs, the local government has not allocated funds to cover those costs, or the amount allocated is insufficient. Another cause is that recipients are burdened with the cost of paying incentives to distributors and transport operators and of raising funds for community construction projects or social activities. However, households are generally willing to pay higher than the stipulated Rastra price because the higher subsidized price is still significantly lower than the market price, resulting in costs 60–80 percent below market prices.

Moreover, the World Bank (2012) also found that recipient households receive rice at lower quantities and higher prices than stipulated. Given this finding, the benefit to households is much lower than it should be. The proportional value of the Rastra program to households—the percentage of household expenditure—should have been 8 percent in 2004, 6 percent in 2007, and 8 percent in 2010; in reality, the value of Rastra rice received as a proportion of household expenditure remained at only 2 percent.

Rice Quality
Since the program was initiated, program guidelines have stipulated a medium quality of rice for Rastra, but other indicators of quality have been subject to change (Departemen Dalam Negeri and BULOG 2004–07; Kemenko Kesra 2011–15). The 2012 general guidelines for Rastra state that rice is to be of medium quality and in good condition, in accordance with the Presidential Instruction on Rice (Kemenko Kesra 2011–15). In previous years, the general guidelines were even more specific, referring to medium-quality rice in good condition and free of pests. In the guidelines covering 2013–15, the specifications for rice to be in good condition and free of pests were removed, so that the quality standard is now based only on the presidential instruction that is in effect (Kemenko Kesra 2011–15). Thus, according to Presidential Instruction no. 5, 2015, BULOG rice is to contain a maximum of 14 percent moisture, a maximum of 20 percent broken grains, a maximum of 2 percent groats, and a minimum whiteness level of 95 percent (Government of Indonesia 2015).

The quality of Rastra rice received by households varies over time and between regions and is subject to frequent complaints. Households often receive rice that is not fit for consumption, because it is yellow, has a bad odor, is infested, is broken, or is powdery. Rastra rice that appears to be of good quality can often still be unpleasant to eat.

The general guidelines already regulate the quality of rice, but quality is hard to enforce, especially because the amount of rice distributed is significant. Rice that is to be distributed should be inspected at the storehouse and at the distribution point. The officials who are supposed to inspect the rice are often insufficiently aware of the technical aspects of grading medium-quality rice. According to BPKP (Suardini 2013, 11), Rastra officials do not examine the quality or check the weight of rice at the storehouse before transporting it to distribution points. The general guidelines also state that rice not meeting the quality standards can be returned to BULOG and will be replaced within 48 hours. In practice, putting that dictate into practice is difficult because rice that is to be returned has to be repacked and transported to the distribution point or to BULOG. The associated costs of those two processes are not included in the calculation of price at the local level. Aside from those hurdles, the quality indicators in the presidential instruction are quite technical and difficult for the general population to understand. The community usually assesses quality on the basis of its appearance, such as the presence of bugs, a high level of broken grains, color, smell, and consistency after cooking. Those assessments are incompatible with the quality regulations, so that rice may meet the official standards but be considered poor quality by the community.

Although recipients may object to the quality of Rastra rice, the low cost when compared with retail prices leads them to continue purchasing it. Households compensate for those shortcomings in the way they use the rice. For example, households usually mix Rastra and retail rice, mill the rice again to improve its color, wash it with soap, or cook it with pandan leaf. Such efforts reduce the benefits to participants.

The low quality of rice has led some households to resell the rice, and there are indications that BULOG sometimes procures rice from previous distributions. A 2014 field study found that households in Central Java could sell the rice to resellers at a price of Rp 5,000–Rp 5,700 per kilogram (Hastuti and others 2014a). Households in some regions are encouraged to sell their rice, and resellers are already waiting nearby at the time of the Rastra distribution. With the presence of such practices, the quality of Rastra rice will continue to decline, along with the benefits.

In 2013, *Komisi Pemberantasan Korupsi* (KPK, the Corruption Eradication Commission) also found indications of similar practices (KPK 2013). The commission stated that lack of precise targeting, rice that is unfit for consumption, and the difference between the Rastra price and the market price are incentives for households to sell Rastra rice to purchase better-quality rice. The practice of buying and reselling rice offers an attractive benefit, and there are always traders willing to purchase it. The KPK investigation identified a trail from intermediary collectors to rice traders, to wholesalers, and then to BULOG partners, which then redistribute rice to regional BULOG divisions.

Payment Systems

According to Rastra regulations, households pay the distributor in cash for the rice when it is distributed at the village level. If an additional cost is incurred for transporting rice from the distribution point to the beneficiaries and it is not fully funded by the regional budget, households contribute to covering those costs. Although household payments are usually made in cash, village payments may vary. From the local distribution center, money collected from beneficiaries is forwarded to the village-level distributor, who then makes a bank deposit or delivers cash directly to a BULOG or a subdistrict government office. BULOG usually allows a one- to two-week grace period from the time the rice is delivered to the local distribution center. BULOG begins the next distribution once the previous account has been paid. However, in some areas, BULOG has a different policy. Villages must pay up-front, before the rice has been distributed. These villages collect payments from households ahead of time or use third-party funding.

Rice Procurement and Storage
Aside from implementing Rastra distribution, BULOG also has a mandate to procure and store government rice, including rice used for the Rastra program, both from domestic and imported sources. Government rice procurement prioritizes domestically produced rice and, through BULOG, purchases rice from farmers across Indonesia who usually have a small amount of land, around 0.5 hectares. The trading chain from farmers to BULOG generally involves small-scale and large-scale traders and BULOG's own trading partners. The capacity to purchase rice in this way relies on domestic rice production, which is unstable, largely because of the influence of climate conditions, natural disasters, and pest infestations. At the same time, the amount of rice required by Rastra is decided annually and does not take into account levels of domestic production. When domestic rice procurement does not meet the total needs of the program, BULOG has the authority to compensate for the shortfall with imported rice.

Efforts to Improve the Rastra Program
Various research organizations, universities, nongovernmental organizations, and other organizations have undertaken studies, provided criticism, and given input to improve the program. Not all of those recommendations have been used, but they have at least encouraged the government to address problems in the program. At several points, modifications have been made to improve Rastra. However, not all modifications have led to improvements; some changes have even been counterproductive.

One reason Rastra has not met its objectives has been ineffective outreach about the program. In the past few years, especially in 2012, program implementers made intensive efforts to inform about the program. The efforts took the form of making public service announcements in the print and electronic media, sending posters and banners to villages, and using direct briefing to local governments. The community engagement approach was not always successful because Rastra provides individual assistance that may cause envy and conflict. In contrast, road and irrigation programs provide broader public good, and in those cases the community engagement approach works relatively well. In 2013, when Rastra became part of the Acceleration and Broadening of Social Protection Program, a program to alleviate the impact of rising fuel prices, the government also provided households with brochures that contained further information about Rastra. Unfortunately, not all households read and understood the information (Hastuti and others 2014b).

Efforts to increase public knowledge about Rastra have had some effect in fostering regional governments' interest in the program, which has taken the shape, for example, of free Rastra programs (that is, regional governments pay for all Rastra rice received by households in their jurisdiction). However, regional governments that are not concerned with Rastra are far greater in number, and some refuse to implement the program altogether. The hope that regional governments can be involved in eliminating differences between the price paid by households and the stipulated price has not been realized. An effort to create a legal umbrella for the involvement of regional governments has yet to succeed in engaging regional governments.[23]

The problem of accurate targeting is an acute challenge that hampers the ability of the program to achieve its aims. In 2002, the government attempted to respond to this problem by changing the name of the program from OPK to Raskin. It was hoped that the inclusion of the word *miskin* (poor) in the full program name would limit the access of nonpoor people. However, another recent name change, to Rastra, could be counterproductive. The full title, *beras sejahtera* ("prosperous rice," meaning rice for prosperous families), could be used as a justification for allowing well-off families to access the program.

In response to the complaint that inaccurate data had caused mistargeting, the government undertook several population censuses through the national agency, BPS: the Susenas socioeconomic survey in 2005, the PPLS for 2008 and 2011, and the 2015 BDT, which is still being updated. Moreover, to respond to the absence of local government involvement in data collection, since 2013 the government has given local governments the opportunity to verify household data through village meetings.

Lack of transparency also produces inaccurate targeting. The official beneficiary list created by the central government is used as a token administrative gesture at the local level. Furthermore, the bargaining position of beneficiaries in ensuring that they can obtain their entitlements is limited because of strong asymmetries in access to information at the local level. Beneficiaries often do not know that the beneficiary list exists or that they are entitled to the allocation of rice.

One important step the government has taken is the agenda for unifying social protection targeting. The goal of unifying records is made possible by creation of the unified database (BDT) for social protection programs, which grew out of the PPLS for 2011. BDT is a national database that contains information on households in the bottom 40 percent of the population, who are potential beneficiaries of social protection programs. Rastra was one of the first social protection programs to use BDT data to identify target beneficiaries in 2012.

In 2012, the TNP2K and the Abdul Latief Jameel Poverty Action Lab (J-PAL) undertook a study and field trial in six districts and cities. The study investigated the effectiveness of two options for dealing with targeting accuracy in Rastra: use of a Rastra card and direct involvement of the community in Rastra distribution at the village level. The study found that the two options, accompanied by intensive social promotion, had a positive effect on targeting accuracy and the amount of rice received. The use of a Rastra card had a greater impact, at a lower cost. The TNP2K and J-PAL submitted the results to policy makers in December 2012 and received a very positive response. Consequently, at the time of the fuel subsidy adjustment in 2013, the Indonesian government launched the social protection card (KPS). The card allows about 15.5 million households to obtain social assistance and protection (Rastra), temporary direct cash assistance (BLSM), and poor students assistance (BSM). The KPS is useful for identifying beneficiaries, especially in the BSM program. Before the card's introduction, the BSM relied on school authorities, especially school principals, to identify target beneficiaries. Households now play a greater role, with students able to take a proactive role by showing their family's card to school administrators. The KPS program can play a strategic role in increasing the effectiveness of beneficiary targeting and complementarity between social protection programs.

Several adjustments have been made with regard to weaknesses in the quality and quantity of Rastra rice; however, these adjustments have not been consistent with the aims of improving the program. In terms of quantity, for example, in 2008 BULOG began to provide rice sacks with a capacity equal to that of household allocations, that is, 15 kilograms. The hope was that local distributors would deliver rice that was already in the correct amount and not burden households with the cost of repacking and weighing. That policy did not last long and did not reach all areas. Since 2013, the general Rastra guidelines have regulated that Rastra rice be made available in 15-kilogram or 50-kilogram packs. The larger package is not ideal for household distribution, but it makes the packing process easier for BULOG, because 50 kilograms is the standard size of rice pack sold at markets. With regard to quality, when the 2013 general guidelines were issued, program management no longer had a general indicator of quality. Instead of indicating that the rice had to be in good condition and free of pests, the only indicators were highly technical and found in a different document, the Presidential Instruction on Rice, which limits the community's ability to assess the quality of rice they are given.

Pilot Transition to Vouchers

Against this backdrop, the government has recently decided to embark on a large-scale pilot of e-vouchers as an alternative to the current in-kind provision of Rastra rice (World Bank 2017). The voucher program would share some similarities with the Supplemental Nutrition Assistance Program (SNAP) in the United States, which is discussed in this volume (chapter 6). Starting in early 2017, the experiment will support more than 1.43 million households and involve some 14,000 merchants in 44 cities.[24] Each target household will receive a voucher worth Rp 110,000 per month. While initial plans included the use of vouchers restricted to rice and eggs (Government of Indonesia 2017), at the time of finalizing this chapter, they included rice and sugar as well.[25] The e-voucher system will be expanded gradually to other cities and districts throughout 2017–19 and be scaled up nationally by 2020.

The transition toward e-vouchers pursues multiple objectives, namely, to improve targeting of households in the bottom 25 percent of the income ladder; provide targeted beneficiaries with better access to nutritious food; give more choices and control for the beneficiaries on when, what type, and how much rice and other eligible food commodities they buy; encourage retail businesses at the grassroots level; provide beneficiaries and small merchants with access to financial services; and, finally, save costs in the government's budget by making the business process more efficient. Voucher cards would serve as debit cards, with cash being transferred to recipients' savings accounts. The savings would not be cashed out, but could only be used at designated merchants to buy eligible food commodities. Although the process is in its infancy and solid assessments will be required, the use of voucher cards may help to reorient Rastra's nature and design parameters toward cash-based assistance in line with other country experiences discussed in this volume.

Future studies could deepen the knowledge and practice on some key questions that would remain relevant regardless of the shape the program might take. For instance, the forthcoming pilot could provide an opportunity to explore the comparative cost-effectiveness of alternative interventions in the form of quasi-cash (vouchers) and in-kind transfers. The pilot could present ideal conditions for an in-depth assessment of costs and impacts among beneficiaries—and do so within a large-scale test as opposed to small-scale experiments. Relatedly, future research could also investigate the levels of community satisfaction with social protection programs in Indonesia, with food subsidies being one area of focus. Moreover, it might be useful to explore the general-equilibrium effects of subsidy reforms under different scenarios (pace of reforms) and modalities (cash or vouchers). This effort could include implications across the main sectors and stakeholders, such as farmers, food prices, employment, and consumer welfare. Finally, Indonesia's possible reform process should be informed by practical lessons emerging from cross-country experiences on how best to manage the transition from in-kind transfers to vouchers. In this regard, this volume might provide timely insights in that direction.

LESSONS LEARNED

Historically, Indonesia placed heavy emphasis on price stability and food sufficiency. After 1998, this approach came at a cost of high domestic prices, which were achieved largely through trade restrictions, floor prices, and barriers to entry into logistical services. More recently, retail food prices are substantially higher in Indonesia than in neighboring countries, which marks a departure from past scenarios in which prices were stabilized at levels modestly above world prices. For example, between 1969 and 2014, domestic prices were 7 percent higher, on average, than international prices; however, since 2008, the difference has grown to about 34 percent (table 7.1).

While the current approach helped to cope with recent global food crises, it also underscores the difference between stability and affordability. Maintaining prices at stable but exceptionally high levels implies that, on the one hand, Indonesian consumers have been massively "taxed" by public trade and agricultural policies and that, on the other hand, as the country advances in its structural transformation, the poor, in particular, are increasingly net food buyers—that is, they do not necessarily benefit from high food prices. For example, according to the World Food Programme (WFP 2015, 115), the most food-insecure districts "have very high consumption to production ratios, meaning that their requirements for consumption far exceed what they produce. They are therefore dependent on markets and purchasing for the majority of their staple foods." Specifically, their consumption-production ratio is 35.4, compared with only 1.9 in the least vulnerable districts.

At the same time, the traditional commodity-based approach of Rastra has been in place for almost two decades, and its core nature and business model have remained largely intact. This chapter has exposed a range of inefficiencies inherent to this model, including issues through the chain of supply and distribution that significantly affect the quantity and quality of social assistance provision.

The experience of the program illustrates the "balance wheel" function of a food-based program in a context where food (rice) self-sufficiency is a core policy priority and where ensuring stable food prices is functional to such a vision. Indonesia was relatively successful in attaining that goal, although at a cost of high food prices for consumers (and producers) and a comparatively limited role for trade. While the general architecture of the program has not changed dramatically, steps have recently been taken to integrate Rastra better into the overall social protection system. The government has spent significant resources on the program, and millions of households have benefited from the provision of affordable rice. However, in practice, several aspects of the program are inconsistent with its design. From the very beginning, the program has faced obstacles, especially in meeting its benchmarks.

Additionally, program implementation costs tend to be high when compared with program effectiveness. In terms of the amount, quality, and frequency of the rice distributions, the rice received by households does not meet the stipulations of the original program design. Target beneficiaries who have been identified centrally do not necessarily become the actual recipients of the program. On average, target recipients who do buy Rastra rice receive only one-third of the rice to which they are entitled. Simple mistargeting or elite capture does not fully explain the receipt of rice by ineligible households. Local social pressures lead to uniform distribution because equal allocation is perceived to be the only fair and hence politically acceptable approach. In this regard, the published literature lays out a range of changes in implementation to improve the targeting.[26]

Available research suggests options for significant reforms of the in-kind component, should it be retained as one of the modalities in the reformed program, ranging from revisiting business procedures to aligning food provision with cash transfers. For instance, the Indonesian government has implemented several social protection programs in the form of cash transfers. In 2005, it set up BLT, a national direct cash transfer program, and then in 2013 introduced BLSM, a community temporary direct assistance program. Both programs targeted the same households as the Rastra program. Numerous studies showed that vouchers and cash transfers—as well as other food-oriented social assistance programs discussed in this volume—outperform Rastra in several dimensions, including the accuracy of targeting, accuracy of the amount of assistance received, and flexibility to meet varying needs of recipients. Another study also found that Rastra is less effective in reducing poverty and improving nutrition than programs based on direct cash assistance or food coupons (OECD 2014).[27] As part of the government's move (at least in terms of pilots) toward voucher-based assistance, the role of BULOG could be refocused on fulfilling its primary function—that is, stabilizing the price of staple goods that are not limited to rice. In this regard, lessons from other case studies summarized in chapter 1 and presented in this volume, such as SNAP in chapter 6, are particularly relevant for Indonesia.

Depending on how it is planned and implemented, such a process may help to put the country on a track that is broadly aligned with the experience of other countries—such as those explored in this volume—that have undergone a more or less complete transition from in-kind food assistance to vouchers or even cash transfers. As those examples illustrate, the journey toward a change in transfer modalities is seldom linear and simple, with several critical issues (for example, the role of BULOG, effects on rice price stability) that will likely entail a thorough process of review. In other words, much-awaited reforms are moving in the right direction, but they seldom happen overnight, and it may not be desirable for them to happen that way.

NOTES

1. The Rastra program has changed names several times. Initially, when the program was first implemented in July 1998, it was titled Special Market Operation. In 2002, to reflect the nature of the program, the government changed the name to Raskin, an acronym for *beras untuk keluarga miskin* (rice for poor families). It was hoped that this title would improve targeting accuracy, expecting that the nonpoor would feel ashamed to receive program benefits. The name Raskin continued to be used, but during 2006–11, its full title shifted to *beras untuk rumah tangga miskin* (rice for poor households) and then to *subsidi beras bagi masyarakat berpendapatan rendah* (rice subsidized for low-income communities) in 2012–15. In 2016, another name change—to Rastra or *beras sejahtera* (literally prosperous rice)—prompted some debate, because it could be interpreted as rice for prosperous families and thus become a justification for giving more well-off families access to the program.
2. This section was drafted primarily by C. Peter Timmer and grows out of his more than four decades as a policy analyst and adviser in Indonesia. It builds on an earlier paper for the World Bank that sought to understand how Indonesia managed to stabilize rice prices for a quarter of a century, from 1973 to 1998.
3. Falcon Team (1985). The team was composed of Walter P. Falcon, M. Margaret Hastings, Leona A. Mears, Scott R. Pearson, and C. Peter Timmer.
4. This section draws especially on Timmer (1995), which sought to distill lessons from 25 years of personal involvement in the process of stabilizing rice prices in Indonesia.
5. See Kaplan (1984) for a fascinating historical account of the relationship between urban masses and their rulers with respect to provisioning of basic foodstuffs.
6. This approach works well when incomes are reasonably stable, but it fails when there is an economywide collapse, as in 1998. See Timmer (2010) for further discussion of the macroeconomic setting for successful rice price stabilization.
7. See Timmer (1990) for an early summary and Timmer (2014) for an evaluation of how Indonesian price policy changed between the food crisis in 1972–73 and the one in 2007–08.
8. President Suharto's determination to avoid rice imports took international trade as a balancing mechanism off the policy agenda. Indeed, Indonesia was supposed to be self-sufficient in rice—after all, the Food and Agriculture Organization of the United Nations had given him a gold medal in 1985 for that achievement. By the early 1990s, President Suharto's economic advisers had convinced him that "self-sufficiency on trend" was a more appropriate policy objective. Limited imports again become operationally feasible, although obtaining permission from the president remained difficult and BULOG was no longer able to count on imports for short-run supply management. The political difficulty in arranging for rice imports remains to this day.
9. See Williams and Wright (1991) for a sophisticated analysis of the limits to price stabilization with finite stocks.
10. See Timmer (2014) for a review of different approaches to valuing grain reserves.
11. Relatively little is known publicly about the financial costs of BULOG's activities to stabilize rice prices. The best estimate is for 1991, a year when BULOG was actively managing the price stabilization effort solely on the basis of its domestic buffer stock. For that year, the full financial costs of BULOG's rice activities were US$233 million, which amounted to 0.11 percent of total GDP and about 1.2 percent of the national budget. See Pearson (1993) for more details.
12. For example, international financial institutions argued that high domestic rice prices were the main factor causing poverty to rise, whereas the government and popular press castigated such views, often dramatically. A highly popular political cartoon in *Kompas,* a leading daily newspaper, showed a large grain harvester representing an international financial institution cutting down peasants.

13. This section draws heavily on World Bank (2006, ch. 2). Timmer was the main author of chapter 2. See Timmer (2004, 2010) for further discussion of the links between a strategy of pro-poor growth based on agricultural development and a stable food system.
14. Indonesia provides several global lessons. It is the original home of the dual economy. Boeke's experience during the Dutch colonial administration of Java led him to identify two types of economic agents—"rational" and "traditional"—with almost entirely separate spheres of economic activity (Boeke 1946). Lewis (1954) built his Nobel Prize–winning model of the dual economy with unlimited supplies of labor on the behavior of such agents (Timmer 2005, 15).
15. The crude IPPG shown in table 7.2 is based on an analytical relationship between the overall incidence of poverty and the observed average income elasticity of demand (based on regression analysis of long-run, time-series data). The income elasticity of food energy for the entire period from 1880 to 1990, estimated to be 0.313, is used as the long-run base, scaled to 1 (italicized in the table). It is multiplied by the long-run growth rate in per capita income, 0.89 percent per year, to generate the long-run average IPPG of 0.89. The income elasticity for each separate time period is then scaled relative to the long-run average and multiplied by the growth rate in per capita income to generate the IPPG for each epoch. The IPPG incorporates both the growth and the distributional dimensions of pro-poor growth and is thus a country-specific version of equation 1 in World Bank (2004).
16. The Dutch forced the Netherland East Indies, the Dutch colonial name for Indonesia, to stay on the gold standard well after regional competitors, including the Japanese, devalued.
17. At 2.37, the IPPG was surprisingly high during the Sukarno era, when economic policy is widely regarded to have been a disaster. But a modest recovery from the quarter century of depression and wars, combined with average per capita incomes rising 1.5 percent per year and large average income elasticity for food energy, suggests that what growth there was actually reached the poor.
18. Data are from the World Bank, World Development Indicators database.
19. The administrative levels of *desa* (village) and *kelurahan* (urban village) are roughly equivalent, with *desa* used in most rural areas and *kelurahan* in most urban regions. This chapter uses "village" to refer to both.
20. RT, or neighborhood unit, is the smallest unit of local administration, consisting of a number of households. RW is a unit of local administration consisting of several RTs within a village.
21. Over this period, BPS verified the 2005 data twice. The first verification was conducted in 2006 because regional government data were then used for Rastra targeting in 2007. BPS verified the data again in 2007, through the Basic Health and Education Services Survey conducted in 15 provinces, and the results were used for Rastra targeting in 2009.
22. Indeed, socialization helps community members to gain more information about Rastra; public announcement of the list of target households informs the community which households are eligible to be beneficiaries; and use of the social protection cards, which are given only to target households, means that only the holders of the card are eligible to get Rastra rice.
23. Expectations were outlined in the Circular of the Ministry of Internal Affairs no. 900/2634/SJ 2013, on the Allocation of Payments for Rastra Distribution Costs from Distribution Point to Distribution Centre.
24. In addition to implementation of the e-voucher pilot, the regular Rastra scheme is still conducted in 470 other cities or districts (*kota* or *kabupaten*).
25. Anecdotal field observations show that rice, oil, and sugar are sometimes provided.

26. In particular, applied research has pointed to several suggestions. Among those, the program could minimize the amount of "missing rice," indicated by an increase in the amount received by target households; improvements in rice quality could be achieved by adhering to the quality standards set by the government; and targeting accuracy and processes for updating information could be enhanced by adopting a dynamic approach that enrolls new beneficiaries while maintaining verification and validation steps that ensure their eligibility. This approach could be achieved by implementing a decentralized on-demand application involving local government and the Ministry of Social Affairs. For example, the size of the benefit—the amount of rice actually received by households—could be adjusted by taking into account the dependency ratio of each household. The program could improve distribution mechanisms through the use of a card or voucher. Cards could empower poor households to demand the full amount of subsidy to which they are entitled (Banerjee and others 2015). A reduction in the price paid by recipient households could be considered. This price reduction should be in line with the stipulated price by setting a maximal subsidized price, by ensuring that governments fund the total cost of distribution to households, or by involving regional governments or the central government. Administrators should consider improving transparency, which can be done through increased promotion and communication, especially related to eligibility, size of the benefit, distribution mechanisms, and frequency of distribution. Finally, governance could be improved by designating a specific agency with the authority and responsibility for program implementation and by designating BULOG as a third party that undertakes provision and distribution.
27. For example, Indonesia has had a number of cash-based programs in parallel to Rastra. These include a large-scale conditional cash transfer scheme (Program Keluarga Harapan—PKH), which in 2016 covered approximately 6 million households. Another cash transfer measure, the Program Indonesia Pintar or PIP, provides cash to enrolled students or school-aged children from the poorest 25 percent of households. PIP currently reaches nearly 19.5 million students.

REFERENCES

Banerjee, Abhijit, Rema Hanna, Jordan Kyle, Benjamin Olken, and Sudarno Sumarto. 2015. "Tangible Information and Citizen Empowerment: Identification Cards and Food Subsidy Programs in Indonesia." Working Paper, J-PAL, Jakarta.
Boeke, Jan H. 1946. *The Evolution of the Netherlands Indies Economy*. New York: Institute of Pacific Relations.
BPS (Badan Pusat Statistik). 2002–14. *Survey Sosial Ekonomi Nasional* (Susenas) [National Socio-Economic Survey] *2002–2014*. Jakarta: BPS.
———. 2015. *Statistik Indonesia 2015*. Jakarta: BPS.
BULOG (Badan Urusan Logistik). 2011. "Prosiding Workshop Optimalisasi Program Raskin." BULOG, Jakarta.
Departemen Dalam Negeri and BULOG. 2004–07. *Pedoman Umum Program Beras untuk Keluarga Miskin (Raskin) Tahun 2004–2007* [2004–07 Raskin Program Guidelines]. Jakarta: Departemen Dalam Negeri and BULOG.
Falcon Team. 1985. "Rice Policy in Indonesia, 1985–1990: The Problems of Success." Confidential report submitted to the chairman of BULOG, Jakarta, September 2.
Government of Indonesia. 2004–16. "Nota Keuangan dan Anggaran Pendapatan dan Belanja Negara [Financial Note and Indonesian Budget] 2004–16." Government of Indonesia, Jakarta.
———. 2015. "Presidential Instruction Number 5/2015 on Policy on Government Provision and Distribution of Rice." Government of Indonesia, Jakarta.

————. 2017. "Guidelines for Implementation of Non-Cash Food Assistance." Government of Indonesia, Jakarta.

Hastuti, Sulton Mawardi, and Bambang Sulaksono. 2012. *Tinjauan Efektivitas Pelaksanaan Raskin dalam Mencapai Enam Tepat.* Jakarta: SMERU Research Institute.

Hastuti, Sulton Mawardi, Bambang Sulaksono, Akhmadi, Silvia Devina, and Rima Prama Artha. 2008. *The Effectiveness of Raskin Program.* Jakarta: SMERU Research Institute.

Hastuti and John Maxwell. 2003. *Rice for Poor Families (Raskin): Did the 2002 Program Operate Effectively? Evidence from Bengkulu and Karawang.* Jakarta: SMERU Research Institute.

Hastuti, Bambang Sulaksono, Sulton Mawardi, Akhmadi, Rahmitha, Valentina Y. D. Utari, Dyan Widyaningsih, Dinar Dwi Prasetyo, Kartawijaya, and M. Imam Zamroni. 2014a. "Mekanisme Penyaluran Raskin." Unpublished fieldnote, SMERU Research Institute, Jakarta.

————. 2014b. *Penggunaan Kartu Perlindungan Sosial (KPS) dan Pelaksanaan Bantuan Langsung Sementara Masyarakat (BLSM) 2013.* Jakarta: SMERU Research Institute.

Hofman, Bert, Ella Rodrick-Jones, and Kian Wie Thee. 2004. "Indonesia: Rapid Growth; Weak Institutions." Paper prepared for the Shanghai Conference on "Scaling up Poverty Reduction," May 28–29 (preliminary draft, April 18), World Bank, Jakarta.

Isdijoso,Widjajanti, Rachma Indah Nurbani Hafiz Arfyanto, M. Sulton Mawardi, Sudarno Sumarto, Nils Grade, Mohamad Marji, Fabienne Babinsky, and Fika Fauzia. 2014. "Food and Nutrition Security in Indonesia: A Strategic Review." SMERU Research Institute, Jakarta.

Kaplan, Steven Laurence. 1984. *Provisioning Paris: Merchants and Millers in the Grain and Flour Trade during the Eighteenth Century.* Ithaca, NY: Cornell University Press.

Kemenko Kesra. 2011–15. *Pedoman Umum Raskin* [General Guidelines for Raskin] *Tahun 2011–2015.* Jakarta: Kemenko Kesra.

KPK (Komisi Pemberantasan Korupsi). 2013. *Laporan Akhir Tahun 2013: Kajian Kebijakan Subsidi Beras bagi Masyarakat Berpendapatan Rendah (Raskin)* [2013 Year End Report: Policy Study of Rice for Low-Income Communities]. Jakarta: KPK.

Lewis, W. Arthur. 1954. "Economic Development with Unlimited Supplies of Labor." *Manchester School of Economics and Social Studies* 22 (2): 139–91.

MacIntyre, Andrew. 2003. "Indonesia as a Poorly Performing State?" Australian National University, Canberra.

Myrdal, Gunnar. 1968. *Asian Drama: An Inquiry into the Poverty of Nations.* New York: Pantheon Books.

OECD (Organisation for Economic Co-operation and Development). 2014. *Transitory Food Security in Indonesia.* Paris: OECD. http://www.oecd.org/officialdocuments/publicdisplaydocumentpdf/?cote=TAD/CA/APM/WP%282014%2914/FINAL&docLanguage=En.

Pearson, Scott R. 1993. "Financing Rice Price Stabilization." *Indonesian Food Journal* 4 (7): 83–96.

Ravallion, Martin, and Michael Lokshin. 2005. "Who Cares about Relative Deprivation?" Policy Research Working Paper 3782, World Bank, Washington, DC. http://ssrn.com/abstract=873669.

Suardini, Deni. 2013. "Hasil Audit Kinerja Raskin dan Rencana Aksi Pengawasan Raskin 2013." Presentation materials. BPKP, Jakarta.

Sumarto, Sudarno, Asep Suryahadi, and Lant Pritchett. 2001. "Safety Nets and Safety Ropes: Comparing the Dynamic Benefit Incidence of Subsidized Rice and Public Works Programs in Indonesia." Paper presented at the Vulnerability and Poverty Workshop, Third Asian Development Forum, Bangkok, June 12–14.

Sumarto, Sudarno, Asep Suryahadi, and Wenefrida Widyanti. 2004. "Assessing the Impact of Indonesian Social Safety Net Programs on Household Welfare and Poverty Dynamics." Working Paper, SMERU Research Institute, Jakarta.

Sumarto, Sudarno, Marc Vothknecht, and Laura Wijaya 2014. "Explaining Regional Heterogeneity of Poverty: Evidence from a Decentralized Indonesia." Working Paper, SMERU Research Institute, Jakarta.

Tabor, Steven R., and M. Husein Sawit. 2001. "Social Protection via Rice: The OPK Rice Subsidy Program in Indonesia." *Developing Economies* 39 (3): 267–94.

Temple, Jonathan. 2001. "Growing into Trouble: Indonesia after 1966." Working Paper, Department of Economics, University of Bristol, Bristol, U.K.

Timmer, C. Peter. 1975. "The Political Economy of Rice in Asia: Indonesia." *Food Research Institute Studies* 14 (3): 197–231.

———. 1990. "Food Price Stabilization: The Indonesian Experience with Rice." Paper prepared for the Asia/Near East Bureau of the U.S. Agency for International Development, Harvard Institute, Cambridge, MA.

———. 1995. "Food Security and Rice Price Stabilization: An Essay in Honor of Bustanil Arifin." In *Beras, Koperasi dan Politik Orde Baru* [Rice, Cooperatives, and New Order Politics], edited by Fachry Ali, 326–51. Jakarta: Pustaka Sinar Harapan.

———. 1996. "Does BULOG Stabilize Rice Prices in Indonesia? Should It Try?" *Bulletin of Indonesian Economic Studies* 32 (2): 45–74.

———. 1997. "How Well Do the Poor Connect to the Growth Process?" CAER II Discussion Paper, Harvard Institute for International Development for the USAID/CAER Project, Cambridge, MA, December.

———. 2002. "Agriculture and Economic Growth." In *The Handbook of Agricultural Economics*, Vol. II, edited by Bruce Gardner and Gordon Rausser, 1487–546. Amsterdam: North-Holland.

———. 2003. "Food Security and Rice Price Policy in Indonesia: The Economics and Politics of the Food Price Dilemma." In *Rice Science: Innovations and Impact for Livelihood, Proceedings of the International Rice Research Conference, September 16–19, Beijing, China*, edited by T. W. Mew, D. S. Brar, S. Peng, D. Dawe, and B. Hardy, 777–88. Beijing: International Rice Research Institute, Chinese Academy of Engineering, and Chinese Academy of Agricultural Sciences.

———. 2004. "The Road to Pro-Poor Growth: The Indonesian Experience in Regional Perspective." *Bulletin of Indonesian Economic Studies* 40 (2): 177–207.

———. 2005. "Operationalizing Pro-Poor Growth." Indonesia country study for the World Bank, Washington, DC.

———. 2010. "Reflections on Food Crises Past." *Food Policy* 35 (1): 1–11.

———. 2014. "What Are Grain Reserves Worth? A Generalized Political Economy Framework." In *Trade, Development, and Political Economy in East Asia: Essays in Honour of Hal Hill*, edited by Prema-Chandra Athukorala, Arianto A. Patunru, and Budy P. Resosudarno, 235–48. Singapore: Institute of Southeast Asian Studies (ISEAS).

Timmer, C. Peter, Walter P. Falcon, Andrew D. Mason, Franck Wiebe, and Jonathan Morduch. 1992. "Approaches to Poverty Alleviation in Indonesia." HIID Report 136/92/255, Harvard Institute for International Development, Cambridge, MA.

TNP2K (National Team for the Acceleration of Poverty Reduction). 2015. "Tantangan Meningkatkan Efektivitas Program Raskin." Research report, TNP2K, Jakarta.

Warr, Peter G. 2011. "Food Security vs. Food Self-Sufficiency: The Indonesian Case." *Indonesian Quarterly* 39 (1): 56–71.

WFP (World Food Programme). 2015. *Food Security and Vulnerability Atlas of Indonesia.* Jakarta: WFP.

Williams, J. C., and B. D. Wright. 1991. *Storage and Commodity Markets.* Cambridge, U.K.: Cambridge University Press.

World Bank. 1993. *The East Asian Miracle: Economic Growth and Public Policy.* New York: University Press.

———. 2004. "Concept Paper on Operationalizing Pro-Poor Growth." Washington, DC.

————. 2006. *Making the New Indonesia Work for the Poor: A Poverty Assessment.* Washington, DC: World Bank.

————. 2012. "Protecting the Poor and Vulnerable in Indonesia." World Bank, Jakarta.

————. 2015. "Presentation Material: The Business Process Review and Re-engineering of Raskin; Finding and Recommendation." Presented at the office of the National Team for the Acceleration of Poverty Reduction (TNP2K), Jakarta, July.

————. 2017. "Terms of Reference: Business Process Review and Re-Engineering—E-Voucher Program." World Bank, Jakarta.